North Africa
Atlantic coast of Morocco, Straits of Gibraltar to Tunisia and Malta

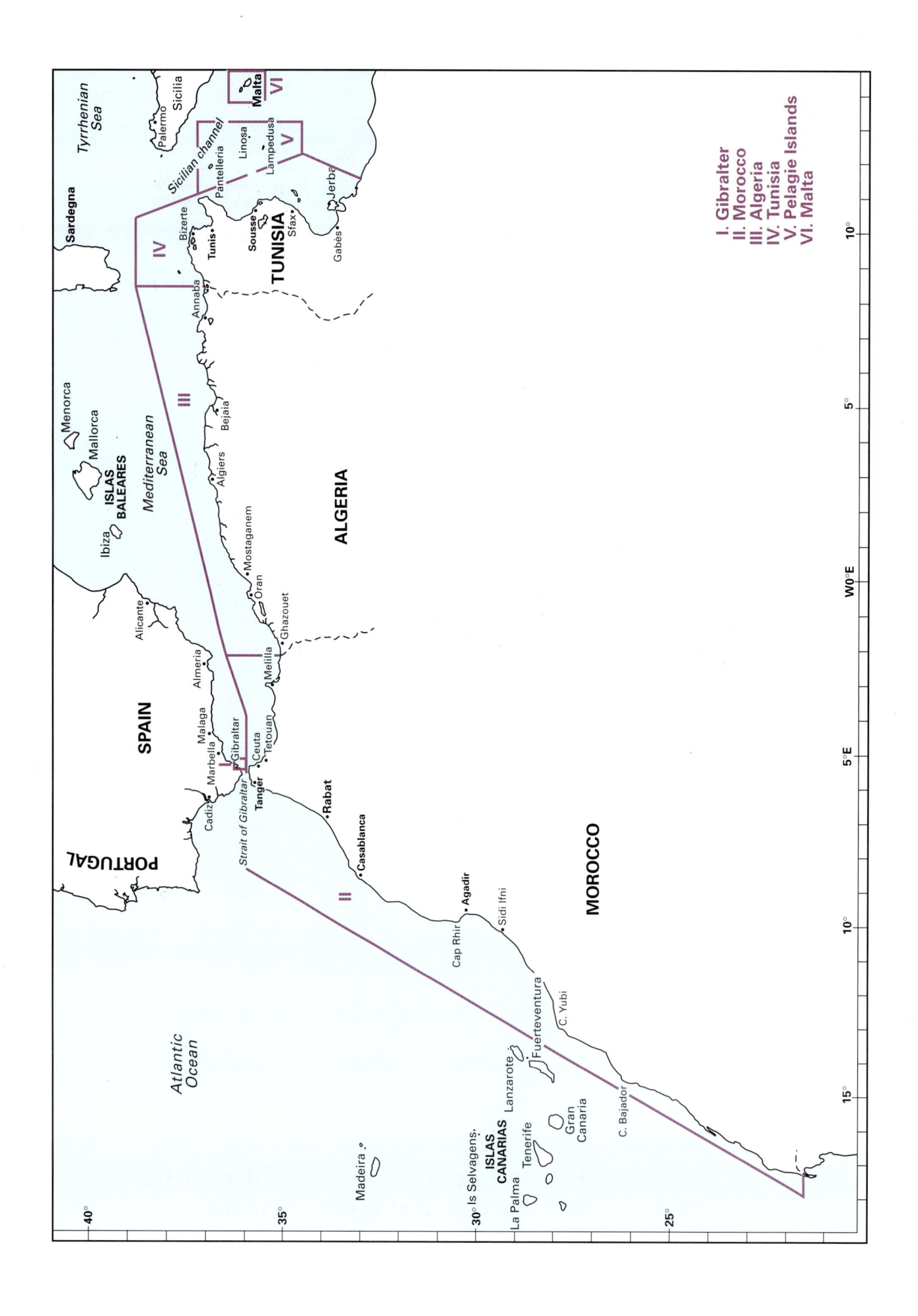

North Africa
Atlantic coast of Morocco, Straits of Gibraltar to Tunisia and Malta

ROYAL CRUISING CLUB
PILOTAGE FOUNDATION
Compiled by Hans van Rijn and
Graham Hutt (Morocco - Atlantic coast)
Revised by Graham Hutt

Imray Laurie Norie & Wilson Ltd
St Ives Cambridgeshire England

Published by
Imray Laurie Norie & Wilson Ltd
Wych House, St Ives, Huntingdon,
Cambridgeshire PE17 4BT, England
☎ +44 (0)1480 462114 *Fax* +44 (0)1480 496109
E-mail ilnw@imray.com.
Website www.imray.com

All rights reserved. No part of this publication may be reproduced, transmitted or used in any form by any means – graphic, electronic or mechanical, including photocopying, recording, taping or information storage and retrieval systems or otherwise – without the prior permission of the Publishers.

First edition 1991
Second edition 2000

© Text: Royal Cruising Club Pilotage Foundation 2000
© Plans: Imray, Laurie, Norie & Wilson Ltd 2000
© Photographs: Hans van Rijn 1991; Graham Hutt 2000

ISBN 0 85288 412 5

CAUTION
Every effort has been made to ensure the accuracy of this book. It contains selected information and thus is not definitive and does not include all known information on the subject in hand; this is particularly relevant to the plans which should not be used for navigation. The Pilotage Foundation believes that its selection is a useful aid to prudent navigation but the safety of a vessel depends ultimately on the judgement of the navigator who should assess all available information, published or unpublished.

CORRECTIONAL SUPPLEMENTS
This pilot book will be amended at intervals by the issue of correctional supplements. These are published on the internet at our web site www.imray.com and may be downloaded free of charge. Printed copies are also available on request from the publishers at the above address.

Printed in Great Britain by Butler & Tanner Ltd, Frome, Somerset

Also by the RCC Pilotage Foundation
Published by Imray Laurie Norie & Wilson Ltd
Islas Baleares
Mediterranean Spain – Costas del Sol & Blanca – Costas del Azahar, Dorada & Brava
The Baltic Sea
Atlantic Spain and Portugal
Atlantic Islands
North Biscay
Biscay Spain
North Brittany
Channel Islands
Lesser Antilles
North Africa
Faroe, Iceland & Greenland
Chile
Published by A & C Black Ltd
Atlantic Crossing Guide
Pacific Crossing Guide
Published by RCC Desktop Publishing Unit
Cruising Guide to West Africa
The Falkland Islands Shores
The South Atlantic Coast of South America

Contents

Foreword, vi
Preface, vi
Acknowledgements, vii

Introduction, 1

Morocco, Algeria, Tunisia, 1

I. General information, 2
  Maritime information, 2
  Sea conditions, 4
  Flora and fauna, 4
  Marine life, 5
  Fishing methods, 5
  Scuba diving, 7
  Anchoring, 7
  Yacht equipment recommended, 7
  Availability of supplies and provisions, 7
  Yacht repair facilities, 8
  Navigation notes, 9
  Buoyage, 10
  Lights, 10
  Weather forecasts, 10
  Radiobeacons, 11
  Coastal radio stations, 12
  Glossary, 12

II. North Africa, 14
  Religion, 14
  Language, 14
  Cultural differences, 14
  Bakhshish, 15
  Eating out, 15
  Shopping, 16
  Chartering, 16
  Wintering, 16
  Connections, 16
  Books, 17

Gibraltar, 18
  Transiting the Straits of Gibraltar, 26
  Gibraltar to Ceuta, 27

Morocco, 30
  General information, 31
  Cruising grounds, 36
  1. Atlantic coast Tanger to Laayoune, 36
     General information, 36
     Weather and sailing conditions, 38
     Ports and anchorages in Morocco, 38
  2. Mediterranean coast. Straits of
     Gibraltar to Saidia, 74
     Ports and anchorages, 74

Algeria, 93
  Introduction, 93
  General information, 95
  Ports and anchorages of Algeria, 98

Tunisia, 127
  Introduction, 127
  General information, 129
  Cruising grounds, 133
  Ports and anchorages of Tunisia, 135
  The Kerkennah Islands, 184

The Pelagie Islands, 202
  Anchorages around Lampedusa, 204
  Anchorages around Linosa, 207

Malta, 211
  Anchorages around Malta, 218
  Anchorages around Gozo, 220
  Anchorages around Comino, 222

Appendices, 223
  Charts, 223

Index, 229

Foreword

The Royal Cruising Club Pilotage Foundation was created by members of the RCC to enable them and others to bring their experience of sailing and cruising to a wider public and to encourage the aspiring sailor to cruise further afield with confidence. It was established in 1977 as a registered charity whose object is 'to advance the education of the public in the science and practice of navigation'. Initial funding was provided by a very generous gift by an American member, Dr Fred Ellis, and the gift of the copyrights of several books from other RCC members has allowed the Foundation to fulfil its remit by producing and maintaining pilot books and cruising guides. It now manages the production and updating of over 20 such books.

The first edition of *North Africa* broke new ground for the Pilotage Foundation and made a start to providing cruising information for the southwestern Mediterranean shore. Graham Hutt has built on the foundations laid by Hans van Rijn, adding to and updating the navigational information · and expanding it to include the Atlantic coast of Morocco. But it is the wealth of background information which will make this book invaluable to those seeking to explore this coast. Graham Hutt has travelled this area for over 30 years both by yacht and on land and the Pilotage Foundation is very grateful to him for making his knowledge and experience available to us.

In order to keep this book up-to-date during its lifetime, supplements are produced by the Foundation and published by Imray. To assist us in doing this we need feedback from users and we ask that you send us (though Imray) updated information and any comments that you feel would benefit others.

Francis Walker
Director
RCC Pilotage Foundation
October 1999

Preface to the second edition

The countries of the Maghreb have held a fascination for me over the past 30 years, since my first trip along the coast in 1966 from Tanger to Tripoli. It was therefore with great interest that I purchased a copy of the first edition of *North Africa* in 1992. It was obvious then that it was incomplete, since there was no coverage of the Atlantic coast of Morocco: the most visited part of North Africa. Most yachtsmen make the journey along that part of coast en route to the Canaries and across the Atlantic from the Straits of Gibraltar, without venturing ashore. It remained an area of foreboding only because there was no information available. The publication of this second edition corrects that situation. I have been visiting these ports for many years with my family and friends and found them delightful and the people very hospitable.

It has been a great honour to have been asked by the Pilotage Foundation to carry out the task of producing this second edition, which could not have been done without the input from yachtsmen keen to keep the yachting community informed of changes.

It is with much regret that we observe the political situations in both Algeria and Libya make it unwise to visit those shores. However, as they become accessible, supplements will be produced to keep you informed.

To balance the above situation, yachtsmen will be delighted to learn that Tunisia, which has been open for many years, is increasing its yachting infrastructure and dredging harbours. In Morocco, the government is trying hard to draw closer to Europe politically and this is having a positive effect on the acceptance of yachtsmen along its shores. Two splendid new marinas have been built close to the Straits of Gibraltar and more are planned.

No work as substantial as this one can be attributed to any one person. Thanks go especially to Hans van Rijn for the original work. My wife Anne and children, Ruth, Sara and Mark have been

Europa Point, Gibraltar

Foreword

good sailing companions for over twenty years on the schooner *Arwen Palantir* and sloop *Safwana*. Together we have visited almost all the ports of North Africa as well as Malta and the islands covered here.

Finally, I would like to thank the Pilotage Foundation for entrusting me with this project.

Graham Hutt
October 1999

Acknowledgements

Much of the tedious computer work updating and correcting text for the whole book has been carried out by Di Stoddard.

Special acknowledgements for assistance by country are as follows:

Morocco

The Ministry of Tourism and Mon. Moulay Hachem Kacimi, for arranging access to ports hitherto never visited by yachts and Mon. Mustapher El Aloui who arranged access to updated information and photographs of new port developments from the Chef de la Division Exploitation du Ports. Mon. Cheikh Azouz and Mdme. Amal Ghamrasni, in the Ports Technical Division, for their help in obtaining aerial photographs and charts.

Mon. Ali Belhaj for assisting with new chart information and verification of new ports.

Annette Ridout for visiting and photographing the Northern Morocco ports.

Serena Van Buskirk, who assisted with the historical information on ports and surrounding areas.

Tunisia

Mon. Houcine Sghaier, President Director General, Agence des Portes, et des Installations de Pêche, and his staff.

Simon Butler, who annotated the first edition with corrections, with help from Phil and Liz Hughes, yacht *Rollon* and Chris and Silve Vign, yacht *Gwalarn Ay*.

Malta

John Lawson, whose recent knowledge of Malta has helped me to correct several errors and omissions.

S & D Yachts whose *Yachtsmens' Handbook and Cruising Guide to Malta* has provided useful confirmation and additions.

Gibraltar

The Gibraltar Tourist Board for their kind help and to Di Stoddard who compiled the information.

Author of *North Africa*, second edition's yacht *Safwana* in Marina Smir, Morocco

Islamic architecture. Mosque in Casablanca

North Africa

Gibraltar from the south

North Africa: an area of great historical interest. (Roman city of Volubulis, near Essaouira, Atlantic coast of Morocco)

Introduction

Morocco, Algeria and Tunisia

Standing on the shores of Spain near the Straits of Gibraltar, the awesome Jebel Moussa looms in the background close to the Spanish enclave of Ceuta. The vast continent of Africa is only eight miles away at this point, but the significance of the separation, politically, economically and culturally is indicated by the turbulent tidal waters between the two continents.

Quickly giving way to calmer, non-tidal warmer waters once into the Mediterranean, the coast of North Africa: the Maghreb, opens out to present an unspoilt and exciting cruising ground with miles of deserted beaches, quiet anchorages, sheer green mountainous coasts and ports with an ancient history where yachtsmen will find a warm welcome. A cruise along the Maghreb coast offers an insight into a totally different culture, but with a history closely linked to Europe.

The Moroccan coast is virtually untouched and the majority of ports that can be visited are small fishing communities. Many ports have been in use for hundreds, and in some cases, thousands of years.

Others are larger commercial harbours, providing good shelter. Although not especially equipped for yachts, facilities are always made available and, more importantly, a typically friendly welcome awaits the visitor once the formalities are completed. Virtually the whole coast of Morocco, from its most eastern Mediterranean port of Ras el Ma, to the Atlantic port of Agadir, can be transited by day-hopping. The Atlantic coast is especially interesting, providing access to the fascinating interior of the country which has the most impressive Islamic monuments in the Maghreb. In spite of its Western orientation and considerable number of European tourists, Morocco retains a strong identity and vigorous culture.

Although at the time of writing Algeria is not considered a safe place to visit due to the political turmoil, this is expected to change. The long Algerian coastline has many safe harbours offering good protection. Several of these are commercial ports, though without much traffic; a result of a declining economy. Several of the smaller ports and anchorages are in beautiful quiet settings. A hospitable reception will be found particularly where yachts are rare. Moreover, steady easterlies in the summer make the Algerian coast a logical route for westbound yachts.

Tunisia offers the most varied and established cruising area of all, with many harbours, from small fishing ports to several marinas. The landscape consists of isolated mountains in the north and shallow, tidal coastal areas in the south where the desert meets the sea. Yachts rarely venture S of Mahdia. The winters are mild and, as there are enough ports with good protection should the weather deteriorate, it is possible to continue cruising in the winter. As a result, an increasing number of yachts spend the winter in one of the Tunisian marinas. There are many interesting historical sites to visit, reminders of the fact that this part of North Africa was once an important Roman province. Overland trips to the Berber dwellings in the south provide for interesting desert excursions.

Aim of this pilot

Although only a short distance from Europe, the Maghreb represents a big leap in cultures. The aim of this pilot is to enable the yachtsman visiting for the first time to feel informed and to quickly adjust in order to fully enjoy and appreciate the rich culture and history of the area. The more adventurous yachtsman will find information on almost every port in North Africa, from eastern Tunisia to the southern Moroccan Atlantic ports bordering Mauritania, as well as on Malta and Gibraltar, with their links with Europe and substantial yachting supplies and facilities.

The charts have been simplified in order to present relevant information only. Much of the harbour information is unique to this publication and is based on experience gained from visiting the ports. It is written with the yachtsman in mind, whether sailing or motor cruising.

The scope of the pilot makes it a very useful companion also for those visiting by land and making use of the roads that exist along almost the entire coastline of the Maghreb.

North Africa

Budgeting
If on a low budget, the cost of living and travel in Morocco and Tunisia (though not in Algeria – due to the exchange rate) can be kept surprisingly low. Many harbours do not charge for mooring and local produce from the market is very cheap, leaving money available for inland travel. The waters are comparatively rich in fish and, in season, giant prawns, grouper, swordfish, tuna, octopus and shark are caught as well as more common species such as mullet, sardines and mackerel.

The quiet unpolluted beaches and interesting sights to visit in the Maghreb provide rich cruising grounds for the adventurous.

Politics
In the first edition of this pilot it was stated that the three North African countries were working to improve the ease with which yachts might cruise their waters. Tunisia is the most advanced in this respect having catered for yachtsmen for many years.

Whilst the Moroccan authorities are anxious to encourage yachtsmen to visit their shores and there are now two splendid marinas, with more planned, it is only fair to say that they nevertheless remain suspicious and inexperienced in dealing with pleasure craft. Bear in mind that smuggling and illegal emigration is a serious problem in Morocco which the EC is pressing the government to improve. However, the authorities have promised a more co-ordinated, consistent and friendly approach. Recent reports indicate that this is being implemented, as more yachts visit their shores.

Algeria remains accessible to yachtsmen, but it would not be advisable to visit until the security situation has improved. Visas are more difficult to obtain than before.

Gibraltar, Malta and the Pelagie Islands
These small countries, along with several islands along the way are covered because of their proximity to North Africa. Gibraltar and Malta have excellent yacht chandlery and repair facilities.

Types of yacht
These cruising grounds do not require a particular type of boat, although a good engine is essential as there are periods in summer without wind – and you will frequently encounter strong winds when entering a harbour in the early evening, when the wind is often at its maximum before dying down at sunset. A few additions or modifications may be worthwhile to ensure a more comfortable time on these shores. See *Yacht equipment recommended*.

The shallower waters in the south of Tunisia will be out of the reach of deep keel yachts.

General information
I. Maritime information
Meteorology
It should be noted that visual signs and methods of forecasting using clouds and barometer, as is usual in Northern Europe, often do not give the same indications in the Mediterranean. It is common to see a fast falling or rising barometer, with no resulting change in conditions. Similarly, cloud formations that we would usually associate with rain or storms approaching, often clear in minutes, leaving blue skies. Sudden winds or squalls can appear very quickly without any warning. These unannounced changes are normally short-lived. This situation changes near the Straits of Gibraltar and on the Atlantic coast of Morocco, where weather patterns are more predictable and forecasts more accurate. Winds along the North African coast and in the Straits of Gibraltar are often very localised. Winds of up to force 8 are often present at Tarifa, whilst in Gibraltar or Tanger, just a few miles away, they can be negligible.

Winds
The N coast of Africa can be divided into sections with varying general wind conditions.
1. **The Atlantic coast of Morocco**
    The northern sector of this coast maintains a predominantly SW airstream occasionally swinging to the NW or NE. In the winter months, strong gales frequently sweep through the area as depressions move NNE from the Canaries through the Straits of Gibraltar. In summer, the wind tends to be steady by day from SW, dropping at sunset. Further south, winds are predominately from the NW, reaching 20kts by day and dying down at night. Gales are rare in summer months.
2. **The Straits of Gibraltar**
    Summer winds are almost always either E or W, about equal duration. If wind strength by day reaches around 20kts, it almost always drops at night. In winter, winds are predominantly E or W, but with frequent swings to the SW, which usually indicates a depression with rain. Very occasionally in winter, NE winds carry very cold air to the area, usually with a long period of settled weather.
3. **The coast of Morocco and Algeria to Oran**
    Roughly, from Ceuta to Oran in Algeria, E and W winds are about equal in frequency in the summer. As in many parts of the Mediterranean, quite often there is too little wind to sail in the summer and the winds do not dictate any favourable sailing direction. In the winter, winds from the W sector are more common.
4. **The coast of Algeria from Oran E to Cap Bon**

General information

From Oran eastward, W winds predominate in the winter. Starting in April/May and continuing during the summer until October, a steady easterly blows in a zone of 25M off the Algerian coast. Around midday it can reach up to 20kts and at sunset it usually dies down. Therefore a summer cruise along the N coast of Algeria can best be planned from E to W. In October winds from the W sector become more frequent until they predominate in the winter. Around Bizerte NW winds are common in the summer and NW to E winds are common in the Gulf of Tunis. Strong warm southerly winds of short duration frequently blow at night near the coast.

5. **From Cap Bon to the Libyan border**
On the E coast of Tunisia the wind regime is markedly different from the other areas with onshore E winds in the summer and offshore W winds in winter. The summer sea breeze usually starts in the morning from the NE and after veering to the SE dies down around sunset. In springtime it can reach up to Force 5–6. In winter the situation is reversed with mostly westerlies.

Between Sfax and Jerba winds are invariably from the E in spring and summer. The winter winds in this area are more evenly distributed around the clock with a slightly higher percentage of W winds.

Wind hazards

Summer gales are rare though not unknown, especially around Bizerte and to a lesser extent Gabès. Winter gales on the N coast of Tunisia are generally stronger and more frequent than on the coast of Algeria and are most often from the NW. In NE Tunisia, especially around Cap Bon, sudden wind shifts are likely. On the E coast of Tunisia gales are rare in summer and infrequent in winter but strong easterlies build up a bad sea at Kelibia, making it difficult to enter the port. Bizerte and Pantelleria have the strongest average winds all year round. Local depressions develop over the Gulf of Gabès in the winter and strong winds are common. Occasionally gales are recorded.

Scirocco is the name widely used in the Mediterranean for southerly Sahara winds which bring hot air laden with dust and, on the N coast of Africa, it is very hot and dry. Fortunately it does not occur very often nor does it last very long.

Winter gales are more frequent in the Straits of Gibraltar and, in recent years, bringing torrential rain that can last for several days at a time, sometimes with wet unsettled weather lasting for weeks. These are the result of depressions moving NNE from the Canaries.

Rain

Rainfall varies considerably in the region from less than 200mm yearly in Gabès to 330mm in Sousse, 420mm in Tunis to almost 800mm in Annaba and Algiers and around 1200mm in Aïn Draham up in the mountains on the N coast of Tunisia. Around the Straits of Gibraltar and the Moroccan Atlantic coast the weather pattern has changed markedly recently: annual rainfall has doubled in the past three years, after many years of drought. Fortunately for sailors, practically all of it falls in winter.

Waterspouts

Waterspouts generally occur in the vicinity of thunderstorms and most commonly at the end of summer. They can cause considerable damage. Their paths seem to follow the clouds and it is usually possible to sail out of their way.

Visibility

Fog is rare, but occasionally occurs in summer in the Straits of Gibraltar where it can be a nuisance. It is a phenomenon associated with an easterly (*levante*) wind and usually forms suddenly around 10am as the land temperature rises, clearing soon after midday in the Eastern Straits. Hazy conditions with a visibility of around four miles is common in

'Flying Saucer' clouds: Indication of strong E winds to come

A familiar cloud over the Rock: indication of E wind (Levanter) conditions, often setting in for a week or more

summer along the Tunisian E coast and the Atlantic Moroccan coast. Visibility is reduced in a *scirocco*.

Temperatures (Celsius)
Air (day and night)

	January		April		July		October	
	max	mean	max	mean	max	mean	max	mean
Melilla	23°	17/8°	29°	21/12°	39°	30/21°	30°	26/16°
Algiers	20°	15/9°	28°	20/13°	36°	29/21°	29°	23/17°
Bizerte	19°	14/8°	26°	20/12°	37°	29/22°	32°	25/17°
Tunis	21°	14/7°	29°	21/11°	42°	31/21°	33°	24/16°
Sousse	21°	16/7°	28°	21/12°	39°	31/21°	31°	26/17°
Gabès	21°	16/6°	32°	22/13°	38°	32/22°	34°	26/17°

Sea Winter 14°, summer from 21° in Ceuta to 26° in Gabès

Sea conditions

Currents
An E current sets along the coast from Gibraltar eastwards, stemming from the flow of Atlantic water into the Mediterranean, replacing water lost through evaporation. Within the Straits, during prolonged periods of easterly or westerly wind, currents caused by a combination of tidal flow, surface wind effect and standing current can reach up to 6kts at HWS. This is more fully explained in the section *Transiting the Straits*.

Once into the Mediterranean it can reach 2kts around promontories and on some of the banks off Al Hoceima. Between Melilla and Jebha, 1½M offshore, an unexplained westerly-going current is experienced, which can be used to advantage. Off the Algerian coast, it runs E between 0·5 and 1kt.

In the Sicilian Channel there is a constant SE current averaging about 1kt in summer. Currents off the Tunisian coast are weaker and less predictable but they can affect navigation when on passage from Pantelleria or Lampedusa.

The Atlantic coast of Morocco has a south-going current of around 0·5kt.

Tides
Tidal ranges on the Moroccan coast from the western Straits of Gibraltar to the Canaries is around 3m, with little difference in timing from Gibraltar, which is a standard port. At Gibraltar it is around 1m, reducing rapidly once clear of Europa Point heading E, becoming negligible 10M into the Mediterranean, until reaching Tunisia.

South from La Chebba, Tunisia, the range is again noticeable and in Gabès the spring range is 1·8m. In the shallow waters around the Kerkennah Islands the range can be 1m and appropriate allowances must be made. There are also strong tidal currents in the channels around the islands. Strong onshore winds can increase the range. In the Ajim Channel between the island of Jerba and the mainland tidal currents are even stronger and navigation is made more difficult by the lack of reliable buoys.

Though rare, the *marrobbio*, a tidal surge with a period of between 10 and 26 minutes, can raise the water level during undisturbed weather. There are also gradual fluctuations during winter, when the mean level in the central Mediterranean can fall as much as 0·5m below normal. These differences are often associated with barometric pressure: high pressure causes lower water levels and vice versa. A range of around 1 metre can be experienced in otherwise non-tidal waters due to these barometric pressure differences, which are more noticeable in the eastern Mediterranean. Take this into account when exploring some of the smaller fishing ports with critical depths.

Swell
In summer, the Mediterranean is usually calm except during prolonged periods of strong E or W winds. A daily wind at the western end usually dies around sunset. However, there are occasional gales which can very quickly whip up huge seas. These usually are short lived. In July and August flat calms are often experienced, lasting for days. In winter, gales are more frequent and occasionally last for several days.

On the Atlantic coast of Morocco, a long swell from the SW or NW prevails. In summer this can be between 1 and 2m. In winter it is often 3 to 5m.

In the Straits of Gibraltar the sea conditions depend very much on the state of the tide and wind direction. Strong E or W winds can create high seas at HW.

Flora and fauna
The flora and fauna of North Africa is closer to that of Southern Europe than to the rest of Africa; the Sahara has been an impassable barrier for most plants and animals. In the S of Tunisia and Libya the Sahara almost reaches the shore but in Morocco, Algeria and Northern Tunisia the coastal areas support a good variety of plant and animal life.

The flora has adapted itself to the cool and humid winters when snow only falls on the high mountains and the mild and wet spring when plants grow quickly. During the long hot and dry summer most of the vegetation wilts or dies and the land looks dry and barren.

The most common vegetation is the *maquis*. The typical Mediterranean scrubby underbrush; erica arborea, dwarf palm, cytisus, holly, evergreen oak and pine trees are the primary vegetation. The prickly pear (*opuntia*) has been introduced from America and eucalyptus from Australia is perhaps too successful in reforestation projects.

The majority of the population lives in the coastal plains and most of the soil is cultivated. In the spring there are big orange- and yellow-coloured flower beds interrupted by blue lupins and yellow lathyrus. Since the plains have been cultivated for centuries, it is hard to imagine what the original landscape looked like but most likely it was made up of grassland, wild olive trees and cork oaks. Today all olive trees are cultivated but some of the original wild cork oak forests remain. The sandy soil on which they thrive has little value to mankind.

The pine and cedar covered slopes of the Rif Mountains in Morocco resemble the Sierra Nevada but, as in Spain, human habitation has taken its toll. Pine forests have been cut for building material or firewood and grazing goats have cleared low shrubs and trees. Through reforestation programmes, financially supported by the developed countries, a continuous effort is made to halt soil erosion, but the effect is offset by the increased need for farmland to feed the rapidly growing population in all of the Maghreb countries.

Numerous species of birds cross the Mediterranean strip as they migrate to and from northern Europe. Small animals like the weasel, otter and genet (genetta, a cat common in Southern Europe), are resident. Until the beginning of this century lions were found in NE Algeria and Tunisia but are now extinct. In the Middle and High Atlas of Morocco, leopards survive alongside more common red foxes and jackals. Wild boar are common in the N of Tunisia and Algeria where hunting is allowed.

Typical domestic animals of North Africa are goats and sheep which are still kept by migrating shepherds. Dromedaries, mules and donkeys, are particularly common in Morocco and Tunisia.

Marine life

In comparison with other parts of the Mediterranean, marine life along the Maghreb coast is relatively rich and sea pollution is far less. The countries are not as developed as in Europe, conservation measures have been taken by the governments and the coast is not as densely populated as the northern shores of the Mediterranean. The fishing fleets of the Maghreb are made up of small vessels which do not scour the seabed as effectively as the larger boats of the Italian or Spanish fleets and both Morocco and Algeria have a continental shelf too narrow to support large scale fishing activity. Tunisia on the other hand has a very wide continental shelf which is possibly one of the richest fishing grounds in the Mediterranean. It still has potential for further exploitation and this is why many new fishing ports have been built recently and why their fishing fleet is expanding. Along the Moroccan and Algerian coast sardines, mackerel, various kinds of sea bream, grey mullets, red mullets, prawns, bonito, swordfish, tuna and shark are common. Along the E coast of Tunisia the mackerel disappears and red mullet become rare but octopus are abundant along with grouper and dentex.

Dolphins are common in the Straits of Gibraltar and along the Moroccan and Algerian coasts, where several pods of differing species live. Some of these families are up to 40 strong. Whenever transiting the Straits or crossing from Spain to Morocco they will accompany your yacht, weaving in and out and crossing your bows at great speed. Pilot whales and occasionally other species of whales and shark will also be seen in the area. Hammerhead sharks, tuna and swordfish are often seen in the area between Ceuta and Cabo de Negro.

Fishing methods

Single boats trawl off the coast and on the edge of the continental shelf in depths up to about 400m.

Large circular nets are set for sardines and mackerel. The main boat, with a crew of sometimes up to 30, lays a floating net in a large circle. One or two of the small auxiliary boats enter the net and attract the fish with powerful lights. Then the bottom of the net is closed and hauled in.

Long lines, with a multitude of short lines furnished with baited hooks, are used mainly for swordfish. The long line is kept afloat with small pieces of styrofoam every 150m or so. Usually only the end buoys are lit and the fishermen patrol the length of the line.

Floating nets are usually laid close to the shore, around harbour entrances and in bays. This is real subsistence fishing as the catch is minimal. It also presents a hazard to sailing boats, particularly in Tunisia as the nets are easily caught around the propeller.

The traditional fishing technique of the Kerkennah Islands uses traps made of palm fronds to divert the fish into nets. The palm fronds are planted more or less permanently in the shallow banks, at right angles to the coast line.

In the S of Tunisia, baked clay pots are used to catch octopus. The pots are strung together and laid on the sandy bottom. Octopus prefer to seek protection in a hole and since the sandy bottom does not provide this facility they crawl in the clay pot.

Tunny nets

The coast of North Africa and Morocco in particular, is famous for its tuna fishing and has been for thousands of years. Tunisia derived its name from the industry. Early coins from the ancient city of Lixus in Morocco bear the tuna fish engraved on them, proof of the importance of this industry as far back as Carthaginian times (around the 4th century BC). Tuna was preserved for export in vast factories, no doubt deriving the salt from the nearby salt pans, in an age when ice was not available. These pans are still in use today, just below the ruins of Lixus and extending to the port of Larache.

This unique sense of ongoing history is a most endearing feature of North Africa. However, this industry also presents a navigational hazard to watch out for. Tuna (tunny) nets are often laid 4M out to sea from the shore. It has been reported that in the area of El Jadida, they can extend further. They are laid out from April to December and are often placed in the same position from one year to the next. These nets consist of a heavy steel cable connected to floats and a deep-weighted net, which

North Africa

pulls down the floats so that they may be almost invisible. Usually, one can assume they are present when small boats are close inshore, with larger ones further out to sea – if they are obviously not trawling. The end marker usually has a flag, either on a buoy, or fixed to a short mast on a small dinghy. These also, often cannot be seen until one is almost upon them.

The nets are supposed to be clearly marked. However, in practice it is very difficult to spot them until a mile or less away and they are almost never lit at night. It is not possible to pass them on the landward side, so substantial deviations have to be made if your vessel is close inshore. They are laid every year between Ceuta and Marina Smir, between Cap Spartel and Asilah and near to Larache, as well as along parts of the coast of Algeria and Tunisia.

Daunting as this may seem, don't feel intimidated by this hazard, for once you are used to spotting the tell-tale signs of these nets, there really is no problem in avoiding them.

Harpoon fishing

The North African coast has probably the most abundant sea life of the entire Mediterranean and there are many places where harpoon fishing can be rewarding for an experienced snorkel diver. Most probably this will be a more reliable way to catch fish than trolling or fishing with a rod. As in Europe, harpooning when scuba diving is considered unethical and is forbidden. The attitude to harpooning when snorkelling is ambivalent. In most harbours locals will be seen with harpoons snorkelling from the breakwaters. It is unlikely that official permission would be given if asked for, so it is best to proceed with discretion.

In 1990 new rules were issued in Tunisia for divers who come specifically for harpoon fishing. These foreign visitors can only receive permission when working from a Tunisian flagged boat. Applications can be sent through a local Tunisian diving club or the FAST (Fédération des Activités Subaquatique de Tunisie), BP 284, 1004 Tunis ☎ 239659.

To what extent yachtsmen cruising Tunisian waters will be affected remains to be seen.

The following are some of the good areas for snorkelling:

Morocco Cabo de Negro, El Jebha (bream, sea bass), Al Hoceima and Ras-el-Ma.

Algeria Beni-Saf, Habibas Islands and the coast E of Bejaïa as far as Annaba.

Tunisia Cap Carthage (sea bass), around Cap Bon and La Chebba.

Hauling 400kg tunny. An industry of North Africa for some 2,500 years

Scuba diving

Diving bottles on board a yacht are a problem to customs officials in many countries, including the Maghreb and diving is sure to attract attention from authorities. This is because the equipment is usually associated with a commercial activity requiring a licence. As long it is only to observe or photograph, it may be allowed but any other activity will certainly require official permission. It is best to check beforehand with local officials to avoid any problems. Diving schools operate in several ports in Tunisia, Gibraltar, Ceuta and Malta and it is possible to participate in daily diving trips, especially in the summer months. Diving bottles can be filled and tested in Gibraltar. In Ceuta, several ports in Tunisia and in Morocco, wherever coral or sponge fishermen operate, one can arrange to get bottles filled.

Anchoring

There is no law prohibiting anchoring anywhere along the North African coast. However, in practice it arouses suspicion unless specific requests have been made at a nearby port. Even then, at night it is likely to encourage a military boat to investigate. In Tunisia, there is less of a problem than elsewhere, because the authorities are more used to yachts. More information is included under each country section. In any event, never anchor before clearing customs.

Yacht equipment recommended

Fenders and warps
In most of the ports yachts lie alongside a quay, so good fenders, warps and anti-chafing gear are necessary. A builder's plank, with a hole at either end so that it can be suspended outside the fenders, is often useful when against a concrete wall.

Batteries
With sun all the year round, solar panels to keep the batteries charged will be found useful, especially in some of the fishing harbours in Morocco, where it is difficult to get an electricity supply.

Water
A large water container or two should be carried for use in the harbours where a hose connection is far away. Carry a long hosepipe.

Anchoring equipment
Although most anchorages are sand with good holding, very few provide overall protection and there can be sudden wind shifts. Consequently, anchor gear must be heavy enough for the boat. Bruce, CQR and Danforth type anchors work well in most anchorages and a Fisherman will be useful in weedy or rocky areas. Typical depths are between 3 and 6m and anchorages deeper than 10m are rare.

Insects
Flies can be a pest; mosquitoes are less of a problem. Good screens will keep both out and also help to keep cockroaches or rodents from boarding.

Navigation
GPS navigation position finders are now very cheap, and will be a great advantage on the North African coast, where buoys are often out of position and lights change signature before charts can be updated, or simply do not function at all.

Communications
The GSM mobile phone system is installed in Morocco, Malta, Tunisia and Gibraltar, providing a link to the world even some miles offshore. With a computer interface, this can also provide Internet and e-mail facilities. Ensure that the International Roaming facility is activated for use abroad. GSM call rates are usually cheaper than using local hotel phones.

Carry
Tools and equipment to hook up to continental type electrical fittings. A long hosepipe and a selection of fittings and jubilee clips.

Photocopies of ship's papers and crew lists which can be left with officials.

A good sun awning; summer temperatures are higher than in the northern Mediterranean.

All charts, maps, guide books, and a French dictionary; all are difficult if not impossible, to obtain in North Africa.

Sufficient provisions, as they can be hard to find, particularly along the Algerian coast.

Availability of supplies and provisions

Fuel
Generally, fuel is available in all harbours, although it may have to be supplied in cans. This can always be arranged and carried by the locals for a small fee.

Water
The quality of tap-water is generally good along the North African coast as far as taste and bacteria-count is concerned but local circumstances and personal metabolism determine whether one can actually drink it unboiled. In Tunisian and Moroccan ports, quality is invariably good, but in some Algerian ports it is suspect. Avoid taps with no pressure. Bottled mineral water is widely available in Morocco and Tunisia but not in Algeria. Water is available by hosepipe in most of Tunisia, Malta and Gibraltar. In Algeria and Morocco it is available in some ports, but in others must be carried a short distance in cans. Again, there are always locals willing for a very small fee to take it to your yacht.

For more specific information look under the general information section of each port.

Gas
Camping Gaz is available almost everywhere. In

North Africa

Ceuta and Gibraltar all types of gas bottles can be conveniently and cheaply filled. In Morocco, Algeria and Tunisia gas is widely used and bottled butane, propane or a mixture of both is widely available and cheap. All three countries have bottles with ⅝in left-handed external thread as used on older English Calor Gas propane bottles. This is the same fitting as used on European propane bottles. Bottles with different fittings will be difficult to get filled in the Maghreb unless taken direct to the refineries.

Bottles can be filled in gas plants in Tanger, Bizerte and Gabès but sometimes foreign types, including *Camping Gaz* bottles, are refused.

In Algeria no foreign gas bottles are accepted.

In Tunisia marina personnel in Al Kantaoui and Monastir fill from local bottles as a service to marina clients.

Although technically, to purchase a bottle locally a contract with the gas company is required, in practice it is often possible to avoid the bureaucracy. Be careful about the type of gas. For detailed advice on fittings and procedures, contact the Boating Industry Liaison Section of Calor Gas Limited, Appleton Park, Slough SL3 9JG England ☎ 01753 40000.

Provisions

A plentiful supply of fresh food is available everywhere. Fruit and vegetables are seasonal. Since deep freeze facilities are not generally used, meat too is always fresh – often alive waiting to be purchased and butchered. Freshly caught fish can be seen on the quays and in the markets. Local bread is delicious and at its best within a few hours of baking. It is baked throughout the day and, since it has no preservative and goes stale quickly, do not stock up with it. Dry provisions like flour, sugar, rice and pasta, etc. are also readily available, except in Algeria where they may be scarce. Canned food is not so easily obtained, so stock up in Gibraltar and Malta and in the large towns. Ice is available everywhere, if needed, since it is used by the fishermen to keep their catch fresh and is often manufactured in the ports.

A wide range of locally produced soft drinks are very good value and many people find them better tasting than their European equivalents. Lager beer is also available in all towns as well as locally produced wine.

Yacht repair facilities

Lift-out facilities

Several marinas are equipped with travel-hoists for hauling out boats, especially in Tunisia, Gibraltar Malta and two in Morocco. However, almost every fishing harbour has a slipway with blocks, props and wedges that can be used in an emergency. In addition, on the Atlantic coast of Morocco, yachts can be careened on a mudflat or in harbour, as the tide range is up to 3m. In Marina Smir there are excellent haul out facilities. Kabila Marina has a light hoist for yachts up to 15 tons.

In Algeria only Sidi Ferruch has a travel-lift (16 tonnes).

In Tunisia there are travel-lifts in the marinas at Sidi Bou Saïd and Al Kantaoui, with one planned for Monastir. There are large travel-lifts in the fishing ports of Bizerte, Kelibia, Monastir (new fishing port) and Sfax and others are planned at Teboulba and Tabarka. In the fishing ports there is usually no high pressure hose available but water and electricity can generally be organised.

Mechanical repairs

There are very competent engineers in most of the larger ports and in many small ones. As in most

Despite primitive workshop facilities, this engine was rebuilt in a day in Morocco and runs better than it ever did!

Most harbours in North Africa have slip or haul-out facilities that can be used in an emergency

third world countries, mechanics take great pride in being able to fix almost anything. Rather than look for a spare part, which inevitably will not be available, a way will be found to either repair the old one or make a new component from scratch.

Spares
Almost all typical yacht spares can be obtained in the large towns and in many small harbours: ropes, fenders, bottle screws, wire rigging, bolts, 'U' clamps and anchoring gear for a boat of any size. Although you will not find stainless steel replacements, in an emergency, sturdy galvanised iron equivalents for most standing and running rigging parts can be found. Good quality polypropylene ropes of any length and thickness can be purchased in most hardware shops.

Navigation notes

With most yachts now equipped with GPS navigation, there is less need to provide the outline coastal features, which are in any case of little practical use due to the haze often present along the coast. In describing harbour entry, this book assumes that a yacht is equipped with GPS. However, please note that in some areas of the North African coast, the GPS position fix may not coincide exactly with the charted position, (at least using Admiralty charts) although local charts are, I am informed, more accurate. Errors are reported as being small and usually only longitudinal, but care should in any case be taken.

Port radio VHF channel information is included, although, in North Africa, any response to VHF calls is rare.

Charts
This survey was conducted with the use of charts produced in Europe, although the three main countries concerned maintain a hydrographic effort of their own, the best by Algeria. The British Admiralty offers complete coverage of the North African coast at a scale of 1:300,000; its coverage of individual countries at larger scales is variable. The other two main European sources of charts are the Service Hydrographique et Océanographique de la Marine of France and the Instituto Hidrografico de la Marina of Cádiz, Spain. Reference to these organisations and their products will be British Admiralty, French and Spanish. See Appendix for details.

Morocco
The Spanish with their interest in Morocco, are an important source of information. Admiralty charts are updated but do not seem to include several well-established harbours. Moroccan charts exist but are difficult to find. Most of the harbour information contained here is based on old charts, updated with information gained from visits.

Algeria
Algeria is well covered by British Admiralty charts. Its hydrographic service publishes charts which are available through the Ministry of Transport in Algiers.

Tunisia
French charts cover Tunisia in great detail but many of the surveys were made more than a century ago and there has been little up-dating during the past thirty years. Ports built within the last ten years nor changes to older ones, to say nothing of new conspicuous marks, appear; nevertheless, navigation around the Kerkennah Islands or in the Gulf of Bou Grara should not be attempted without French charts. British Admiralty charts, although mainly to a smaller scale than the French charts, are more up to date and the range includes useful larger scale charts of areas important to shipping.

Tunisia does not have a hydrographic office but copies of French charts are available from the Service de Topography. The main office is near Tunis international airport, about 600m E of Stade Olympique in El Menzah and next to the *Météo* office which has a conspicuous satcom dome on the roof and a branch is located at Sousse on Avenue Bourguiba, opposite the Monoprix.

Notices to Mariners
The *marine marchande* in Tunisia issue *Avis aux Navigateurs* on a regular basis. These notices are distributed to their offices in major ports and to the British embassy and are read before the weather on Tunis Radio and Sfax Radio. The contents deal with buoys, lights, tunny nets laid, firing exercises, etc.

In Morocco notices to mariners along with weather fax information is provided daily and posted in the customs house and harbourmasters office.

Daily notices are posted on the notice boards of the marinas in Gibraltar.

A note about the plans
1. Co-ordinates of ports are taken from about midway in the entrance.
2. Description of lights is sometimes changed from the *Admiralty List of Lights* when their description is not very clear or simply incorrect.
3. When two charts are quoted for a port the first one is large scale (1:300,000) and the second is the smaller scale (1:60,000).
4. Distances are given to various ports.
   For Morocco Mediterranean coast from W to E.
   For Morocco Atlantic coast N to S
   For Algeria from W to E.
   For Tunisia the route is from N to S.
5. Spelling of names is taken from the Admiralty charts as long as their spelling agrees with Michelin map 172 for Algeria and Tunisia. Common differences are noted.
6. Co-ordinates for harbour entry lights are only given for the large commercial ports.

North Africa

7. Some Admiralty charts give the tides as 'not to exceed 0·6m' presumably to be on the safe side. For practical purposes however the tides can really be neglected but where no specific tidal information was available the 0·6m max. range is quoted. In practice tides can be forgotten except on the Atlantic coast and further S in Tunisia.
8. Prices for harbour dues and hauling out are only given as an indication. They are often negotiable.
9. Bearings are true and from seaward.
10. Depths are in metres.
11. Light characteristics are based on the author's observations and from information provided by yachtsmen.
   Positions given are from the Admiralty List of Lights which may differ slightly from the positions shown on the charts.

Key to symbols used on plans

- harbourmaster/port office
- fuel
- customs
- post office
- slipway
- anchorage
- anchoring prohibited
- visitor's berths

About the distances between ports

Distances to nearby ports for Tunisia are shown as follows:
e.g. Beni-Saf
Ras el Ma 54M, Ghazaouet 28M – Oran 54M
The hyphen indicates the position of the port described, ports to the left are to the west and the ones to the right of the hyphen are to the east.

Buoyage

Buoyage is practically non-existent in Morocco and Algeria. Parts of the Tunisian shallows are buoyed but except for those which are important to commercial shipping, the position, characteristic (particularly lights) and even the existence of buoys cannot be relied on.

Lights

Every effort has been made to acquire accurate information on lights. However maintenance is poor and, for instance in Tunisia, though the Navy is responsible for lights it has no institutionalised way of reporting defects. Do not expect to find lights to correspond exactly to the information in this or any other book. Generally lighthouses and harbour lights in the bigger commercial ports are reliable but in the small ports and even the marinas they are not.

Clearing formalities

Unlike sailing in Europe, where once cleared by customs you are free to travel anywhere without further formalities, in North Africa, yachts have to officially enter and clear each port visited. This formality is speeded up by informing the authorities of your next port of call. Technically in Tunisia, once cleared, all that needs to be done in the next port is produce the papers without the need to complete further formalities. However, the reality is often different.

Officials from the customs, immigration police, local police and harbour authorities will all visit your yacht on arrival. They are usually very courteous and the routine filling of forms is a friendly affair that does not take long. Full details of your yacht and a crew list is necessary at each port, so carrying photocopies of the relevant information is very helpful.

If the skippers name is not on the owners logbook, a letter of authorisation by the owner is necessary and will avoid problems. The officials like to see a ships stamp on forms, although this is not strictly necessary.

If you intend to change crews or if an individual is leaving by land or air, it is important to inform the immigration department to avoid problems when you leave.

Visas

Specific visa requirement information should be obtained from the relevant embassies or consular officials in advance of travel, but most nationalities do not have any problem in Tunisia or Morocco. If a passport holder is not in possession of a visa, this is usually overcome by the authorities issuing a shore pass as they would for ships crews while the passport is held until departure. Most nationalities require a visa before visiting Algeria, with the exception of Swiss and French nationals.

Restricted items

Guns and large quantities of alcohol have to be declared. Spirits may be bonded onboard by the customs authorities until departure if a suitable lock-up exists, or kept by the customs department until leaving. Guns, even a Very pistol, provoke a lot of paperwork when declared. Drugs are forbidden, except for medicinal purposes.

Weather forecasts

Probably the most useful general weather forecast for the North African coast is given by Monaco Radio on SSB although it will have to be interpreted to predict winds along the Tunisian coast.

The Algerian SSB stations in Oran, Algiers and Annaba are difficult to receive, even along the coast, and are a partial retransmission of French weather forecasts.

Weather and radio information

In several Algerian and some Tunisian ports weather forecasts are available from the *capitainerie*, *marine marchande* or sometimes a small *Météo* office in the port which will be gladly supplied to yachts. These are mentioned in the port descriptions.

All weather forecasts for Tunisia are in French.

Tunis Radio and Sfax Radio provide a good, although not always accurate forecast on SSB and this is probably the best for winds along the Tunisian coast. The National Broadcast Authority has a useful report on Radio Tunis Ch 2 (Chaine International) on medium wave. Also useful for the winds out at sea are the transmissions of the Italian station Radio Due which are retransmitted in Tunisia.

For the area of Gibraltar, including a 50 mile radius covering Northern Morocco, good forecasts can be obtained from Gibraltar Radio throughout the day on FM92·6 and AM1458kHz. These stations can only be received if you are in the immediate vicinity of Gibraltar.

Accurate forecasts can be obtained from the local harbour authorities.

Mention should be made of the amateur radio Maritime Mobile net, which also gives a forecast on 14303Mhz every weekday at 1730UT, covering the entire Mediterranean and any other areas required. Propagation is not always good, but usually a helpful yachtsman who is receiving will offer to relay the information.

Forecast frequencies and times

Time (UT)	Station	Frequency	Language
0715, 1715	Monaco Radio	8728·2kHz	French English
0805, 1705	Tunis Radio	1820kHz	French
0630, 1230 1630, 2130	Radio Tunis Ch 2	962kHz	French
0500, 1335, 2035	Radio Due	846kHz	Italian
0933, 1733	Sfax Radio	2719kHz	French

The forecast on Tunis Radio(SSB) starts with the AVURNAV, the *Avis Urgence aux Navigateur*, the Notice to Mariners.

The weather report begins with a general description of the weather systems followed by the 24hr forecast for the three regions of Tunisia

Zone du Nord, the coast from Tabarka to Cap Bon

Zone du Nord Est, the coast from Cap Bon to Mahdia and

Zone du Golfe de Gabès, the coast from Mahdia to Zarzis.

At the end of the forecast the tendency for the following 24 hours is given.

The wind speed is given in knots, wave height in feet and visibility in nautical miles.

Radiobeacons

No beacon is reliable: many are frequently off-air. All have 24hr transmission scheduled unless otherwise indicated.

Morocco and Spain
Cap Spartel *SP* (···/−−·) 312kHz 100M 35°47'·40N 05°55'·55W
Tarifa *O* (−−−) 299kHz 50M 36°00'·13N 05°36'·47W
Ceuta *CE* (−·−·/·) 311kHz 50M 35°53'·84N 05°18'·6W
Tétouan Aero *TUN* (−/··−/−·) 388kHz 35°37'·33N 05°17'·65W
(*Note* this beacon is well inland)
Al Hoecima Aero *ALU* (·−/·−··/··−) 401kHz 35°11'·0N 03°50'·30W
Nador Aero *NDR* (−·/−··/·−·) 414kHz 35°09'·57N 02°55'·63W
Cabo de Palos *PA* (·−−·/·−) 313kHz 50M 37°38'·17N 00°41'·42W
Cabo de la Nao *NO* (−·/−−−) 294·6kHz 50M 38°44'·17N 00°14'·20W

Sardegna
Carbonara Aero *CAR* (−·−·/·−/·−·) 402kHz 100M 39°06'·27N 09°30'·93E
Tortoli Aero *ARB* (·−/−···/·−·) 289kHz 25M 39°55'·38N 09°41'·72E
Olbia Aero *SME* (···/−−/·) 357kHz 50M 40°53'·95N 09°30'·82E
Capo Ferro *CF* (−·−·/··−·) 291kHz 100M 41°09'·25N 09°31'·47E
Alghero Aero *ALG* (·−/·−··/−−·) 382kHz 50M 40°35'·17N 08°15'·83E
Capo Sandalo *IP* (··/·−−·) 310kHz 100M 39°08'·92N 08°13'·42E
Cagliari Aero *CAG* (−·−·/·−/−−·) 371kHz 25M 39°12'·85N 09°05'·87E

Algeria
Ras Aiguille *AG* (·−/−−·) 296·5kHz 100M 35°52'·60N 00°29'·25W
Mostaganem Aero *MOS* (−−/−−−/···) 334kHz 100M 35°54'·55N 00°08'·23E
Mostaganem North Jetty *MN* (−−/−·) 301kHz 5M 35°56'·06N 00°04'·19E
Ras Tenes *TS* (−/···) 313·5kHz 30M 36°33'·05N 01°20'·49E
Cherchell Aero *CHE* (−·−·/····/·) 397kHz 100M 36°35'·68N 02°11'·62E
Ras Caxine *CX* (−·−·/−··−) 287kHz 200M 36°48'·83N 02°57'·37E
Algiers *AL* (·−/·−··) 309·5kHz 20M Fog 36°46'·69N 03°04'·75E
Ras Matifou *MF* (−−·/··−·) 291·5kHz 30M 36°48'·75N 03°14'·83E
Bejaia East Jetty *BI* (−···/··) 314·5kHz 10M 36°45'·22N 05°06'·17E
Bejaia Aero *BJA* (−···/·−−−/·−) 423kHz 50M 36°42'·38N 05°01'·50E
Jijel Aero *DJI* (−··/·−−−/··) 340kHz 50M 36°48'·9N 05°52'·20E

Tunisia
Cap Blanc *BC* (−···/−·−·) 309·5kHz 100M 37°19'·72N 09°50'·13E
Tunis Khereddine Aero *KDN* (−·−/····/−·) 385·5kHz 36°49'·4N 10°18'·5E
Cap Bon *BN* (−···/−·) 296·5kHz 200M 37°04'·22N 11°02'·67E

North Africa

El Attaia, Kerkennah *KR* (–·–/–·) 298·5kHz 100M
34°44'·50N 11°18'·33E
Jerba Aero *JER* (·–––/·/·–·) 371kHz 33°52'·70N
10°44'·90E

Italy
Lampedusa Aero *LPD* (·–··/·–––) 373kHz 50M
35°29'·88N 12°36'·73E
Pantellaria *PT* (·–––/–) 302·5kHz 100M 36°49'·56N
12°00'·81E

Sicily
Cozzo Spadaro *PZ* (·––··/––··) 286·5kHz 100M
36°41'·25N 15°07'·83E
Augusta *AT* (·–/–) 294kHz 100M 37°13'·05N
15°13'·50E
Catania Aero *CAT* (–·–·/·–/–) 345kHz 80M
37°27'·38N 14°57'·95E

Malta
Valletta, Luqa Aero *LQA* (·–··/––·–/·–) 416kHz
35°53'·67N 14°32'·32E
Birzebbuga, Luqa Aero *MLT* (––/·–··/–) 395kHz
35°49·00N 14°31·80E
Ghawdex, Gozo Aero *GZO* ––·/–––/–––) 320kHz
36°02'·30N 14°12'·52E

Coastal radio stations
Times are UT

Morocco
Tanger (CNW) 35°49'N 05°48'W
RT (MF) Transmits on 1911, 2182, 2635kHz. Receives on 2182kHz (H24)
Traffic lists on 1911kHz at 0740, 1140, 1540, 1740
VHF Transmits and receives on Ch 16 (H24), 24, 25, 26, 27.
Al Hoceima (CNA) 35°10'N 03°58'W
VHF Transmits and receives on Ch 16 (H24), 23, 25, 27, 28

Algeria
Ghazouet (7TE) 35°04'N 1°09'W
VHF Transmits and receives on Ch 16 (H24), 24, 25, 26, 27, 28
Traffic lists Ch 28 at 0303, 0703, 0903, 1103, 1303, 1503, 1703, 1903, 2103, 2303
Oran (7TO) 35°46'N 00°33'W
RT (MF) Transmits on 1735, 2182, 2586, 2719kHz. Receives on 2182kHz
Traffic lists on 1735 at every even H+35
VHF Transmits and receives on Ch 16 (H24), 24, 25, 26, 27, 28
Traffic lists on Ch 25 at 0303, 0703, 0903, 1103, 1303, 1503, 1703, 1903, 2103, 2303
Arzew (7TW) 35°43'N 00°18'W
VHF Transmits and receives on Ch 16 (H24), 24, 25, 26, 27, 28
Traffic lists on Ch 27 at 0303, 0703, 0903, 1103, 1303, 1503, 1703, 1903, 2103, 2303
Tenès (7TN) 36°30'N 01°19'E
VHF Ch 16 (H24), 24, 25, 26, 27, 28
Traffic lists on Ch 24 at 0333, 0733, 0933, 1133, 1333, 1533, 1733, 1933, 2133, 2333
Alger (7TA) 36°40'N 03°18'E
RT (MF) Transmits on 1792, 2182, 2691, 2775kHz. Receives on 2182kHz
Traffic lists on 1792kHz every odd H+03

VHF Transmits and receives on Ch 16 (H24), 24, 25, 26, 27, 28, 84, 87
Traffic lists on Ch 84 at 0330, 0730, 0930, 1130, 1330, 1530, 1730, 1930, 2130, 2330
Bejaia (7TG) 36°45'N 05°05'E
VHF Transmits and receives on Ch 16 (H24), 24, 25, 26, 27, 28
Traffic lists Ch 26 at 0333, 0733, 0933, 1133, 1333, 1533, 1733, 1933, 2133, 2333
Skikda (7TS) 36°53'N 06°54'E
VHF Transmits and receives on Ch 16 (H24), 24, 25, 26, 27, 28
Traffic lists Ch 25 at 0303, 0703, 0903, 1103, 1303, 1503, 1703, 1903, 2103, 2303
Annaba (7TB) 36°54'N 07°46'E
RT (MF) Transmits on 1911, 2182, 2775kHz. Receives on 2182kHz
Traffic lists on 1911 at every even H+50.
VHF Transmits and receives on Ch 16 (H24), 24, 25, 26, 27, 28
Traffic lists on Ch 24 at 0303, 0703, 0903, 1103, 1303, 1503, 1703, 1903, 2103, 2303

Tunisia
Bizerte (3VB) 37°17'N 09°53'E
RT (MF) Transmits on 2182, 1687·4, 2210kHz. Receives on 2182kHz.
VHF Transmits and receives on Ch 16 (0700–1900), 23, 24
Tunis (3VX, 3VT) 36°54'N 10°11'E
RT (MF) Transmits and receives on 1768·4, 2182, 2670kHz. Receives on 2182kHz
Traffic lists on 1768·4kHz at 0250, 0450, 0950, 1350, 1750, 2150, 2350
VH Transmits and receives on Ch 01, 10, 12, 18, 21, 25, 26, 16
Kelibia (3VL) 36°50'N 11°07'E
VHF Transmits and receives on Ch 16 (0600–1800), 26, 28
Mahdia (3VM) 35°31'N 11°04'E
RT (MF) Transmits on 1696·4, 1771, 2182kHz. Receives on 2182kHz
VHF Transmits and receives on Ch 16 (H24), 27, 28
Sfax (3VS) 34°44'N 10°44'E
VHF Transmits and receives on Ch 16 (0600–1800), 02, 22, 24

Glossary
Weather forecast terms

French	English
prévisions météo	weather forecasts
abondant	heavy
affaiblissement	decrease
agité(e)	rough
amélioration	improvement
anticyclone	anticyclone
apercu	short summary
après midi	afternoon
assez fort	rather strong
augmentant	increasing
aujourd'hui	today
averse	shower
avis	warning
avis de coup de vent	gale warning
basse pression	low pressure
en baisse	falling
banc de brouillard	fog bank
beau	fair, fine
belle (mer)	smooth

Glossary

bon(ne)	good	nuages	clouds
en bordure	on the border, edge of	nuageux	cloudy
brouillard	fog	nuit	night
brise	breeze	orage	thunderstorm
brise de mer	sea breeze	orageux	stormy
brise de terre	land breeze	ouest	west
bruine	drizzle	ouragan	hurricane
brume légère	haze	passagèrement	temporarily/passing over
brume mouillée	mist	persistance	continuing
brume sèche	haze	perturbation	disturbance
brumeux	hazy, misty, foggy	pluie	rain
calme	calm	pluvieux	rainy
centre	centre	précipitation	precipitation
comblant	filling	pression	pressure
coup de vent	gale	prévision	forecast
courant	current/airflow	probabilité	probability, chances of
couvert	overcast	prochaine	following
creusant	deepening	profond	deep
cyclonique	cyclonic	rapidement	quickly
demain	tomorrow	rafale	gust
se déplacant	moving	recul du vent	backing
dépression (bas)	depression (low)	région	area
devenant	becoming	ressac	surge, backwash
direction	direction	rester, restant	remain, stay
se dispersant	dispersing	sans nuages	cloudless
dorsale	ridge	situation générale	general synopsis
éclair	lightning	suivant	following
éclaircie	bright interval	sporadiques	scattered
échelle de Beaufort	Beaufort scale	stationnaire	stationary
état de la mer	sea state	sud	south
est	east	temps	weather, time
étendu	extensive	tempête	storm
extension	extending	tonnerre	thunder
faible	slight, weak	vagues	waves
force du vent	wind force	valable	valid
en formation	building	variable	variable
fort	strong	vent	wind
fraîche	fresh	vent frais	strong breeze
frais	fresh	vent à rafales	gusty
fréquent	frequent	virement	veering
front	front	visibilité	visibility
front froid	cold front	voilé	cloudy/overcast
front chaud	warm front	zone	area
gelée	frost	Sea state	Wave height
grain	squall	Peu agitée	Slight (0·5–1·25m)
grand frais	near gale	Agitée	Moderate (1·25–2·5m)
grêle	hail	Forte	Rough (2·5–4m)
en hausse	rising	**Terms found in French Charts**	
haut	high	jusant	ebb tide
houle	swell	flot	flood tide
isolé	isolated	marnage	max. range of the tide
jour, journée	day	**Terms used in custom clearing**	
au large	at sea	acier	steel
léger	light	allant a/destination	going to/destination
légère	light	année de construction	year of construction
légèrement	lightly	bois	wood
lentement	slowly	chantier	ship yard
locale	local	combien de cheveaux	horse power
matin	morning	date et lieu de naissance	date and place of birth
mauvais	poor	delivré	issued (date)
même	the same	douane	customs
mer	sea	d'ou vous venez?	where do you come from?
mer forte	rough sea	destination	destination
modéré	moderate	equipage	crew
se modérant	moderating	expire le	expires on
néant	none	fabriqué de	constructed in (date)
neige et pluie	sleet	heure d'arrive	hour of arrival
noeuds	knots	heure de départ	hour of departure
nord	north	jauge brut/net	tonnage gross/net

North Africa

largeur	width
lieu de l'emission	place where issued
loch	log
longueur	length
marque	brand name
matricule	registration (country)
moteur	engine
né le	born on
nom du bateau	name of the boat
numero d'immatriculation	registration number
passagers	passengers
pavillon	flag/nationality
proprietaire	owner
polyester	grp/polyester
port d'attache	port of registration
venant de/provenance	coming from
puissance	horse power
renouvellé	renewed
sondeur	echo sounder
tirant d'eau	draught
tonnage	tonnage

Sample crew list and boat data

Nom du Bateau (name of the boat):
Nationalité (nationality):
Port d'attache (port of registration):
Matricule (registration number):
Longueur (length):
Largeur (width):
Tirant d'eau (draught):
Jauge brut/net (tonnage gross/net):
Année de construction (year of construction):
Chantier (shipyard):
Moteur (engine):
Provenance (coming from):
Destination (going to):
Date d'entrée (date of entry):
Date de sortie (date of departure):
Proprietaire ou skipper (owner or captain)
Né le (date born):
à (place):
No. de passport (passport number):
Délivré le (date of issue):
par (by whom):
Renouvellé (renewed until):
Expire le (date of expiry):
No. de visa (visa number):
Délivré le (date of issue):
par (by whom):
Profession (profession):
Addresse du proprietaire (owner's address):
Passagers (number of passengers):
The same data for the crew as for the owner or captain.
Equipement (equipment):
Radio (VHF, radios and transmitters):
Radar (radar):
Marque (brand):
Sondeur (echo sounder):
Type (model No.):
Loch (log), Satnav, Loran, etc.

II. North Africa

Religion

The official religion of the Maghreb is Islam which is inextricably linked with the way of life and the political systems. Islamic beliefs, observances and laws are well described in the travel guides listed, but a few relevant notes are included here.

There are five prayer periods every day, announced from the minarets. Friday is the weekly holy day. The most important annual celebration is Ramadan, the month of fasting, when Muslims do not eat, drink or smoke between sunrise and sunset. One should be discreet in public about eating, drinking and smoking during this period in order not to cause offence. Many restaurants are closed during the day and shops and markets only open later in the afternoon. The evenings give way to celebrations and special patisseries are made during this period.

It is forbidden for Muslims to eat pork. Alcohol is widely available and a wine and beer industry thrives in the Maghreb although, strict Muslims would not indulge.

Language

Arabic is the official language in the Maghreb, but in most places French is also spoken. Along the coast of Morocco many of the older people speak Spanish and the young guides in Tunisia and particularly Morocco often speak other European languages. In commercial ports, the officials will usually speak a little English. Signs in Algeria are often only in Arabic, not Arabic and French as is common in Tunisia and Morocco. Berber is widely spoken in Morocco and Algeria and there are many dialects: Kabyle, Soussi, Tamazight, Tashalhyat, as well as Derija, the colloquial Arabic and Classical Arabic, which is the written form that remains consistent throughout the Arab world.

It will help considerably in dealing with officials and for the first steps ashore to speak a little French.

Cultural differences

There are substantial differences between the way Europeans behave, think and believe, and the way a Muslim does. Devotion to extended family, the call to prayer, obedience to the *Qu'ran* and Islamic teaching are but a few. It is easy to observe behaviour and draw conclusions based on our own culture, misinterpreting differences. In the Maghreb for example, as in many Mediterranean countries, holding hands and walking arm in arm is as customary amongst men as with women, and is in no way an indication of orientation.

It is common to see devout Muslims praying in public if they cannot get to a mosque. This highlights an important aspect of Muslim life: they speak by open action in a way we usually do not. Although many Christians make a public confession of their faith in various ways, few would so publicly worship God as an individual, in the way a devout Muslim does.

Perhaps one of the most remarkable and pleasant aspects of the Arab culture, is the hospitality afforded to a complete stranger. In areas where few yachtsmen visit, you will be invited to visit homes and receive a warm welcome by the whole family. Arabs have a deep sense of responsibility to care for strangers and provide hospitality. It is not uncommon to arrive in some ports and be invited to an official's home for cous-cous. This is a genuine act and they will be honoured by your accepting the invitation.

Attitudes towards women

The relationship between men and women in the Arab world is quite different from that in the west. Films, television and the inconsiderate behaviour of some tourists have helped to reinforce the idea that western women are promiscuous. Some men are quite curious about western women who can be made to feel uncomfortable by their attention and this is particularly true in some tourist centres. Considerate behaviour and dress code for women and men will command respect from locals and consequently avert any potential problems.

In order to really enjoy the pleasures of the Maghreb and the hospitality of the people, it is necessary to suspend prejudice and respect their culture.

Bakhshish

This could be a problem for those who are untravelled and has the potential to ruin your visit if not appreciated.

Bakhshish is money paid as a tip, often to speed up a bureaucratic process. It is a common practice throughout the world, though not so evident in Europe and North America. It usually involves a very small amount of money, a small gift: a packet of cigarettes, in a country where salaries are very low. It is best to respect this practice as part of the local tradition. Keep it in perspective as a minor issue and avoid making value judgements about it. Try to think of giving bakhshish as analogous to tipping in restaurants, or as a gift to people who have helped you. After all, there are few other charges to pay.

In its mildest form bakhshish involves pressure on you to pay for unsolicited services. For instance, on returning to your parked car someone will appear out of nowhere and ask for a fee for 'looking after it'. Since you only need to pay a few pence and, after all, he must have been watching it to have noticed your return, it is better to give something and abandon any sense of resentment at paying a few pence for what you did not request. It can be used to advantage by asking for somebody to keep an eye on your yacht, bike or car. It will only cost you a dollar or two for a day, but will ensure your security and give food to someone who has a very small wage to survive on.

There is a more serious form of bakhshish which may involve paying to do what you are in any case entitled to. When police or customs officials come on board, they may well expect a gift of cigarettes, money, wine or spirits. This is perfectly normal, especially in Morocco. Although they will never coerce you to give, it will save a great deal of aggravation and possibly hours of your time if you are prepared to comply. It is wise to carry on board cartons of cigarettes especially for this purpose.

Hammams

The Arab word *hammam* means 'healthy spot' and in the Maghreb this is the name for the public steam baths which are found in every town or village. Rather like a Turkish bath, it is a very interesting and refreshing experience to visit a *hammam*. They are always quite clean, certainly when compared to some marina showers, and a lot less expensive. Some of them have trained masseurs. A swimsuit is needed but generally soap and towels are supplied and you splash yourself with buckets of hot and cold water. Where *hammams* were found they are listed under the port description but, although often inconspicuous, they are found everywhere. There are either separate *hammams* or separate hours for men and women.

Eating out

Through the influence of tourism in Tunisia and Morocco and the French occupation in all three countries, a variety of restaurants will be found everywhere.

In Tunisia and Morocco restaurants range from high class with French cuisine in the big cities to the most simple eating houses frequented by villagers. Interesting places which may not appear spotless may serve the best meals; go by your nose but allow your system time to acclimatise before embarking upon something really adventurous. Desserts, apart from fresh fruit and flans, are not common in the more basic restaurants but can be brought in, as can something from a patisserie to eat with a *thé à la menthe* in Morocco or *thé noir* in Tunisia. Coffee is taken strong with a lot of milk or as expresso. Restaurants catering for tourists have a familiar menu of wine, starters, main dishes and desserts, similar to European cuisine.

Prices vary from as much as £10 per person for good French cuisine to as little as £1.20 for a meal in a local eating house. The better restaurants serve wine, which is often locally produced. Morocco has a flourishing wine industry. Lunch is usually served from 1200 onward and dinner from 2000. Small restaurants may only open at lunchtime.

In Algeria restaurants are harder to find and cater

North Africa

Market day

mainly for the affluent, since eating out is not particularly cheap when the bill is paid with officially exchanged Algerian dinars. Ice-cream parlours are prolific in the Maghreb and the quality is quite good. In Malta, most restaurants cater for cheap tourist menus.

Some typical dishes
Cous-cous, made of durum wheat and eaten with vegetables, chicken, meat or fish, is a most popular food in the whole Maghreb.

Bread is always eaten with any salad or appetiser and to soak up sauces. Chicken is always on the menu and good fish can be had along the coast.

Morocco
Harira, a spicy, thick, filling soup which can be a meal in itself.
Briouates, deep-fried pastry parcels filled with minced meat, prawn or chicken. Found in the better restaurants.
Tajine, meat and vegetables stewed in an earthenware pot and eaten with bread.
Cornes de Gazelle, batter covered almond pastries.

Tunisia
Brik à l'Oeuf, a thin pastry with a filling of egg, parsley and sometimes tuna fried in oil. Learn how Tunisians eat them or you will end up with a yellow mess.
Salade Mechouia, a relish from grilled or roasted peppers and tomatoes, garnished with olives and hard boiled egg.
Chakchouka, an egg dish with green peppers and harissa.
Ojja, a variety of chakchouka with a tomato base. Makes a tasty appetiser or light meal.
Harissa, a hot red pepper paste but not as hot as the Indonesian varieties. Mixed with some olive oil and eaten with bread or as a dip for olives it is a nice appetiser.
Baklava, puff pastry filled with ground nuts mixed with honey.

Shopping
Bartering is the normal and expected way to arrive at a price and the merchant has less respect for a buyer who does not barter. Rules are hard to formulate but here are some guidelines:

Do not get involved in serious bidding on an item that you do not really want to buy.

Determine for yourself what a certain product should cost or how much it is worth to you.

Do not feel embarrassed to leave a shop and compare prices in a neighbouring shop.

There is no bartering in government handicraft shops, food markets, supermarkets, non-tourist oriented clothing stores, restaurants and in taxis if they have a working meter – check this first.

The fixed-price government handicraft and tourist shops are well worth a visit to give you a general idea of the maximum price you can expect to pay in the *souk* after bartering.

Chartering
In Tunisia, chartering can only be arranged by a company with a Tunisian partner. In practice, privately chartered yachts based outside Tunisia have been allowed in and have even changed crews in some ports but all depends upon local officials and attitudes may change from year to year.

In Morocco and Algeria a charter yacht is unlikely to encounter any problems, but crew changes must be notified to the immigration authorities.

Wintering
Many ports in Tunisia and some in Morocco are well appointed and safe places to winter in. Tunisia is by far the cheapest, with Monastir being the most popular (full in 1998), followed by El Kantaoui and Sidi Bou Saïd. It is possible to winter in Sidi Ferrouj ,in Algeria and in Marina Smir and Kabila in Morocco, but these are expensive options. Other Moroccan ports are also available: Tanger, Casablanca and Agadir – but these are undergoing extensive alterations currently.

Gibraltar and Malta are other places to winter but need advance booking and are also very expensive compared to Tunisia.

Connections
Good international airports operate throughout North Africa, Malta and Gibraltar. Information is given in each country section.

Bartering for spices

Books

Do consult some of the excellent guidebooks on North Africa, both for further information on the ports and for places you may want to visit on excursions from them.

The Rough Guide to Morocco, (Mark Ellingham and Shaun McVeigh, Harrap-Columbus) is probably the best general guide on Morocco and is written with enthusiasm. It has detailed information on travel, hotels, costs, sights and history. Indispensable when travelling inland.

The Rough Guide to Tunisia, (Peter Morris and Charles Farr, Harrap-Columbus), of the same excellent quality as their guide on Morocco.

Morocco, Algeria & Tunisia: a travel survival kit (Geoff Crowther and Hugh Finley).

Lonely Planet The best alternative to the individual *Rough Guides* on Morocco and Tunisia. Not quite as detailed as the *Rough Guides* but it probably has the best coverage on Algeria for which there is no specialised guide in English.

A Guide and History of Morocco (Nina Banon – Societe Nouvelle),

Marreucos (Guias Acento) and *Morocco Handbook* (Anne and Keith McLachlan – Passport Books) are also excellent publications.

Italian Islands, (Dana Facaros & Michael Pauls). Published by Cadogan Books. Amongst coverage of all the Italian Islands including Sardinia and Sicily, it has a good section on Pantelleria and the Pelagie Islands.

Road maps

Road maps are indispensable when making a journey inland, one of the attractions of visiting North Africa, but they are difficult to find there.

RV Reis and Verkehrsverlag *World Maps* cover Morocco, with another covering all of Northwest Africa. These are available in most petrol filling stations in Spain and France. Roger Lascelles map of Morocco is also excellent. Also available are Hallwag or Kummerly & Frey's maps of Morocco.

Michelin's map 172 covers Algeria and Tunisia and is more detailed than the maps produced by the Tunisian Cartographic Office.

Cookery books

Mediterranean Seafood, Alan Davidson. Penguin. A handbook with all the names of Mediterranean fish, crustaceans and molluscs in several languages and over 200 recipes from Mediterranean countries. Indispensable in the markets and fishing harbours with their unfamiliar fish. The recipes are practical and do not require ingredients exotic to the Mediterranean.

Mediterranean Cookery, Claudia Roden. It contains 250 delicious and easy recipes of traditional Mediterranean cooking prepared with locally available ingredients.

Further reading

Italian Waters Pilot, Rod Heikell. Imray Laurie Norie & Wilson

Imray Mediterranean Almanac. Editor Rod Heikell. Two yearly

Votre Livre de Bord-Mediterranée, Bloc Marine

Mediterranean Pilot (NP 45) Vol. 1, British Admiralty.

Mediterranean Cruising Handbook, Rod Heikell. Imray Laurie Norie & Wilson

Atlantic Islands. RCC Pilotage Foundation. Imray Laurie Norie & Wilson

Atlantic Spain and Portugal, RCC Pilotage Foundation. Imray Laurie Norie & Wilson

Mediterranean Spain – Costas del Sol & Blanca. RCC Pilotage Foundation. Imray Laurie Norie & Wilson

A Bridge and Galley Guide to Tunisia, Ann P. Maurice and Bryan E. Lockyear. Out of print.

Guide Practique de Sardaigne et Côtes de Tunisie, Jacques Anglès. Edition du Pen Duick

Fodor's North Africa. A guide to Morocco, Algeria and Tunisia. Reprinted in 1989.

Traveller's Guide to North Africa from IC publications. The history, economy and culture of Mauritania, Morocco, Algeria, Tunisia, Libya and Egypt.

The Travellers' Guide to Malta and Gozo, Christopher Kininmonth.

The Haj, Leon Uris. A fictious account of Arabic lifestyle and values based on historical events. Doubleday and Company, Garden City, New York.

On the shores of the Mediterranean, Eric Newby. Penguin. His journey through the Mediterranean countries.

The Lemon, Mohammed Mrabet translated by Paul Bowles. An account of life in Tanger under international rule.

The Sheltering Sky, Paul Bowles. A couple's travels in Morocco.

Midnight Mass, Paul Bowles. Several short stories set in Morocco.

Berlitz Guide to Algeria.

It will be advantageous to obtain the books required from Europe, as they are difficult to find in the Maghreb, except for some of the titles in Morocco.

North Africa

Gibraltar

36°09'N 5°21'W

Tides
Gibraltar is a reference port
MHWS	MHWN	MLWN	MLWS
0·1	0·7	0·3	0·1

Charts
	Approach	Port
Admiralty	773, 142, 1448	144
French	7042	7026
Spanish	445, 4451, 4452	–

Lights
Approach
1. **Tarifa** 36°00'·1N 5°36'·5W
   Fl(3)WR.10s40m26/18M 113°-W-089°-R-113°
   White tower 33m Siren(3)60s Masonry structure 10m
   Radiobeacon O 289kHz 50M Racon
2. **Punta Carnero** 36°04'·7N 5°25'·5W
   Fl(4)WR.20s42m18/9M 018°-W-325°-R-018° Siren
   Mo(K)30s Yellow round tower, green lantern 19m
3. **Gibraltar (Europa Point)** 36°06'·7N 5°20'·6W
   Iso.10s49m19M Oc.R.10s15M F.R.44m15M Horn
   20s 197°-W-042°-R(Oc&F)-067°-W-125° White
   round tower, red band 19m
4. **Gibraltar** Aeromarine 36°08'·7N 5°20'·5W
   Aero Mo(GB)R.10s405m30M

Entrance
5. **North mole east head** 36°09'N 5°21'·9W
   F.R.28m5M Tower

General
Gibraltar's location on the southern tip of the Iberian peninsula, its proximity to Morocco and its predominantly English-speaking community, makes it an ideal place for yachtsmen in the area to store, take on fuel, carry out repairs and explore Spain. It offers a safe place to lay-up, repair and maintain ship with all facilities available and with many European and US agencies represented for servicing and spares. It also has an airport serving the UK.

There are now three marinas, all on the western side of the Rock in the Bay of Gibraltar. (Known as the Bay of Algeciras to the Spanish.) It is a popular place and the marinas are busy. Two are very close to the airstrip, which is convenient for crew changes, but noisy. It is often far cheaper to have equipment and spares exported by air to Gibraltar as 'Ships Stores in Transit' than to buy them off the shelf there.

Since 1992 there has been much land reclamation on the eastern side of the commercial basin and on the south shore on the way to the marinas, i.e. on the N side of the N mole. Many elegant apartment complexes and high-rise flats have been built here, also the large Safeway supermarket.

Gibraltar is a good safe place to leave a yacht in order to explore Spain and even to visit Morocco on the ferry if you do not want to explore the Atlantic coast by yacht. Marina prices are reasonable and English is spoken everywhere, although the Gibraltarians communicate with each other in Spanish. The Spanish perception of Gibraltar as a haven for drug and tobacco smugglers and as a place of money laundering has implications at the border for those wishing to cross into Spain. There are frequently long delays at the border for those travelling by car, as most are searched, although this does not normally affect pedestrians.

Approach
Gibraltar is clearly visible at all times, except in fog, which is rare. At night the Rock is illuminated to the west by the town and to the east by the bright red lights marking the radio antennae on the north face, which is itself illuminated by spotlights. To the south is the lighthouse on Europa point. In contrast, the precipitous east face of the Rock is dark. There are no marinas or anchorages on this side. A safe entry can be made via the Bay of Algeciras in almost any conditions. Beware of squalls in the bay, particularly during an easterly, when strong downdraughts are frequent. Note the dangerous wreck in position 36°09'·24N 05°21'·32W marked by a green can buoy.

Entrance and Formalities
Boats going to Marina Bay or Sheppards Marina must first report to the Immigration and Customs station; two huts located opposite the airport runway, close to the marinas, next to the fuelling station. The short pontoon is very low and the staff officers are unhelpful and will never offer assistance to yachts arriving, whatever the weather. The reporting station flies the 'Q' flag. Queensway Quay Marina has its own arrangement and formalities are completed on arrival, in the marina office by filling out a form. Queensway Quay Marina has its own customs and immigration clearance via the Marina Control Centre.

Berthing
After clearing customs for Marina Bay or Sheppards, call either marina on VHF Ch 9 or 12, asking for a berth number. A layout of both marinas will be seen in the Immigration hut. Alternatively, go to the Visitors' Pontoon for Sheppards, (the long pontoon closest to the customs house) or to Queensway Quay Marina.

Facilities
Water and electricity Available at every berth at Marina Bay and Queensway Quay and via a long fixed hose at Shepherds.

Provisions Safeways supermarket is a short walk from Queensway Quay and not far from Sheppards or Marina Bay. There is a Safeways bus (No.10) which runs from the bus station near Main Street and terminates at the Frontier. On Gibraltar's Main Street and its adjacent streets and alleyways, almost anything can be obtained. A good selection of fresh fruit and vegetables is available just outside the frontier gate in the La Linea market. This is a favourite place for Gibraltarians to shop. Peraltos supermarket is tucked back behind the bus station on the right. It has a good selection of canned and frozen foods. A new supermarket called Checkout, selling

Tesco's products, opened in December 1998 and has branches in Main Street, near Marks & Spencer and at Marina Bay. The fish, meat and vegetable market is a covered market on the right as you pass through Casemates Gate. There is a market held in John Mackintosh Square on Wednesdays, Fridays and Saturdays. Shops are normally open Monday to Friday between 0930 and 1930. Many close between 1300 and 1500, and most close Saturday afternoons and Sundays.

Post office In Main Street. Post by 1030 for urgent mail to UK. Sub post office, Winston Churchill Ave.

Banks In Main Street. Gibraltar has well-established banking services for both offshore and local customers with a full range of international banks, including several UK institutions. A full list of financial services is available from the Tourist Board. Banking hours are generally between 0900–1530 except Friday when some are open in the afternoon. There are also several *Bureaux de Change* agencies in Main Street, one at the airport and another in a circular office opposite the airport. Currency is Gibraltar pounds and pence, on a par with the British pound, but its value is greatly reduced outside of Gibraltar.

Chandlery Just about everything for the boat is available at Sheppards, which probably has the best range of yacht chandlery in the Mediterranean. There are also chandlers located at Marina Bay. See section *Communications* for details.

Repair and haul out Sheppards Marina has a 40-ton travel-hoist and a 10-ton crane. Mechanics are on hand or can be contracted locally. Only repair facility in Gibraltar ☎ 77183/75148 *Fax* 42583

Fuel Diesel (and water) at the Shell or BP stations by the customs pier opposite Sheppard's and Marina Bay. Shell ☎ 48232 BP ☎ 72261

Gas Available from New Harbours ☎ 70296.

Charts Available from the Gibraltar Chart Agency, 4 Bayside, Gibraltar, ☎ 76293.

Weather forecasts

Both Radio Gibraltar (GBC) and British Forces Radio (BFBS) broadcast local weather forecasts from the RAF Met. Office. GBC includes a sailing forecast for 50M around Gibraltar.

GBC 91·3, 92·6MHz, 1458kHz

General synopsis, situation, wind direction and strength, sea state, visibility, for area up to 50M from Gibraltar in English (1300 broadcasts in Spanish)

Weather messages Mon–Fri 0610, 0930, 1030, 1230, 1300, 1530, 1715. Sat: 0930, 1030, 1230, 1300. Sun: 1030, 1230.

BFBS 1 93·5, 97·8MHz ☎ 54211

Storm warnings on (F3E) on receipt. Shipping forecast, general synopsis, situation, wind direction and strength, sea state, visibility together with HW/LW times:

Weather messages Mon–Fri 0745, 0845, 1130, 1715, 2345. Sat, Sun 0845, 0945, 1230. (Sun also 1645 1702, 1745).

Forecast for Gibraltar area: general synopsis, situation, wind direction and strength, sea state, visibility, together with HW/LW times: Mon–Fri: every H+06 (0700–2400). Sat, Sun, every H+6 (0700–1000, 1200–1400) LT.

BFBS 2 89·4, 99·5MHz ☎ 54211

Mon–Fri 0757, 0857, 1010, 1357, 1857. Sat 0857, 0958, 1357. Sun 0857, 2259.

Sheppard's Marina

Waterport, Gibraltar ☎ 77183, 75148 *Fax* 42535 VHF Ch 9, 12.

Sheppard's has been established as a yacht facility in Gibraltar since 1961. As such, it was the pioneer in its field, not only in Gibraltar, but for many hundreds of miles around. Since then the Company has developed and expanded successfully into several areas associated with the yachting trade. It has, over the years, become a regular stopping point for all aspects of marine maintenance, equipment supply, berthing, repairs and fitting-out for Mediterranean or Atlantic-bound yachtsmen of all nationalities. It also offers new yachts sales and brokerage.

Office facilities are available including *poste restante* to the above address.

Berthing

Sheppard's offers safe berthing for 150 vessels. The system of concrete piers with floating pontoon berths, in a sheltered location, provides very secure berthing in all weather conditions all year round. There are both alongside and stern-to berths.

Facilities

Water and electricity Accessible to each berth.

Repairs Facilities include workshops for mechanical and electronic repairs plus rigging, light engineering and welding. Calybre Ltd, subcontractors based on-sight, offer a fine painting and GRP facility. (☎ 75869). They are particularly well known for their spraying, osmosis treatment and invisible GRP repairs. The yard is equipped with a 40-ton travel-lift and 10-ton crane with 15-metre jib.

The chandlery is very widely stocked with electronics, spares, hardware, engines, generators, paints, inflatables and all materials needed for maintenance, repair and fitting out. The shop staff are knowledgeable about yachts and able to provide technical advice (☎ 75148).

Charges Daily berthing charges fall into 2 categories: 12m and under (class I), over 12m (class 2) (1998) Class I stern-to Summer (June–Nov) £0·38/m. Winter (Dec–May) £0·32/m. Alongside £0·70/m. Class 2 stern-to £0·48/m, £0·42/m. Alongside £0·90/m.

There is a multihull surcharge of 50%. Length is over-all including any projections. There is a 10% reduction on half-yearly accounts paid in advance. Water for tank-filling is included but there is a £0·50 per day socket rental charge.

Standing daily rate first fortnight L0·15/m thereafter £0·30/m

Water and electricity, hire of pressure hose and ladders extra.

Weather

Posted daily at the office.

Marina Bay

The Tower, P.O. Box 373, Gibraltar ☎ 73300 *Fax* 42656 VHF Ch 73 24hrs.

Marina Bay is a tranquil 250 berth marina nestling

North Africa

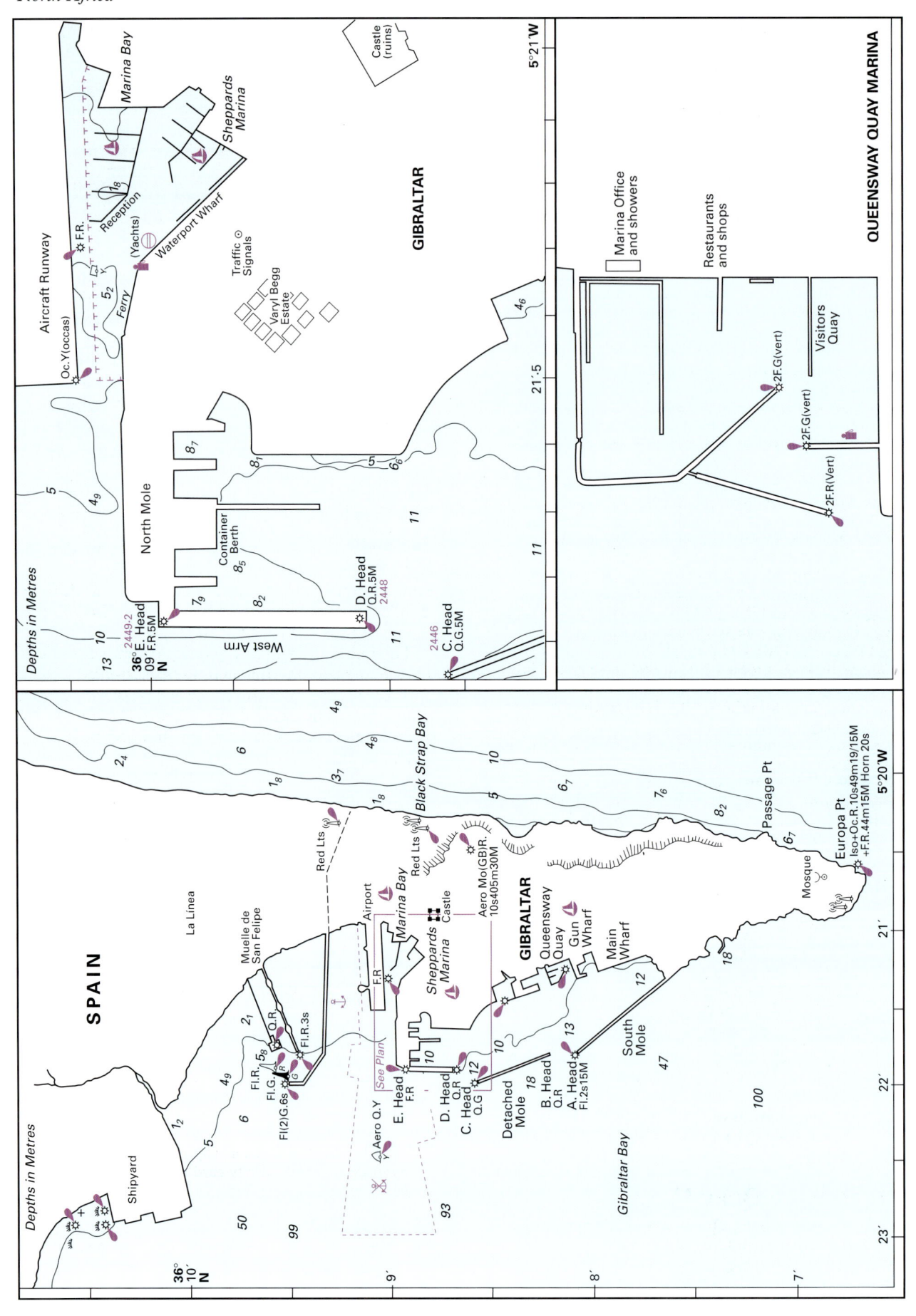

QUEENSWAY QUAY MARINA

on the west side of the Rock surrounded by an elegant complex of shops and apartments, restaurants, chandleries and shops offering an extensive range of services and duty-free shopping. These include a chemist, grocery market, video rental, launderette and hairdresser. Cutty Sark Kiosk (next to Biancas Restaurant on the quay) for notices, pilots, newspapers etc. and duty-frees. Neptune House, the principal building on the quay offers offshore banking, secretarial services, *poste restante*, dentist and medical clinic. The marina office is located on the outer end of the main pier.

Berthing
Berths are allocated by the staff who are on hand from 0800–2200 daily. If making a night entry, find a vacant berth and report to the office later, which is situated at the end of the Main Pier.

Facilities
Each berth is fitted with total-facility units containing points for water and electricity, telephone, fax, satellite TV and security connections and is installed with a custom-made computerised system. Depth alongside 2–5m and boats of up to 96m can be facilitated.

Water Available at every berth charged at 5p per gallon. (All prices 1998).

Electricity Available at every berth charged at 15p per kWh. Plugs can be hired at 32A: £10·00, 63A: £35·00. 63A (3Ph): £40·00.

Repairs Only available at Sheppard's Marina
☎ 77183/77183 *Fax* 42535

Charges Basic fees for a 12–15m vessel are £9.60 in summer (1/5–31/10) and £6.75 in winter.
Cash discounts Monthly – 10% Half-yearly – 20% Annually – 25%
Credit cards Monthly – 5% Half-yearly – 15% Annually – 20%
There is a Government levy of 47p per day or part thereof on all categories of boats.

Multihulls There is a surcharge of 50% on corresponding length fee. (Total length includes extensions i.e. davits, bowsprit, to nearest whole metre.)

Showers and WC On ground floor of pier office building. Facilities for the handicapped.

Security Security guards 24 hours. ☎ 40477.

Transport No 9 bus from the frontier to the bus station stops in Winston Churchill Avenue in front of the tower blocks at the northern end of Glacis Road, but it is only a 10 minute walk to the bus station and city centre. Turn right onto the main road. Bear left past the Bank of Scotland which will take you through the Landport tunnel and you will soon see ahead of you Casemates Gate, the bus station and Main Street.

Weather
Daily bulletins are posted at the Pier Office.
☎ BFBS Radio 53416

Queensway Quay Marina
Ragged Staff Wharf, Queensway, Gibraltar.
☎ 44700 *Fax* 44699 VHF Ch 73.

Queensway Marina is the Western Mediterranean's newest marina. Designed by Robin Knox-Johnson, Phase I was opened in May 1994, providing 130 berths. The new Queensway Quay development includes luxury apartments, a restaurant and many business enterprises. There is also duty-free shopping along the wharf and in Gibraltar's Main Street just 5 minutes' walk away.

Approach
Head for Europa Point and pass through the outer breakwater. The marina is located at the site of the old Naval Torpedo Boat Camber inside Gibraltar Harbour between Gun Wharf and Coaling Island.

Berthing
The Visitors Berth is the first pontoon once inside the marina, to the south. Longer stay berths are in the more sheltered northern end of the marina. Call up the duty piermaster on channel 73 prior to entry and he will allocate a berth and assist with lines. Mooring is stern-to concrete floating pontoons. A limited number of deep-water berths varying from 3–7m in depth at LWS, with power points and water, are available along the southern wall of the marina.

Since 1994 modifications have been evidenced. The floating pontoons, which were originally in a N/S configuration, have now been re-orientated to face E/W and a pontoon has been added. The individual finger pontoons proved unsuccessful and were consequently removed. An additional breakwater has been added across the marina entrance thus reducing incoming swell a little.

The marina and quay are being extended to the N of the present marina and it is envisaged that a further 7 berths, accommodating vessels between 35–50m, will be available for stern-to berthing in the near future. The area is to be dredged to a LWS depth of 3m.

Formalities
Customs and immigration may be arranged via the Marina Control Centre (MCC) on arrival. This is situated at present at the NW end of the marina but is to be re-sited to the NW end of the Ordnance Wharf. Office hours 0830–2145 (summer), 0830–2015 (winter).

Facilities
Every berth has access to a Service Module, most of which contain electricity, water, intercom and telephone. Access to the floating pontoons is by coded lockable gates. Car park by the MCC. Office facilities available from the MCC include fax and photocopying, bookswap, *poste restante* to the above address.

Water Available at every berth charged at 1p per litre with a minimum charge of £1. Hoses can be hired and tap connections bought from the MCC.

Electricity Output 240v 16/32 amps, with 3 phase 415v also available. Charged at 15p per kWh and obtained by inserting an electricity card available from the MCC who will explain its use. Card values range from £1·00–£20·00. Electrical leads are available for hire and plugs bought from the MCC.

Fuel and oil May be ordered in advance through the MCC. Minimum delivery is normally 200 litres but if several vessels require fuel at the same time this restriction will not apply. (There may be a surcharge

North Africa

at weekends.) Pay by credit card at the MCC or cash direct to the bowser driver. At the arranged time, tie up alongside the steps on the wharf at the southern end of the marina. Alternative fuel may be obtained from the fuelling berth at Waterport (Shell and BP).

Repairs Only available at Sheppard's Marina ☎ 75148/77183 *Fax* 42535.

Charges A 12–15m vessel would be charged in summer (1/5–31/10), £9·95. Winter (1/11–30/4) £6·95.

All fees payable in advance. There is a 50% surcharge on corresponding category length for multihulls.

(LOA includes all davits, bowsprits etc to the nearest metre).

Long stay discounts:
Cash monthly – 5%, 6 monthly – 20%, annually – 25%.
Credit card 6 monthly – 15%, annually – 20%.

Showers and WC Situated in the MCC. Facilities for the disabled. Bath available for £3·50. These amenities close 30 minutes earlier than the rest of the establishment. Toilets for after-hours' use can be found along the main quayside to the rear of the large anchor. Lock code available from Reception.

Laundry Queensway Quay Launderette: Self-service and service washes available. Queensway Quay Dry Cleaners ☎ 45594.

Security Access to pontoons (after hours) is by a coded digital lock.

Transport Local buses from the bus station. No. 3 bus to the frontier from Line Wall Road near the Museum.

Weather
Daily reports for an area of 50M radius of Gibraltar is posted early each morning. A weather station is on view at the MCC. See above radio weather bulletins.

Anchoring
Anchorage is possible immediately north of the runway, which runs E to W. For safety reasons, yachts are prohibited from anchoring close to the runway or in a direct line with the flight path to the west. Closer to the Spanish shore of La Linea is a newly completed long jetty.

Communications
International code for Gibraltar	350
Ambulance and Police	199
Fire	190
Operator	100
Health Centre	70112/78337
House calls	77003
St Bernard's Hospital	79700
Airport: Flight enquiries	44737/75984
Customs	78879
Immigration	48531
Chandlers Sheppard	75148
Gibraltar Tourist Board	74950
Border	42777
Pumpkin Marine	71177
Med Marine Ltd	48888
Consulates	74950

Port VHF Ch 16; 06, 12, 13, 14.
Pilots VHF Ch 16; 12, 14.
Lloyds Windy VHF Ch 08, 16; 12, 14 office hours (0900–1400 Mon–Fri).

Eating out
Enjoy the relaxed atmosphere of the waterfront restaurants within the marina complexes or the many restaurants, pubs and fast-food houses in the town, particularly in Main Street. A full list may be obtained from the Tourist Board. A friendly welcome awaits yachtsmen at the Carpenters Arms, above the Methodist Church in Main Street. Good food for excellent value can be obtained here.

A *pizzaria* is located in Watergardens, near the entrance of Sheppards Marina.

Transport
Buses There are six local bus routes which run at approximately 15 minute intervals and cover most of the main tourist attractions. Details can be obtained from the Tourist Board ☎ 79450, Rock City Services ☎ 75660, or (Route 10 Safeways/Frontier) Calypso Tours ☎ 76520.

Hire cars May be arranged from the airport or from several car hire firms in the town and taken into Spain.
Avis ☎ 75552/79200 Budget ☎ 79666. For full list contact the Tourist Board ☎ 74950.

Local taxis ☎ 70052/70027/79999 but are not permitted to cross the border into Spain.

Air Services to the UK and Morocco (but not Spain).

To visit Spain one may take a bus or taxi (or hire car) to the border where taxis wait on the Spanish side. La Linea Bus Station is fairly close and from here an excellent (and cheap) bus service networks the whole of Spain. If time is short, you may take advantage of the RENFE inter-city train service as a faster way to see Spain. The nearest station is in Algeciras where there are also ferries to Tanger and Ceuta. There is a connecting bus from La Linea bus station to Algeciras bus station from where you will have to either walk or get a taxi to the station or port.

Top of the Rock, a short walk from the marinas: famous for its barbary apes. It is said that if ever they leave the Rock, so will the British

Gibraltar: The northern anchorage and entrance to Marina Bay

Tourism

There is much to see in Gibraltar with the many monuments to its rich naval and maritime history to visit, duty-free shopping in the colourful, cross-cultural High Street and *souks*. A trip to the top of the Rock can be made by cable car, taxi or a walk which takes around an hour. Spain, Morocco and the Western Straits can be seen on a clear day from the top, along with the famous resident barbary 'apes', which are actually tail-less monkeys from the Atlas Mountains. It is unknown how they came to be in Gibraltar, but in 1915, the army took on their care in order to curb their nomadic roaming. In fact, during the Second World War, their numbers declined almost to the point of extinction, and it is told that Sir Winston Churchill ordered more to be imported from Morocco fearful of the legend which deemed that Gibraltar would cease to be British the day the apes left the Rock! St Michael's Cave, half way up, is well worth a visit. Concerts are sometimes held here and the acoustics are magnificent.

As Gibraltar is a mere 2 square miles in size, much can be seen in a day. The quickest and most comprehensive way to sample her history and spectacular views is to take an Official Rock Tour which lasts approximately 90 minutes. (Or you can negotiate a tour of your choice, which can include cable car rides if desired).

Starting from the frontier the tour includes visits to:

Catalan Bay (which was home to the Genoese settlers in the 18th century).

Water catchments (an impressive sand-slope covered with corrugated iron on the east face of the Rock previously used for water conservation).

Europa lighthouse (commands a spectacular view across the Straits)

Upper Rock Reserve (a nature reserve rich in flora and fauna).

Jews' Gate (panorama of the Rif Mountains of Morocco).

Saint Michael's Caves (the cathedral cave, a unique hall of crystallised nature thought to have been inhabited in Neolithic times. During the Second World War it was prepared as a hospital, but never used).

O'Hara's Battery (outstanding views from the top of the Rock). One can see the complex machinery associated with the large 9·2-inch gun on the summit).

Apes' Den (a chance to be photographed with the Barbary Macaque monkeys).

Military Heritage Centre (housed in Princess Caroline's Battery; a collection of military artefacts).

Great Siege Tunnels (excavated during the Great Siege of 1779–83 to permit the mounting of a gun on the north face and subsequently extended to form an impregnable line of artillery).

Gibraltar, a city under Siege (optional: exhibition within the oldest buildings on the Rock).

Lime Kiln (optional: last remaining lime kiln in Gibraltar dating back to the late 19th century).

Moorish Castle (the Tower of Homage which dominates the hillside and approach to Gibraltar dates back to AD 1333 and displays battle scars sustained during ten sieges in the 14th and 15th centuries and was refuge to hundreds in 1540 when Corsairs sacked the town. A Spanish governor held out here for 5 months against the Duke of Medina Sidonia).

The Gibraltar Museum & Moorish Baths (a film and accompanying photographs and artefacts tell the history of Gibraltar). The basement houses the best preserved Moorish Bath House in Europe.

Nelson's Anchorage (the unique Super Gun located close to the site where Nelson's body was brought ashore after the Battle of Trafalgar).

Parson's Lodge (optional: a historic battery guarding the entrance to Rosia Bay).

Alameda Botanical Gardens (named after the popular Alamo tree, this garden was opened in 1816 on the site of the Grand Parade ground where British troops mustered for the famous Night Sortie).

Other tours can be arranged through travel agents or the tourist information offices. Worthy of mention are the Tunnel Tour of the Second World War tunnels, ☎ 54451, and the tour of the Lower St Michael's Cave ☎ 55829 or 40561 Mr Walker.

It is possible to conduct your own walking tour of the City Gates and Fortifications, with the aid of the *Official Guide of Gibraltar*, issued by the Gibraltar Tourist Board and *A Guided Tour of Gibraltar* by T J Finlayson. Other helpful books are *Gibraltar Guidebook* and *Discover Gibraltar*. It is also possible to visit the main sites by local bus. A detailed Bus Routes sheet may be obtained from the Tourist Offices.

Many places of interest may be encountered in Main Street, a colourful multicultural mixture of local shops and *souks* and British department stores such as Marks & Spencer), below a dignified colonial-style facade.

The centre is a 5–10 minute walk from Sheppards or Marina Bay, right along the main road (Glacis Road), over the roundabout and bearing left through Landport Gate. This was originally the only landward entrance into Gibraltar and was rebuilt in 1729 on the site of previous Spanish and Moorish gates and through which the troops emerged for the surprise sortie against the Spanish during the Great Siege. Casemates Square, site of the 15th-century Spanish quarter, which had been demolished due to almost total devastation following the Great Siege, then rebuilt in 1731. It had been the venue for many executions!.

Enter the city through Casemates Gate passing the main market on your right. About half way along Main Street on the right, you will encounter the House of Assembly, Mackintosh Square, the British War Memorial, Tourist Information Office and City Hall. Nearby on the left you will find the Catholic Cathedral of Saint Mary the Crowned. Make a short detour left to the end of Library Street and opposite you will see the Garrison Library and offices of *The Gibraltar Chronicle* whose most famous scoop reported the victory at the Battle of Trafalgar. Returning to Main Street, a little further on, you will come to Cathedral Square. Detour right, down Bombhouse Lane, if you wish to visit the Museum and Moorish baths. Back up to the square again, the Anglican Cathedral of the Holy Trinity is worth a visit, also the King's Chapel a little further on. Opposite you will find the Supreme Court and next-door, the Convent (which has now become the Governor's Residence). A little further on the left, is Wesley House, the Methodist Church and Carpenter's Arms upstairs, which serves very reasonably priced home-made meals and snacks in a very welcoming atmosphere. (Open 1000–1400 Mon–Fri). The new Queensway Marina is situated on Ragged Staff Wharf at the base of Charles V wall and only a 5-minute walk from the centre of town. Towards the end of Main Street, through Southport Gate, a visit to Trafalgar Cemetery is of interest. Here you will find a few graves of sailors killed in the battle of Trafalgar and in particular a gravestone commemorating two sailors purported to be killed by the same cannonball.

The cable car station is just a short walk from here and is open from 0930–1800 daily except Sundays. The last car up is at 1715 and the last one down at 1745. The fare includes entry to St Michael's Cave and the Apes' Den ☎ 77826. Continuing on, you will come to the Alameda Gardens, above which you will see the elegant Rock Hotel and the Casino.

The most direct way to find the Moorish castle and Galleries is to climb the flights of steps leading to the uppermost road (Willis's Road) from Bell Lane (opposite the post office) and bear left. It is a fair walk.

The Gibraltar Memorial can be found in the Linewall Boulevard.

It is a ten-minute walk from Sheppards marina to the frontier and airport. Turn left along Glacis Road and cross the runway.

Tourist information

Details of more sites and other tourist information, including details of Consulates, Restaurants, Natural History etc, can be obtained from the Gibraltar Tourist Board's excellent and comprehensive Fact Files which are issued free. The Tourist Board also provides a very good street map.

Its offices are located at Duke of Kent House,

Cathedral Square, ☎ 79450; The Piazza, Main Street, ☎ 79482; Four Corners, Winston Churchill Avenue, ☎ 50762; Arrivals Hall, Gibraltar Airport. ☎ 73026/47227; Customs Hall at the border; Gibraltar Museum, 18-20 Bombhouse Lane; John Mackintosh Hall, 308 Main Street. The staff are very friendly and extremely helpful.

History
The ancient Rock of Gibraltar has witnessed the unfolding of a unique and chequered history over the centuries from its inimitable vantage point at the intersection of two continents and two oceans.

Gibraltar claims to have some of the oldest inhabitants with Neolithic human remains having been found.

Recent scientific announcements that there is no genetic link between these remains and humans, has not diminished its claim as the cradle of civilisation. However it has undoubtedly been a place of sojourn for many civilisations. For centuries the Rock served as an important landmark and provided shelter for ancient mariners, who came in their small ships, and a place or worship. (Evidenced by remains of Phoenician, Carthaginian and Greek pottery, amulets and artefacts bearing classical and Egyptian gods found in caves at the foot of the Rock.) The Phoenicians built settlements by rivers close to the Rock and the Romans built cities nearby, but neither they nor the ancient Greeks built a city here.

The Rock was once named Monscalpe and according to Greek mythology was, together with Mons Ably near Ceuta, (across the Strait), one of the twin pillars of Hercules. During the Arab invasion in the 8th century under Tarik ibn Zeyad, the Rock was known as Gibel Tarik meaning: the Mountain of Tarik which eventually metamorphasised into its modern day name of Gibraltar.

Around AD 400, the decline of the Roman Empire led to invasions by Barbarian races from the east. The Vandals and Goths swept through Spain and the Vandals marched on to conquer North Africa while, from 414–711, the Goths occupied the Iberian Peninsula.

The death of the Prophet Mohammed in 632 precipitated a rapid expansion of Islam. By the beginning of the 8th century the Arabs were poised to invade Spain and succeeded in conquering the whole of the Peninsula with the exception of the Cantabrian mountains and the Pyrenees. Thus began a Moorish rule over Gibraltar which was to last more than six centuries (bar a 24-year lapse between 1309 and 1333) with the landing of Tarik ibn Zeyad in AD 711, a Berber chief and Governor of Tanger. During this time, the peninsula was divided into Arab Kingdoms and by the 11th century, Gibraltar was under the dominion of the Arab Kingdom of Seville, except for a short period under Berber rule from Malaga. Following the increasing threat of invasion by other North African tribes Tarik ordered the construction of a few fortifications. However, it was not until 1160 that the first town of Gibraltar and fortress were founded by Abdul Mamen, Caliph of Morocco and leader of the Almohads. A small walled city then grew up on the western side of the Rock on an area from the Tower of Homage to what is Grand Casemates Square today: the *Medinat al Fath* or City of Victory.

By 1252 Arab influence was declining following inter-tribal skirmishes and fighting between Arabs and Christians, thus only two kingdoms remained under their control (Murcia and Granada).

Spain was gaining the upper hand and in 1309 Alonso Perez de Guzman and his troops laid siege to Gibraltar and took the upper Rock from where they shelled the town, causing much destruction. After a month, the garrison surrendered and the inhabitants were free to leave. Few remained and the Spanish were left to rebuild the fortifications and shipyard.

In 1333 Gibraltar was recaptured by the Muslims and was once again under siege, this time led by Abdul Malik, the Prince of Morocco. The garrison held out for four months before finally capitulating.

More sieges followed and in 1462 Gibraltar was recaptured by the Spanish, initially under the King of Castille but its strategic importance waned under the Spanish King Henry IV as he broadened its municipal boundaries concentrating on agriculture and boosting the economy. As a result his defences were weakened and more sieges and petty feuds followed.

In 1474 the Catholic Queen Isabella came to the throne and in 1501 issued a decree declaring Gibraltar Crown Property. The following year she granted a Coat of Arms; the Castle and Key, with the inscription: Seal of the Noble City of Gibraltar, the Key of Spain.

Gibraltar remained under Spain until the beginning of the 18th century. In 1702 the King of Spain died childless leaving only foreign relatives, precipitating the eleven year War of Spanish Succession. Britain had first become interested in Gibraltar during the time of Cromwell. However, it was during the struggle to attain the Spanish throne, between Archduke Charles of Austria and Philip of Anjou, (grandson of Louis XIV of France), that Cromwell the English Lord Protector seized the opportunity of capturing the Rock. He sent a combined Anglo-Dutch fleet led by Admiral Sir George Rook, on behalf of Charles, which undertook a massive bombardment of Gibraltar. The acting Governor eventually surrendered. As it turned out, it was Philip who won the throne, becoming Philip V, King of Spain but due to the collapse of the Archduke's cause, Gibraltar remained under British control. This was ratified under the Treaty of Utrecht in 1713 and Gibraltar thus became a British garrison.

Although Spain and Gibraltar resumed trading, the peace was a tentative one and in 1727, the Spanish besieged the Rock but the attempt was unsuccessful and lasted only a few months. However Spain was determined to have Gibraltar back and in 1779 began The Great Siege lasting

North Africa

almost four years. The garrison demonstrated incredible fortitude and endurance and would have starved had they not received supplies from British fleets on three almost annual occasions. They were outnumbered almost five-to-one but against such odds, and using the Rock to its best advantage, they held their own. Tunnels were blasted out of the Rock and a gun carriage designed facilitating the placement of guns high in the Rock face above their opponents. In November 1871 they launched a surprise counter-attack which considerably evened up the numbers! At this, and on the realisation that they could not starve them out, the remaining army changed tactics and assembled seemingly impregnable floating batteries consisting of naval vessels from which they mounted a devastating assault destroying most of the town. (Hence there is little evidence today of the original Spanish and Moorish architecture.) Even this challenge did not defeat the intrepid garrison who retaliated by raining down red-hot cannonballs, heated from their furnaces, which eventually penetrated and blew up the batteries affording them an incredible victory and grand finale to the great siege as they re-established supremacy of the Rock.

Recent history
In the 19th century Gibraltar was rebuilt with even stronger fortifications and began to develop as a commercial centre comprising a fairly diversely cosmopolitan population of merchants. It was Nelson's home port and following the Battle of Trafalgar his body was brought here in 1805, reputedly in a barrel of rum.

In 1830 Gibraltar became a Crown Colony and a Judiciary was set up independent of the executive and legislative powers vested in the Governor.

At the beginning of this century, when Germany was increasing in military might, Britain responded by strengthening her Navy in Gibraltar and building a harbour and dockyard. It was from this Naval base that the Straits were patrolled during the World Wars and the allied warships repaired. An airfield was constructed and miles of tunnels were dug out of the Rock creating a self-sufficient city with generators and telephone exchange, a hospital and food stores in case of another siege. In fact they were never utilised.

Out of the post-war years mushroomed a growing desire for self-government and in 1945 the Civil Council was reinstituted only to be reversed three years later with the formation of a Legislative Council but in 1969 Britain issued a new Constitution granting them self-government in domestic affairs.

In 1963 Spain revived her claim on Gibraltar and began a campaign of increasing restrictions at the border culminating in 1969 with its closure. Gibraltar survived another 16 years of isolation before it was finally reopened. However, even today the border problems continue and the question of Gibraltar's identity still remains.

Transitting the Straits of Gibraltar

Many yachts will be using Gibraltar as the departure point for trips to Morocco. Many elements combine to produce a complex system of tides and currents in the Straits, an appreciation of which will greatly help yachtsmen heading west. Having spent many fruitless hours trying to make a westwards passage through the Straits some years ago, thoroughly convinced by the Admiralty tide tables that the current was with me, whereas in fact I was losing ground while making 6kts. These paragraphs are included to assist the yachtsman transitting the Straits.

Eight miles separate Europe from Africa at its narrowest point in the Straits. The water at the western end of the 30 mile stretch is some 2–3m higher than at the eastern end, thus causing a constant surface flow into the Mediterranean. This is due to evaporation in the Mediterranean, which is three times faster than the rate at which the combined waters from rivers flow into it and the fact that the Atlantic is tidal with a predominantly westerly swell, whereas the land-locked Mediterranean, is virtually non-tidal. This produces a standing E-going surface current of between 1 and 2kts. Differences in salinity between the Atlantic and the Mediterranean forces the heavier water down, causing a subsurface current in the opposite direction. Wind also accounts for a surface current effect, depending whether it is easterly (*levanter*) or westerly (*poniente*), which confuses the equation further. Then there are tides, which are well documented in Admiralty tide tables. At the eastern end of the Straits the range is only half a metre and negligible once a few miles into the Mediterranean, whereas at Tanger the spring range is 3m. Barometric pressure differences also affect the height of water.

On the north side of the Western Straits is Tarifa. Winds in excess of 30kts are said to blow there for 300 days of the year, whereas at the same time winds at the eastern end may be negligible, resulting in conditions at one end of the strait being very different from those at the other. Currents also vary in different parts of the Straits, and even run in opposite directions at the same time, as shown on the tidal chart. From these conflicting and confusing parameters some guidelines can be extracted.

Eastbound vessels
For yachts entering the Straits from the west, there is no real problem going eastwards, unless there is a strong easterly wind, in which case passage will be rough, especially around Tarifa. If strong winds are forecast, stay in Tanger or Barbate until it drops, or anchor in the lee of Tarifa if strong E winds are encountered once en route. During periods of light easterly winds, sea mist or fog may be persistent in the Straits, especially during the mornings. The best time to depart for the trip east is soon after LW.

From Tanger, keeping close inshore, the light and increasing E-going current off Punta Malabata will be useful. If going to Gibraltar, most vessels cross to Tarifa from Punta Malabata, or from Ciris, 12M further east.

Westbound vessels
In strong westerlies it is almost impossible to make headway west, due to the combined E-going current that can, with unfavourable tide, reach 6kts or more, with heavy steep swell and overfalls off Ceuta Point, Tarifa and Punta Malabata.

In good conditions, to make use of the favourable current, set off from Gibraltar 2 hours after HW. Keeping close inshore, a foul current of around a knot will be experienced off Punta Carnero. A favourable W-going current 4 hours after HW will assist passage during springs, although this is weak E-going at neaps. Crossing from Tarifa to Tanger it is usually wise to use the engine to make a fast passage to combat the increasing E-going current, or anchor in the sheltered W side of Tarifa and wait for the next favourable tide, around LW to make the crossing. It is possible, using the engine, to make a fast passage from Gibraltar without encountering heavy adverse currents.

From Ceuta, the timing is similar, setting off 2 hours after HW, keeping close inshore to make use of the counter current.

Gibraltar to Ceuta

Crossing from north to south and vice versa can normally be undertaken at any state of tide, since winds through the Straits are normally E or W, although it is important to account for leeway to counter the tide and currents. Remember, in general, a combined current of 1–2kts is usually E-going, in addition to tidal effects. Beware of rough overfalls and stronger currents around Europa Point and Ceuta Point. Entering Ceuta harbour this is particularly noticeable one mile NE off the entrance.

The above information is based on several articles regarding tides, current and wind effects in the Straits of Gibraltar, as well as many hours testing out the theories in over 50 journeys transitting them. The currents in the Straits are still full of surprises and for sailing purists who do not want a motor-assisted transit, this can be very frustrating.

Ceuta, looking north with Gibraltar behind city

North Africa

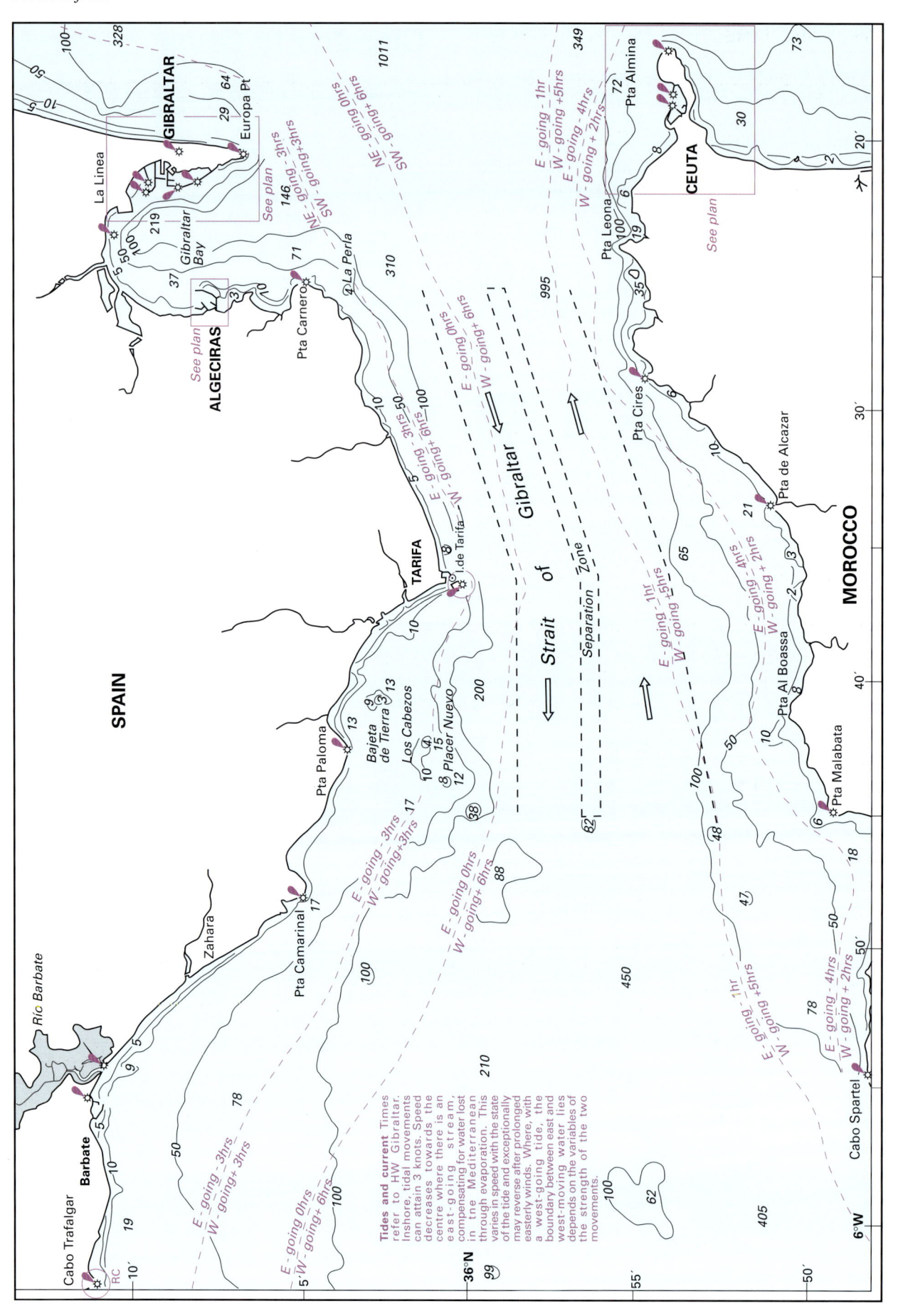

Tides and current Times refer to HW Gibraltar. Inshore, tidal movements can attain 3 knots. Speed decreases towards the centre where there is an east-going stream, compensating for water lost in the Mediterranean through evaporation. This varies in speed with the state of the tide and exceptionally may reverse after prolonged easterly winds. Where, with a west-going tide, the boundary between east and west-moving water lies depends on the variables of the strength of the two movements.

Gibraltar to Ceuta

TIDAL STREAMS - DIRECTION AND RATES

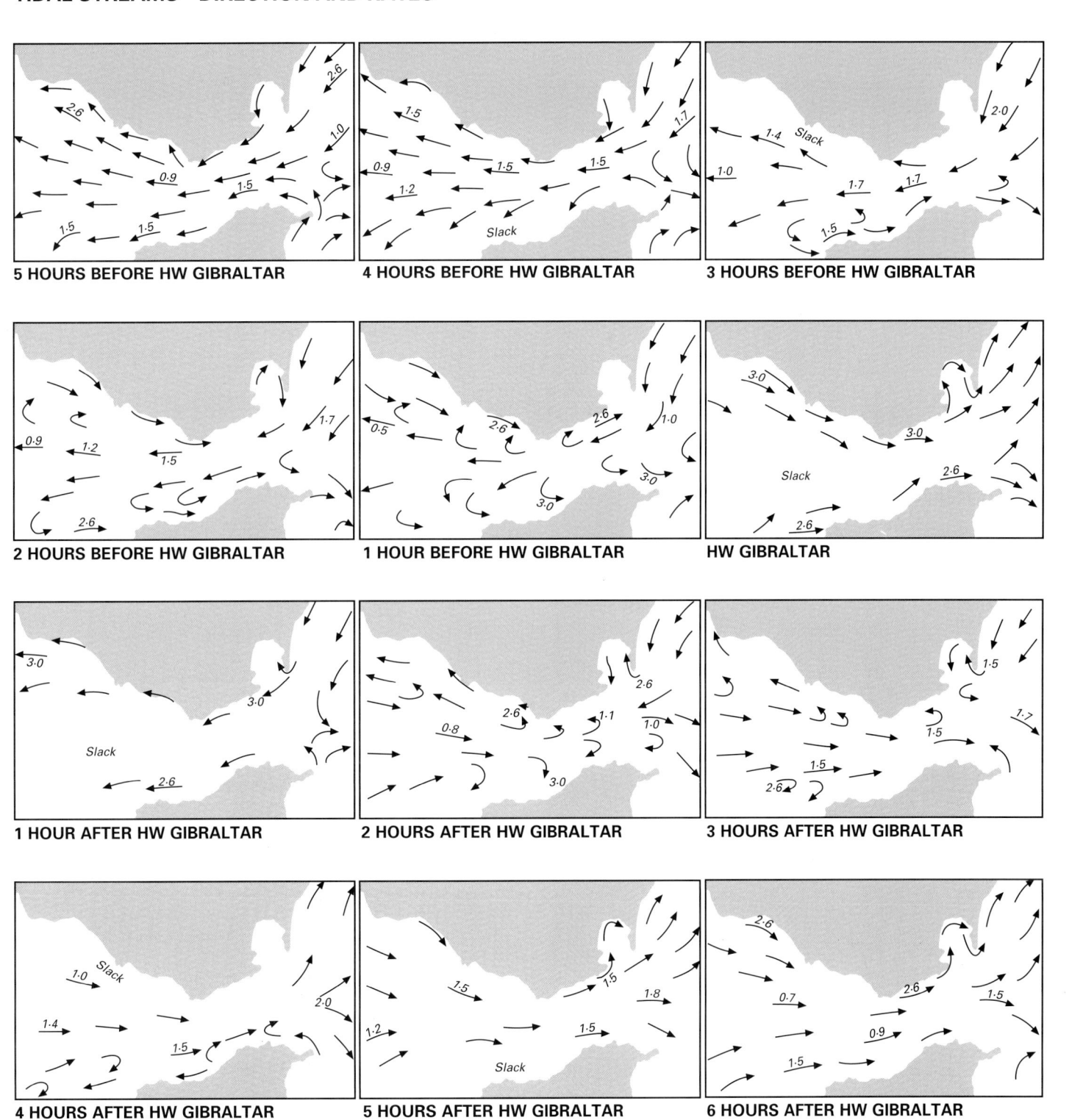

5 HOURS BEFORE HW GIBRALTAR

4 HOURS BEFORE HW GIBRALTAR

3 HOURS BEFORE HW GIBRALTAR

2 HOURS BEFORE HW GIBRALTAR

1 HOUR BEFORE HW GIBRALTAR

HW GIBRALTAR

1 HOUR AFTER HW GIBRALTAR

2 HOURS AFTER HW GIBRALTAR

3 HOURS AFTER HW GIBRALTAR

4 HOURS AFTER HW GIBRALTAR

5 HOURS AFTER HW GIBRALTAR

6 HOURS AFTER HW GIBRALTAR

TIDAL STREAMS EXPLANATION
The figures shown against the arrows are the mean rates at springs

North Africa

Morocco

Capital Rabat
Commercial capital Casablanca
Area 458,730 sq km
Population Approximately 29 million
GDP per person $620
Average annual population growth 2·5%

Introduction

Although only a few miles from Gibraltar, Morocco is completely different from the European mainland and one of the world's most fascinating places to visit. The Rif mountains bordering the Mediterranean coast may appear deserted but they are dotted with small villages and isolated fishing communities wherever there is a small bay or narrow strip of beach. Further inland are the great cities of the plains, old capitals of powerful Sultans whose territories once stretched from Mauritania to the Pyrenees and from the Atlantic to Tunisia. Further south rise the majestic Atlas Mountains, home to the original Berber inhabitants, where many of the old rulers started their conquests. Beyond the High Atlas, the mountains give way to the Sahara.

Morocco has retained its traditional values and lifestyle more than any of the other North African countries (The Maghreb). It is an intriguing and delightful place: a country where visitors are welcome but where the government has not encouraged the sort of tourism that has destroyed the cultural fabric, as in so many towns elsewhere. Where tourist accommodation has been built, almost nowhere has it impinged on the ancient parts of the towns. In Tanger for example, the hotels are mainly along the seafront, completely separate, but within easy reach of the old part of the town. Likewise, the ports remain very Moroccan: typical busy fishing ports going about their business as they have for centuries. Do not expect to find luxurious well-appointed marinas as seen in Europe, although two such marinas: Marina Smir and Kabila, are described. These are well located for excursions to Chefchouen and Tetouan.

A brief history

Although there were Phoenician trading posts along the coast and the Romans had built quite a large city near Volubilis, Morocco was not subjugated to any central authority before the 7th century. The Berber tribes each had their own territories in 'Maghreb el-Aksa', the land furthest to the west. Only after the Arab conquest in the 7th and 8th centuries did some sort of central rule emerge, possibly helped by the first successful invasion of southern Spain in 711 by Muslim-converted Berbers. The Moors, as they were called, continued north until halted at the Pyrenees in 731 by Charles Martel. In 680, the Governor of Kairouan (in present day Tunisia), Oqba Ibn Nafi, had reached the Atlantic coast of Morocco and introduced the Islamic religion to the indigenous Berbers. When Islam split into Sunni and Shi'ite sects in the 8th century, many of the latter moved west from Damascus and eventually arrived in Morocco. Among them was Moulay Idriss who was accepted as the new leader by the inhabitants of Volubilis which at that time was still a major city. In 791 Moulay Idriss was poisoned by Sunni Muslims but his short reign marks the first Moroccan dynasty, the Idrissids. Moulay's son Idriss II ruled Morocco from the north to the oases south of the Atlas for over 20 years and founded Fes as his new capital. Situated between the other two great cities of western Islam, Cordoba in Spain and Kairouan in Tunisia, Fes became a flourishing trading as well as religious centre. The power of the Idrissids weakened after a short time and the sultanate fell apart again in separate principalities. In the 11th and 12th centuries Morocco was ruled by two great Berber dynasties, the Almoravids and Almohads.

Today's aspiration for a Greater Morocco with regard to the Western Sahara goes back to the Islamic Golden Ages under these dynasties. The Almoravids set up Marrakech as their new capital and, having lost territory in Spain to the Christians, their leader Youssef bin Tachfine restored Muslim control as far north as Valencia in 1107. The Almohads, driven by religious zeal, eventually overthrew the Almoravids. Under Yacoub el Mansour they defeated the Christians in Spain again in 1195 and for the first time in history the Maghreb was one huge empire from the Atlantic to Tunisia and Spain to Senegal. With the wealth this brought, a new capital was built in Rabat and many new mosques and minarets were built in cities as far apart as Sevilla in the north and Marrakech in the south. When the Almohads tried to push the Christians north of the Pyrenees they were defeated in 1212 and a gradual decline set in until the Moors were finally defeated in Spain with the fall of Grenada in 1492.

In the following centuries the Portuguese set up seaports on the Atlantic Coast and the Maghreb became part of the Ottoman Empire. The most remarkable event of this period was the establishment of the pirate 'Republic of the Bou Regreg', on the Atlantic coast around Rabat, in the beginning of the 17th century. Spanish ships were the main target of their attacks but they strayed as far north as Ireland and traded weapons with the English and French. Towards the end of the 17th century the new dynasty of the Alaouites emerged from the south and during the 55 years of Sultan Moulay Ismail's reign the entire country was subjugated again. Morocco enjoyed its last 'Golden Age' and Meknes became the new Imperial Capital. At his death in 1727 Ismail left a great empire and from his numerous sons, Sidi Mohammed emerged as the new sultan. Morocco continued to prosper but after Mohammed's death in 1790 the country fell back into a state of civil war. The 20th century is marked by a growing European influence and at the Treaty of Fes in 1912 Morocco was divided into French and Spanish Protectorates. Spain took the north where since the 15th century they occupied the enclaves of Ceuta and Melilla, and a strip of Sahara down to French Mauritania, and France controlled the area south of the Rif mountains. Spain showed little interest in developing their part of the Protectorate but under the inspired leadership of Marshal Lyautey, the French introduced their own administrative system alongside the Moroccan bureaucracy and built new French towns next to the Arab medinas, as well as new roads and irrigation systems to develop the country. Before the beginning of the Second World War moderate nationalist feelings had surfaced, but during the war Moroccan forces fought alongside French troops. After the war this Moroccan loyalty was not rewarded and Istiqlal, the party for independence, grew stronger. When in 1953 Sultan (later King) Mohammed V openly supported the independence movement he was exiled but this only increased his popularity. Under pressure from increased violence and unrest he was allowed to return to Morocco in 1955 and in 1956 France and Spain signed treaties with the King for the complete independence of Morocco.

Recent history
The Alaouite dynasty, rose to power in the 17th century. Mohammed V, the grandfather of the present king, Mohammed Vl, led the country to independence after French colonial rule ended in 1956. After the sudden death of his father, Hassan II, still in his early twenties, assumed control in 1961. Helped by the fact that he was a direct descendant of the Prophet and as such also the religious leader, he maintained control of his country through good leadership and shrewd political manoeuvring.

In July 1999, King Hasan II died and Mohammed Vl inhereted the throne at 36 years of age.

One of King Hassans II's remarkable initiatives was the Green March in 1975 when 350,000 unarmed Moroccans moved into the Western Sahara which until then had been a Spanish colony. Attention was deflected from internal problems and the population was united for the common cause of a Greater Morocco. This initiative brought its difficulties. Supported by Algeria, the population of the new territory started a war for independence and relations with Algeria were strained for many years although they have recently improved. The Western Sahara issue is still not resolved, although renewed efforts by the UN are currently under way. Through a new Maghreb unity, Morocco hopes to find new markets for its agricultural products and gain access to the rich oil and gas reserves of Algeria and Libya. Morocco is a large producer of phosphates but has no other significant natural resource. Phosphates and derivatives account for 60% of export earnings and agricultural exports, tourist revenues and remittances from Moroccans working abroad make up the rest. Morocco's export of agricultural products has been severely cut since the full integration of Spain and the rest of Europe into the EU.

Spain retains sovereignty of two small enclaves on the Moroccan coast: Ceuta and Melilla. These, along with two small islands are all that remain of the Spanish colonial rule.

One of the most fascinating aspects of Morocco is the sense of ongoing history, which is clearly evidenced everywhere, both in the nature of the port activities and the historical constructions. The continuing and practical use of donkeys, working alongside the most modern vehicles, provokes a feeling of timelessness. The story you see in the architecture and the ruins around the ports, is one of a rise and fall of empires: Portuguese 16th-century global maritime trade, 20th-century French/Spanish colonial empires and Moroccan dynasties. Over time their prominence and prosperity has ebbed and flowed like the tide. With high unemployment and other internal problems, the new King is determined to bring the country closer to Europe and into the 21st century, giving more freedom to the people.

General information

Money
Morocco's currency unit is the Dirham (Dh) with an exchange rate of approximately Dh15=£1–00 and Dh9.5=$1–00. (1999). Moroccan traders often express prices in francs, where 100 francs equal 1Dh. In coastal towns in the north, Spanish Pesetas can often be used.

Eurocheques, travellers cheques and cash are accepted at banks and international giro cheques can be cashed at post offices. With an American

Ancient Portuguese fortress near Tanger

Express credit card, traveller's cheques can be bought from the American Express representative, Voyage Schwarz, which has offices in Tanger, Casablanca, Rabat, Marrakech and Agadir. Using a *Visa* credit card, varying amounts up to Dh8,000 can be withdrawn at automatic cash machines, depending on the bank. Many shops take *Visa*, including, surprisingly, many of the small shops in the *souks* and *casbahs*.

Taking Dirhams in or out of the country is not permitted, though small amounts do not seem to cause any concern. Changing left-over notes is possible when receipts have been kept but it is preferable not to draw more than is needed. Notes can also be changed in Gibraltar or Algeciras. The Spanish enclaves within Morocco, Ceuta and Melilla, use Spanish pesetas. Credit cards, Eurocheques, traveller's cheques are accepted and there are no exchange controls.

Provisioning

Supermarkets exist only in the larger towns, but between the small shops and markets most requirements can be met. All fresh produce is seasonal and often grown locally. The quality is excellent and, due to less intensive farming techniques, fruit and vegetables generally are very good. Chicken and meat are not tampered with and because refrigeration is often not available, meat is freshly butchered; the heads of slaughtered animals are displayed by the butcher as proof of freshness. Shopping at the markets is fun. After a round of all the stalls a bag full of good quality fruit and vegetables may cost no more than £2. Tanger has a particularly fascinating market and the small villages are rewarding, especially on the weekly *souk* (market) days. Farmers from the mountains bring their produce which varies from livestock such as chickens, rabbits or a goat to fruit and vegetables. Donkeys get new shoes, saddles are repaired and at the end of the day the farmer leaves again with a new supply of staple articles. Chickens in the small villages are delicious and can be bought alive; the merchant will be happy to dress them on the spot. Once used to these different customs it is difficult to revert to the plastic wrapped products from the European supermarket.

Locally produced bottled soft drinks are very good value for money, as is the local beer. Local wines are not on a par with European wines and are expensive. Canned food is not usually available. There are supermarkets and shops in the Spanish enclaves. Ceuta is a free port operating in competition with Gibraltar. Bonded stores in Gibraltar are on the shelves in Ceuta at comparable prices without the hassle of customs formalities. Generally, prices in Ceuta and on the Spanish mainland are around 20% cheaper than in Gibraltar, but will vary with exchange rate.

Water

Generally there is a sufficient supply of good quality water but it is not always a convenient hose pipe length away. Sometimes a small charge is made, especially if you require assistance carrying cans aboard.

Electricity

Nominal voltage is 220V, 50Hz. This is available in the marinas and is often possible to arrange in other ports with a long lead, even if no specific provision is made, except in some of the very small harbours.

Fuel

Ceuta and Melilla have very cheap, good quality diesel. In Morocco it is more expensive but available from pumps in several ports and elsewhere it can be obtained in drums, which can be delivered for a small fee.

Harbour charges

Since most of the harbours in Morocco are fishing ports with no facilities or infrastructure to accommodate yachts for more than a few days, it is unusual for formal charges to be made. However, precisely because of the ambiguity of the situation, there is potential for its exploitation: be prepared for the unexpected with a little bakhshish (see section on bakhshish) – or even to pay port charges when they are levied unexpectedly and without explanation upon departing a port. This has been experienced in Al Hoceima and El Jadida. These charges may be negotiable and no doubt the government will in due course bring out guidelines. It is courteous to give a gift to the harbour watchman, who you will always find to be an invaluable assistant during your stay.

The two yacht marinas in Morocco which are built along European lines, Marina Smir and Marina Kabila, both near Sebta (Ceuta) offer every facility a yacht requires and naturally have a daily rate. It should be noted that at present, these two little-used marinas, charge a daily rate higher than most in Europe and, in contrast to marinas in Spain and Gibraltar, the price is not negotiable, except for long term stays of several months or more.

Marina Smir has excellent haul out facilities for any size of yacht and Kabila has a small travel-hoist. With Gibraltar and Puerto Sotogrande (10M NE of Gibraltar) nearby, both with 40-ton travel-hoists, the area is well served with repair facilities. Diesel engines of the types used in Morocco can be repaired or even completely overhauled at very low prices in almost any Moroccan port. Emergency repairs to other engines can be carried out anywhere. Fuel systems for any make of diesel engine can be repaired but it takes time to find the right workshop.

With a tide range of over 2–5m, it is possible to careen a yacht either on a mud-flat or in one of the harbours on the Atlantic coast.

Telephone

Overseas calls can be made at post offices but there are often queues. There are now kiosks in most towns selling telephone cards, which can be used on any public international phone. The larger hotels also have facilities, although very much more expensive and usually without STD dialling. The GSM mobile phone network is very well advanced and works in almost every town as well as several miles offshore along much of the coastline. Ensure the International Roaming facility is activated with your providing company. The mobile GSM system is often cheaper than using the local public phone system.

Health precautions

There are no mandatory inoculations except for yellow fever if coming from an infected area. Pharmacists are well trained but stock only a limited range of drugs. A good anti-diarrhoea drug should always be carried on board. Repatriation insurance in the case of major surgery is advisable. Many yacht insurance policies include this.

Tourist information

The ONMT (l'Office National Marocain du Tourisme, also called Syndicat d'Initiative), has offices in all major cities in Morocco. Their London office is at 174 Regent Street ☎ 44 (0)171 437 0073/74. They have useful city plans and general information but for any serious information the travel guides listed under 'Books' in the General Introduction are indispensable.

Tipping

Tipping follows the same rules as in Europe although it is not uncommon to have tips refused in the small villages along the coast. In European style restaurants and tourist areas, tipping is expected. It is useful to have European or American cigarettes on board as a gratuity for small services.

Public holidays

New Year's Day 1 January
Feast of the Throne 3 March
Labour Day 1 May
Green March 6 November
Independence Day 18 November
Islamic holidays are listed in the *General Introduction*.

Business hours

Banks are normally open Mon–Fri 0830–1130 and 1500–1630.

Shops are normally open 7 days a week from early morning to late in the afternoon with a long lunch break. As everywhere, markets have the best assortment in the mornings.

Time zone

Morocco is on UT (GMT) all year round: 2 hours behind Southern Europe time in the summer.

Photography

There is no particular problem providing pictures are not taken of military objects which include naval patrol boats. When taking pictures of people keep in mind that there is an Islamic religious objection to making an image of a person, though, with modern publicity and television this is fading. Objections can usually be smoothed away with a small tip.

Harbour security

There are no particular problems in any port in Morocco. The army and police have a discrete presence in every harbour. If the yacht is to be left for any length of time in a port, pay a guardian to keep an eye on it. Look on it as harbour dues; all fishing boats have guardians and it is a way of providing a little income for often poor families. When arranging a guardian keep in mind that a fisherman brings home between Dh 500–1000 per month £35 to £70. It is possible to employ a watchman for just a few dollars a day.

An exception to the above is Melilla which has a reputation for burglary and petty theft. Ceuta has improved security with the addition of a new marina.

Maritime security and anchoring

Smuggling and illegal emigration are a constant problem to the Moroccan authorities. Even though there does not seem to be a law forbidding anchoring along the Moroccan coast, care must be exercised because of the *kif* (marijuana) trafficking. Yachts close to the shore are sometimes checked by military boats to ensure they are engaged in legitimate activities. Thus, beware of lingering or anchoring near the shore without first informing the authorities that you wish to do so. Generally, local officials will not allow yachts to anchor in the vicinity of ports. Although much of the coast looks deserted, there are hidden military posts along the entire coastline at regular intervals and it will not be long before you will be made aware of this if you venture too close without first obtaining clearance. This is particularly true of the coastline between Melilla and Ceuta and in the Bay of Tanger. There are good fishing areas and lovely bays on the north coast which may be used if the nearest harbour authorities are informed in advance.

In case of an emergency or change of plan try to inform the authorities of your position by VHF on Ch 16. Never go ashore without authorisation in deserted parts of the coast or without first clearing customs, since you will almost certainly be arrested.

Harbour entry

Generally, except in the large commercial ports, entry at night is not advisable. Most of the harbours are fishing ports, often with no specifically designated place for yachts. It is easier to see the best place to moor by daylight and to avoid the many lines crossing between the boats which frequently also cross the harbour entrance. Some of the harbours are difficult to navigate, with entrances prone to silting although, once inside, they are quite safe. Daylight is also generally considered to be more auspicious, especially if you are engaged in something as unusual as sailing a yacht!

Entry formalities

Every port has its own variation of entry procedure, but the formalities are no great problem, although often protracted. Officials will show up soon after arrival. Immigration police, or the *gendarmerie* in the small ports, will always visit to check passports, which they sometimes retain, together with the ship's papers. These are returned shortly before departure, so if planning an early start, allow time to get them back. Customs officers will visit along with the harbourmaster. Some of the smaller harbours are not official ports of entry, but this is not usually a problem unless you want to travel inland, in which case your passport may be retained and a shore pass issued.

Entry into the small ports is an interesting experience. The officials will probably all arrive together and the yacht may also be honoured by a visit from the *caïd* who equates to a French prefect or mayor, appointed by the government. Officials are friendly and speak French or Spanish and sometimes, a little English. Entry procedures are free of charge.

Tips, which might be considered as bribes, must be avoided, but the practisce of bakhshish exists and it is not uncommon to be asked for cigarettes or whisky by the officials.

The main concern for customs officials boarding your yacht appears to be guns. If you have a weapon onboard, it must be declared and it will be bonded while in port. Note that this and other cargo and crew information is exchanged between the ports by fax. Alcoholic beverages on board for personal use are not of great concern but large quantities should be declared and may be sealed in a locker until your departure. Generally, a glimpse inside the boat will satisfy official curiosity. The *capitainerie* and *marine marchande* operate in all ports but generally are not interested in yachts staying only a short time.

When making a trip inland be sure to take passports or your shore pass if one is issued in lieu, as these are required by hotels.

Note Formalities and inspections in some harbours, particularly on the northern coast, have in the past been rather excessive and unnecessary. This has been the case at Al Hoceima – where as many as 10 officers may board your vessel – Marina Smir and Kabila, where yachts have undergone a thorough searching taking an hour or more, for no apparent reason both on arrival and departure. However, things are changing with the recently declared policy of encouraging yachtsmen. Letting the harbour authorities know your next destination will greatly assist your passage through the formalities.

Yachts are a rarity in Morocco at present, so many of the port authorities simply do not know how to handle them, especially in the context of a working fishing port. No doubt as more sailors visit and as the authorities gain greater familiarity with the yachting community, they will learn to discriminate between pleasure sailors and those very few who are involved in less agreeable activities, and the government will develop a more systematic and practical approach. Being friendly and retaining a sense of humour is essential.

The Kif trade
The growing and processing of *kif* (marijuana, hashish), is an important economic activity in the Rif mountains on the north coast with some communities totally sustained by it. This local habit is of little concern to a yachtsman, but in order to avoid misunderstanding about the purpose of your own visit, it is advisable not to participate. It is legal to grow and sell the drug, but illegal to buy or transport it. There are many smuggling routes to Europe and shipment by yacht is one, as witnessed by the numbers of yachts confiscated in Europe and many more in Moroccan ports with the crews in Tanger jail. Police often photograph yachts when cruising along the coast, which is regularly patrolled. Although the official attitude to *kif* is unambiguous, officials in some of the smaller ports seem happy to ignore it. It is by far the biggest source of income in the otherwise poor north and it is not uncommon to be asked, even by officials, to buy a few kilos. This may be done either to test the purpose of your visit or to propose a real transaction, though a serious attempt at a business deal will almost never be made directly. Providing you are aware that there is a traffic it is easy to avoid it. It is important to know that the dealers profit is not only made by selling *kif*, but also by informing the police of his customers! He often gets the *kif* back in the end to re-sell, thus profiting three times from any sale.

Visas
Most Europeans, North American, Australian and New Zealand citizens do not need a visa to enter Morocco for visits up to 90 days. Citizens of the Netherlands, Belgium, Luxembourg and South Africa do require them and they are best obtained in their country of residence, normally taking 24 hours to process. There are Moroccan consulates in Malaga and Algeciras, Spain, but it takes longer to obtain visas there. Visitors with Israeli or South African stamps in their passports may be refused entry into Morocco although there does not seem to be a consistent policy. It is possible to renew or extend a visa. In practice, yachtsmen rarely have a problem, whatever their nationality and can usually obtain a shore pass even if a visa is theoretically required.

Embassies
UK 17 Blvd de la Tour Hassan, Rabat ☎ 07/720905-6
  Consulate: 9 Rue de Amerique du Sud, Tanger ☎ 09/941557
USA 2 Av. de Marrakech, Rabat ☎ 07/762265
  Consulate: 29 Rue el Achouak Chemin des Amoureux, Tanger ☎ 09/941557
Canada 13 Bis Rue Joafar Assadik, Agdal, Rabat ☎ 07/771375
Netherlands 40 Rue de Tunis ☎ 07/33512
  Consulate: Immeuble Miramonte, 47 Av. Hassan II, Tanger ☎ 09/931245
Denmark 4 Rue de Khemisset, Rabat ☎ 07/32684
  Consulate: 150 Meskini, Casablanca ☎ 02/314491
Sweden 159 Av. Pres Kennedy, Souissi, Rabat ☎ 07/754740

Consulate: 3 Rue du Lt. Sylvestre, Casablanca
☎ 02/304648
Norway 22 Charia as-Souira, Rabat-Chellah
☎ 07/761096
Consulate: 3 Rue Henri Regnault, Tanger
☎ 09 933633

Irish, *Australian* and *New Zealand* citizens are advised to use UK consular facilities while in Morocco.

International travel

Air Tanger, Casablanca, Marrakech and Agadir all have airports operating international flights.

Sea Several ferries operate from Tanger and Ceuta to Algeciras. In summer a fast boat operates between Marina Smir and Benalmadena. (near Malaga). A ferry operates from Melilla to Malaga and Almeria.

Overland travel

Morocco has a good public transport infrastructure:

Trains The railway system covers most of the northern cities and is the most comfortable way to travel. It is worth paying the very small price difference to travel first class.

Buses and coaches There is a regular bus service connecting almost every town and village in Morocco. This is a slow method of travel, except for the inter-city CTM coaches, but interesting, since you will pass on minor roads and see the countryside. Most larger towns and cities are served by a coach service. Many of these are modern air-conditioned vehicles.

Taxis Inter-city service taxis will wait until full and then take passengers from one town to another and drop off along the way. The price for this is comparable to a bus service but very much quicker. Petite taxis operate within towns and cities and are very cheap, but since the meters rarely work, a price should be agreed in advance to avoid argument at your destination. Petite taxis will only carry a maximum of 3 passengers, whereas the more expensive Mercedes taxis will take more.

Donkey and cart Although most villages towns and cities have taxis operating, you can always be sure to get a ride on a donkey/mule and cart. A rather bumpy, but delightful way to travel for short distances. Some railway stations outside the towns are served in this way to transfer passengers the short distance to the town centre. Some towns also have a regular horse and cart service for both sightseeing and as a regular taxi service.

Car hire This is available in the larger towns, but is very expensive compared with Europe or the USA. Typically 700 to 1,000 Dirhams ($70 to $100) per day for a small car for 3 days and cheaper for longer periods. If you do hire one, be careful when passing through towns and villages, where speed restrictions as low as 40 kilometres per hour are in effect but often not marked. With plenty of police available and an increasing use of radar in the country, you are sure to be stopped and fined if exceeding the limit.

Own vehicle If you have a motor cycle onboard, this can usually be used without any problem or paperwork. If you take in a car from Spain, formalities can be completed fairly quickly in Tanger or Ceuta. You will need your original registration document and the vehicle needs to be in the driver's name. Complications arise if you are using a friend's vehicle, unless you have a legal document giving authorisation. Most European insurance companies (with the exception of Spain) do not automatically include Morocco, but insurance agents are located in the ports to provide short term cover. Hire cars from Ceuta may be taken into Morocco by arrangement with the company, but not those hired in mainland Spain.

Tour guides

As with *bakhshish*, understanding this issue in advance can make the difference between having a relaxing time in Morocco and leaving the country exhausted by minor struggles with the ubiquitous 'volunteers' who intend to help you with the details of life for a small fee – whether you want it or not! This is particularly problematic in Tanger. Europeans are accustomed to deciding when they need assistance and so it can be disconcerting to find that payment is expected for services rendered without ever being consulted: a porter to help with bags, a tour guide, an attendant to wash and watch over your car, etc. Even when asked in advance, it may seem that declining is simply not an option. If you genuinely have no intention of accepting such offers/demands for payment, or if you are aggressively pestered as is common in Tanger and Tetuan, be sure not to engage in any conversation beyond a polite 'no thank you', for verbal engagement is taken as a sign of interest. 'No' is taken to mean 'perhaps'. However, do consider that it can be a tremendous relief to relinquish some of one's autonomy and simply permit people to help whilst enjoying the luxury of highly personalised attention. Once you have chosen a particular person to help you with a task and settled on a price you both think is fair, you can rest assured that he will personally fend off all other contenders for the honour and usually do his job very attentively.

At times you may want a guide. In El Jadida, for example, a tour guide will willingly spend an entire day taking you round the extensive sights for some 50 Dirhams – just $5·00 (although more may be appropriate). Many guides, official or not, speak excellent French and English and know a good deal about the history of their towns. Spending several hours with an articulate guide now and then can teach you much about Morocco, its culture and history.

Many guides will have a personal agenda (e.g. taking you to visit 'my brother' the carpet merchant) so be sure to steer your own course through the *souk* without getting bamboozled into buying what you do not want. In Marina Smir, Kabila and M'diq there are usually taxi drivers who will take you to

North Africa

Tetuan, Chefchaouen, the Oued Laou market and the surrounding villages for a very reasonable fare. For a small extra charge they are often prepared to act as a tour guide, ensuring that you are not disturbed on your excursion. Insofar as you can anticipate them, it is wisest, financially, to outline all such desires in your initial negotiations.

In sum, rather than cling to a 'do-it-yourself' approach in Morocco, it often makes more sense to think through your needs and wishes so that you can negotiate clearly when the opportunity arises, and then allow the abundant volunteers (who may desperately need a few extra Dirhams) to help you execute them. Rather than resist it, let this different system work for you from the start.

Note For any train or bus excursion, it is wise to know the schedule yourself. Tourists are occasionally followed onto trains and told that they must get off a train and change to another in some town or other, only to find that such route/schedule revisions were concocted to lure them into the shops of the family of the 'guide' who gave them this advice. In any case, if you want to make your own way around Moroccan cities, a general piece of advice is that you will be much less hassled if you always at least look as if you know where you are going, even if you do not!

Cruising grounds

The N coast of Morocco borders the Atlantic for some 30M from Cap Spartel to Ceuta from where the Mediterranean coast extends 165M to the Algerian border. Most of this coast is flanked by the inaccessible Rif Mountains, interrupted by beaches in the bay S of Ceuta, the Bay of Al Hoceima and the coast E of Cabo Tres Forcas. Several strategically located rocks and islets off the coast are still in Spanish hands as well as the enclaves of Ceuta and Melilla. There are few anchorages with good shelter. The Spanish ports of Ceuta and Melilla are conveniently located to stock up on items not available in Morocco. Although Morocco is visited by the largest number of European tourists in the Maghreb, around 1–5 million a year, this is hardly noticeable along the coast. The ports offer a unique view of the traditional Moroccan lifestyle and yachts will find a friendly welcome everywhere.

The west Atlantic coast, although not spectacular from seaward, offers a glimpse of the past in the form of many ancient cities and ports which, in some cases have been in use for thousands of years. It is possible and practical to visit the entire coast of Morocco without having to spend a night at sea.

Good all-weather ports

Entry safe by day and night and in bad weather:
Mediterranean coast: Tanger, Ceuta and Melilla (not in strong easterlies). Gibraltar.
Atlantic coast: Casablanca, Jorf Lasfar, Safi, Agadir.

1. Atlantic Coast. Tanger to Laayoune

General information

As you contemplate visiting the Atlantic ports of Morocco, whether en route to the Canaries, or for tourism within the country, remember that some of the ports you are sailing into have been in use for thousands of years. You are sailing in the wake of Phoenicians, Carthaginians, Romans, Portuguese (all involved in the trans-Saharan slave and gold trades, and as a stopover on their long voyage to the East Indies), Spanish (17th- and 20th-century occupations) and many pirates. These, along with sailors and sultans native to these parts, have all left their mark on this coastline. From these shores, Thor Hyerdahl set out in *Ra* to prove that ancient seafarers, using boats constructed of reeds and bamboo, crossed the Atlantic long before Columbus.

Moreover, four of the five Atlantic ports which the Portuguese fortified in the 15th century, can be visited and are included in this book. These cities – Asilah, El Jadida, Safi and Essaouira – essentially retain their massive limestone ramparts and are some of the most gracious, clean and quiet of Moroccan cities. The small port of Asilah, for example, has a history going back at least 3,600 years. Called Zilis by the Phoenicians, this was one of the most important trading cities of Tingitan Mauritania. The 15th-century fortifications which can be seen today, largely intact, are of Portuguese origin. Other ancient harbour towns are Azzemour, just north of El Jadida, a Carthaginian port built for ships trading between Portugal and Guinea; El Jadida, one of the most protected cities of its time, and still standing with its full ramparts intact; Safi and Essaouira; both pre-Roman. All these cities were fortified by the Portuguese and their limestone ramparts and elegant façades of houses within them, lend an unusual graciousness and grandeur, enhanced by the natural cleanliness brought about by the sheer impenetrable faces of limestone from which they were constructed. Many of the cities themselves are equally well preserved.

As I write, new marinas are planned for Asilah, Agadir, Casablanca, Tanger and Mohammedia. When completed, they will undoubtedly enhance the sailing on this coast. Completion of some of these projects could be several years away, and there is much to be said for visiting these places as they stand now, while sailing can be full of unexpected adventures! Consequently, this part of the book too is provisional: sailing in Morocco is in its infancy. One thing is certain: the spontaneity with which the locals will welcome yachtsman.

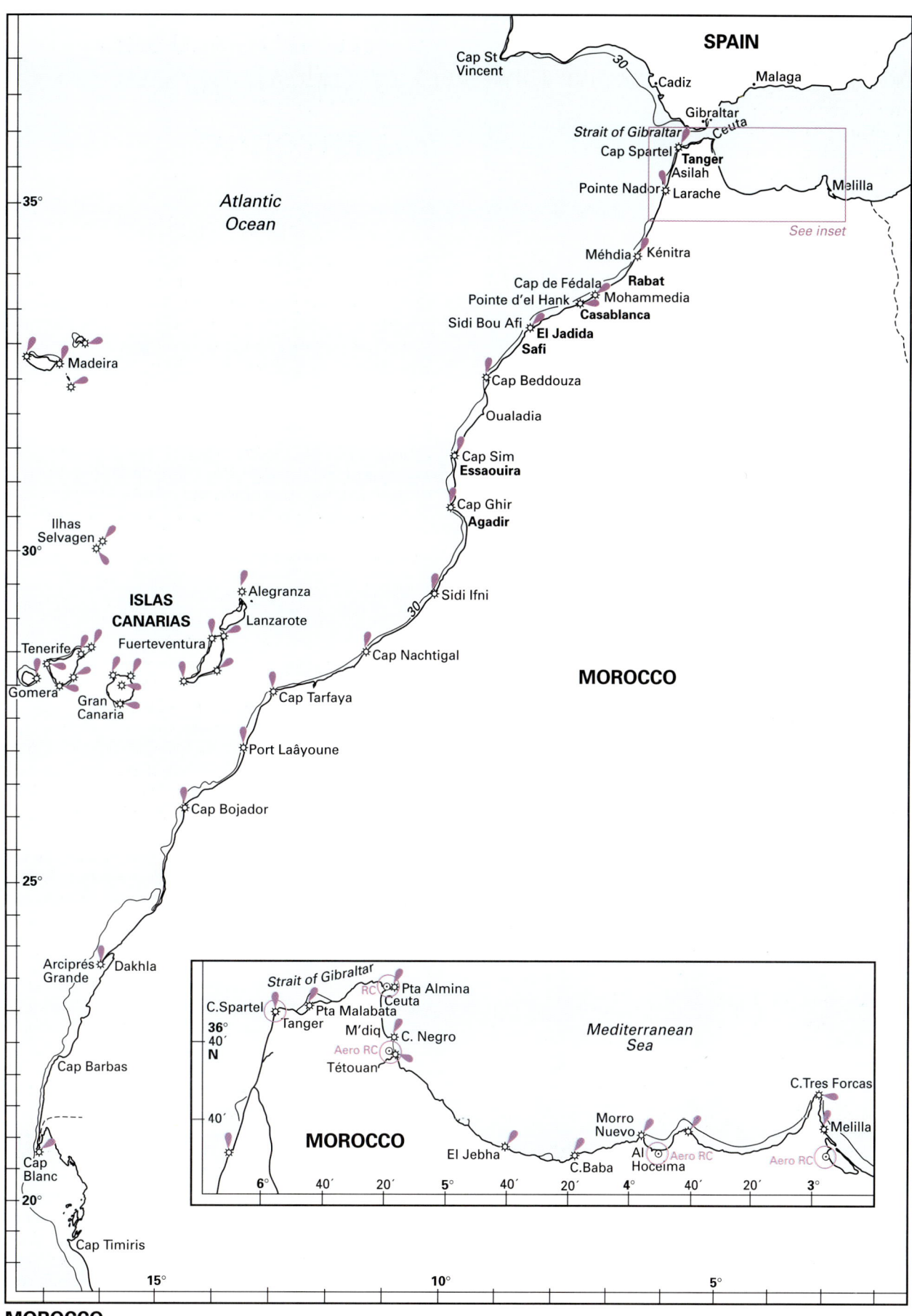

MOROCCO

Map labels (Atlantic coast, north to south)

- SPAIN
- Cap St Vincent
- Cadiz
- Malaga
- Gibraltar
- Strait of Gibraltar
- Ceuta
- Cap Spartel
- **Tanger**
- Asilah
- Pointe Nador
- Larache
- Melilla
- *See inset*
- Méhdia
- Kénitra
- Cap de Fédala
- **Rabat**
- Pointe d'el Hank
- Mohammedia
- Sidi Bou Afi
- **Casablanca**
- **El Jadida**
- **Safi**
- Cap Beddouza
- Oualadia
- Cap Sim
- **Essaouira**
- Cap Ghir
- **Agadir**
- Sidi Ifni
- Cap Nachtigal
- Cap Tarfaya
- Port Laâyoune
- Cap Bojador
- Arciprés Grande
- Dakhla
- Cap Barbas
- Cap Blanc
- Cap Timiris

Atlantic Ocean

- Madeira
- Ilhas Selvagen
- **ISLAS CANARIAS**
- Alegranza
- Lanzarote
- Fuerteventura
- Tenerife
- Gomera
- Gran Canaria

Inset

Strait of Gibraltar
- C. Spartel
- Pta Malabata
- Tanger
- RC
- Pta Almina
- Ceuta
- M'diq
- C. Negro
- Aero RC
- Tétouan
- **MOROCCO**
- El Jebha
- C. Baba
- Morro Nuevo
- Al Hoceima
- Aero RC
- C. Tres Forcas
- Melilla
- Aero RC
- *Mediterranean Sea*

MOROCCO

North Africa

Weather and sailing conditions

Conditions are quite different from those in the Mediterranean. The Atlantic coast tends to have stable weather from June to October, with light winds form the SW or NW. Temperatures are usually lower than along the Spanish coast, although the humidity increases as you move south past Casablanca. If a strong westerly wind gets up while you are at sea, or a depression passes through, there is little you can do except keep well out to sea. Some ports can be entered in any conditions and these are listed. The swell several miles out is far less than that encountered close inshore. This is due to the steady shelving of the sandy bottom, which causes huge rollers to break near the shore, even in fairly light winds. When entering rivers, watch out for the unexpected roller to sneak up from behind. It is an alarming experience to have a succession of two-metre, steep-sided rollers hit your stern when the sea is otherwise flat and you are in a confined channel!

During winter, light NE or SW winds can be expected for much of the time. Fronts associated with fast moving depressions occasionally move NE from the Canaries, causing squalls and sometimes more prolonged periods of strong winds, particularly from November to April. Winter daytime temperatures are not normally less than 16°C.

A weatherfax is a great asset when sailing in the Atlantic and is a better longer range indicator of weather than in the Mediterranean. If you have a personal computer onboard, a weatherfax programme can be purchased quite cheaply and connected to your HF-SSB radio. This will enable you to see any depressions moving from the Canaries, where in stable conditions, a high or low pressure system usually sits, sometimes for weeks, giving a steady airflow and minimal swell. Using a GSM mobile phone connected to a laptop computer, forecasts can also be obtained via the Internet. It only takes a minute to download once the connection is established.

The Atlantic swell is irksome at first, but in summer it is only about a metre in height, usually from the SW or NW. In winter it is frequently around 3 to 5m, even in light winds.

Most yachts travelling south to the Canaries with the intention of crossing the Atlantic, do so in October or November to catch the change in the trade winds and Gulf Stream, which are more favourable in December and January.

Tides

There is a 14-minute time difference between HW Gibraltar and HW Casablanca and little more as you move south. Gibraltar and Casablanca are standard ports and local tide tables can easily be obtained from either port. Most harbour authorities are happy to give a photocopy of their tables.

Current

Generally, a steady surface current of about half a knot, moving south, can be expected for most of the Atlantic coastline as far as Agadir.

Tanger

35°47'·5N 5°47'·5W

Distances
Cadiz 56M – Gibraltar 31M, Ceuta 27M

Tides
MHWS MHWN MLWN MLWS
2·4m 1·9m 1·0m 0·6m

Charts

	Approach	Port
Admiralty	92, 142, 773	1912
French	1701, 7042	1701
Spanish		4461
US	52039	52042

Lights
Approach
1. **Cap Spartel** 35°47'·6N 5°55'·3W
   Fl(4)20s95m30M Dia(4)90s Yellow square stone tower
2. **Punta Malabata** 35°49'·1N 5°44'·8W
   Fl.5s77m22M White square tower on dwelling
3. **Monte Dirección** 35°46'·1N 5°47'·3W
   Oc(3)WRG.12s89m11-16M On terrace of white house 140°-G-174·5°-W-200°-R-225° F.R lights on radio mast 1·1M SW; on hospital 1·8M WNW and Grand Mosque 1·7M NW

Harbour
4. **Breakwater head** 35°47'·6N 5°47'·5W
   Fl(3)12s20m14M White tower
5. **S mole head** Oc(2)R.6s7m6M
6. **NW inner jetée** Iso.G.4s6m6M
7. **Entrance inner harbour N mole** F.G.4m6M
8. **Entrance inner harbour S mole** F.R.4m6M

General

The commercial port of Tanger (also spelt Tangier or Tangers) is a pleasant and practical harbour in which to make a first acquaintance with Morocco. The old fishing port, called Port de Plaisance, can accommodate around 14 yachts, racked out, on the same jetty as the harbourmasters office, next to the customs house. This jetty is shared by the pilot boats and is often quite crowded, but safe. In another basin there is a small yacht club where shallow draught boats can lie in greater privacy, though visiting yachts have difficulty accessing the club. Both basins are well protected, entrance is easy and formalities are handled efficiently. Security in the port is excellent. A pass issued by the passport police is necessary to enter the port from the town and a night guard is always on duty at the yacht quay. Tanger offers excellent opportunities for trips inland and the railway station is immediately outside the harbour gate.

Approach

Approach from the W is assisted by the radiobeacon on Cap Spartel (also known as Cabo Espartel and Cape Spartan) and its lighthouse with a 30M range.

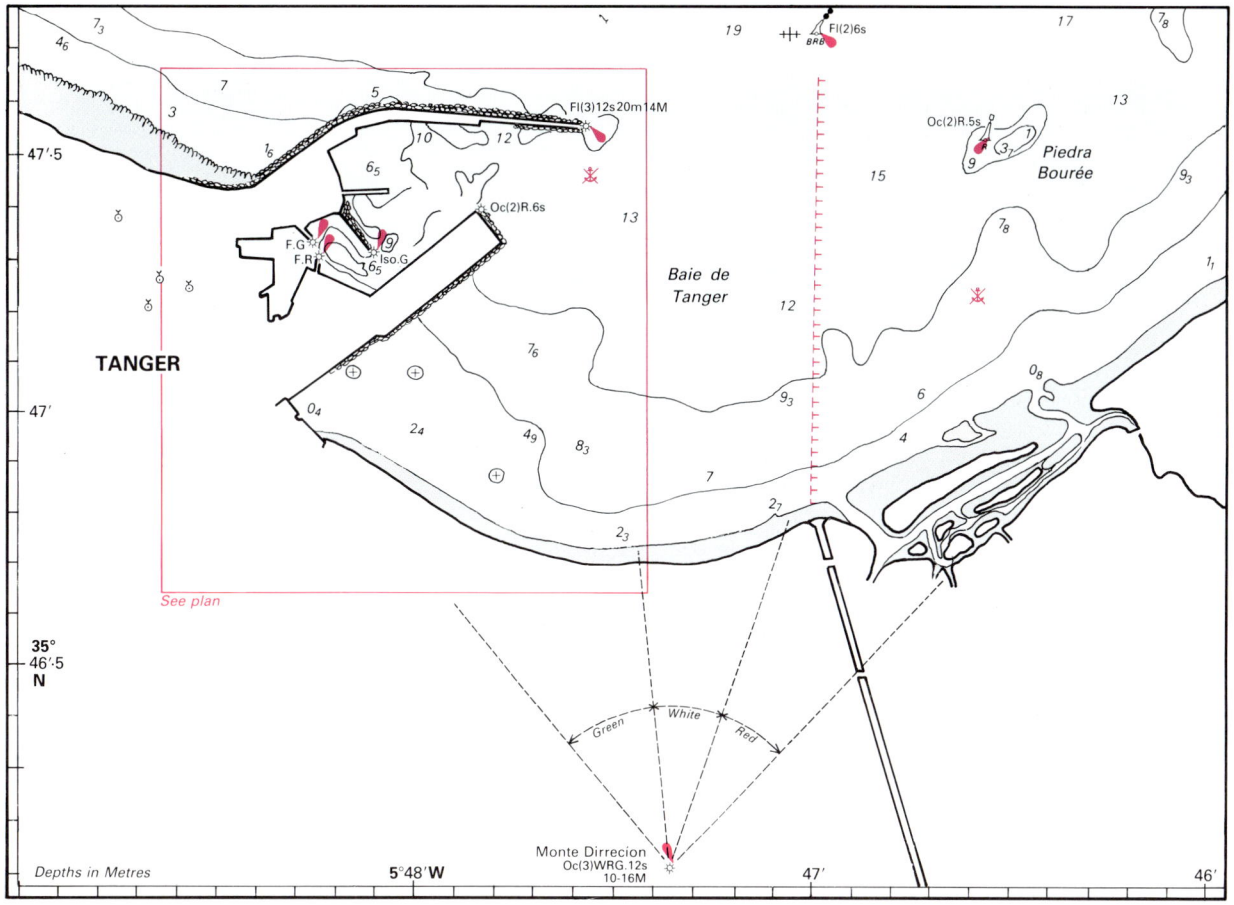

TANGER

From the E, the steep headland of Punta de Malabata with its lighthouse provides a good landmark. Closer to the port the white tower at the end of the N breakwater and the ports large cranes are visible from a good distance off, as is the white minaret of the Grand mosque, with the Catholic church spire nearby. If arriving from the tideless Mediterranean, do not forget that currents and tides are an important consideration here. (See section *Transitting the Straits*.) Strong currents and overfalls are present near the E entrance to the Bay of Tanger, especially around HW.

Entry
Proceed carefully into the fishing port; yachts drawing more than 2m will have difficulty in entering at low water, particularly near to the E wall of the harbourmasters building. Watch out for mooring lines from fishing boats lying to the quay.

Berthing
Tie up alongside the N quay of the fishing basin. This quay used to be reserved for visitors, but now also berths the pilot launches, several impounded yachts and large open boats used for tuna fishing. In summer it can get quite crowded. Towards the S end of this quay, the bottom shallows to a depth of approximately 1·5m. Yachts drawing 2·2m have had no trouble lying alongside the E half of the quay. Deep draught boats can take the ground at low water and lean against the wall which is without obstructions. Recent work to extend the quay immediately under the harbourmasters office has removed the shallow ledge that posed a hazard on the E side.

If alongside the quay, use a plank outboard the fenders as surging takes place in this busy harbour and the concrete is rough and oily.

Deep draught boats can tie up alongside the quay on the S side of the outer harbour, but the swell and surging is considerable there.

Shallow draught boats may find room at the small yacht club in minimum depth of 1·3m.

Reportedly there is an exceptional tidal range once each winter when the quay in the fishing port floods at HW.

Formalities
VHF Ch 6, 14.

Customs and immigration police are very efficient and come to the yacht. They will usually show up within minutes of arrival. Since Tanger is a commercial port with a free port section, the police issue a *permis d'escale* in lieu of passports which are retained until departure. This card has to be shown when passing the guarded harbour gate on re-entry.

Facilities
Water and electricity In the fishing port water is available at a charge per 1,000 litres from a hose near the pilot

North Africa

TANGER

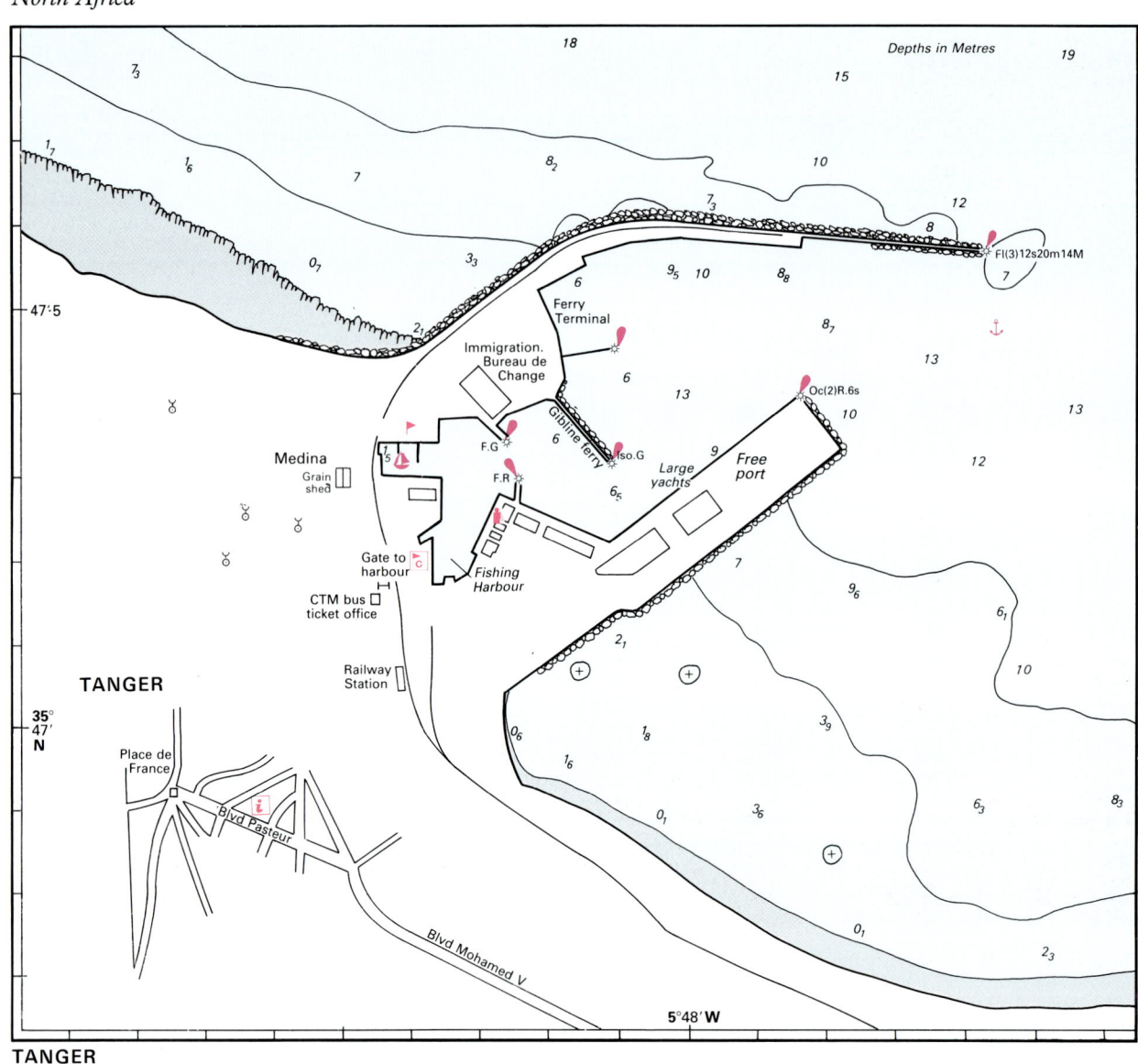

berth. Containers can be filled from a water tap in the toilet of the grain shed: marked on the plan.

Electricity Can be arranged for a small fee, but requires a long cable. In the yacht club water and electricity are available for visitors.

Fuel Diesel is available in drums.

Provisions A small *alimentation général* in the harbour sells a little bit of everything from bread to photocopies. The main markets in the Medina are a short walk from the port in Rue du Portugal and Rue de la Plage close to the Grand Socco square where there is abundant fresh produce at very reasonable prices. Between Ceuta, for canned and processed articles, and Tanger, for fresh and many dried products, a yacht can provision well for a long sea voyage. Tanger has a sizeable textile industry and for live-aboards it is worth shopping in the modern town around Rue Mexique.

Gas Gas bottles can be filled at the SGP plant outside Tanger near the intersection of road P38 to Tetouan and the railroad.

Showers The yacht club has showers and washboards for clothes washing and permission to use them when lying in the fishing port is never refused. As an alternative it is worth exploring the douche public (*hammam*) in the Medina, 5 minutes walk from the port. Men and women can use it during the same hours.

Repairs Emergency engine repairs can possibly be carried out.

Post office The main post office on Boulevard Mohammed V has a 24 hour telephone service.

Tourist information On Boulevard Pasteur, 200m from Place de France in the new town.

Bank There are several banks in the port near the ferry terminal and there is a small change shop on the way out of the port. In the town most banks are found on Boulevard Mohammed V or Boulevard Pasteur.

Eating out

There is a wide range of restaurants ranging from the most simple eating houses in the Medina to good European style restaurants in the modern town. *The Rough Guide* has a good listing.

The port of Tanger with yacht basin

History

Known in history as Tingi, Tanger was well known to Phoenicians and Carthaginians who used the port as an anchorage before setting off across the Atlantic or voyaging south. The Carthaginian navigator Hanno mentioned the city when he visited the area around 500BC on his way to Guinea. It was famous for its salted fish and anchovy sauce, which were held in huge vats nearby. Anchovy with garlic sauce is still a speciality of the area today. During the Berber dynasties, Tingi was associated more with Mauritania than the Roman rulers of Carthage until around 50BC, particularly after the fall of Carthage in 146BC. The Romans gave Tingi the status of a colony under the province of Spain in order to bring it under the influence of the Empire. In AD3, Tingi became the capital of Tingis Mauritania under the rule of Diocletian, retaining the Spanish connection. Vandals occupied Tingi in 429 under the rule of King Genseric, who also ruled Spain. He then set about conquering North Africa and Tingi became part of the Byzantine empire until Moussa ibn Nasser captured it in 705 during the Islamic conquest which swept Westwards from the Middle East. A large Berber army was assembled under Tariq, a Syrian, who later invaded Spain through Gibraltar giving his name to the Rock – Jebel Tariq. (Mountain of Tariq). Berber tribes of the Rif rebelled against the new rule and the forced conversions to Islam, and re-conquered Tingi for a short time in 739. The town became the centre of a power struggle between the Idrissids and the Omeyyads until coming under Tunisian dominance in 958. During successive take-overs, the port flourished as a gateway trading post for ships en route through the Straits.

The Portuguese, after an unsuccessful attempt to occupy the town in 1437, finally succeeded in 1471. Spanish, Portuguese and the English all occupied the town. The British withdrew after the dispute between Charles I and the British Parliament 1679, leaving the way clear for Moulay Ismael, who was mounting a blockade, to occupy the town. By 1810, after a long period of decline, there were only 5,000 inhabitants left.

Later in the 19th century, several European countries vied for control of Tanger: France, Spain, Britain and Germany. In 1906 a treaty was signed giving Tanger a special international status as a free port. This lapsed when Morocco gained

North Africa

Tanger Harbour entrance viewed from W. Cathedral spire just visible to left of Grand Mosque, almost in transit

independence. Apart from Moroccans, the population at the time was a cosmopolitan mix of European and American writers, artists, bankers and entrepreneurs. In 1956, the international status ended and the banks and companies moved back to Europe but Tanger has still retained some of the cosmopolitan character from those days.

Tourism
The European town is a pleasant ensemble of wide streets and green squares with restaurants, coffee bars and shops of all kinds. Place de France, in the heart of the new town, is surrounded by several terraces frequented by the new expatriate community and offers a splendid view of the Bay of Tanger.

The ancient Medina is close to the port, remaining much as it has for over a thousand years. Filled with small shops, it is easy to get lost in its narrow winding streets. Although without the medieval feel of the medinas in Fes or Marrakech it gives a good idea of the lifestyle on the south of the Strait, which is so different from that of Europe. Tanger is the gateway to Morocco and in many ways is a microcosm of much that can be found in cities throughout the whole country.

Transport
Excellent trains to Rabat, Casablanca, Meknes and Fes. Ticket offices for buses are at the harbour gate but the buses leave from the outskirts of Tanger. Regular ferry services to Algeciras, Gibraltar and Sète. The airport is 15km out of town.

Car rental All the big companies are to be found on Boulevard Pasteur or Boulevard Mohammed V.

Asilah
35°28′N 6°02′W

Distances
Cap Spartel 20M, Tanger 25M, Larache 16M

Tides
	MHWS	MHWN
Range	3·6 m	2·9m

Slack water is 1hr either side of HW and LW.

Charts
	Approach	*Port*
Admiralty	3132	–
French	–	–
Spanish	447	4461
US	–	–

Tanger new club moorings and harbourmasters offices

Lights
1. **Dique N** F.R.8m mounted on low concrete tower
2. **Dique S** F.R.10m mounted on low concrete tower
   Cap Spartel (Cabo Espartel) 35° 47·6'N 5°55·3'W
   Fl(4)20s30M Dia(4)90s Tower 95m RC

General
Coastline from Tanger to Asilah
From Tanger, the spectacular Cap Spartel (Cabo de Espartel) can be seen immediately after leaving the bay. This area is often shrouded in mist, especially in the mornings and particularly during easterly (*levante*) winds. Rounding the promontory can be tricky if there has been a prolonged period of westerly wind, building up a standing surface current with tidal races from the Atlantic as well as a long heavy swell. East-going currents up to six knots can be experienced in the area immediately N of the cape, with high over-falls at HW, so it is important to make the exit from the Mediterranean with favourable tides if the wind is westerly. (See section: *Transiting the Straits* for more information on currents in the Straits.)

Once rounded, the high mountainous cape soon gives way to a flat landscape with miles of golden sand dunes, deserted beaches and a favourable current, leaving the 1,000ft high Cap Spartel looking like an island. Asilah is 20M from the cape. Once into the Atlantic, going south, there are virtually no safe anchorages or natural bays outside of harbours. The heavy ground-swell caused by the gradual shelving is more noticeable 2–3M from shore, so it unwise to get too close except in settled weather. A hazard to look out for is the tuna nets, which typically extend four miles out to sea (see *General sailing notes* in the introduction). These are present around the entrance to Asilah.

Because of the difference between sea and land temperatures in summer, there is often a sea mist all along the Atlantic coast, reducing visibility to between two and four miles. Prevailing winds tend to be either NE, or SW, except when depressions are passing. The current follows the coastline south at a rate of about 0·5kt between Cap Spartel and Asilah.

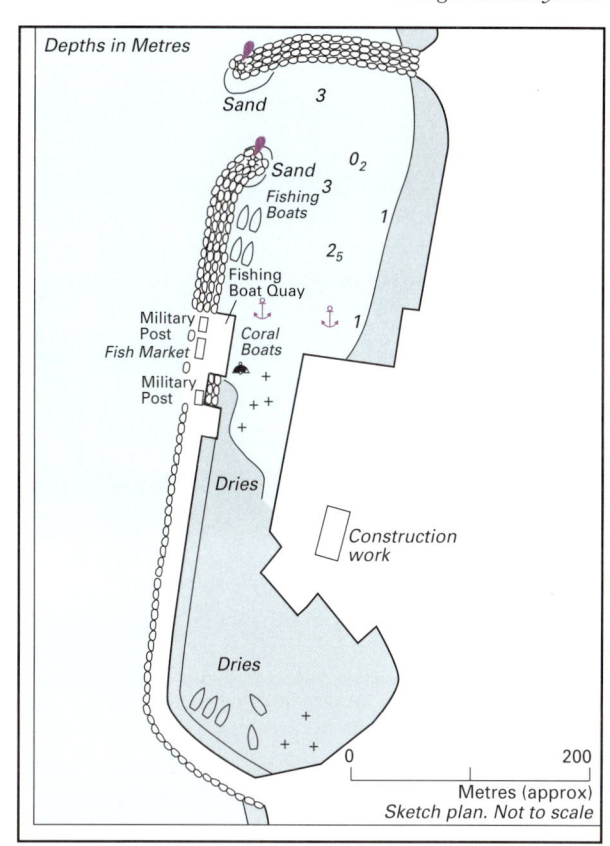

ASILAH

Approach
Entry into Asilah is straightforward. The harbour breakwater is clearly visible between the open beach to the north and the city walls, which begin a few hundred yards beyond the harbour. Atlantic rollers enter the mouth of the harbour in strong westerlies, reducing the depths of around 5m, so timing is important if a swell is running.

Entry
Turn sharply to starboard after clearing the entrance to avoid being picked up by a roller, and head towards the short quay running parallel to the breakwater. Several large fishing vessels are usually anchored in the lee of the breakwater.

Berthing
Minimum depths once inside the harbour are 2·5 to 3m in the centre, but only as far as the southern end of the jetty wall. Beyond that, although boats are moored, the harbour dries out and there are projecting rocks which can be clearly seen at LW. In winter, beware of breast lines extending from the coral boats moored alongside, which are laid out across the harbour to pull them off the quay during strong easterly winds. These are not used in summer, when the weather is more settled and the boats go out every day.

Moor alongside the coral boats, or anchor in the lee of the breakwater south of the entrance in sand. The harbour jetty is only some 70m long and several

Asilah viewed from the west

North Africa

Asilah: yachts lie alongside the coral-fishing boats

vessels moor alongside the high wall. Fishing boats moor at the north end and coral boats at the south. This is an advantage, since with the larger boats inboard, climbing the ladder up to the quay is made easier. Locals are very friendly and always ready to assist. The coral and fishing boats leave early in the morning every day in summer except Fridays, but an attendant fisherman will re-tie your mooring lines, avoiding the necessity to get up early. If you do anchor out, the fishermen will offer to take you ashore in their small smacks for a few Dirhams, avoiding the need to launch your tender and then having to worry about it while ashore.

Formalities

Although not officially a port of entry, the customs officials and police are very friendly and willing to give temporary visitors the right to stay by holding their passports until they are ready to depart without stamping them. If you intend to stay in Asilah and require an entry stamp for travel inland, it is possible to obtain this by visiting Tanger port overland, but it would be wiser to call in at Tanger on the way to Asilah if you intend to travel from this port. Local police will pick up the captain by taxi and take him to their nearby offices to complete the necessary paperwork.

Facilities

Water May be obtained in cans if necessary, but no hosepipe facilities exist at present.
Electricity None on the quayside but the coral boats often have generators running and can provide a mains power point for a few hours if necessary.
Fuel This can be arranged by locals and brought to the yacht in cans.
Provisions Local shops have all the usual items.
Gas Calor gas readily available and also the large old style screw top bottles.
Post office and banks In the centre of town. (See end of section on *Tourism*.)
Repairs As in almost any port in Morocco, most types of mechanical repairs can be undertaken in Asilah, but no specific yacht facilities are available. A small slipway S of the jetty hauls out fishing boats.

Eating out

Many good restaurants line the sea front just outside the harbour. As with all coastal towns, fish is naturally the local speciality and, due to the Spanish influence, there is a predominance of Spanish cuisine. Restaurant Alcazaba, opposite the main gate to the medina is excellent, as are several of the eating houses along the promenade.

Notes

1. A new port is planned ten miles south of the cape, which will eventually replace Tanger, for freight and oil-tanker traffic, leaving Tanger as a fishing and passenger port, with a yacht marina. Although the land has already been requisitioned for the new port, work has not yet begun (December 1998).
2. A new marina is planned for Asilah. This is a prime place for such a venture, being the first Atlantic port and within easy reach of the station and therefore connecting to all the major tourist cities inland.

Tourism

At present, Asilah is the first port on the Moroccan Atlantic coast. It is a clean, quiet port and very unlike any other in Morocco. The medina of Asilah lies within the 15th-century Portuguese walls, just beyond the southern end of the harbour. Although smaller, it is less claustrophobic than most in Morocco and very clean, giving a feeling of spaciousness. It is one of the most pleasant to shop in, providing good value for tourists all year round. On offer are a good selection of arts and crafts representative of the different regions in Morocco: Berber carpets from southern, as well as the northern tribes close to Asilah, the multi-coloured painted wood furniture typical of Fez and Rabat, fine objects carved in *thuya* wood from Essaouira,

Asilah medina. Wall murals are unique features of this quiet town

ceramics from Safi, etc. One generally feels graciously invited to look around, rather than intimidated. Bargaining in Asilah is also a far less aggressive affair than in Tanger and other towns, nor do 'guides' and touts bother you here. Since the medina is small, an added attraction is that after walking around a few times, you get the comfortable feeling of knowing the place. Wonderful wall paintings and modern murals are to be seen within the medina and are a feature of the annual festival described under *Local specialities*.

At the southernmost point of the ramparts above the sea, lies a bastion from which there are marvellous views of the coast, town and a local shrine with beautiful tiled tombstones. From here, continuing along the ramparts will take you inland and, in the morning, out to the bustling city market which lies outside the walls along Avenue Hassan II. This is a good place for provisioning. In the evening, noisy street traders and people dining in restaurants, crowd the pavements outside the medina, providing a contrast to the quiet residential streets and business-like atmosphere prevailing inside the walls.

Turning left on leaving the port leads to a long promenade along the seafront, where every evening Moroccan families stroll. This leads to a stretch of beach, which continues northwards for miles. Uphill from this promenade, interspersed here and there in tree-lined streets, among low buildings, are very pleasant cafés and small restaurants. Banks cluster at the Place Mohammed V and the post office is a short walk NW from here.

Brief history
Asilah has been known by a number of names (Azilah, Arzila, Arcila and Asilah), all of which clearly derive from *Zilis*, the name it was given when founded as a commercial port by the Phoenicians in the second century BC. Subsequently it was occupied by the Carthaginians and Byzantines and destroyed by the Romans; rebuilt in the 9th century by the first coherent Moroccan dynasty (the Idrissids) and soon afterwards assaulted by the Normans. It was rebuilt once again by the Omeyyad Caliph of al-Andalus in 966. Leon el Africano, an erudite and well-travelled man born in Granada in the late 15th century, wrote in his *Description of Africa* that when the sovereigns from Cordoba ruled in Mauritania (as Morocco was known in Muslim Spain), they restored Asilah and 'put it in better condition than before (the Norman attacks). The inhabitants of Asilah became very rich, educated and warlike.' Although a little less warlike today, these adjectives seem appropriate for this gracious, cultured town today.

Like other northwest African ports, Asilah was attractive to the Portuguese for its situation en route to the East Indies and at the Atlantic margin of the Saharan gold trade. In 1471 some 30,000 Portuguese soldiers disembarked from nearly 500 boats at Asilah (an amazing fact considering the tranquillity and size of the port today), took the city and built the massive fortifications and sea-wall which still stand and define the medina today. Just over a hundred years later, Portugal's King Sebastian, who hoped to win all of Morocco for Christendom, landed in Asilah en route to the fateful Battle of the Three Kings at Ksar el Kebir, just SE of Larache. In this battle he and two Moroccan kings lost their lives and, in its aftermath, so many Portuguese nobility had to be ransomed, that Portugal went bankrupt, losing all its Moroccan ports. It was subsequently absorbed by Spain.

In 1691, after a hundred years of Spanish domination, Asilah reverted to Moroccan rule. History was again repeated by the inclusion of Asilah in the Spanish Protectorate from 1911–1956. The intervening period, between roughly 1690–1910, is marked by pirates, whose headquarters at Asilah provoked mid 19th-century bombardment by both the Austrians and Spanish, as well as by the famous bandit-turned-Regional Governor, Moulay Ahmed Raisuli. His Hispanomuslim-style palace, built in the first decade of this century, looks out over the sea towards the far end of the medina. There are plans for this palace, now known as the Palais de la Culture, to become more accessible to visitors as it plays an increasingly vibrant role in the cultural life of the town.

Local specialities
Today, Asilah is primarily a small fishing port and an extremely relaxed tourist resort. Most of the holiday-makers are Moroccans. In winter it is very quiet. The lovely long stretches of soft white sand on either side of the port, (especially to the north, where they stretch half way to Tanger) provide the opportunity for privacy, even in the tourist season. Here, as on many other Moroccan beaches, you can also hire a camel.

Coral and sponge fishing are local speciality industries. Boats go out most days with diving gear, returning in the late afternoon with spectacular corals. There are several varieties, including huge bright orange tree-like structures. It is possible to join the boats for a day to see how they operate. Several of the fishermen and coral divers speak English. With environmental awareness becoming an issue in Morocco, there are many who now oppose this trade, believing it to be destructive in the long run.

Asilah is most famous for its month-long cultural festival, which takes place every year in July or August. People from all over Morocco and abroad come for this event, where arts, crafts, music and many other attractions are well organised and include artists and musicians from all over the world, including the USA and the Middle East. This is a time when you are particularly fortunate to be visiting Asilah by boat, for hotel rooms are always fully booked. Much of the town's fresh, modern appearance and the excellent restoration work that has been carried out in the town, is attributable to the Mayor of the city, who was once Minister of Culture and currently an ambassador.

North Africa

Larache
35°12'N 6°09'·3W

Distances
Asilah 16M Mehdia 62M

Tides
	MHWS	MHWN
Range	3·6m	2·9m

Charts
	Approach	Port
Admiralty	3132	–
French	–	–
Spanish	447	4461
US	–	–

Lights
Entry signals
•/Red Lt – caution for entering.
Two • – port closed except for motor fishing vessels.
Blue flag with PC/2 Red Lts – port closed.
Approach
1. **Outer bar Ldg Lt 102°** *Front* Iso.2s4M White ▲ on red mast 6m 352°-vis-212°
   Rear 200m from front Iso.2s4M White ▼ on red mast 8m 352°-vis-212°
   Inner bar Ldg Lt 145°30' *Front* F.R.2M White mast 12m 015·5°-vis-275°
   Rear 70m from front F.R.2M Church tower 055·5°-vis-235·5°
   Training wall head F.G
   Iso.G.4s7M Green mast 4m
Harbour
2. **N breakwater head** Fl(2)6s10m14M Horn(3)40s White tower 7m

General
The port of Larache is difficult to enter, but once inside it is spacious and safe. Although deep-draught fishing vessels of over 50ft in length do operate daily from this port, keel yachts would be best advised to continue on to Mehdia except in exceptionally settled weather.

Approach
Coastline from Asilah to Larache
This 15 mile stretch of coastline is similar to that from Cap Spartel to Asilah, with long stretches of sandy beaches, except that the backdrop of mountains is more evident here through the haze, which is often present in summer. Beware of tuna nets laid out along this stretch of coast (see *General information*).

Entry
Lying at the entrance of Oued Loukkos, Larache is well protected from the Atlantic, as the river curves sharply to the right once inside the sandbars. Larache can only be entered with a keeled yacht in

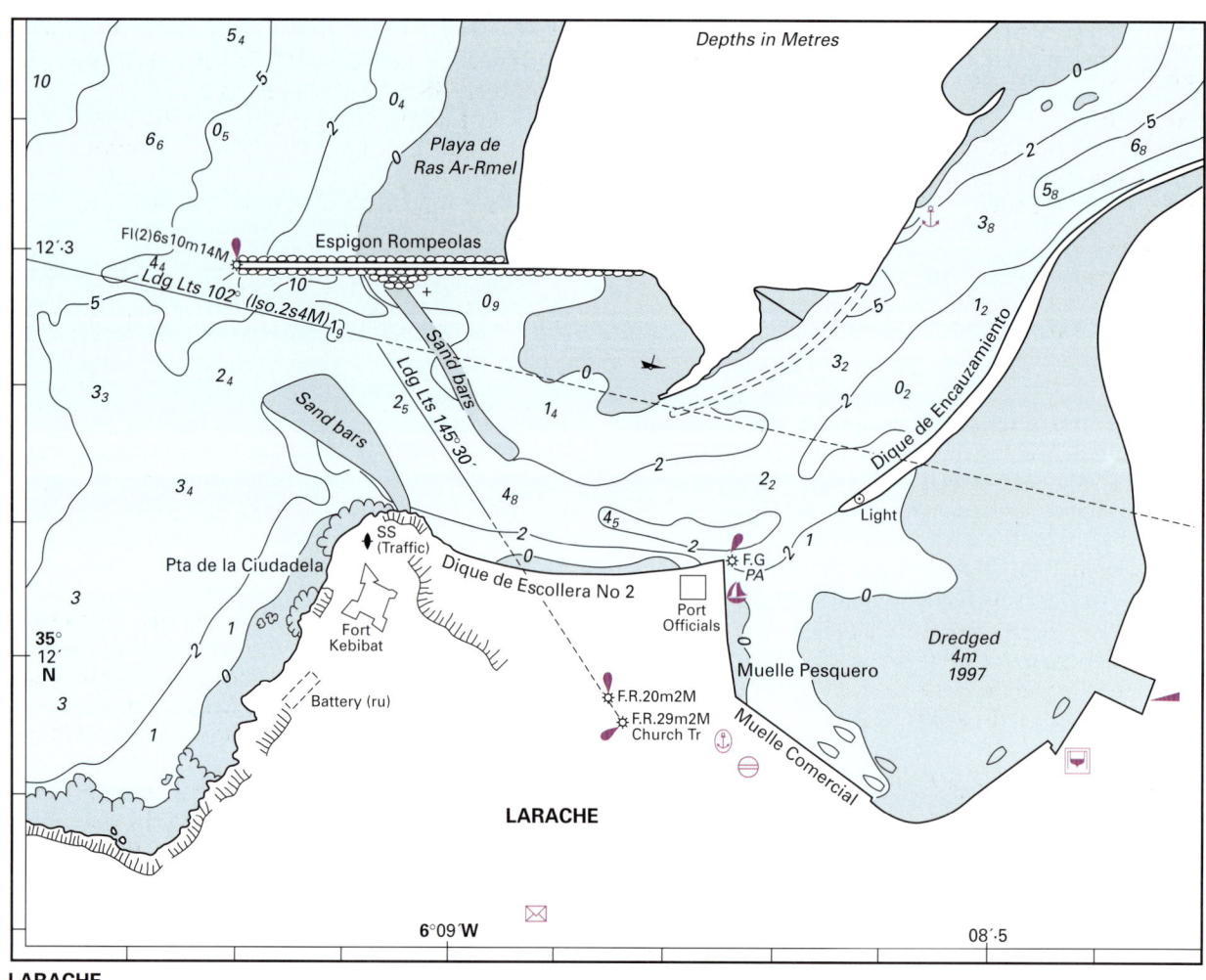

LARACHE

good weather conditions around HW and never at night. You would be strongly advised to wait for a fishing boat to guide you through this tricky river entrance. Moroccan seafarers are always happy to act as pilot and take pride in doing so. Two sandbars stretch right across the river near the entrance, with a distance of some 15m between them, forming a channel as shown on the plan. They lie barely submerged at LW, with strong over-falls caused by the fast running current, but a channel with a minimum depth of 1·5m at LW allows access between them to the port. Entry to the channel is via a gap on the left seaward sand-bank, and, after traversing diagonally across the river, exit from the channel into the port is through a gap near the opposite riverbank. Transitting the channel would be very difficult with a strong current running, so good timing with respect to tide is essential.

In this busy port, there are several large fishing boats with draughts of 2m or more, so, although access is rather difficult, it is certainly possible. Small fishing boats can be observed entering and leaving at all times of the day. The port authorities and harbourmaster monitor VHF Ch 16 and say they are willing to give assistance to yachts who want to enter the port.

Berthing
Depths of 3 to 4m at LW can be found once inside the harbour. Go alongside the seaward jetty just under the harbourmaster's office, where a police launch will usually be moored.

Formalities
Larache is a port of entry and officials will visit the boat. Customs and police are located within the port and are very friendly.

Facilities
Water Is available from a tap on the jetty.
Fuel Can be obtained in cans.
Provisions Local markets have a good selection of fresh food.
Gas Camping Gaz available in the town.
Post office and banks In the Place de la Libération and Avenue Mohammed V, are banks, the PTT, a tourist office *(Syndicat d'Initiative)* and a (Spanish) Catholic church.
Repairs All types of mechanical repairs can be undertaken here.

Eating out
The main road from Tanger to Rabat passes through the centre of town which is close to the port. Consequently, there are many small bars and restaurants lining the entire route. Spanish influence dominates the local cuisine.

Tourism
Small fishing boats can be hired for a few Dirhams for trips across Oued Loukkos to one of Larache's principal attractions: an immense extension of tree and café-lined fine sandy beaches, or to the ruins of ancient Lixus, some 3M inland on the river. (Cost 50–100 Dirhams.) Both Lixus and the beach can also be reached by taxi and the city buses. Lixus is the site of the mythological Gardens of Hesperides to which Hercules travelled in search of golden apples in his eleventh and penultimate labour. The megalithic stones in its Acropolis confirm its importance in prehistoric times, although its ruins are mostly Phoenician, Carthaginian and Roman. There are several temple sanctuaries from the various historical ages with confirmation of the Christian presence in Morocco in the years before the Islamic conquest. These can be seen in the ruins of a Christian basilica. From this Acropolis, there is a splendid view of Larache port and the town, and of the active salt pans below the ruins (see *Local specialities*). Between the hill and the main road can be seen the ancient vats used for storing anchovy sauce or garum.

Larache itself, is perhaps less compelling than these peripheral attractions. Because it is on the main road from Tanger to Rabat, heavy trucks trundle through the centre, making it somewhat dusty. Nonetheless it is beautifully situated on a hill overlooking water on two sides, has a relaxed, friendly feel and an aura of faded elegance, owing to the fact that it was the principal port of the Spanish Protectorate (1911–1956). Many Spanish colonial buildings still stand, ranging from the arcaded buildings in the Place de la Libération, (formerly Plaza de Espana) and the domestic architecture in the new town, to the extraordinary hispanomauresque-style Moroccan National Academy of Music (1915) in the little Place de Makhzen which overlooks the port.

Today Larache (population some 70,000) is still a busy fishing port and, in summer, a tourist resort with few foreigners but many Moroccan families who have returned for summer holidays from their homes abroad.

To get there from the port, one must either traverse the old medina (immediately uphill), or head to the right, under the ruins of the 16th-century fortress Kebibat and along the Avenue Moulay Ismail, which overlooks the sea. The Place, which divides the old and new cities, is surrounded by old hotels, restaurants and cafés.

Just below Larache are some famous bird-watching sites and more Roman ruins (Benasa, Volubilis) but these are closer to Mehdia, and are described under that port.

History
Larache was founded in the 7th century, when some of the Arabs who brought Islam to Morocco from the Middle East, settled across the river Oued Loukkos from Lixus. Although Lixus itself was by this time on the decline, Larache has been inhabited continuously since then.

In the late 15th century, the threatening presence of the Portuguese in Tanger, Asilah, El Jadida and other towns along the coast, convinced the Sultan of Fez to establish a fort to defend the city of Larache and control the mouth of Oued Loukkos. Today, the ruins of this fort lie just outside the medina gate Bab el Kasbah. Larache became a pivotal port for

North Africa

the Muslims, and was successfully defended against Europeans for over a century. It is said that when the Portuguese lost the nearby Battle of the Three Kings in 1578, those taken prisoner were brought to Larache to build the Castillo de la Ciguena. (Stork's Castle – a massive fortress also in the Place de Makhzen overlooking the port.) Although Larache fell to the Spaniards in 1610, it was regained and repopulated in 1689 by Sultan Moulay Ismail. This Alouite Sultan also took Tanger and exercised absolute power during his reign from 1672 until 1727. Through his concentrated approach he built a network of major coastal fortresses, extending his authority all the way to Senegal. Before its colonisation by Spain in 1911, Larache spent relatively little time under European control. This accounts for the fully Moroccan style of its medina, which contrasts sharply with that of El Jadida, for instance, and with the Andalusian style of the new town built after 1911.

Given its close proximity to Fez, Larache could have been as important a port as Tanger and Casablanca, were it not for its dangerous sandbars. The city has always diversified its fishing and trading activities with agriculture. Many of the ships used by the famous pirates of Sale and Rabat were also built here.

Local specialities

Apart from the fishing industry, Larache is the first of many towns on the Atlantic coast with an important salt-panning industry. Large areas between the main road and the beach are segmented off and salt water is allowed to sit and evaporate for a year or more. The resulting salt surface is then raked off, heaped into stacks and, when dry, marketed. Some of the lower ruins at the ancient city of Lixus, are those of first century (BC) salt factories, attesting to the antiquity of this specialised practice in the Larache area.

Mehdia and Kenitra

34°11'·6N 6°40'W
(River Oued Sebou entrance)

Distances
Larache 62M Mohammedia 46M

Tides
	MHWS	MHWN
Range	3·6m	2·9m

Charts
	Approach	Port
Admiralty	856, 3132	1912
French	6145	7550
Spanish	215	–

Lights
River Oued Sebou
Entry signals
Flag S flown if bar practicable. R over G flag if bar is impassable.
Mehdia
Approach
1. **Entrance Ldg Lts 102°30'** *Front* DirF.G.12M Green ▲, white stripes, on black metal framework tower 10m
2. *Rear* 800m from front Oc(3)12s74m16M Red tower on white dwelling

Kenitra
Approach
South bank fixed.
Transit lights
1. Leading (arc) DirF.G.12M Green ▲, white stripes, on black metal framework tower 10m
2. *Rear* Oc(3)12s74m16M Red and white tower
3. **Ldg Lts 060°** *Front* F.R.2m7M Tide gauge
4. *Rear* 213m from front F.R.5m8M Black and white beacon

Harbour
5. **Jetée Nord head** Oc(2)R.6s17m5M Red and white tower
6. **Jetée Sud head** Iso.G.4s16m6M White tower 10m

General
This 60 mile coastline from Larache to Mehdia consists of white beaches, scrubland and low cliffs. White tombs can be seen just above the beach at Moulay Bousselham, some 20M south of Larache. Behind the beach dunes is a large lake, which is the habitat of several rare species of birds.

The large port of Mehdia (also spelled Mehdya and Mehdiya) lies 1½M inland from the entrance, on the south bank of the river Oued Sebou. The river is navigable, winding its way to Kenitra, some eight miles further upstream. The port, which begins with the fishing quay, covers two miles of the river bank. Between Mehdia and Kenitra is a large important military airbase, built by the Americans and now in the hands of the Moroccan Air Force.

Keep well out to sea in the tuna fishing season as nets usually extend four miles from the shore, but could stretch further.

Approach
The entrance leading into the mouth of the river is formed by two breakwaters projecting half a mile out to sea. Although entry is not recommended at

Mehdia dinghy pontoon. Anchor 10 to 15 metres out

Tanger to Laayoune

MEHDIA

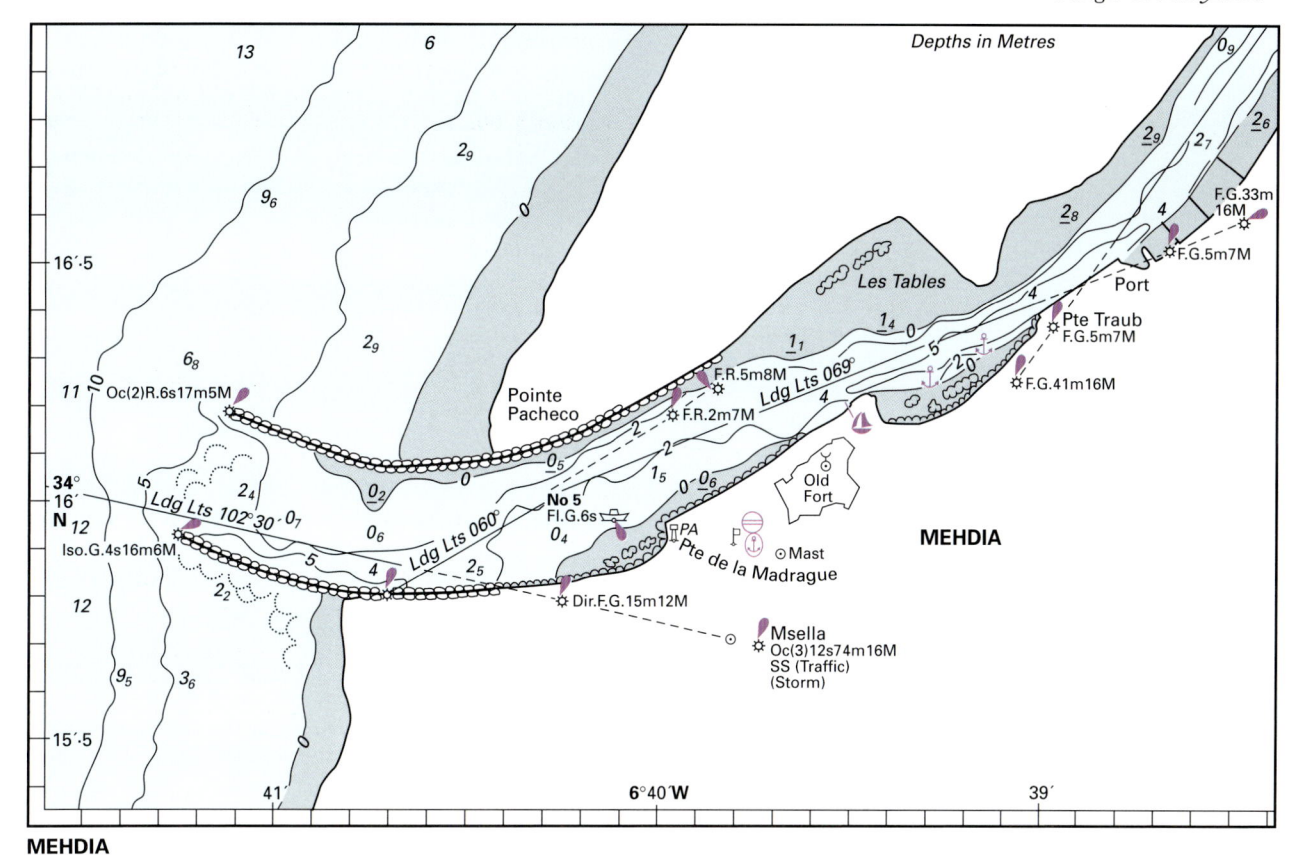

night, a transit can be easily identified between the southern breakwater light and a lighted tower further upstream. Lighted buoys, supposedly positioned midstream, do not appear to be in situ.

Large ships transit the river at high water as far as Kenitra, always with a pilot onboard. Several sand banks make it essential to pay great attention both to the chart and to the state of the tide. A fast-running current of 3 to 4kts out of the river is due to the 2 metre height difference upstream. This is enough to neutralise the neap flood current at HW and cause prolonged periods of slack water at springs. During the rainy season, the river floods its banks and is often one metre higher than charted.

Minimum depth at LWS is around 2m in the channel between sandbanks. Keep well to starboard on entry to avoid the first sandbar, which lies mid-river and extends to the north bank. Head for the tower indicated on the chart on a course of 102°. Keep a good lookout astern, since huge rollers can occasionally enter, even when the Atlantic is calm, especially when passing the first sandbar near the entrance. Local fishermen wait at the entrance, watching the wave patterns before making a fast entry upstream. If in doubt, it is possible to anchor on the northern side of the entrance and wait for calmer waters.

The fishing port, with its market and long buildings, will be seen 200m past an ancient circular gun emplacement on the S riverbank. Several fishing boats are usually moored either alongside the jetty, or anchored nearby.

Berthing

Yachts can berth alongside the fishing jetty for entry formalities. A short distance further on is a pontoon for tenders, with steps leading up to the large car park in the port. Depths by the pontoon, which is very close to the edge of the river, are very shallow at low water and yachts should not attempt to go alongside. A short distance from the bank there are depths of over 3m with good holding in soft mud. Stern and bow anchors are needed to keep fore and aft of the fast-running current. Fishing boats use the bank opposite to careen.

A mile further upstream is the larger freighter and tanker port of Mehdia with cranes looming on the quay. This part of the port is not recommended for yachts as it is an industrial zone with high-sided jetties, but no doubt it could be used for larger yachts, or if you are not confident about anchoring. There are many convenient places where a yacht may anchor in the river between the two port areas.

Formalities

Formalities can be carried out on the fishing quay or at the main harbour upstream. Mehdia is a port of entry, although, because the port is split between the fishing and commercial port, officials will probably come from the commercial port.

Facilities

Water Available in cans.
Fuel Available in cans or by bowser arranged with the port.
Provisions A small open market lies above the road running past the port with fresh fruit, vegetables and

49

meat. A more abundant supply is available a short taxi journey away in Kenitra.
Gas Obtainable in Kenitra.
Post office and banks In the centre of Kenitra.
Repairs Emergency repair can probably be undertaken but there are no specific yacht repair facilities.

Eating out

The nearest restaurant is a few minutes walk W of the port gate. Known as 'Belle Vue Restaurant', it is perched on the hillside above the road with good views across the river. If you are in the mood for a more lively scene, it would be worth making the trip into the new town, where cafés and restaurants on the seaward side of the road have inviting terraces overlooking the beach.

Local transport

Taxis can always be found waiting in both the fishing and freighter ports. Buses also use this coast road, and stop at both port gates.

Tourism

The old town and *kasbah* are located directly across the road from the port on a hill with access via steep steps. A constant stream of locals can be seen descending to buy fish in the port. At the top of these steps is a shantytown. Wealthier residents live further SW, near the beach in the new town. An impressive 17th-century Spanish/Alouite fortress overlooks the harbour from the hilltop, commanding panoramic views of the Oued Sebou, port, breakwaters and the town. The spectacular entrance, recently restored, gives access to the remains of the fort. Off to the SW is the nature reserve of Lac de Sidi Bourhaba.

Mehdia's extensive beaches start on the southern breakwater where the new town begins. Plage Mehdia is the beach serving the inhabitants of Kenitra, an industrial city some 6M inland along the Oued Sebou. In August these beaches are crowded and lined with brightly coloured tents. With miles of soft white sand and continuous rollers, like much of the Moroccan coastline, this is a surfers' paradise.

Since the area around Mehdia is flat and wet, miles of reedy marshland give protection for many species of wildlife, especially at Lac de Sidi Bourhaba, which is a picnicking area and an outstanding place for bird-watching, famous for its birds of prey and thousands of ducks in winter. Another protected nature reserve nearby is Merdja Zerga, where flamingos winter. A little further north lies Moulay Bousselham, again a large area of flatland nature reserve around a lake, protected from the sea by low cliffs. This is a popular place in summer and there is a small village to cater for the (almost exclusively Moroccan) tourists, with a street of cafés and small restaurants. The area took its name from the Egyptian, Moulay Bousselham, who was an important saint to whom the conversion of the Atlantic coast of Morocco to Islam is attributed.

Eight miles north, off the main road to Tanger, lie the Roman ruins of Tamuzida. Meknes and Fez are directly inland and the ancient city of Rabat is 15M south. All are well worth a visit, although it may be more convenient and safer to leave the yacht in Mohammedia or Casablanca for this excursion. On the other hand, if you are interested in sailing up the Oued Sebou and mooring in the very safe harbour of Kenitra, this would be a superior base from which to make such excursions.

History

It is thought that the port was founded in the 6th century BC as a Carthaginian trading post. The Almohads built naval shipyards here, and by the 16th century the port, then known as Al Mamoura and located just south of the Oued Sebou, was an active commercial port. In its struggle to resist European occupation (the Portuguese took the port in 1515 but were unable to hold it), the character of Al Mamoura changed. It soon ranked with Sale and Algiers as one of the principal pirate ports of North Africa. The Pirates of Sale were renowned and feared by all seamen transiting the area. Finally, the Spanish took Al Mamoura in 1614. They built the huge fortress high on the hill above the present port, which was later seized by Sultan Moulay Ismail in 1689 and renamed El Mahdia, *the citadel delivered*, hence the present-day name of Mehdia. Moulay Ismail set to work fortifying the *kasbah*. The bastions and cannons are still in place and its ruins reflect how extensive a community it encompassed. They included a *hammam* (public baths), a mosque (still in use), an inn and a Governor's Palace. The shantytown, which presently huddles around its eastern face, no doubt perpetuates settlement which began in the 17th century with the *kasbah* itself.

In the late 19th century, the French used this *kasbah* as a military base. It unfortunately sustained extensive damage in their clashes with the American Expeditionary Force which landed at Kenitra in November of 1942. In 1947 the Americans returned to establish an important military base, now under Moroccan command.

Kenitra

Kenitra is an interesting trip 8M further up the winding river Oued Sebou and is an excellent port to leave your yacht for excursions to Rabat, Fez, Meknes and Volubilis; the magnificent Roman ruins just north of Meknes. Good rail links to these cities are available from the station located a short distance from the port.

The river is very wide and navigable and large freighters are able to transit at high water. It is possible to moor alongside the main quay in Kenitra, since there are rarely more than two or three ships in the port. The quay is high, so look for a place where a ladder has been built into the wall. This port, obviously built with splendid facilities for many more ships than are now visiting, is consequently very quiet, safe and clean. Friendly police and customs officers are present and there is a very relaxed atmosphere.

KENITRA

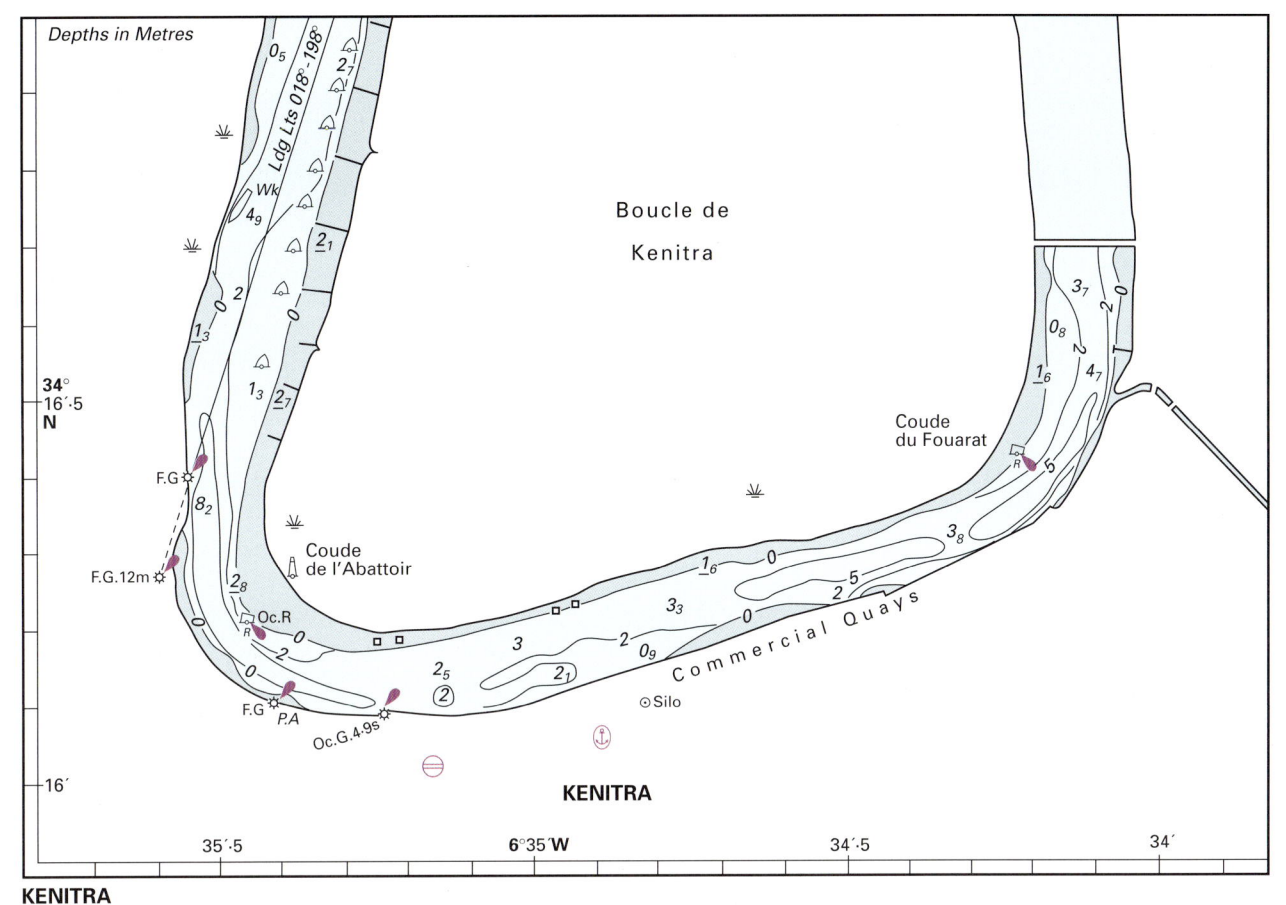

The port gates open into the town which, although not attractive as a tourist destination, has many places to eat out as well as to purchase any supplies needed. All mechanical repair facilities are available here and a small boatyard is located at the end of the port.

History
This small industrial city of some 300,000 inhabitants is especially well known for its history as a military base. Its impressive port was originally developed by the French in 1913 to replace Larache, lost to the Spanish in 1911, and for a while it was known as Port Lyautey.

The town, like the port, has a rather forgotten air about it. This is commonly attributed to the fact that Kenitra was the base for a 1972 coup on the monarchy, which resulted in the withdrawal of financial support for the town. However, it must also be considered that since Moroccan independence in 1956, the relative importance of commercial ports has shifted considerably. The prominence of Kenitra was integrally linked with the French Protectorate. Nowadays there are no colonial divisions, better roads, and more accessible ports in Morocco.

Rabat
34°02'N 6°50'·8W

Distances
Mehdia 16M Mohammedia 33M

Tides
Differences on Casablanca (standard port) – 5mins
MHWS   MLWS   MHWN   MLWN
+0·2m −0·3m +0·1m −0·2m

Charts
	Approach	Port
Admiralty	856, 3132	–
French	6145	7551
Spanish	–	216

Lights
Entry signals
R flag at masthead of signal station – entrance prohibited.
R flag at half-mast – entrance dangerous for small boats.
Approach
1. **Rabat LtHo** 34°02'·1N 06°50'·8W
   Oc(2)6s31m16M Yellow tower black lantern 24m 290°-unintens-020° F.R on radio mast 12M NE
2. **Rabat Salé** 34°03'N 06°46'W Aero Fl.10s on top of control tower

Coastline from Mehdia to Rabat

This 16-mile stretch is unremarkable, with sandy beaches and cliffs. As you approach the river Oued Bou Regreg, the walled town on the northern bank

North Africa

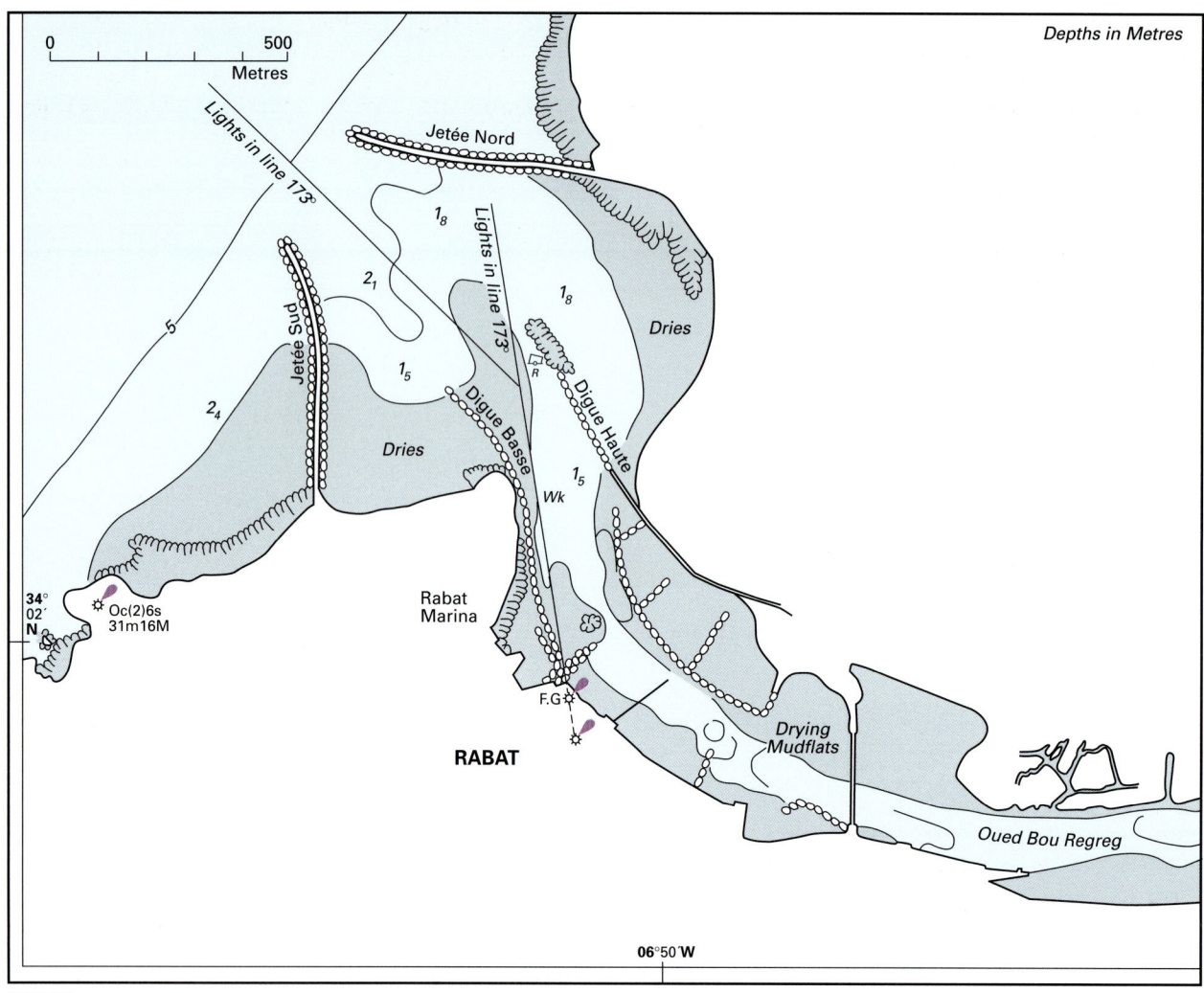

RABAT

is Sale, and its twin city Rabat extends to the south. High walls encircle Rabat on both the seaward and river sides.

General
Although once a large commercial harbour (in Merinid times a canal led from the river, under the Port Gate of Sale, to docks within the town walls), few yachts today venture into Rabat due to the difficulty of negotiating the sandbar which now restricts entry to high water. Even then the estuary is only navigable with difficulty if any swell is present. Thus, Rabat is listed here with its history less for its attraction as a good harbour, than for its importance as an ancient port city, now the capital of Morocco, which can be visited from adjacent ports.

Two breakwaters lead into the centre of the river and a shallow sandbar lies across its mouth, which, except in exceptionally settled weather, is clearly visible by the rollers breaking over it. Fishing boats tend to ride the rollers to clear the bar. Once over, there is a short span of deeper water before the bottom shelves to a drying sandbank either side of a narrow channel. The entry is well lit, but should never be attempted at night. Large areas of drying flats can be seen on either side of the river at LW. The flood tide has a maximum rate of 2kts and ebb of 4kts.

Berthing
Yachts have been seen anchored well inside the river, parallel to the *kasbah* ramparts where the sandy bottom dries out, but, it would be difficult to get ashore at low water and certainly very few yachts visit. However it is likely that yachts' crews would be given a good welcome here. It would be possible to anchor on the extensive drying mud flats either side of the river.

Formalities
Rabat is not a port of entry.

Facilities
Provisions Available in the town.
Post office and banks In the centre of town.

Eating out
Restaurants of all classes and cultures are in Rabat: Lebanese, Chinese, Korean, Indian and even a McDonalds: all to be found along with traditional large and small eating houses.

Tourism

Composed of sister cities – Rabat and Sale – flanking the mouth of Oued Bou Regreg, Rabat is a beautiful and photogenic city. It is easy to navigate the town which is filled with superb historic monuments. Its extensive medinas are rich in Moroccan foods and merchandise. Unlike Marrakesh and Fez, no guides are necessary in either Rabat or Sale. On the Rabat side, the old city stands in marked contrast to the new, providing a clear illustration of the concept of the first Resident-General under the French Protectorate, Marshal Lyautey, that the new French infrastructure and its physical manifestations should be kept distinct from, and conform to, traditional Moroccan forms of power and urban spaces. Thus the Ville Nouvelle was situated apart from the medina of Rabat, in a pattern which would be followed in other major Moroccan cities. Although this was a controversial urban planning policy at the time, the result seems well worth the degree of preservation of old Moroccan medinas, unique in North Africa.

Rabat City

There is a lot to see in Rabat, which has some of the most outstanding city walls and gates in the world. Hassan Mosque was built in the 12th century, but seems to have been left incomplete at the death of Yacoub el Mansour in 1199. The views across the old city and Sale from the minaret, which was intended to be 100ft higher, are spectacular. The mosque was destroyed in 1755 by an earthquake in Lisbon.

The mausoleum of King Mohammed V (grandfather of the present king) is built on the site where he gathered people in 1955 to thank God for Moroccan independence.

The Almohad walls at the Kasbah des Oudayas (Gate Almohad) were fortified by pirates (see below) in the 16th and 17th centuries, adding bastions such as the Tower of the Corsairs at the end of Calle Laalami. Within the *kasbah's* winding streets, is the 1150 Almohad mosque (oldest in Rabat) restored by renegade English architect, Ahmed el Inglesi in the 18th century (who also built Marine Gate at Essaouira). Moulay Ismail built a palace adjoining this *kasbah* in the 17th century, now the Museum of Moroccan Arts, fronted by beautiful Andalusian-style sunken gardens built in 1915–1918. Café Maure is a delightful place from which to view the sea and Sale, imbibe mint tea and taste the charms of Morocco. Here, in the Old Wool Market, is the site where captives of the Pirates of the Republic of Bou Regreg were sold into captivity in the 16th/17th centuries, just outside their *kasbah*. Along Rampe S. Maklouf (river road) are many antique shops.

Walking up Ave Mohammed V past the railway station leads to the 18th-century Grand Mosque of Rabat. From here turn right onto Ave Moh. Hassan and a few hundred yards further along on the left is the entrance to the *mechoua*. This extensive palace area includes another mosque, the houses of government (Dar el Makhzen) and the extensive royal palaces which housed some 2,000 people (members of Alouite dynasty, retainers, cavalry, guards etc).

Not far from here are the ruins of Chella, site of the port town Sala Colonia from Phoenician to Arab times (Sale moved across the estuary in the 13th century), and the burial site of the Merinid sultans who used Rabat as a *ribath* during 13th and 14th centuries. The Merinid ruins are still in good enough condition to locate the mosque with its ablutions court and prayer hall, and the tomb and *zaouia* (place of religious retreat, a separate courtyard with minaret which housed up to 16 men in retreat) of Abou el Hassan who ruled a vast empire from Tunisia to Spain between 331–1351 and was known as the Black Sultans being the son of an Abyssinian mother.

The National Archaeological Museum (near Grand Mosque and the Royal Palace) houses remarkable treasures, including superb bronzes and mosaics of Volubilis, a nearby Roman city.

Sale

Sale can be reached by crossing main Hassan II bridge (especially if you travel by taxi) but also by

One of the many ancient gateways into Rabat Madina

small boats which constantly cross the Bou Regreg. You will immediately notice a change from Rabat to a far more conservative, Muslim, non-European style. The medina is very traditional, with wares grouped by trades/guilds. Following the Rue de la Grande Mosque, you arrive at the Great Mosque of Sale. Surrounded by active *zaouias* and the famous, now inactive, Abu Hassan Medersa, a 14th-century Merinid religious school. Built in Hispano-Muslim style (visitors to Granada's Alhambra will be struck by similarities), it is related to the great Bou Inania *medersa* in Fez and Meknes. It is adorned with beautiful traditional decoration and commands superb views over Sale, Bou Regreg, to Rabat.

History
The name Sale derives from Sala Colonia, the Phoenician and later Roman trading port, which is now silted up, located on the south bank of Oued Bou Regreg in the area today known as Chellah. From the 8th century, Sala Colonia was occupied by Berbers who followed a form of government inspired by the Koran but based on Berber custom known as Kharajite. Aggravated by the presence of such heretics, the conservative Zenata tribe built a *ribat* (fortified monastery) on the site of the present-day Kasbah des Oudaias, as a base from which to attack and convert them. Two centuries later, a second and far more extensive *ribat* was built by the Almohad Sultan Yacoub el Mansour 'the Victorious' (over the King of Castile in 1195); due to its association with these *ribats*, in time the south side of the river came to be known as Rabat.

Of the ports included in this guide, the history of Rabat and Sale is distinctive in that it is integrally linked with that of the Spanish Province of Andalusia. The immense 3-mile ring of walls around Rabat were specifically built to house and organise troops preparing to defend and extend the Muslim territories of the Almohad dynasty in Spain. Planned as the capital of this Berber dynasty (which spread from Tripoli to northern Spain), Rabat was conceived on imperial proportions. Its Hassan Mosque, built but left incomplete circa 1197, was to be the second largest in the Muslim world, with a capacity for 40,000, the entire army of the Sultan. The cultural unity of Spain and Morocco at this time is evident in the striking correspondence between the minaret of this mosque (the Tower of Hassan), the Koutoubia in Marrakesh and the Giralda of Seville: all three were designed by the same architect. Subsequently, in 1260, when the Merinid dynasty was beset with political instability, Alfonso X of Castile seized the moment and sacked the port of Sala Colonia. This prompted the definitive movement of this population to the north side of the Bou Regreg – in effect, the foundation of present-day Sale.

Sale became a thriving city. Its rich Merinid constructions all attest to its vitality as the principal port of Morocco from the 13th to 16th centuries. Meanwhile, however, Rabat languished. When Leo Africanus (a Muslim from Granada) visited in 1500, he found no more than 100 houses and few shops.

After the conquest of Granada in 1492, the last Muslim kingdom in Spain, intolerance against even converted Muslims mounted until their final expulsion from Spain in 1611. At this time many thousands of Andalusian refugees came to settle in Sale and Rabat. Rabat's Almohad walls were so extensive that the newcomers constructed the Andalusian Wall (along what is now Blvd Hassan II) to define and protect a smaller city, the present medina, built in the style of the Andalusian cities from which they had come. To this day, the medinas of Rabat and Sale are renowned for preserving the architectural style, customs and music of medieval Andalusia.

Immediately upon arrival, many of the refugees began to take revenge on the Spanish in particular, and Christians in general, through piracy. Sale and Rabat were proclaimed the independent corsair Republic of Bou Regreg. Famous for selling Robinson Crusoe into slavery, and enormously successful between 1620–1630, alone they took over 1,000 European ships from the Atlantic. In time they ranged as far afield as Plymouth and Ireland. These famous 'Sallee Rovers', based in the *kasbah* of Rabat, were not subdued until Moulay Ismail incorporated them (and their revenues) into his state in the late 17th century. Moulay Ismail installed the warlike Oudaia tribe in the *kasbah* to subdue the corsairs, and within its walls built himself the palace which is now the Museum of Moroccan Arts. Rabat became one of a string of this sultan's intense development of fortified Atlantic ports (including Tanger, Larache, Mehdia, Safi and Agadir).

Recent history
When the French made Rabat their capital in 1912 it consisted of various distinct elements: the *kasbah* of the Oudaias, the Andalusian medina, the *mechouar* or palace complex of the Alaouite dynasty begun in 1768, the ruins of Sala Colonia (Chellah), and the separate city of Sale. The space between the medina and *mechouar* was open grazing land. Thanks to the urban planning policy of Marshal Lyautey, the Ville Nouvelle (New Town) occupies the space between the medina and the Almohad walls beyond them, and the old city of Rabat remains intact. Today, as the capital of Morocco, Rabat has grown into an agglomeration of nearly 1·5 million inhabitants, extending far beyond the Almohad walls and encompassing the formerly distinct city of Sale.

Local specialities
Sale is well known for its ceramics. A complex of some 20 potteries lies upriver and can be reached by petit taxi from Rabat or after crossing to Sale by boat (ask for *al fajarrín* and point upriver!). It is interesting to see the traditional processes, though the wares themselves are not necessarily so. The new Sale style uses as principal motifs traditional Berber facial tattoos and the *fibula*, a triangular

silver brooch used to fix both ends of a cloak around a woman's shoulders: a Roman practice continued in the traditional garb of Berber peoples across the Maghreb. In the contemporary urban Moroccan context, the fibula has recently become a symbol of the Berbers in their struggle for recognition. Depending on your taste, you may find these new Sale wares more attractive as they are more delicate and based on pastel colours, but they are also more fragile than traditional Moroccan ceramics such as those of Safi, Meknes and Fez. In this potters' complex are also a few contemporary artist potters of interest, and a large Moroccan handicrafts shop.

In Rabat, there is a carpet market on Thursday mornings in Rue des Consuls (near the *kasbah*), to which people from surrounding mountain towns and dealers bring a diverse selection of carpets. A huge Thursday market, Suq El-Jamis, takes place near the national highway outside Sale, and gathers artisans from both Rabat and Sale.

Sable Dór
General
This new marina will be one of the best in Morocco. It is located near the prestigious area of Temara, some 8M S of Rabat. The marina breakwaters have been built but no infrastructure is yet in place.

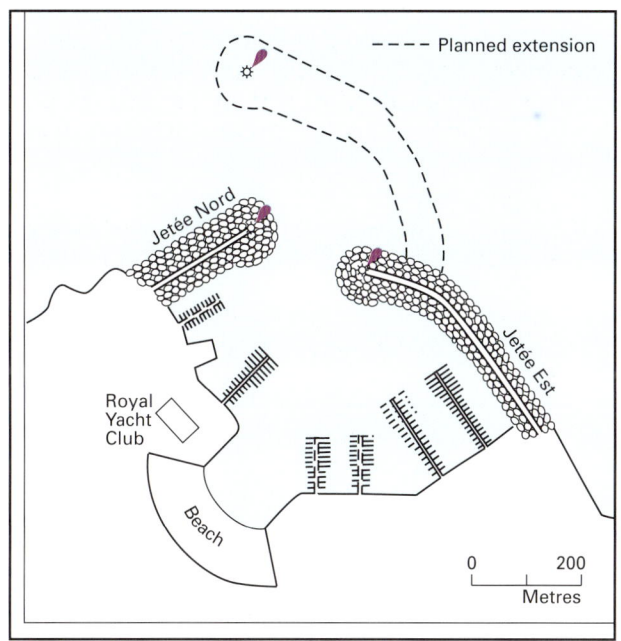

PORT DE SABLE D'OR

Mohammedia
33°43'·1N 7°24'W

Distances
Mehdia 46M Casablanca 13M

Tides
	MHWS	MHWN
Range	3·5m	2·7m

Charts
	Approach	Port
Admiralty	856, 860, 3132	861
French	6142	6142 (inset)
Spanish	527	5271

Lights
Approach
1. **Punta Almina** 35°54'N 5°16'·8W
   Fl(2)10s148m22M Siren(2)45s White tower on building

Harbour
2. **Entrance Ldg Lts 265°** 33°43'·0N 7°24'·1W
   Front DirOc(3)12s11m18M 262·5°-intens-267·5° White column, black bands 10m
3. *Rear* 110m from front DirOc(3)12s14m18M 262·5°-intens-267·5° White column, black bands 13m
4. **Jetée Nord head** Iso.WG.4s8m9/5M White tower, green tank 5m 191°-G-240°-W-191°
5. **Jetée Sud head** Oc(2)R.6s8m6M Red tower, red tank 6m

General
This 33-mile stretch of coastline from Rabat consists of sandy beaches and rocky areas. Running parallel to the beach, are two ranges of hills, the first a mile inland and the other 5M from the coast. Features of the coastline are the village of Temara, where the mosque minaret can be seen 7M S of Rabat, and the steel works of Skhirat, where a high mast is conspicuous, some 15M SW of Rabat. An islet, Sidi el Bou Derbala stands out at 33°50'N 7°09W. Another minaret at Mansouria is conspicuous 9M SW of the islet. Current is half a knot SW along the coast.

Approach
The port lies on the SW side of the bay of Fédala, with the Cap Fédala easily identified by the white oil storage tanks which can be seen from a distance of 20M. Ships are often moored 2M NE of the harbour entrance, where offshore oil pipeline berths are located. A light on Cap de Fédala (Fl(2+1)) is also visible for 20M. Two underwater obstructions N of the port will not worry yachtsmen, being 9m deep. Depths in the entry channel are in excess of 5m.

The first leading light, (130° Oc(2)WG.6s) is on a black and white chequered pedestal. The harbour entrance is marked by lights atop two white towers with black stripes, both DirOc(3)12s.

The north head jetty is marked by a white tower with green stripes, whilst the south head jetty has a white tower with red stripes.

Entry
Minimum depths in the harbour are around 5m.

North Africa

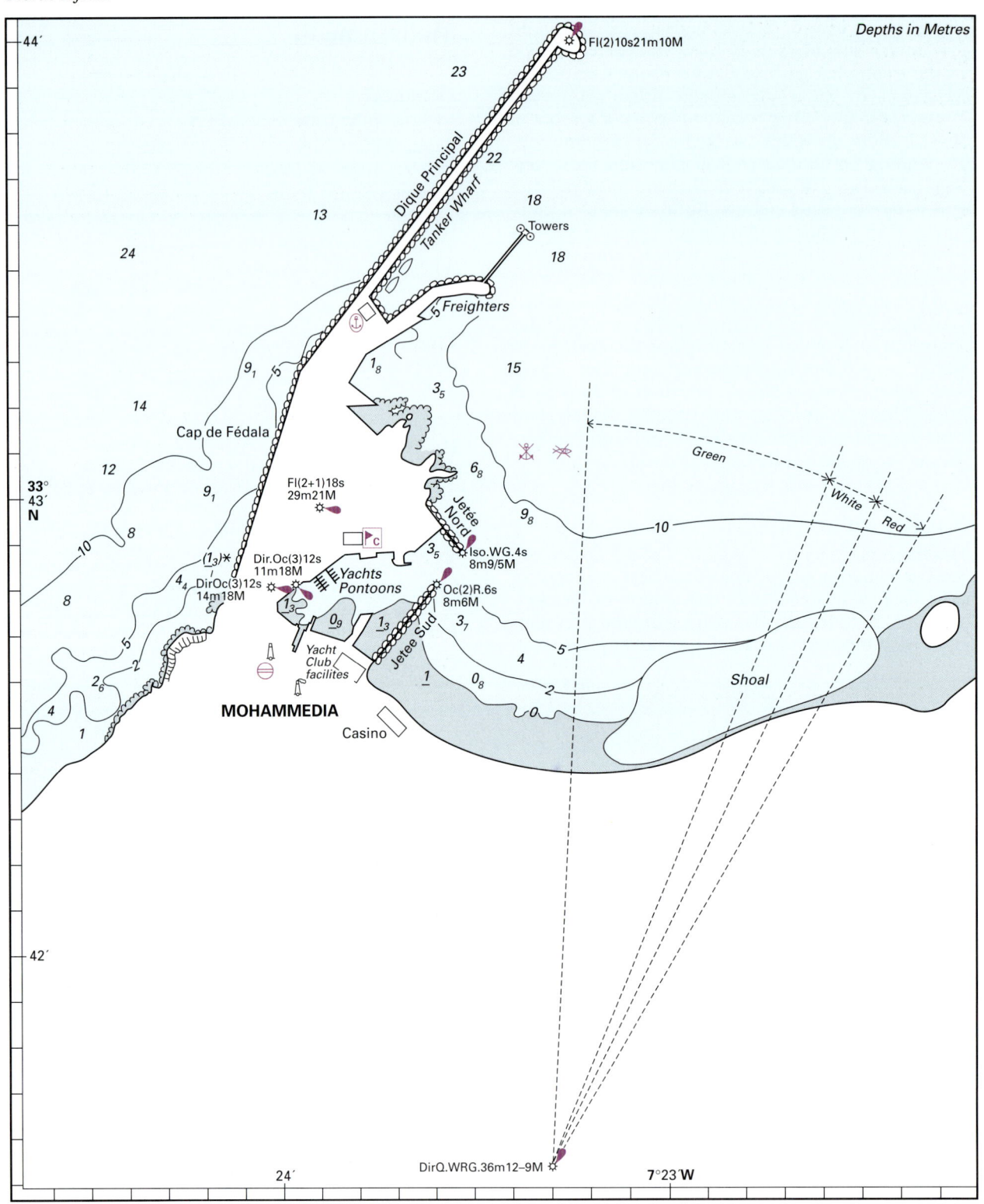

MOHAMMEDIA

Yachts should proceed south, past the two outer moles, and then west into the inner harbour, where two pontoons will be seen on the north side of the harbour.

Berthing
The above are the *club nautique* berths and are always full, but the club manager will usually allow visiting yachts to anchor ahead of the boats on the pontoons, taking a line to one already moored. Alternatively, anchor west of the pontoons in depths of 3–5m.

Formalities
Mohammedia is a port of entry and officials will visit your yacht. VHF Ch 16, 11, 13.

General
Mohammedia is the nearest there is at present to a

Mohammedia yacht club moorings

marina on the Atlantic coast and there are plans to develop the facilities into a full marina. The two pontoons currently serve members of the *club nautique*, whose staff are very friendly and helpful. The club facilities are situated across the harbour, separate from the fishing fleet. The marina is currently taking yachts normally moored in Casablanca, which is closing to allow construction of a new marina there, so moorings and facilities in Mohammedia are very stretched. This situation is likely to remain for 3 to 4 years.

If you are able to moor, or at least take a line to the pontoon after anchoring forward of the existing yachts, electricity and water are available. A very well-equipped exclusive yacht club complex is located on the south side of the harbour and is available to visiting yachtsmen at the discretion of the manager. Facilities include a swimming pool. The fish market is located near the main gate and also the club facilities.

Facilities
Water and electricity Available on the pontoons.
Fuel Available by arrangement with the yacht club.
Provisions There is an excellent hardware shop called Fast Ways, (diagonally across from the Hotel Sabah), which is well stocked with tools and equipment. There are grocery shops along the Avenue des F.A.R. and at its end, off to the left of the *kasbah* on Boulevard Moulay Youssouf, lies the town's marketplace.
Gas Available by arrangement with the *club nautique* staff.
Post office and banks In the centre of town.
Repairs Emergency repairs can be undertaken. A 30-ton floating crane is available.

Eating out
Mohammedia has some superb restaurants. Inquire at the tourist office (14 Rue al Jahid) or consult a recent guidebook for a current list of these. This is a town where it is worth the trouble to ask around and be selective!

Tourism
Mohammedia is one of Morocco's major commercial ports. Emerging from the well-tended marina and port gardens heading east into town, the most direct route takes you past a series of warehouses on a dusty track for a hundred metres. This leads to the port entrance, (visible from your mooring) the fishing harbour and the yacht club, set in a large garden. As well as a swimming pool, the club has a sailing school to encourage the children of those who summer in Mohammedia, (primarily families from Casablanca) to take up the sport. On the far side of the breakwater is the projected site of the new marina, and beyond this, a long stretch of beach.

The town of Mohammedia spreads out SE of this point. Although there are no historical monuments to visit, aside from the *kasbah* which dates from 1773, it provides an excellent reminder that there is much more to Morocco than the richly-stocked *souks* and densely-packed old medinas you may have previously visited. This is a prosperous and elegant resort town with large trees and colourful shrubs along its residential streets.

History
The port of Mohammedia (formally known as Fédala) has been active since the 14th century, especially in the 17th and 18th centuries, when it engaged in horse trading with Europe. In 1960, a long period of decline was reversed by the inauguration of an important oil refinery. King Mohammed V presided over this event and the name of the town was changed to Mohammedia. This recent period of growth has also been marked by the prosperity brought by increased tourism, witnessing the construction of elegant hotels and a golf course.

Local specialities
Each July there is a popular festival in Mohammedia, consisting of cultural events, arts and crafts exhibitions, marathons, etc. For centuries Mohammedia has been a centre of horse breeding and training. An important racecourse is located in the town.

Casablanca
33°37'·1N 07°33'·9W

Distances
Mohammedia 13M Al Jadida 50M

Tides
Standard Port
    MHWS MHWN
Range 3·7m   2·9m

Charts
	Approach	*Port*
Admiralty	3132, 856, 860	861
French	6111	5697
Spanish	527	50

North Africa

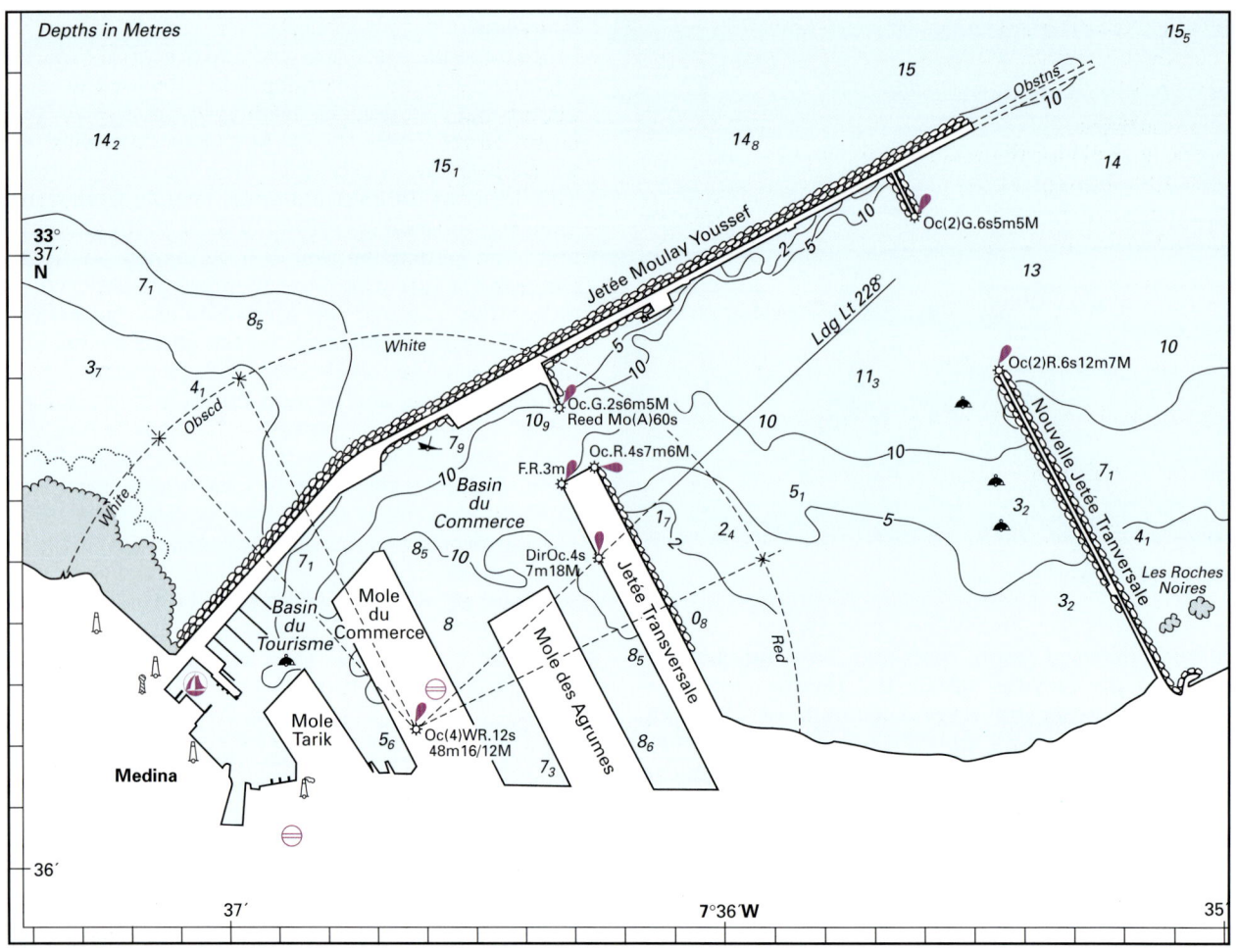

CASABLANCA

Lights
Entry signals
- ball over black cone/3G(vert) Lts — dangerous swell, Force 5 within next 24hrs
- ball over 2 black cones/GRG(vert) Lts – very dangerous swell, force 6 or above within next 24hrs

Approach
1. **Oukacha LtHo** 33°37'·1N 07°33'·9W
   VQ(2)2s29m18M 110°-vis-255°
   White tower, red lantern RC
   Auxiliary F.R.12M 055°-vis-110°
2. **Roches Noires** Oc.WR.4s21m16/12M
   090°-R-162°-W-090° White round tower, red lantern

Harbour
3. **Approach Ldg Lts 228° Muelle de Fosfatos**
   Front DirOc.4s30m18M 225·5°-intens-230·5° Red tower, white stripes
4. *Rear* 770m from front Oc(4)WR.12s48m16/12M shore-W-245°-R-285° 138°-obscd (silo)-153° Red grain silo
5. **Azemour** (cape light) 33°20'·6N 8°18'·3W
   Fl(2)WR.6s45m15/11M 075°-W-100°-R-245° White tower

General
The principal commercial port in Morocco and home of the navy. The yacht basin, at the far end of the port is very sheltered and safe. Currently (Dec 1998) extensive changes are taking place as land and buildings are being requisitioned in the basin to make way for a new marina. Consequently, visiting yachts may find it difficult to moor here until the new pontoons are in place. Entry is safe and straightforward in all weathers although a considerable swell can be experienced with a NE wind.

From Mohammedia the coastline begins with long sandy beaches, giving way to cliffs.

Approach
Some distance from the main mole, Jetty Moulay Youssef, on a transit of 228° are two buoys (leading Fl.G, followed by Fl(3)G) marking the mid-channel approach. Large vessels are often anchored to the W of these buoys. By day and night the most conspicuous feature is the huge mosque to the W of the port. Depths in the entrance are substantial and do not become noticeably shallower until well inside the yacht basin.

Berthing
Follow the mole Moulay Youssef SW, past the naval yard to the end of the port, where entry to the yacht harbour will be observed. New moorings will be seen just before rounding the yacht club and old customs house. These are exclusively for the use of military personnel and should not be approached. Currently the mooring facility consists of a single jetty, soon to be replaced by new pontoons (see

above). Go bow or stern-to this pontoon. Minimum depths are around 2·5m on the E side, and 1·8m on the W side.

Formalities
Officials will visit the yacht and are very efficient and friendly. Immigration police can be contacted by phone on ☎ 317628 and will visit before you leave. Port VHF Ch 16, 12, 14, 24hrs.

Facilities
Water and electricity On the quay via a very long hose and wire.
Fuel Can be arranged and brought to your yacht by the boatyard watchmen.
Provisions Shops, supermarkets and fruit and vegetable markets abound in Casablanca.
Gas Available from many shops or ask the boat watchmen to arrange it for you.
Post office and banks In the centre of town.
Repairs All repairs can be undertaken here although at present there is no lift-out facility. Opposite the pontoon is a wall which dries out at LW. With a range of 2·9m most underwater jobs can be carried out here.

Eating out
Within the yacht basin is a moderately priced restaurant with good atmosphere, Restaurant Port du Peche. This also acts as the club nautique meeting place until the new facilities are in place. Good fish restaurants are also to be found along the Corniche, at the far end of which is Ain Diab, where there are also some Japanese and Korean restaurants.

The best restaurant in Morocco is said to be Sijilmassa on Rue de Biarritz, a Moroccan-style restaurant complete with bellydancers (go armed with DH 10 notes!). Near the Boulevard Mohammed V are several other reasonably priced Moroccan-style restaurants – Ryad Zitoun (31 Bd Rachidi ☎ 223927) Ouarzazate (Rue Mohamed El Qorri) and the Bahj (Rue Colbert) – and the more expensive Al Mounia (Rue du Prince Moulay Abdallah).

Note The new marina will accommodate some 300 yachts with all modern facilities. However, it may be two or three years before these facilities are in place.

Tourism
Casablanca is a huge sprawling city, a mixture of ancient and modern. Leaving the yacht basin via a gate shared with the naval yard takes you to the main road: left into town and right along the Corniche. This leads to the immense and stunning Hassan II Mosque. The mosque, given by the nation to King Hassan on his 60th birthday in 1989 was inaugurated 1993. It was designed by French architect Michel Pinseau at a cost of $500 million and took 35,000 workers 50 million hours to complete. It is the tallest religious building in the world, with a minaret 575ft (175m) high. At some times in the Moslem calendar, a laser beam shines from the top of the mosque, pointing towards Mecca, the holiest city of Islam. Standing at the furthest point west in the Muslim world, this is the largest mosque outside the Saudi Arabian cities of Medina and Mecca. The central courtyard can hold 20,000 people while 80,000 more can pray on the surrounding esplanade. Guided tours are available for Dh100.

Beyond the Mosque is a fashionable area of Saudi palaces, elegant beach clubs and the Marabout of Sidi Abderahmen: a picturesque cluster of white tombs rising on a rocky outcrop just offshore.

At the lower end of the old medina is the 18th-century Borj Sidi Mohammed ben Adullah, built to resist Portuguese raids and in its eastern section is the Grande Mosque, built in the late 18th century until after the recapture of Anfa from the Portuguese. Several nights a week there is a coloured-lights display at the fountain in the Place des Nations Unis.

Near the square is the pleasant Parque de la Ligue Arabe, the largest green space in Casablanca, with palm trees, arcades and cafés in the shade. It was opened in 1918 and adjacent to that is the exuberant design of Cathedrale de Sacre Coeur, built in 1930 and now used as a school.

Also recommend, is a visit to the church of Our Lady of Lourdes at the medina entrance, with its remarkable expanse of stained glass windows. The church was built in the 1950s and the windows designed by Gabriel Loire.

History
There is evidence of Phoenician 7th-century BC and Roman occupation at Casablanca. The Almohads conquered the town in 1188 from the Berber tribe Barghawata, and developed it as a port. The Portuguese established a settlement here in the 14th century on the site of the village of Anfa, which soon became a centre for pirate activities and was destroyed by the military: an act repeated in 1515. The Portuguese re-established themselves in the late 16th century, renaming the town Casa Blanca, (white house) remaining until 1755, when an earthquake destroyed the settlement. The town was rebuilt at the end of the 18th century by Sultan Mohammed Ibn Abdellah, who constructed the spectacular Grand Mosque.

In the 20th century the French constructed an artificial harbour under the patronage of Sultan Abd al-Aziz, which marked the beginning of Casablanca's rapid expansion into a modern commercial capital. The medina, which was formally the Jewish quarter until the establishment of Israel, was extended during this period.

The new city centre has monumental *Mauresque* buildings, wide avenues, white commercial and residential buildings, as well as the Pastiche Medina designed by Albert Laprade (a specialist in Moroccan traditional architecture). See MacLaughlan's list of *Historic Casablanca Architecture – a checklist* for more information.

Casablanca is not an important city in terms of historic monuments or ambience, but it is the economic capital of Morocco. The port handles a

North Africa

vast range of traffic from European cruise liners to phosphates. Its population by the turn of the century had barely reached 20,000, not a tenth of that of Fez at the time. Since then, however, it has risen to be the main port and industrial powerhouse of Morocco, with a population unofficially estimated to be around 4 million people.

El Jadida
33°16'N 8°30'W

Distances
Casablanca 50M Jorf Lasfar 11M.

Tides
	MHWS	MHWN
Range	3·6m	2·8m

Charts
	Approach	Port
Admiralty	3132	–
French	6120	6119
Spanish	216	527
US	–	–

Lights
Approach
1. **Oukacha LtHo** 33°37'·1N 07°33'·9W
   VQ(2)2s29m18M 110°-vis-255
   White tower, red lantern. RC
   Auxiliary F.R.12M 055°-vis-110°

Harbour
2. **Jetty Nord head** 33°15'·6N 8°29'·8W
   Iso.WG.4s7m13/9M 120°-G-235°-W-120° Square concrete tower, green band 5m
3. **Jetty Sud head** F.R.10m7M White column red top

General
El Jadida is a quaint, busy fishing harbour with many attractions and a friendly welcome for yachtsmen.

Heading southwards from Casablanca, one leaves to port one of the most impressive landmarks in Morocco: the Grand Mosque of King Hassan II, described under Casablanca. Even more spectacular by night, this, the highest mosque in the Arab world, stands out for miles, diminishing the lighthouse of Point d'Oukkacha. Rocks and tombs, with a background of low-lying hills, form the coastline from Point del Hank to El Jadida.

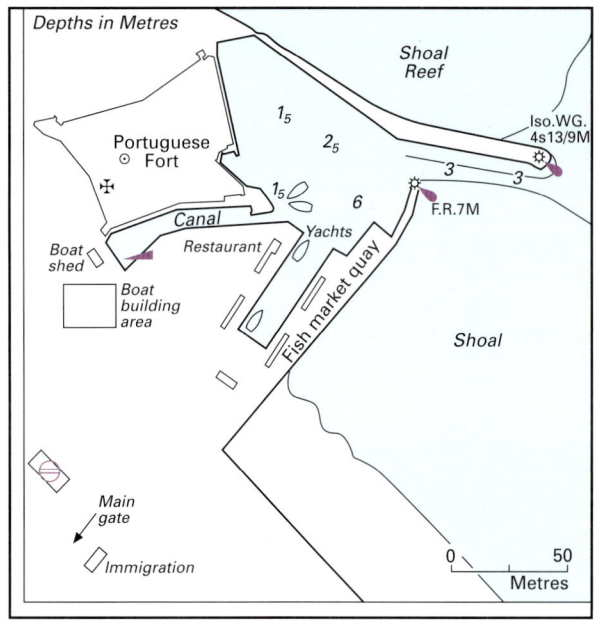

Approach
Entry to El Jadida is possible at night, but be sure to correctly identify the port and starboard lights on the north and south breakwaters. Several vessels have mistakenly identified the green and red flashing lights inland on a pharmacy and an antenna, which are brighter and have alarmingly similar characteristics. Confusing them will land you on the shallow coral reef which extends over a mile out to the north of the port and which surrounds Cap de Mazagan.

A wreck half a mile south of the harbour should also be avoided. It is lit at night, but the area is often shrouded in mist, especially in summer.

Entry
Entry on a course of 220° heading for the northern breakwater will take you into the harbour and clear of the dangers. Keep to the right of the breakwater, as there is a sandbar in the centre. Depths in the entry do not go below 3m, except in the troughs of a deep Atlantic swell.

There is no night radio watch, although during the day channels 12 and 16 are supposed to be monitored.

Once inside, depths of 6m exist in the main channel of the harbour, until transiting the short canal, which gradually reduces to 1·5m where fishing boats will be seen moored.

Berthing
There is no need to go further than the restaurant on the far side of the harbour, where a short wall leads to steps. Moor alongside, with ropes secured to the railing beneath the restaurant and to the large bollard (formed by the buried muzzle of an ancient iron cannon) on the corner of the jetty. A tidal range of 3m should be considered when mooring. Some surging can be expected here during westerly winds. Minimum depth alongside is 3·5m.

This jetty belongs to the Association Nautique, which is a well-run sail training centre with dinghies and sailboards, used by the youngsters of the town. It can therefore get a bit noisy during the afternoons, but discipline is very good and you will not experience any problems from the happy children swimming and sailing around. Any assistance by way of woodworking tools, etc. for the repair of their equipment would be very much appreciated by the club and greatly facilitate your stay.

Formalities
VHF Ch 6 and 12.
El Jadida is a port of entry and the police, customs and immigration officials will come to the yacht to complete the paperwork. The officials are very

EL JADIDA

friendly, although the customs officers here expect a 'gift' before completing their task and will return with their boss, who will also expect to be reimbursed for his effort. Keep the cigarettes or whisky handy!

Facilities
Water Available from a tap on the jetty by permission of club nautique.
Electricity Not generally available, although it is possible to run a cable from the restaurant located next to the jetty by arrangement with the owner.
Fuel Available and may be brought to your yacht in cans, or fill up at the fishing quay, where a pump is located.
Provisions Many shops are located just outside the port with a good range of items. Follow the old city wall to the right for the fish, meat and fruit markets.
Gas Can easily be arranged with Ahmed, the gatekeeper.
Post office and banks Located just outside the main port gate in the centre of town. Several banks here have automatic cash facilities and up to Dh8,000 can be withdrawn on *Visa* cards. *Diners Club* cards are also accepted.
Repairs This is one of the best ports for engine repairs, which do not exist in the port itself, but mechanics and tradesmen will come to the boat. In the town are workshops catering for complete overhauls for any engine and the engineers, who may not be literate, are nevertheless as competent as those in Europe and very much cheaper. Ahmed can arrange anything necessary.

View north from behind restaurant and Club Nautique

Eating out
The local marina restaurant serves a basic menu at a reasonable price. Since the town is a holiday resort, it is full of restaurants of every type and size.

Charges
As most of the ports in Morocco there are no formal charges for the use of the port, although it has been known for the harbourmaster to make an unexpected levy, apparently on orders from Jorf Lasfar. This does not seem to be an official charge and is negotiable.

Tourism
A small gate from the restaurant and club nautique leads into the main harbour. The gate is manned during the day by Ahmed; a friendly old fellow who has been working there for thirty years. He can arrange anything for visiting yachts from tour guides to engine overhauls and will appreciate 'a souvenir' in return. Ahmed will happily look after your yacht and ensure its safety while you leave for excursions.

Once outside the port, to your left will be seen the famous beach of Sidi Bouzid, with a long elegant corniche, where vacationers from all over Morocco promenade on summer evenings and socialise in cafés, bars and discotheques. Straight ahead lies the Place Mohammed V, the functional centre of El Jadida where you will find banks, PTT (post and telegraph), at the south end of the plaza, a helpful tourist office (NW corner of the plaza), photographic shops, traditional cafés, etc. And to the right, past a long block devoted on the seaward side to the city market, you will come upon the high

Splendid Moroccan design and workmanship in the facade of this hotel in El Jadida: Hotel Anduluz

walls of a wonderful old Portuguese fortress-city, well worth a visit.

Today, the Cite Portugaise, as the old fortress/city is known, is a beautiful, relaxed and interesting place to visit. From the ramparts one gets a sense of the original situation of the city, its moat (now limited to one side), and its harbour (now silted up). Wandering its streets, one enjoys elegant old Portuguese architectural details. Descending into its immense cistern, one is stunned to silence by a vast shimmering space, its ribbed Gothic vaulting supported by 25 huge pillars. This cistern, featured in films such as *The Harem* and Orson Welles' *Othello*, seems secret and indeed it was completely forgotten after the 1769 fall of the city, only to be casually found by a shopkeeper in 1916 as he was increasing the size of his store.

Because El Jadida is a university town, it is possible to find especially well-versed and enthusiastic guides to show you some of these sights in detail; and because it is an easy-going place with none of the confusion and 'volunteer' pressure of bigger cities, it is just as possible for you to explore them alone.

Although the railway line passes through the town, it is now only used for freight. However, a good bus service operates and the station can be found at the far end of the ramparts of the Cite Portugaise. In the summer it would be wise to purchase bus tickets to Casablanca and Marrakesh a day in advance of any excursion. Taxis can also be found everywhere.

Because it is so quiet and safe, and your yacht will be well guarded by Ahmed, El Jadida is a particularly good port to use as a base for excursions. Marrakech, for instance, is less than 2 hours away.

History
The name El Jadida derives from *Al Brija al Jadida*, which means 'the new little port', and indeed the city has had several incarnations. The Portuguese began to build this massive fort to consolidate their Atlantic trade advantage in 1513 on the site of an abandoned Almohad fortress. Called *Mazagao* or Angel's Bastion, it gradually grew into a city and as other Portuguese ports like Agadir and Azzemour were conquered or regained by Moroccans, Portuguese exiles resettled here. Two hundred and fifty years later Mazagao was one of the last and best-situated Portuguese bastions along the Moroccan coast, only falling to Sidi Mohammed Ben Abdallah in 1769 after a prolonged siege. When the Portuguese finally sailed out through the Porte de la Mer Mar (located at the end of the principal street into the old city and visible below from the SE restored Bastion de l'Ange as one tours the ramparts), they left the city partially burned and mined, so that after much loss of life, the triumphant Moroccans were forced to abandon it.

Forty five years later Mazagao was rebuilt, re-baptised *El Jadida* (the new), and resettled. The moats on two sides were filled in, connecting the formerly detached, impenetrable fortress with the land. Gradually Muslim inhabitants settled around it, while Europeans and Moroccan Jewish merchants, who were pivotal to trade with the interior, congregated within the walls of the old city. The Jewish cemetery is just north of the walled old city and, standing on the Bastion de l'Ange looking north within the city, the former synagogue can be recognised by the Star of David high on its facade. Also visible, is the former Catholic Church, complete with its cross. A new law in Morocco forbids the destruction of such non-Muslim places of worship and paves the way for their restoration.

In 1912 the city, again called Mazagan, became an important regional administrative centre in the French Protectorate. The final reversion to the name El Jadida in 1956 marks the end of the assorted colonial intrusions into Morocco which began with the Portuguese five centuries ago.

Local specialities
Primarily a fishing town, because of the splendid beaches this is a popular tourist resort. The town is renowned for its beautiful women. Well worth a visit, is the Hotel Palais Andalous. This splendid building in typical Hispanomuslim style, recalls in its spectacular ceramics and elaborate stucco work, many features of the Alhambra in Granada and the palace built by Muslim artisans in Seville and Reales Alcazares.

Jorf Lasfar
33°10'N 8°37'W

Distances
El Jadida, 11M Safi 60M.

Tides
	MHWS	MHWN
Range	3–6	2–8

Charts
	Approach	Port
Admiralty	3132	–
French	6170	–
Spanish	216	216 (inset)
US	–	–

Lights
Approach
1. **Cap Bedouza** 32°32'·6N 9°17'·0W
   Fl(2)10s65m22M Turret on fort

Harbour
2. **Dique Principal head** Fl(2)R.10s18m8M
3. **Epi head** F.R.15m8M
4. **Contradique head** Fl.G.4s14m8M R light on tower 1M S

General
Although not recommended as a port worth visiting, Jorf Lasfar is mentioned because it is one of the largest and safest shelters to run to in bad weather, with easy access in any conditions. It is primarily intended for the export of phosphates which are mined in this area, mostly in Ganturs 100M away. Morocco has the largest reserves of phosphates in

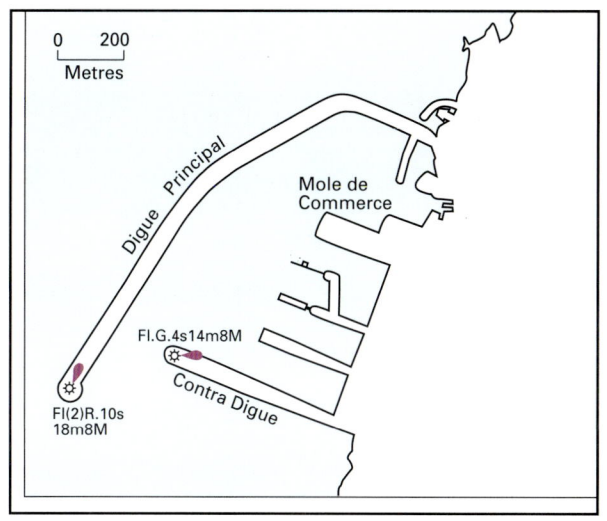

PORT DE JORF LASFAR

the world, and they have been mined since Roman times. Jorf Lasfar was formerly a small fishing port where *gambas* (large prawns) were landed.

From El Jadida, this part of the coastline starts with the low lying coral ledge surrounding Cap Mazagan. To avoid this reef, keep at least 1½M out from El Jadida before heading south. When leaving El Jadida and rounding the cape, Jorf Lasfar can be seen in the distance. The coastline rises into a rocky cliff 60m high approaching the port.

Approach
The port can be clearly identified from several miles away by the cranes and large ships moored inside. The entry channel is on the south side of the breakwater, with a high tower painted with red and white stripes on the clifftop above the entrance. Entry presents no problems for any vessel and is well lit at night.

Berthing
The port is new and no details are available regarding depths, however, since this is the main phosphate port in Morocco and can handle very large deep-draught vessels, minimum depths for any yacht can be assured. Yachts would not normally wish to stay here, but the authorities say they are welcome. Like El Jadida, radio watch is said to be maintained on VHF Ch 12 and 16 during the day.

Formalities
Port of entry, officials will visit the yacht.

Facilities
There are no facilities currently available for small vessels, although they are welcome. There are no villages within walking distance, nor any supplies available in the immediate vicinity. However, El Jadida is just a few miles away and is served by the main coastal road which passes the port with a regular taxi and bus service.

Tourism
The ruins of the ancient Berber city of Tit, near Moulay Abdallah is 3M NE of the port. Tit (meaning 'eyes' – the watchtowers would have been looking out to sea) was built as a fortified monastery, one of several built on the Atlantic coast in the 12th century to counter the threat of Norman invasion.

Safi Port and Oualidia Lagoon
32°19'N 9°15'W

Distances
Jorf Lasfar 60M Essouira 56M

Tides
	MHWS	MHWS
Range	3·4m	2·7m

Charts
	Approach	Port
Admiralty	3132	–
French	6169	6103
Spanish	529	254
US	–	–

Lights
Approach
1. **Ldg Lt 150°** *Front* Q.11m12M 060°-vis-240° Red and white mast
2. *Rear* 150m from front Q.14m12M 060°-vis-240° Red and white tower
3. **Pointe de la Tour** 32°20'·0N 9°16'·8W Oc(4)12s90m18M 302°-vis-164° Yellow tower
4. Fl(2)WRG.6s11m14/13M 085°-G-097°-W-103°-R-113°

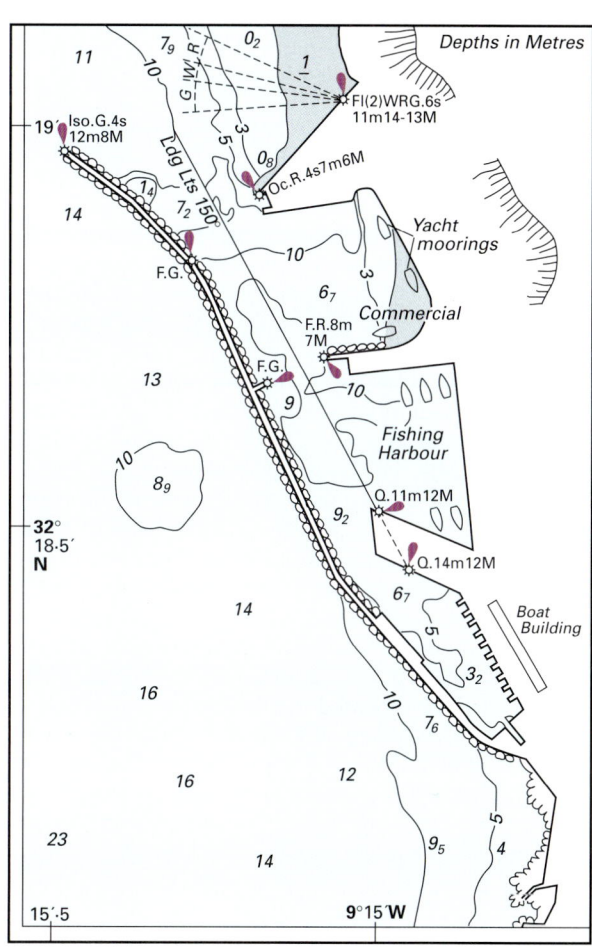

SAFI

North Africa

5. **Spur W of entrance** F.G.10m6M
Harbour
6. **Grande jetée head** Iso.G.4s12m8M White and green tower F.G 400m and 800m SE
7. **Elbow** F.G.6m3M 133°-vis-335° White and green pedestal
8. **Jetée Transvaal Nord** Oc.R.4s7m6M Grey and red hut
9. **Mole de phosphates head** F.R.8m7M
10. **Root** 32°18'·7N 9°14'·8W Oc(2)6s28m12M 012°-vis-145° Yellow tower 2F.R are shown from chimney 1·36M SSE

Coastline from Jorf Lasfar to Safi

This coastline is rocky, with long stretches of low-lying cliffs and 50 foot sand dunes. A large inland lake and connecting lagoon lie behind dunes near Oualidia.

Nearing Cap Cantin (Beddouza), 7M to the north, the white mosque of Sidi Bou Seksou is conspicuous. Rocks extend about a mile from the cape, and the sea starts breaking much further out in the relatively shallow 5 metre depths. It is advisable to give the cape a clearance of at least 3M. Sardine nets are laid out from May to December in the area between Cap Cantin and Essaouira. A wreck lies four miles NE of Cap Safi.

Sea mist is often encountered along this part of the coast in summer. The prevailing wind from N-NNE is usual in the months between April and October, getting up before midday, often reaching 30kts in mid-afternoon and dropping at night. Winter winds are more moderate and prevail from the SW–NW with occasional storms.

Oualidia Lagoon

32°31'·5N 9°02'W

This lovely peaceful lagoon, half way between El Jadida and Safi, is worth visiting in exceptionally calm weather and provides a spectacular anchorage. Summer homes and cafés cluster around a natural mile-long bay, formed by two rocky cliffs running parallel to the shore. Two breaches allow entry into the lagoon. A sandbar across the north entry passage reduces depths to around 2m at LW, according to local fishermen. The southern entrance has rocks on either side of a narrow passage, and a minimum depth of 1·5m at LWS. Huge rollers often overwhelm the entrance, even in light winds, so entering and leaving here is not an adventure for the fainthearted!

Several small fishing boats operate from inside the lagoon beaching at the SE, but this is not considered a port and certainly has no facilities for yachts. It would be advisable to inform the authorities in El Jadida or Jorf Lasfar if you intend to go inside the lagoon, although there seems to be no prohibition.

King Mohammed V had his summer residence here and the recently abandoned remains of what used to be a majestic palace, can be seen on the seashore. On the inland waterway that extends for a considerable way NE from the bay, oysters are

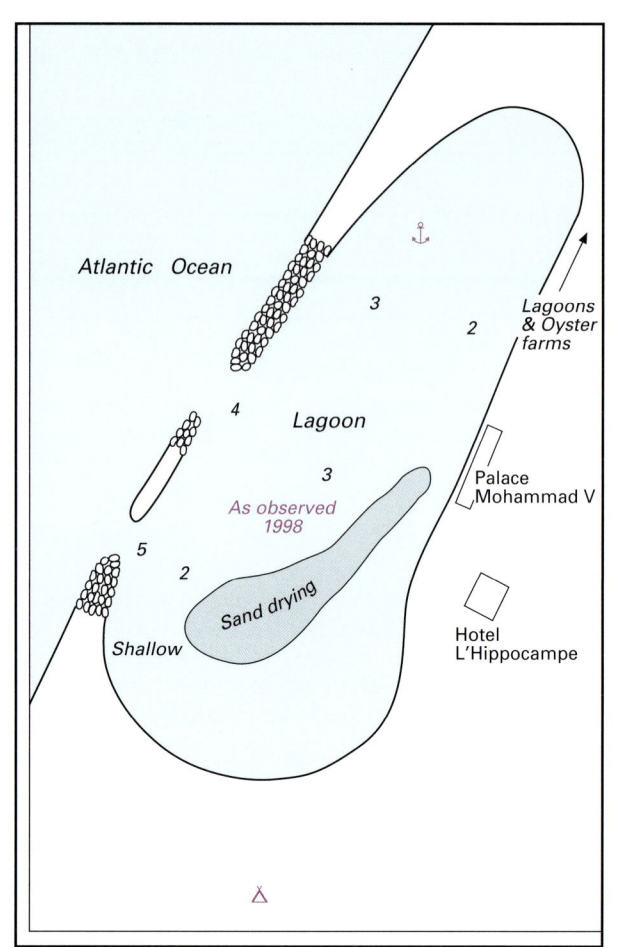

OUALIDIA

cultivated. Oualidia is a wonderful place for swimming, fishing and bird-watching. Many species of migrating birds stop-over here. High on the hills above the lagoon are several terraced restaurants commanding picturesque views and serving seafood menus. On the same road, halfway up and tucked back into a residential area on the left, is the charming Hotel Hippocampe, with its adjoining restaurant.

Approach to Safi

A large silo nearly 70m high, can be clearly seen at the southern end of the harbour. A long mole projecting NW leads into the port. The end of the mole is well lit and the channel is dredged to a depth of at least 7m. Large freighters enter the port.

Berthing

Safi is a very busy fishing port with a large area to the south of the harbour dedicated to boat-building. It is a well sheltered harbour from all wind directions, although a swell does run into the port during strong westerly winds. A separate quay to the NE of the harbour serves the larger freighters. This is the best place for yachts, being much quieter than the inner fishing harbour. Go where directed by the harbourmaster, whose tower is just before the freighter terminal. Cement and phosphates are transported from the port, making it a somewhat dusty place in summer.

Tanger to Laayoune

Oualidia lagoon: a good anchorage in exceptionally calm weather

Artist at work in Safi. Note the hands stencilled with henna

Formalities
Safi is a port of entry and officials will arrive at your yacht. Port VHF Ch 16, 9, 10, 11, 12 24hrs.

Facilities
Water Is available from large hose connections.
Fuel Can be delivered to your boat by bowser or in cans.
Provisions Most supplies are available from the well-stocked shops just outside the port.
Gas Camping Gaz and propane/butane refills are available from local hardware shops.
Post office and banks In the centre of town.
Repairs No yacht repair facilities are available in the port, but as in most Moroccan towns, engineers can easily be arranged in the town and any supplies can be purchased there.
Charges None officially at present.

Eating out
As usual, the medina contains many places where one can eat well and inexpensively. There are several nicer restaurants around Place de l'Independence near the Wafa Bank. North of the city on Route Sidi Bouzid, are magnificent views of Safi, leading up to the restaurants Le Refuge (French and seafood) and La Corniche (Moroccan and seafood). Take a petite taxi for this excursion.

Local transport
Safi is a safe place to leave your yacht for excursions inland. Europcar rental has an office located in Place Ibnou Sina. The train and bus stations are located some 1500m south of Place de l'Independence, on the extension of Rue de R'bat and Avenue du President Kennedy, respectively. A railway line connects Safi with all the coastal towns to the north, as far as Tanger, but recent information suggests that this coastal line is now only used for freight once south of Casablanca. The line running inland to Marrakesh, Meknes and Fez still carries passengers.

Tourism
The fish-market on the quay is one of the most fascinating in Morocco. All types of fish can be seen and purchased, including very long conger eels, caught nearby. Due to the cold currents which bring sardines close to shore just to the north, Safi has been one of the most important sardine fishing ports in the world for centuries. Many boats under construction can be seen near the port main gate to the city. Boat building is a family business, with the designs being carried in the minds of those families for centuries, without reference to printed plans. Each boat carries a distinctive traditional family characteristic, handed down for generations.

The port lies just outside the NW corner of the city walls which were built by the Almohads in the 12th century. Uphill, to the left of the port, also outside the northern wall, lies the Potters' Quarter (see *Local Specialities*). The coastal road to the right runs past the medina, which extends uphill away from the sea, then past the Portuguese Dar el Bahr (Castle/House of the Sea), built in 1523 to guard the port and house its governor. The road continues to a new part of town and Place de l'Independence, where you will find the Post office and banks etc. The Ville Nouvelle (new city) where government offices, modern residences and apartment buildings fan out from Place Mohammed V, lies a considerable way uphill. The tourist office is located just south of this Place but, while friendly, offers little to make the difficult journey from the port worthwhile.

Safi is a highly active industrial city with a large number of artisans amongst its population of some 300,000. Without a beach, or the grandeur of a city like Rabat, it can seem like quite a change of pace

Safi town and harbour viewed from south

from other ports. However, its teeming medina is well worth a visit, as are the Portuguese fortresses Dar el Bahr and Kechla, at the top and bottom of the medina. The top level of the Kechla, stocked with British cannons, provides excellent views of the city and harbour. The lower level houses the Bahia Palace, an 18th-century governor's palace and an interesting Ceramics Museum. Within the medina, at the north end of Rue du Socco (just before exiting the medina and arriving at the Potters' Quarter), is an attractive and rich pottery market. Finally, in the lower south-western portion of the medina, near the Great Mosque, are an old *madrasa* (Islamic teaching school) and the late Gothic Portuguese Chapel, intended to be the choir of a cathedral, which was left unfinished when the Portuguese withdrew in 1541.

History
Safi, a pre-Roman port, was first intensively developed by the Almohads during the 12th to 13th century. At that time Asfi, as the city was known, was renowned as a religious and intellectual centre in an occidental Muslim world which stretched well up into Spain. Along with Moroccan political cohesion however, its importance and power gradually declined, enabling the Portuguese to conquer it in 1508. They shored up the *kasbah*, built the several fortresses and chapel referred to above, but were ousted in 1541 by the Saadians, who also recovered Agadir and Essaouira at this time. The Saadians built the Great Mosque in the medina and probably the Kechla, whose origin is disputed. Thereafter, a succession of sultans culminating with Moulay Ismail in the early 18th century, added religious buildings, restored portions of the ramparts and built up trade with Europeans.

Safi's present concentration on phosphates dates from the French colonial years of this century. After independence, Maroc-Chimie built the huge processing plant which lies along the coast just south of the city. This has made possible the diversification of the local industries, leading Safi to become one of the key ports of Morocco.

It was from Safi that the Norwegian explorer Thor Hyerdahl sailed his papyrus, bamboo and reed-built boat, in an attempt to prove that the ancient Egyptians could have crossed the Atlantic to found the Inca and Aztec civilisations, accounting for the many similarities between the two ancient civilisations. These similarities have remained a mystery to ethnologists, because they have not accepted that the Atlantic could have been crossed before Columbus. Hyerdahl succeeded on his second attempt in 1970, reaching Barbados after 57 days.

Local specialities
In addition to viewing its fascinating traditional boat building, anyone interested in Moroccan ceramics and the history of European painted and glazed ceramic vessels (based largely on techniques which entered both Europe and Morocco through medieval Muslim Spain) will find a visit to Safi's Potters' Quarter highly rewarding.

Safi has one of the principal urban popular ceramic traditions in Morocco. Its pots, vases and plates can be purchased all over Morocco (and abroad), but there are distinctive colours and patterns which mark traditional Safi wares, just as there are for the ceramics of cities like Fez, Meknes and Sale. One can get an idea of the evolution of the traditional Safi style in the Ceramic Museum of the Kechla. Many pots still conform to it. Safi potters have also recently invented some new styles, which may dismay the purist, but are far less time-consuming to produce. These seem to be very popular among tourists, ensuring the continuation of the local pottery industry at the very least. The tiles for the distinctive green-tiled roofs of many religious and official buildings in Morocco (such as those on the Kechla itself) are also produced at Safi. Walking around the Potters' Quarter, one can see them drying in the sun.

Unlike the hand-coiled, unglazed wares made at home by women in rural areas of Morocco, urban ceramics are made by men in *ateliers*, concentrated just outside the city walls, as was customary in medieval Europe. This is due to the smoke and fire hazard posed by the kilns and to the need for access to water and the constant delivery of clay and wood. The techniques in use at Safi are also very ancient, as pots are thrown on sunken kick wheels and are fired in specially-shaped two-tiered, wood-burning kilns. Until recently, when industrially-prepared colours became available, each atelier would have ground its own mineral colours according to their own special recipes. Safi pots are still painted by hand and it is possible to observe all phases of the manufacturing process, from a lump of clay to the fired, painted product.

At the base of the hill towards the medina, is a

small ceramic *souk* worth investigating. (Here are also a few galleries of contemporary Safi artists.) In fact the ceramic *souk* near Bab Chaaba, at the upper end of Rue du Socco in the medina, may offer a better selection. Considering all the time and effort evident in the Potters' Quarter, you will find prices for these wonderful ceramics extraordinarily cheap.

Essaouira
31°30'N 9°46'W

Distances
Safi 56M Agadir 65M.

Tides
       MHWS MHWN
Range 3·6m   2·8m

Charts

	Approach	*Port*
Admiralty	3133, 863	863 (inset)
French	6206	6204
Spanish	529	254
US	–	–

Lights
Approach
1. **Sidi Mogul** 31°29'·6N 9°45'·9W
   Oc.WRG.4s18m14-9M 034°-G-124°-W-136°-R-214°-W-260°-W(unintens)-350°-W-034° Tower

Harbour
2. **Jetty head** 31°30'·5N 9°46'·6W Q.8m12M Horn 60s 208°-vis-108° Column
3. **Spur** Oc(2)R.6s2m6M Red pedestal Obscd seaward
4. **E Mole head** Fl.G.4s2m5M Pedestal.

General
This stretch, 56M from Safi, evidences a change from rocky cliffs to desert. Features along the coast include: a tower 80m high, 3M SW of Sidi Rhouzia (32°15'N 9°16'W) and, 4M further south, a red cliff, Jorf el Houdi, distinctive in its sugar-loaf shape. Another similarly shaped cliff lies 7M further SW.

A mile north of Oued Tensift River, 3M south of Soueira Kedima, the ruins of an old Portuguese fort can be seen. The wide Oued Tensift looks inviting, but has a shallow sand-bar, making entry impossible. Ten miles further SW, the tomb of Sidi Yssahak is conspicuous. Several more white-painted tombs can be seen between Sidi Yssahak and Cap Hadid (31°42'N, 9°41'W). This cape should be given a clearance of 3M, as submerged rocks extend offshore. Jebel Hadid, a mountain range a short distance inland extending from Oued Tensift to Cap Hadid, can be clearly seen from several miles offshore. 10M north of Essaouira, is the tomb of Moulay Bouzerktoun. This white-painted tomb on a low-lying cliff connects to a small fortress, now occupied by shepherds, with a well to the west of the outer wall serving a small settlement nearby. Sandy beaches are the main feature approaching Essaouira, with the snow-capped Atlas mountains visible in the background.

The NW swell along this part of the coast is rarely less than 2m high for most of the year. Current is negligible. Winds are generally from the SW, except for strong northerly winds which often occur from April to August. From August to November, winds are usually light. Winter storms usually begin in December, bringing strong SW gales until March, with a swell of around 5m.

Approach
A rocky reef extends west of the harbour and an island to the south. Entry should be made between the eastern dique and the island Isle de Mogador, on a course of 128° heading for the lighthouse Phare de Mogdoul. Enter once the breakwater is 10° abaft the beam, where minimum depths of 2·5m will be found in mid-channel. The harbour diques are well lit at night, but usually lines are stretched across the entrance of the harbour after dusk.

Berthing
The harbour gives good protection in all weather conditions, although a land breeze funnels through the entrance. Minimum depths of 3m are to be found in mid-harbour. Although mooring rings can be seen on the jetty, do not approach the end section of the eastern wall, as a shallow rocky ledge extends from it. Instead, moor alongside the jetty next to Chez Sam restaurant, close to the harbourmaster's office.

Formalities
Essaouira is a port of entry and officials will come to the yacht. The port authorities are very friendly, if quite inquisitive.

Facilities
Water On the quay by arrangement with the restaurant Chez Sam.
Fuel Can be brought to the boat
Provisions Local shops and the market are near to the port and can supply most provisions.
Gas Camping Gaz readily available.
Post office and banks In the centre of town.
Repairs Most repairs can be undertaken locally. A slipway at the north end of the port can facilitate haul-out of vessels. Although unaccustomed to keel yachts, these small boatyards are generally well able to cope with unusual situations and any hull shapes, using various wedges and blocks.
Charges None at present.

Eating out
Unlike Safi, where the police exclude all casual visitors from the port, in Essaouira the public are encouraged to mingle with the fishermen and to eat in one of the restaurants inside the port. These are of two kinds: an open area with tantalising aromas where fresh fish are grilled by several independent fisherman-chefs along the quayside, and a more traditional restaurant at the end of the port (Chez Sam). The small open air grills allow you to choose your fish from well presented selections, negotiate the price per kilo and see it cooked to perfection in front of your eyes. Chez Sam has excellent seafood, atmosphere and service, and lunch at the grills is a must! The Chalet de la Plage on the corniche is slightly more expensive than other restaurants, but

North Africa

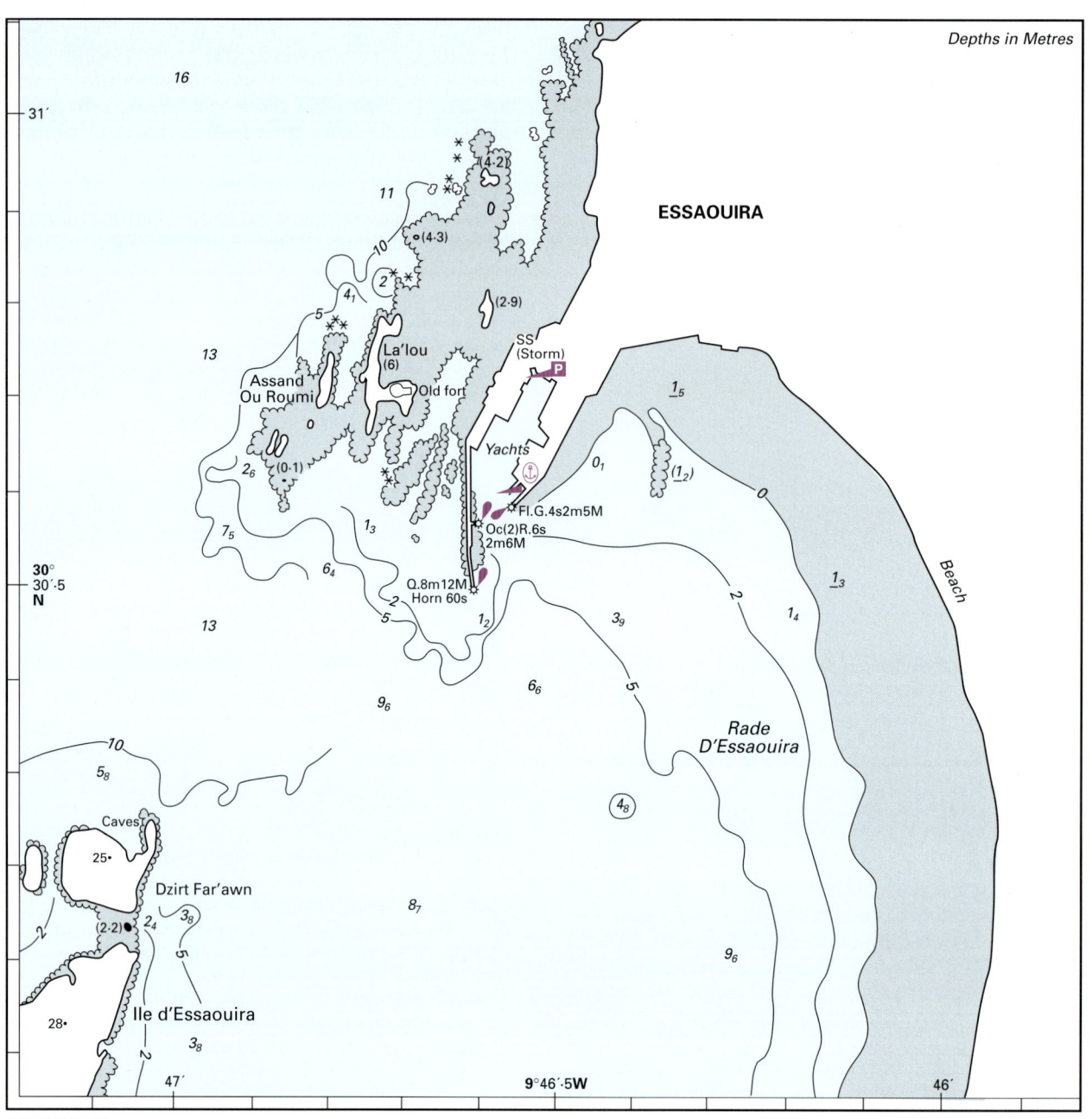

ESSAOUIRA

its lovely terrace bar and the quality of its food make it well worth it. For superb Moroccan food in a truly superb Moroccan setting, dine at the small Hotel Villa Maroc (10 Rue Abdellah Ben Yassin, just to the right and behind the clocktower). Chez Toufik near the clocktower, and café-restaurants Essalam and Bab Laachour in Place Prince Moulay el Hassan, all also come well recommended.

Tourism
The change from a rural industrial area to the more placid life of the nearby Sahara desert becomes more apparent in Essaouira. After the busy port of Safi, Essaouira is a pleasant, unhurried town and the port reflects this in its relaxed atmosphere.

Designed by a French architect-engineer in the 18th century, Essaouira is much more orderly than most Moroccan cities and is very easy to get around.

Passing through the gate in the harbour wall takes you to Place Moulay el Hassan, a long open avenue and hub of social life. In addition to a Tourist Office, banks, cafés and some fine restaurants are located in this plaza: Jack's Kiosk is an important landmark. Every essential can be found at Jack's, from newspapers, magazines and second-hand books in diverse languages, to international telephones, a fax machine and assistance with travel arrangements ranging from local tours to international flights.

More conservative than in the north, women here tend to be more closely veiled. Some restaurants near Place Prince Moulay el Hassan have separate dining rooms for them.

From Place Moulay Hassan towards the sea, the profusion of beautiful objects made and sold in the woodworkers' *souk* (see *Local Specialities*) can be seen. Or proceed north-eastwards, towards the spice and jewellery *souks*. Before the predominantly Jewish jewellers left Essaouira in the late 1950s, this Souk des Bijoutiers was renowned for its jewellery; today some silverwork is still done here. Beyond these *souks*, at the far north end of the medina, is the Mellah, or former Jewish quarter, now abandoned. By the mid-19th century, Jews comprised one third of the population of the town, some 4,000 people. But by the late 1960s, prompted by changes in attitude relating to Moroccan independence and fear of reprisal for aggressive Israeli military actions, most of them had left.

Darb Laalouj is a cross-street on this general north-south axis which houses many woodworkers as well as the excellent Museum of Sidi Mohammed Ibn Abdellah (Museum of Traditional Arts and Heritage of Essaouira, closed Tuesdays). This museum, once the home of a pasha, contains carpets, traditional weapons and musical instruments with superb marquetry inlay, objects showing the long history of the tradition of thuya marquetry and woodworking in Essaouira, displays which suggest the meaning of Berber symbols found on diverse art forms, etc.

Near the western end of Darb Laalouj lies the entrance to the Skala de la Ville. Impressive European cannon line these great sea ramparts and from their North Bastion, one can get an overview of the Medina and Mellah.

The Isles Purpuraires were renowned in Roman times as the source of dyes for the imperial robes of the Caesars. King Juba II (to whom Caesar Augustus had granted the Kingdom of Mauritania Tingitana circa 25BC), established factories here for the extraction of drops of colour from a certain type of mussel. Subsequently, attending Caligula's games in Lyon, Juba's son and successor, the extravagant Ptolemy, wore purple robes of such magnificence that he was assassinated for his presumption by the Emperor. Nowadays these islands are renowned for another rarity, their birds, especially the Eleanora's Falcon, and visiting is restricted. Permission can be obtained to visit the islands by boat, as explained in the Tourist Office in Place Prince Moulay el Hassan.

The climate is more tropical in Essaouira. With a constant high Atlantic swell and a breeze for most of the year, this is an ideal location for surfing. Many surfers head south of town (off the road to Agadir) to the extensive sandy beaches known as the *plages sauvages*.

An early morning bus leaves for Marrakesh from the Hotel des Isles, just south of the port overlooking the beach. This bus is timed to link up with trains from Marrakesh to Rabat and Casablanca. Otherwise, the new bus station is unfortunately some 2km east of the north gate of town (Bab Doukkala), and due both to its distance and to the unsavoury nature of the 'suburbs' and Quartier Industrielle en route, taking a taxi there is advised. (There is a petit taxi rank by the clock tower near Place Prince Moulay el Hassan.) Grand taxis and buses for all other destinations leave from this new bus station. Note that on the return trip, however, grand taxis are usually willing to let you off at Bab Doukkala or the clock tower.

History

Essaouira was visited from at least the seventh century BC. by the Phoenicians, but its first prominence in the ancient world dates from the first century AD, when it was known in Rome as the source of imperial purple dyes and fine marquetry woodwork. For a short time after 533 Essaouira was occupied by the Byzantines, who reinstituted Christianity in Morocco after the Vandal depredations which had led to the sack of Rome, but when the first wave of Arabs spreading Islam swept across North Africa in the late 7th century, they found avid converts in Moroccan Berbers. By the 10th century the town, already an important port which transmitted all goods from southern Morocco, was known as Amogdul (the well-guarded), after the Berber Muslim patron saint of the city, Sidi Mogdul, who is buried 3km away.

The Portuguese distorted 'Amogdul' into 'Mogdura' (a name later transformed by the Spanish into Mogadur and by the French into Mogador). Some vestiges remain of the Portuguese royal palace of 1506, built at the port entrance. As always, these colonisers sought to dominate the export of goods coming across the Sahara and from the south of Morocco, but in the region of Mogdura they also developed a profitable sugar cane industry. In 1541, however, the Portuguese were forced to abandon Mogdura along with Safi and Agadir.

In 1764, the Alaouite Sultan Sidi Mohammed Ben Abdellah (1757–90) decided to make this a key military and commercial port. Enraged by its treacherous alliances with Europeans, his goal was to eclipse and pacify Agadir, and he charged a French architect prisoner, Theodore Cornut, with devising a new plan for Mogdura. Its wide, orderly streets and French-style city walls and ramparts date from this moment. In Arabic the town was renamed Essaouira, or 'fortified place', and well fortified it was: the immense artillery platform of La Skala defended the city from sea attacks, while city walls repelled insurgent tribes on land. The Sultan ordered all foreign consuls at Agadir to move their bases to Essaouira, and summoned the wealthiest businessmen of the kingdom, including many Jewish merchants. By 1780 Essaouira had some 40% of the maritime trade of Morocco, at least a thousand European residents, and an extremely diverse body of Moroccans. In the 19th century Essaouira was the only Moroccan port south of Tanger open to European trade, and thanks to its protected trade status it continued to flourish.

Under the French Protectorate this cosmopolitan city entered a severe decline due to the promotion of the ports of Casablanca and Agadir and, in the late 1950s, to the exodus of the Jews. Although it was

North Africa

popular in the 1960s and '70s with occasional hippies such as Jimi Hendrix, Essaouira has only recently recovered its balance as a small-scale but thriving fishing and market town and tourist destination. However, it is home to many famous artists.

Local specialities

According to Cicero, the magnificent marquetry tables of Essaouira were highly prized in Rome. To this day, the quality of woodworking here is as breathtaking as the wood principally used for its execution. Thuya, a beautiful walnut-like wood derived from a coniferous tree rare elsewhere, grows abundantly around Essaouira. It is used extensively in the production of ornamental objects: bowls, boxes, candlesticks, lamp-holders, carvings and desktop items, both for everyday use by Moroccans and for the tourist trade. Since thuya is very brittle, it is not ideal for the construction of larger pieces of furniture, although a few large ornate chests and tables are made from it. The root is very hard and has the same characteristics as burr walnut. The trunk has a grain similar to walnut but more exotic. Local craftsmen always give the wood a highly polished finish using the traditional French polish technique. Banding and cross banding are used to create decorative effects similar to those characteristic of Sheraton furniture; in Essaouira, local craftsmen obtain exactly the same contrasts by using white lime wood in place of the boxwood of Sheraton, and by burning lime to produce a hard black wood resembling ebony. Mother of pearl and silver wire are also used as inlay to produce decorative effects.

The woodworkers' *souk* runs along the rampart walls along the Rue de la Skala, and on streets perpendicular to it. Essaouira is unusual in that there seems to be no pressure to purchase and on the base of most items can be found the price – or at least the starting point for negotiations. A reduction of about 30% can be expected after haggling. As in Safi, you will also be invited to see the craftsmen at work producing these beautiful handmade items. Note particularly the exact fitting lids and the very high quality of finish on almost everything. Many of the abstract forms made from the natural twisting roots are truly spectacular and very cheap. For some contemporary pieces which play upon these natural abstractions, visit the Galerie d'Art Frederic Damgaard (Av. Oqba Ibn Nafia), the owner of which is a talented Danish furniture designer.

Agadir
30°25'·18N 09°37'·9W

Distances
Essaouira 65M Lanzarote 112M

Tides

	MHWS	MHWN
Range	3–7m	2–8m

Charts

	Approach	Port
Admiralty	3133	863
French	6178	5955
Spanish	217, 530	181

Lights
Approach
1. **Cap Sim** 31°23'·9N 9°49'·9W Fl(3)15s104m21M Turret on fort black/white bands
2. **Cap Ghir** 30°38'·1N 9°53'·1W Fl.5s85m22M White tower

Harbour
3. **Grande Jetée** Oc(2)R.6s8m8M Reed(2)30s Red and white tower
4. **E breakwater** Fl(2)G.6s5m4M White tower, green top

Port d'Anza
5. **W mole** Fl.R.4s.5M White and red tower
6. **E mole** Fl.G.4s.5M White and green tower

Coastline from Essaouira to Agadir

With a backdrop of the snow-capped Atlas Mountains, this shoreline consists of rocky cliffs, mountains, long beaches and desert scrubland. Cap Sim is formed by a cliff 100m high with a rocky reef extending 1 mile W of the cape. The lighthouse is a large tower with black and white bands, with four smaller towers surrounding it. A 3 mile clearance should be given to the cape. A conspicuous tower (31°10'N 9°40'W) 10M ENE of Cap Tafelney, stands on Jebel Amsittene, which is 1,000m high. A reef extends 3½M from Cap Tafelney. From Cap Tafelney to Cap Rhir (30°38'N 9°53'W) the coastline is mountainous. This promontory is 360m high and the lighthouse can be clearly seen. Agadir lies 18M S of the cape. Currents along the coast are south, ½ to ¾kts. Just S of the harbour entrance, currents going NE at 2kts have been encountered.

Brief squalls can be experienced at any time in this area, especially around the capes, caused by the extreme differences of temperature between the snowy mountain tops of the Atlas range and the hot desert sands. Generally during summer, periods of calms can be expected, with land and sea breezes alternating from the W to E. In winter, Atlantic depressions sweeping through the Canaries give rise to a very heavy and dangerous swell, sometimes reaching 12m. Fog is frequent from June to October.

General

Agadir is the most important of the southern Moroccan ports. For most yachtsmen this will be the preferred departure point for the Canary Islands and across the Atlantic, being 112M from

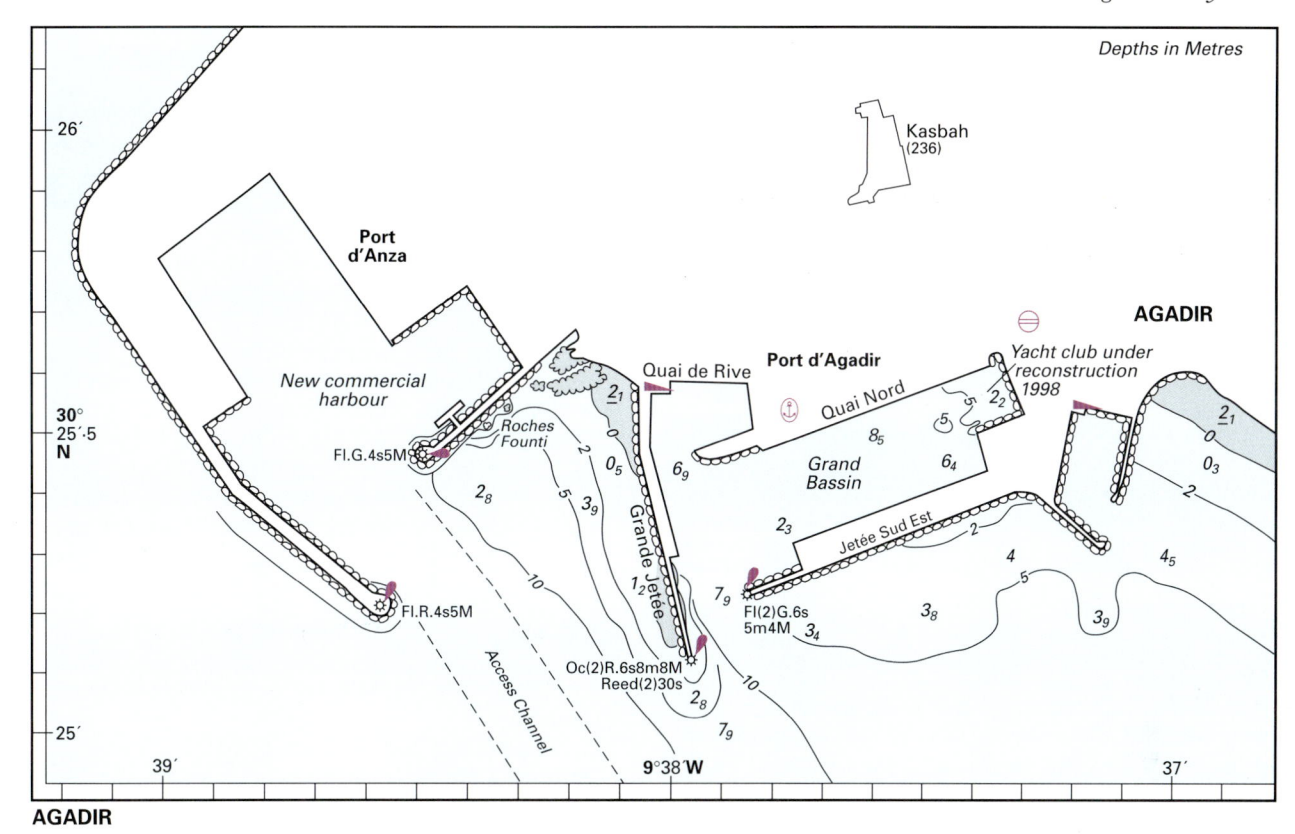

Lanzarote. The Moroccan Saharan coastline continues south for another 600M. Agadir is a new town and the harbour is artificial, although sheltered by Pointe Arhesdis. The harbour is busy and a swell caused by the traffic in and out is noticeable.

A new harbour, Port d'Anza, is almost complete (1998) adjoining the present port to the NW. Plans are in hand to develop a new marina, but it is not known if this is in the new harbour or the old one.

Although entry is difficult in strong westerlies, this is a well protected harbour which can be entered at any time. Beware of tunny nets laid out from April to September, which can extend 4M from the shore.

Approach
Three lighted buoys form a transit with the inner W mole giving entry from the south into the harbour, following the Grande Jetée.

Entry
Depths in the entrance are in excess of 7m. Once round the E breaker turn right, past the ferry terminal on the right and the Moroccan Navy berths left, and continue to the Eastern end of the harbour.

Berthing
Some moorings are available, but they are usually occupied by local boats. Anchor in 4 to 5m as close to the yacht moorings as is practical. It may be possible to anchor stern or bows to the pontoon, if there is a space. It is often possible to moor alongside another yacht if the harbour area is too crowded to anchor.

Agadir

North Africa

Old Agadir yacht basin

Formalities
Agadir is a port of entry and the port officials are very friendly and relaxed. The harbour authorities do not come to the yacht: head for the yacht club office and you will be directed to the customs and police offices.
Port VHF Ch 16, 12, 24hrs.

Facilities
Water Available on the quay.
Electricity No supply unless you can get to the pontoon.
Fuel Can be supplied in cans, or from the fishing harbour.
Provisions Local shops very close to the port have all the usual commodities. A small shop selling drinks and bread is located within the port.
Gas Camping Gaz available in the town along with the larger old style bottles.
Post office and banks In the centre of town.
Repairs There is a slipway for emergencies in the fishing harbour. All the usual Moroccan chandlery items are available here, including polypropylene rope, galvanised rigging screws and other fittings.
Charges A small charge is made for berthing by the yacht club.

Eating out
Many superb local and tourist type restaurants are in the town. Inevitably, fish is the main local dish.

Tourism
Agadir is a new town and all that remains of the old city, destroyed in an earthquake in 1960, is the restored *kasbah*. These ruins are worth a visit and are a solemn reminder of the incredible forces of nature which we are powerless to subdue.

Local specialities
This is a modern tourist town, complete with a casino. Tourism is the largest industry here, with a local airport serving the town with international flights, mostly via Marrakech and Casablanca. As you travel south on this Atlantic coast, the fish get bigger and better.

Atlantic coast of Morocco – continuing south

Further south facilities are sparse, but the following are mentioned because of their location as landmarks along hundreds of miles of deserted beaches. There are plans to develop some of these facilities into ports. The coastline is mainly desert, with 500M of sand and spectacular dunes. The area is very exposed with no bays or safe anchorages for protection in poor weather. Many wrecks can be seen on the beaches between Agadir and Dakhlak.

A light, Cala Nun (Cap Drâa) Fl(2)25M (28°40'·5N 11°07'·5W) lies on the beach five miles S of Cala Nun between Sidi Ifni and Tan Tan. It does not relate to either port but is a coastal marker beween the two at the the entrance of an unnamed river.

Sidi Ifni
29°22'·8N 10°11'W

Tides
Tidal range here reduces to 1·9m MHWS and a mean range of 1·6m.

Chart
Admiralty 3133, 863

Lights
Approach
1. **LtHo** NE of the jetée Fl(1+3)30s57m25M F.R 80m on 4 radio masts 2·2M ENE
Harbour
2. **Jetty head** Iso.R.4s11m5M Fl.R.3s marks inner jetty head
3. **Overhead transporter** Fl.4s10m5M

Facilities
Consist of a double fingered jetty, with good anchoring for yachts in settled weather. Anchor in 2·5m of sand in the SE lee of the inner jetty. Although not a port of entry, there are local shops nearby which can be visited with the permission of local police.

Tan Tan
28°29'N 11°20'W

Chart
Admiralty 3133

Lights
Approach
1. **Cap Nachtigal LtHo** (NE of the port) Fl.5s35m15M Tower.
Fishing Harbour
2. **Main SW Jetty head** F.13m Black pedestal
3. **Spur head** F.R 11m Red pedestal
4. **Cross Jetty head** F.G.11m Green pedestal

Until recently this was a small fishing port which can be used by yachts. The port is being enlarged to accommodate larger ships. The breakwaters have recently been extended and the port facilities considerably enlarged for commercial use.

Atlantic coast of Morocco

Tan Tan

Tarfaya
27°53'·1N 12°57'·2W

Lights
1. **Lighthouse** Fl(2)10s17M 27°55'·3N 12°56'·3W Masonry tower 13m 3F.R(vert) on radio mast 1·6M NNE

A small port on the point of C Juby is being enlarged and dredged.

Tarfaya new port development

Laayoune
27°07'N 13°26'W (Fishing harbour)
27°04'N 13°27'·8W (Muelle de Forbucraa – long mole)

Chart
Admiralty 3133, 863

Lights
1. **Fishing Mole** Fl(2)4s
2. **Barge Berth head** WR.11m18M W7M/R5M. 010°-W-070°-070°-R-010°.
3. **Muelle de Forbucraa** 27°03'·9N 13°27'·7W Fl.5s 48m18M Reed Mo(U)120s
4. **North end** F.G.17m3M White and green post.
5. **South end** F.R.17m3M White and red post.

General
Facilities here consist of a small fishing harbour to the N, and a mile SW, a two mile long pier extending towards a disused phosphate berth, now used mainly as a fuelling jetty and for landing provisions for this isolated town. A cargo jetty is located half way along the S side of this pier.

The harbour provides limited shelter for the local fishing fleet. Anchorage is possible inside the south-going mole of the fishing Muelle de Forbucraa head (27°03'·9N 13°27'·7W) Fl.5s18M. Light (on end of barge berth jetée) WR.18M. Lights at 30m intervals along jetty.

Laayoune, not easily missed: the jetty is 4 miles long!

Dakhla
23°41'·8N 15°55'·3W

Light
Muelle Transversal No 3 Head Q(3)G.6s8m4M Grey truncated conical tower 5m RC 1·7M N. Obstruction light on radio mast 0·7M WNW, on TV mast 0·6M WNW

General
The last port of Morocco, on the Tropic of Cancer,

73

North Africa

Dakhla: Long jetty built to clear the shoaling sands

180M from the border with Mauritania. A huge natural south-going protective finger provides shelter from the west, but is open to the south. A long dique extends to offer deep water facilities for commercial shipping. Resolving the political issue of this area makes it expedient to develop the facilities here and the government is keen to include the area in its plan and make it an important addition to the maritime infrastructure. Phosphates and other minerals abound in the region and the fishing grounds are amongst the best in the world.

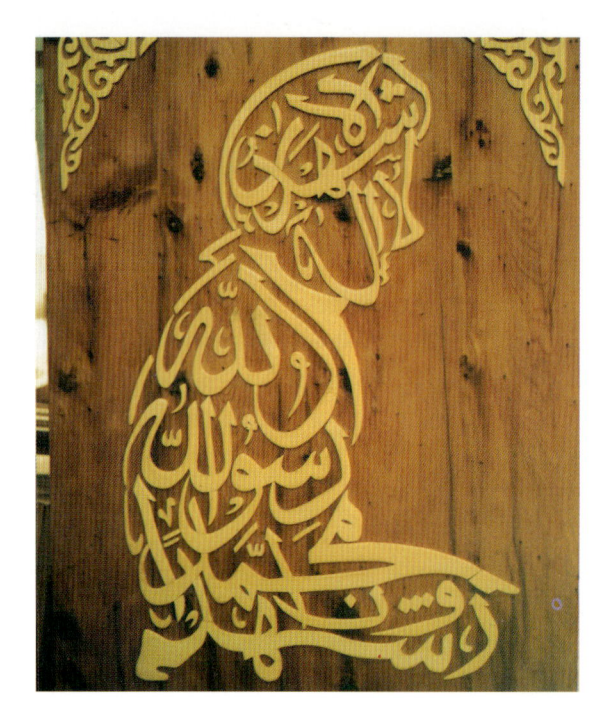

A fine example of Islamic art

2. Mediterranean coast. Straits of Gibraltar to Saidia

This section covers the Western Straits into the Mediterranean, including the Spanish enclaves and islands to the Algerian border.

General

Sea level at Tanger is some 2 to 3m higher than in the Mediterranean. When sailing through the Strait into the Mediterranean with the predominantly westerly wind behind, a feeling of going 'downhill' is reinforced by the fast moving currents that are almost always E-going, even when the tide is going W. Most yachts call in at Gibraltar or begin their journey to Morocco from there, hence Gibraltar is covered in this pilot.

The constant flow of water from the cold Atlantic into warm waters of the Mediterranean give rise to an abundant fish life in the Strait. Many dolphins and different species of whales are invariably seen accompanying the yacht for parts of the journey. Heavy overfalls and currents are present in the areas E of Tanger bay, Tarifa Point and Ceuta.

Ksar-es-Seghir

35°51'N 5°33'·5W

Light

The light of Punta de Alcazar, mounted on the pier head of Ksar, was destroyed in 1988, but has recently been replaced. Characteristics not yet known.

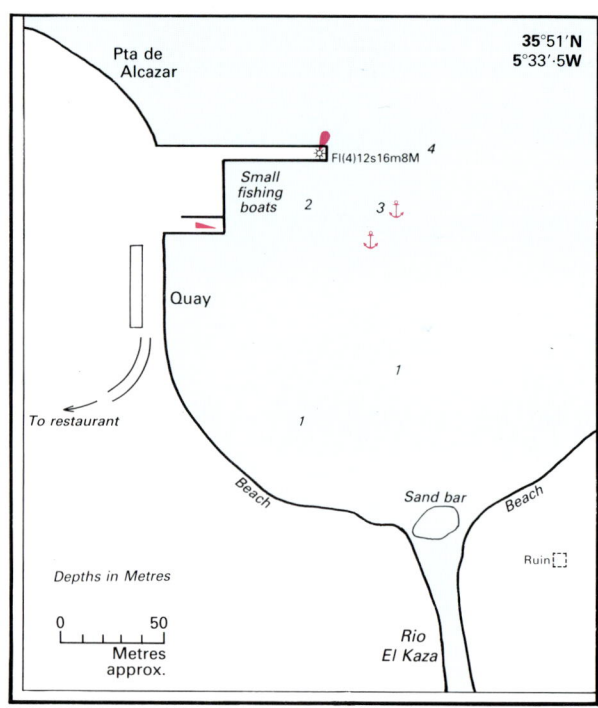

KSAR-ES-SEGHIR

General

Ksar-es-Seghir, midway between Tanger and Ceuta, is a useful anchorage when current and wind from the W makes the passage of the Strait eastwards a useless effort and, though within sight of Gibraltar and Tanger, its remoteness makes a refreshing contrast to the big ports. The small pier jutting out E from Punta de Alcazar is home base for a small fleet of open fishing boats. Landing is prohibited: this is not a port of entry and has no facilities. This small village is on a route known as *Routa de Contrabandistas*: the smugglers route, which runs between Ceuta (Sebta) and Tanger. For this reason, there is a heavy police and military presence in the hills above. However, yachts have been allowed to anchor in the bay to await the tide change.

Anchorage

Anchor SE of the destroyed light but keep an eye on the echo sounder as depths decrease to less than 2m towards the quay and S towards the beach. The spring range is about 1·5m. Protection from the W is reasonable but swell from the NW may roll around the pier and to the E it is quite open. On the S side of the bay is a river which can be explored by dinghy. There is a restaurant and bar a short distance from the landing up on the hill and some basic provisions are obtainable – if you can negotiate your way ashore with the local police.

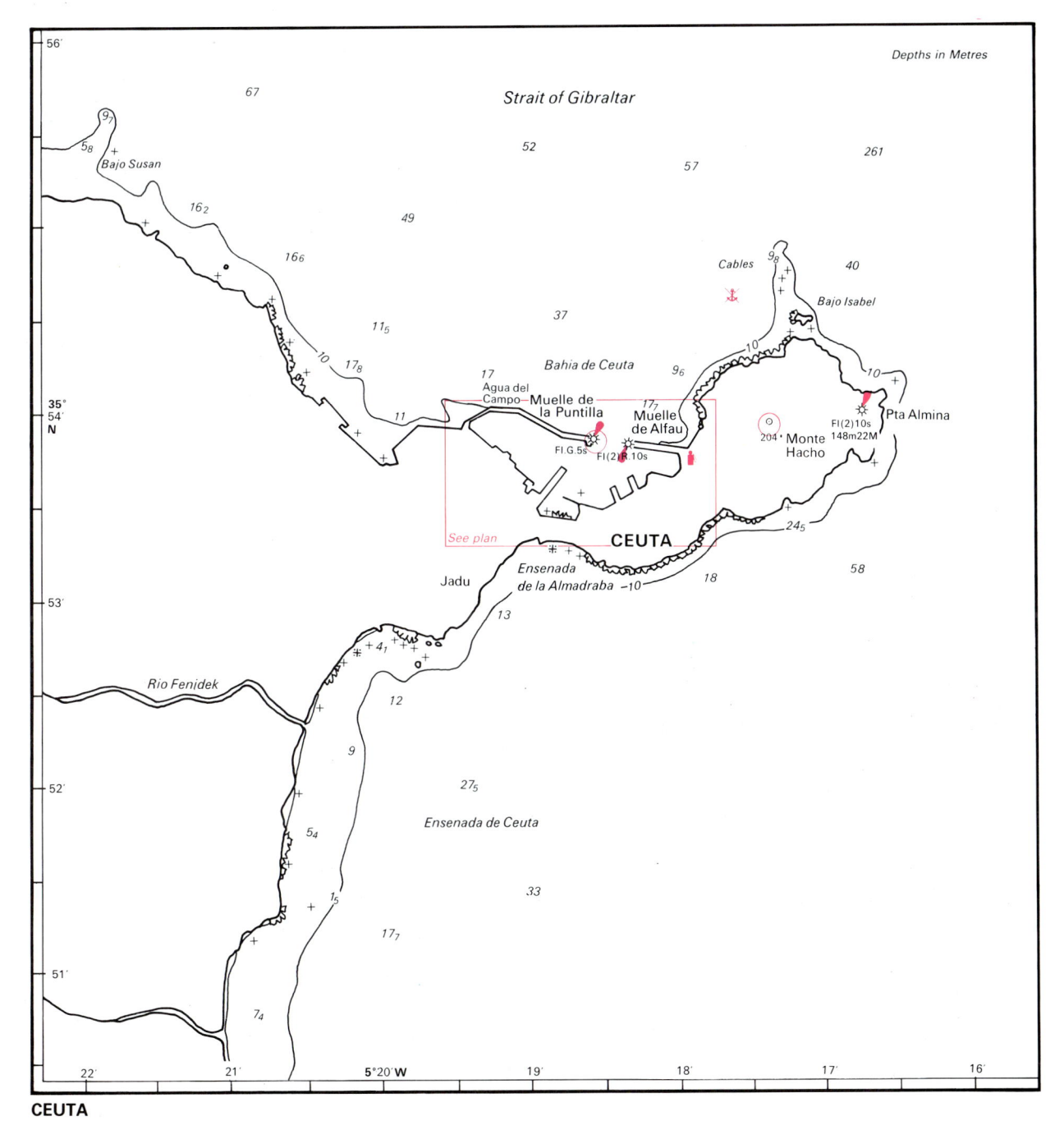

CEUTA

North Africa

Ceuta (Sebta)
35°53'·5N 5°18'W

Distances
Tanger 27M, Gibraltar 15M – M'Diq 16M

Tides
MHWS	MHWN	MLWN	MLWS
1m	0·8m	0·4m	0·2m

Charts
	Approach	Port
Admiralty	92, 142, 773, 3578	2742
French	7042, 7300	7503
Spanish	44C, 105, 445, 451	4511
US	52039	52048

Lights
Approach
1. **Punta Almina** 35°54'N 5°16'·8W
   Fl(2)10s148m22M Siren(2)45s White tower on building

Harbour
2. **Dique de Poniente** Fl.G.5s13m10M Siren 15s Conical concrete tower F.R on Tank Farm 1·3m W
3. **Dique de Levante** Fl.R.5s13m5M Conical concrete tower
4. **Spur E corner** Fl(2)G.8s7m1M Green post
5. **Muelle de Espana head W corner** Fl(2+1)R.12s7m1M Red post green band
6. **Nuevo Porto Deportivo breakwater head** Fl(4)R.11s8m1M Red round mast
7. **Breakwater** Fl(4)G.11s6m1M Green metal post
8. **Head** Fl(4)G.11s5m1M Green round metal mast
9. **Muelle de Ribera W** Oc.G.4s8m1M Green round metal mast
10. **E end** Fl(2+1)G.21s7m1M Green round metal mast, red band.

General
Ceuta, (known as Sebta in Morocco) has been a Spanish enclave since the 16th century. After Moroccan independence in 1956 Spain retained it because of its strategic location. Ceuta is still an important Spanish military base and, as a duty-free port, it has become a shopping centre for Spanish families from the mainland and for Moroccan guest workers returning home from their work in Europe during the summer as well as many Moroccans who daily cross the border to purchase commodities cheaper, or not available in Morocco.

Formally considered unsuitable for yachts, Ceuta now has a splendid new marina and is an excellent place to stock up: probably the best and cheapest in the western Mediterranean. Fuel is much cheaper than on the Spanish mainland, or in Morocco with petrol currently costing Pts64 ($0.42) per litre and diesel Pts45 ($0.29) per litre (May 1998). Security has been greatly improved for yachts with the introduction of gates to access the pontoons and magnetic locks with keys only available to yacht crews.

Approach
The hills on the W side of Ceuta are high (850m) and very steep; Ceuta itself is low-lying and the hill to the east, Monte Hacho is only 200m, but the lighthouse at Punta Almina, where the coast turns S for some miles, is prominent. There are low-lying rocks to the E of the entrance, N of Monte Hacho. The final approach has to be made from the N quadrant so care must be taken with the set and tide in the strait, especially in strong westerly winds. Ferries from Algeciras will be seen entering or leaving the harbour every few hours throughout the day.

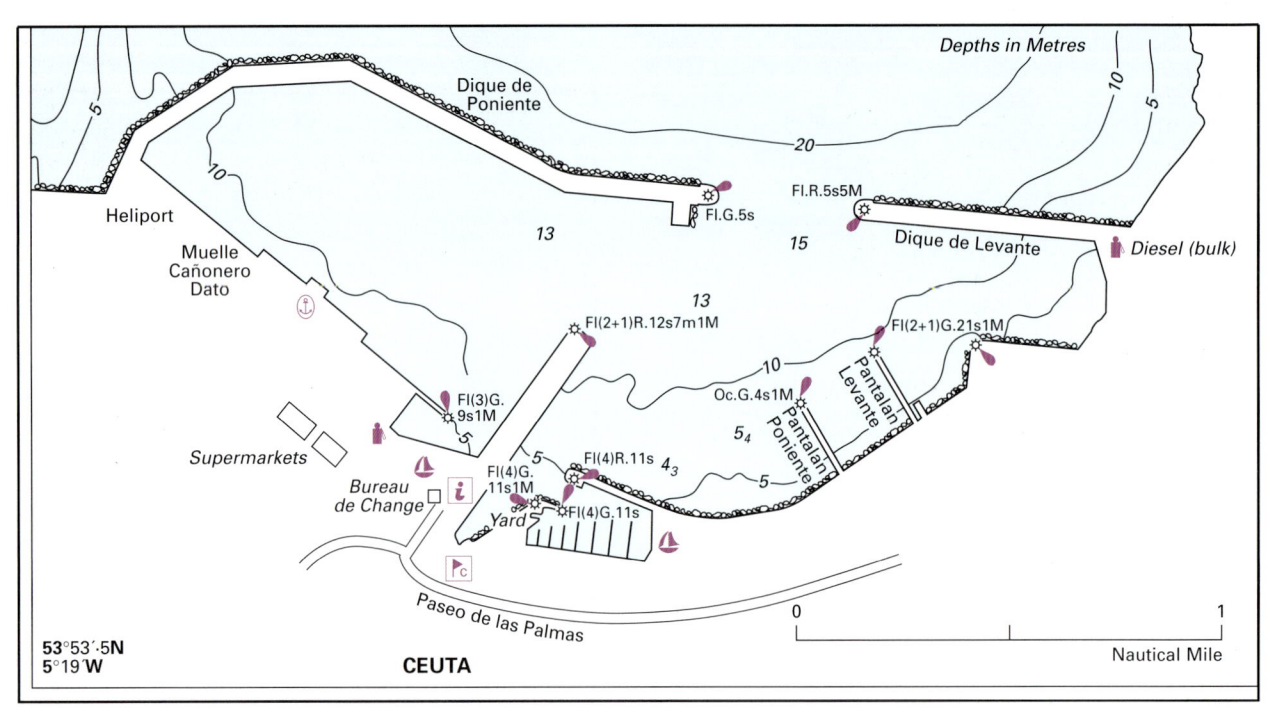

CEUTA

The new marina Ceuta (Sebta)

Entry
Once through the outer moles, continue SSW where a large limestone observation tower will be seen with a nearby light mounted on a lower white-painted tower. The marina is just beyond the tower.

Berthing
Pontoons will be seen once round the tower. The outer pontoons nearest the tower have depths of around 4m. Moorings are available for up to 200 boats.

Formalities
Marina Office ☎ 908 502274, Port Authority ☎ 956 502274. VHF Ch 16, 9, 12, 13, 14, 15 24hrs.

As in Spain, there is no need to seek out customs and immigration, although they may call at the yacht and check that papers are in order.

Facilities
Water and electricity At each berth on the quay.
Fuel From a pump on the quay. Large quantities (over 300 litres) can be bought at a lower price from a fishing boat supply point in the NE corner of the commercial port. Allow time for the attendant to show up and beware of the oily quay.
Showers and toilets A security key to the pontoons and toilet facilities is available from the marina office. This is located on the first floor of *club nautico* at the western end of the marina.
Provisions Two large supermarkets are close to the marina and both have a wide choice of articles especially suited for yachts such as powdered milk, canned butter, meat, dried hams, fruits and vegetables, beer, wine and spirits at lower prices than the Spanish *hipermercados*. Other shops sell everything from food to diving equipment, fishing tackle, portable radios, television sets, cameras, etc. These are very much cheaper than in Gibraltar and on the Spanish mainland.
Gas Available in the town or by arrangement with the marina office. If you have an odd fitting, ask a taxi driver for the gas plant, Butano SA. You can wait while your bottles are being filled. All types of bottles can be filled including Calor Gas butane bottles with snap-on fittings and propane bottles.
Post office and banks In the centre of town. There are change shops around the ferry terminal but check their exchange rates and commissions.
Repairs A light hoist (8 tons) is located in the marina. Most emergency repairs can be taken care of and a wide range of nautical chandlery is available here.
Charges Excellent value at $11·00 per day for a 15 metre yacht, with a negotiable discount for longer stays.

Eating out
There are many restaurants of all categories in the centre of town.

Tourism
There are several museums illustrating the rich history of Ceuta. The fortifications, which are mainly of Portuguese origin, are worth a walk around and there are fine views across to Gibraltar from Monte Hacho. The tourist office, located on the way out of the port, has more detailed information. The walk to the centre along the palm tree-lined Paseo de las Palmeras is pleasant but the centre is very crowded with banks and shops.

The border with Morocco is 3km away: a short taxi ride, or a regular bus service operates from the town to the border. If you want to visit Morocco from here, buses and taxis await on the Moroccan side. Tetuan is half an hour from the border and the two modern marinas of Kabila and Marina Smir are ten minutes away by taxi.

A daily ferry service operates to Algeciras.

Restinga (Marina) Smir
35°45′N 5°20′·1W

Distances
Gibraltar 26M, Ceuta 12M – M'Diq 4M

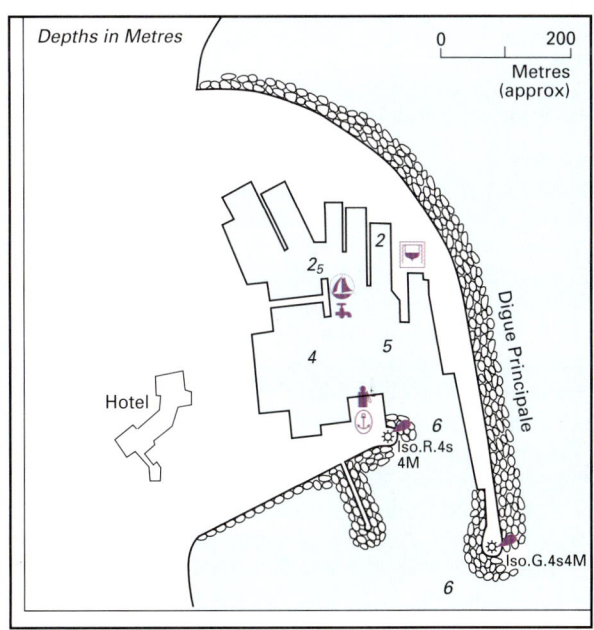

RESTINGA SMIR

North Africa

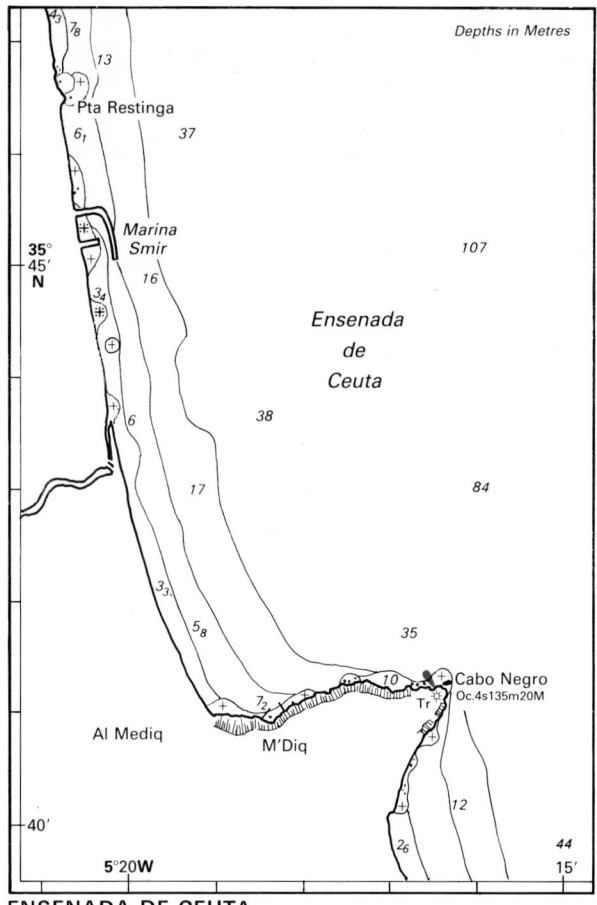

ENSENADA DE CEUTA

Tides
MHWS	MHWN	MLWN	MLWS
1·0m	0·8m	0·4m	0·2m

Charts
	Approach	Port
Admiralty	773, 142	–
French	7042	–
Spanish	445, 451	–
US	52040	–

Lights
Harbour
1. **N mole** Iso.G.4s11m4M
2. **S mole** Iso.R.4s7m4M

General
The first marina to be built on the Mediterranean coast of Morocco, Marina Smir was constructed on a deserted beach 1 mile S of Point Restinga, between Ceuta and M'Diq. Work was carried out by a Romanian company in exchange for phosphates, with Saudi finance for the hotels and apartments built around the port. The port facilities are owned by Marina Marbella and it is run on Spanish lines. Unfortunately it is more expensive than most Spanish marinas and is usually empty, although berthing for over 300 yachts are available.

Once inside, this is a superb marina and very safe in all weather conditions. Entry can be difficult in strong E winds due to the swell that builds up around the entrance. The marina is very clean, and a secure place to leave your yacht for inland excursions.

Approach
Entry from Ceuta is straightforward by identifying Jebel Zem Zem, marked on the charts, and heading to the left hand slope of the mountain. To the right will be seen a large white hotel complex: Club Mediterranée, which lies less than two miles W of the port. The breakwater is difficult to see until about two miles off, as it blends into the surrounding beach dunes. However, there are no other constructions nearby and the large travel-hoist will be seen first. Beware of tunny nets laid out 4M NW of the port on a direct line with Ceuta. A small boat with a stub mast marks the end of the nets. This marker is often not lit at night.

Entry
Minimum depths in the entrance channel are 4m. On entering the port keep in mid channel and head for the control tower and fuelling jetty, where customs and other port officials will be waiting.

Berthing
Marina officials will direct you to a berth after customs and immigration formalities are completed.

Formalities
Port ☎ 977126 VHF Ch 9.

Smir is a port of entry and immigration officials, customs and local police are all conveniently located on the entry pier and are very efficient. There is an extensive police and military presence in the port.

Note The port gained a very bad reputation over the past few years as the police have carried out extensive and indiscriminate searches on yachts on arrival and departure. This was largely due to problems caused by smugglers from Gibraltar using the port as a base for operations. However, with the improvements since the change of government in Gibraltar and the ban there on the use of RIB launches, problems are not as frequent.

Facilities
Water and electricity On the quay at every berth.
Fuel Available from pumps at the control tower jetty.
Shower and toilet facilities By arrangement with the tower who issue a key. Very clean.
Provisions A local shop selling fresh provisions is located just outside the port. M'diq is a short distance by taxi and is a small town with most items available.
Gas Available from nearby M'Diq.
Post office and banks In M'Diq town and in Tetuan.
Telephone Located in the marina office block. All connections are manual via an operator.
Repairs Facilities for haul out are excellent, with a 200-ton travel-hoist and very clean conditions. Mechanics and other workers can be arranged with the marina.
Prices A 12-metre yacht is charged Dh172 per day, plus Dh 35 per day for water and electricity, plus tax at 20% – over $25 per day. These are summer rates. There is a deposit to be paid for the use of an electric plug, which is usually necessary, since it is an unusual fitting.

Eating out
Several restaurants are located within the port complex, including Chinese, Lebanese and high-

class Moroccan restaurants. These are very expensive and one might consider a short excursion to M'Diq, where many open-air or more up-market fish restaurants can be found either along the seafront or on a parallel street. Aladdin's Lamp: a restaurant with several distinctive Persian style round towers, will be found four miles from M'Diq on the road to Tetuan and provides excellent typically Moroccan dishes at very reasonable prices and is well worth the taxi fare.

Tourism
Although there is nothing to see in the immediate vicinity, Marina Smir is an excellent place to leave your yacht for excursions inland. Nearby are the towns of M'Diq, Tetuan, Chefchaoun and Ouad Laou, where a typical Berber market is well worth a days visit. Superb beaches are on either side of the marina.

Local specialities
Along the road outside the port leading to M'Diq and Tetuan are several stalls selling ceramic pots, cous-cous, cooking ware, plates and ornaments. Local Berber markets can be found in the surrounding villages.

Marina Kabila
35°43'·3N 5°20'·08W

Distances
Marina Smir 2M M'Diq 4M

Tides
Range 0·5m.

Charts
	Approach	Port
Admiralty	773, 142	–
French	7042	–
Spanish	445, 451	–
US	52040	–

Kabila Marina with the Rif mountains in the background

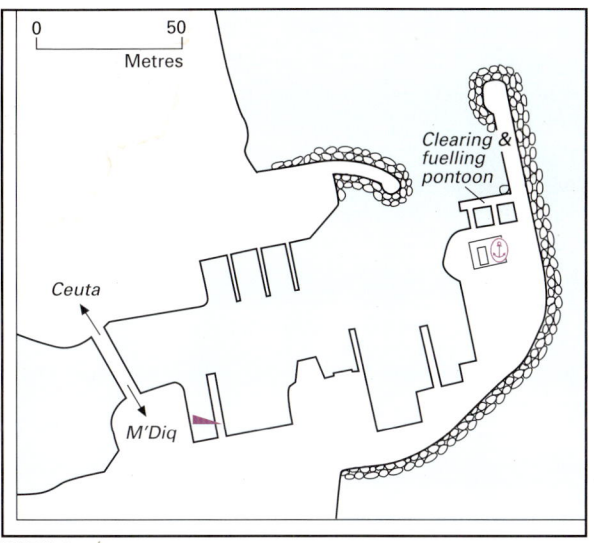

KABILA

Lights
1. **E pier head** Fl.10s
2. **Entrance E spur** Fl.R.5s
3. **Entrance W breakwater** Fl.G.5s

General
Kabila Marina, laying 2M E of Marina Smir is another holiday complex, with the smaller marina well laid out with a capacity for 150 yachts. Like Smir, it is hardly used, except in August. The Marina staff are very friendly and helpful and prices are lower than at Smir. This is a much quieter place in July and August, than Smir, where the local disco can be heard throughout the night.

Approach
From the Straits of Gibraltar, head for the left-hand slope of Jebel Zem Zem. Marina Smir will be seen with its travel-hoist. Kabila is difficult to identify until close, when the white three-storey control tower will first appear, located 2M south of Marina Smir. Current is negligible in this area. Entry is not recommended in strong easterly winds. Beware of tunny nets located E of Marina Smir.

Entry
The entry silts, but minimum depths of 2·5m are found on the left side of the channel. Keep well over near the outer breakwater on rounding the light. Depths increase once round the breakwater. Head for the visitors quay, 30m directly ahead, under the 3-storey white administration building.

Berthing
You will be directed to a choice of berths once formalities have been completed. There is little room for large yachts to turn because of the silting, so in strong winds it is advisable to go to Marina Smir.

Formalities
Port ☎ 975005/975264 VHF Ch 9.

Customs, police and immigration authorities are located in a separate building next to the tower and are very efficient and friendly. Like Marina Smir, entry and exit formalities here have in the past been protracted, but no reports of difficulties have been received recently. The situation is expected to improve further as the Moroccan government encourages more yachtsmen.

Facilities
Water and electricity At each berth.
Fuel Available from the visitors berth by arrangement with the marina office.
Provisions A local shop is located within the tourist complex next to the marina. M'Diq is nearby and can provide most essential supplies.
Gas Available in M'Diq.
Post office and banks In the centre of M'Diq and in Tetuan.
Repairs Engineers can be arranged with the marina staff and a small hoist is available up to 15 tons.
Charges Around 30% less than Marina Smir.

Eating out
As for Marina Smir. In summer, bars are open in the complex adjoining the marina.

Tourism
As for Marina Smir, this is an excellent and safe marina for local inland excursions.

M'Diq
35°41'N 5°18'·5W

Distances
Kabila 4M Ceuta 16M – El Jebha 42M

Tides
MHWS MHWN MLWN MLWS
1·0m   0·8m   0·4m   0·2m

Charts
	Approach	Port
Admiralty	773, 142	–
French	7042	–
Spanish	451	
US	52040	–

Lights
Approach
1. **Cabo Negro** 35°41'·2N 5°16'·4W Oc.4s135m20M White tower

Harbour
2. **E pier head** Q.12m13M Horn 60s 090°-vis-270°White tower, black lanterns
3. **Entrance W pier head** F.G
4. **Entrance E pier head of spur** F.R

General
A very picturesque and busy fishing harbour, under spectacular red cliffs in the lee of Capo de Negro. This was the only harbour in the bay of Ceuta until the two marinas were built within the past six years. Yachts are no longer encouraged to use M'Diq and the harbour is officially closed to pleasure boats, although several small yachts still visit unhindered. Fishing boats fill the harbour, which is exposed to the SE.

Inside is a Royal Moroccan Yacht Club, catering mainly for the needs of its own members, most of whom have now moved their boats to Kabila. The

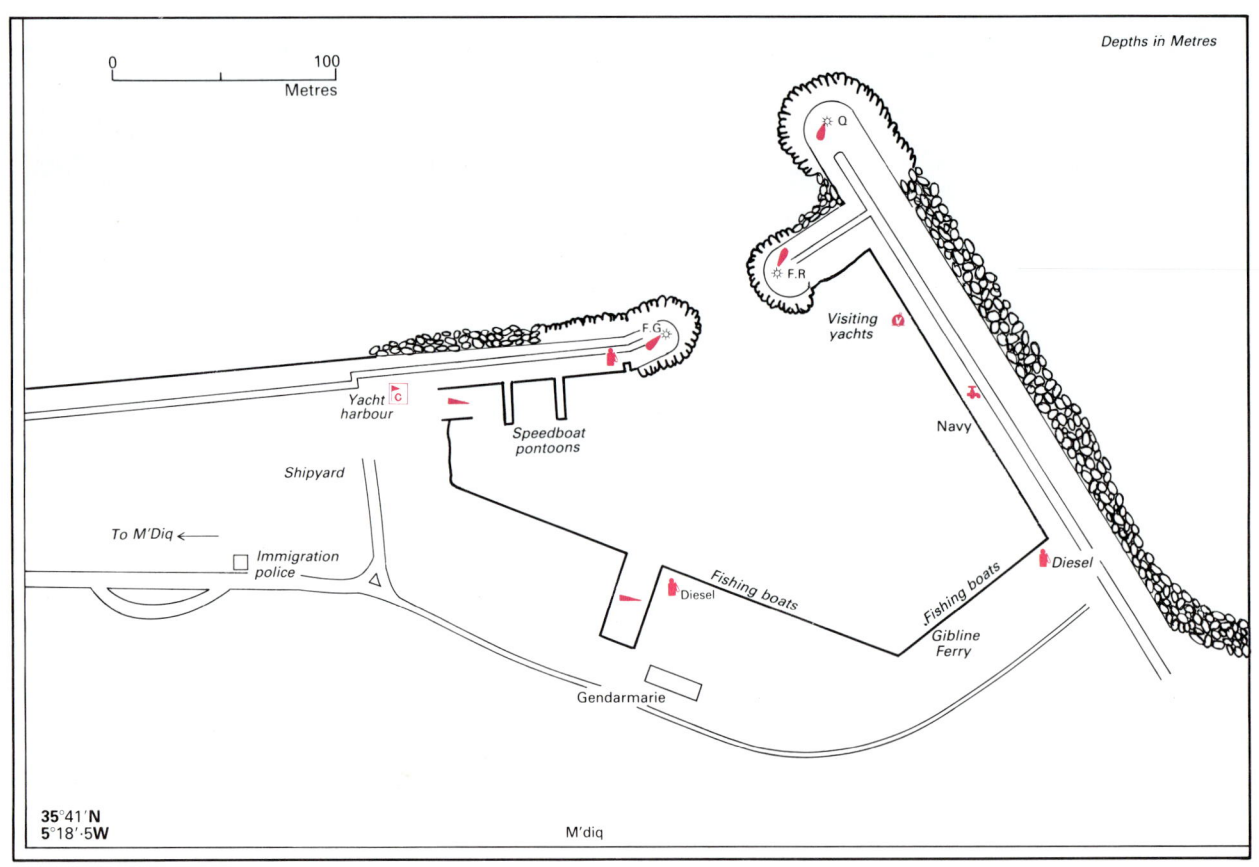

AL MEDIQ

Straits of Gibraltar to Saidia

The fishing port of M'Diq

The fishing port of Jebha set in a deep valley of the Rif mountains, viewed from NNE

North Africa

beaches north of M'Diq are popular among Moroccan holidaymakers and in the summer there may even be a few European tourists. The fairly nondescript village is a short walk from the port and aside from several restaurants and a good craft shop it has no particular attraction.

Approach
By day, in good weather, there are no particular problems. The entrance is not easily visible until fairly close, but is easily identified by the red cliffs above and the striking Cabo de Negro, to the east. The port lies just E of the low-lying village and new apartments are scattered around the hills behind it.

Entry
Once in the entrance proceed carefully as there is not much room to manoeuvre and there are numerous semi-submerged mooring lines. A night entry is not recommended and entry in strong E winds is not advisable because of the swell in the entrance.

Berthing
Small yachts might find room in the yacht club but normally the place for visitors is along the crowded E pier which has room for about five yachts lying to their own anchors bows or stern-to. The yacht club charges minimal harbour dues and the public quay is free of charge.

Formalities
All officials in the port.

Facilities
Water and electricity Water is available from a tap on the E pier and electricity with a long lead. The yacht club has several water taps and electricity sockets.
Fuel Diesel available from a pump between the fish market and slip and petrol from a pump at the yacht club.
Provisions Good provisions can be found in several small shops in the village about 20 minutes walk from the port. The craft shop on the left-hand side, at the beginning of the main street, has a good assortment of leather clothing with very reasonable fixed prices (uncommon in Morocco).
Showers If lying at the yacht club, their showers may be used.
Post office, telephone and bank In the village.
Repairs Local craftsmen work on the boats in the yacht club and there is a small shipyard for wooden fishing boats. It may be possible to get simple repairs done.

Eating out
Several eating houses and simple restaurants are located in the village. In summer time the restaurant in the yacht club is open and serves spectacular fish dishes.

Tourism
M'Diq has no special attraction but Tetouan, 16km from M'Diq, is a striking town and well worth a visit. It is situated in a wide valley on the northern edge of the Rif mountains and, when the Oued Martin was still navigable, small boats sailed up to it. During the time of the Spanish Protectorate it was the capital of Northern Morocco and some of the architecture is reminiscent of the Moorish buildings in Andalucia. Spill-over tourism from the Costa del Sol has left its traces and Tetouan's attraction is slightly overshadowed by the problem of dealing with the many young guides, but do not let this stop you from visiting. There are frequent buses between M'Diq and Tetouan.

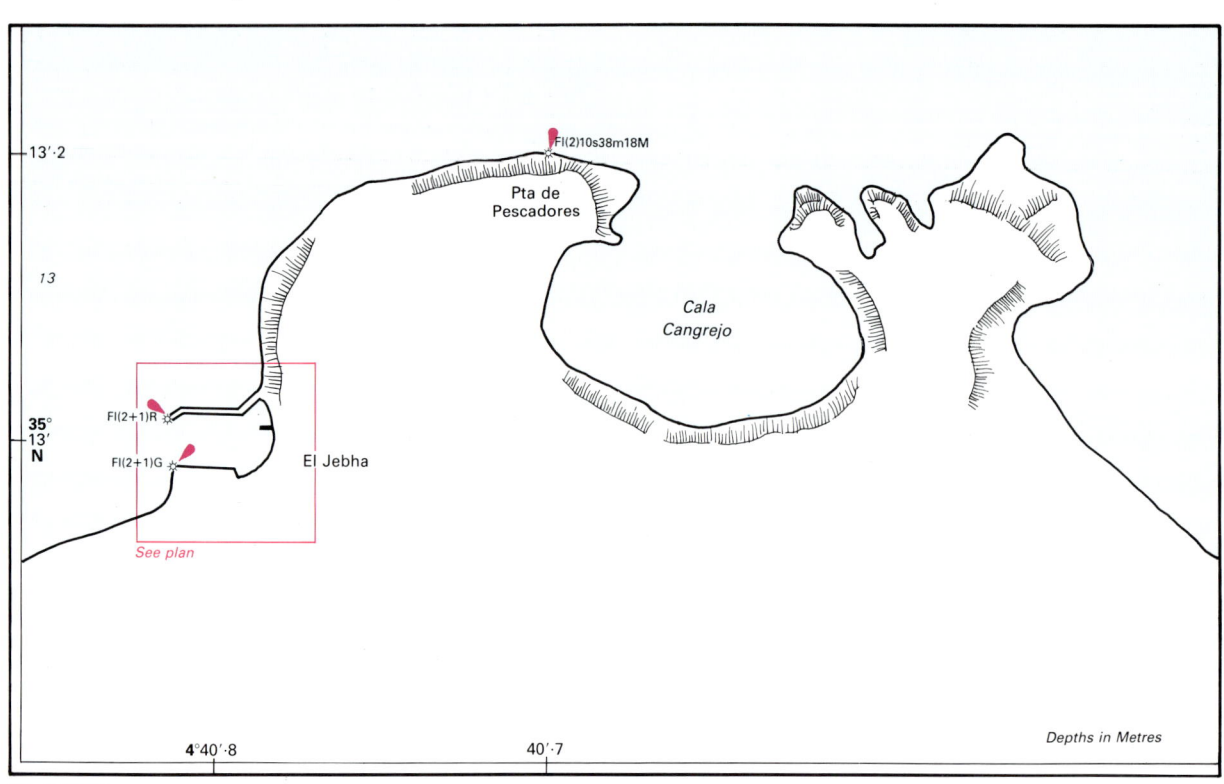

EL JEBHA

Fishing in the area is rewarding, with many large fish around Cabo Negro. Various types of shark, swordfish, tuna and other large fish are regularly caught in the area. Permission has to be obtained from the authorities to anchor in the area.

El Jebha

35°13'N 4°40'·8W

Distances
M'Diq 42M – Peñón de Véléz 20M, Al Hoceima 40M

Tides
MHWS MHWN MLWN MLWS
0·9m   0·7m   0·4m   0·2m

Charts
	Approach	Port
Admiralty	773	–
French	1711	–
Spanish	–	–
US	52040	–

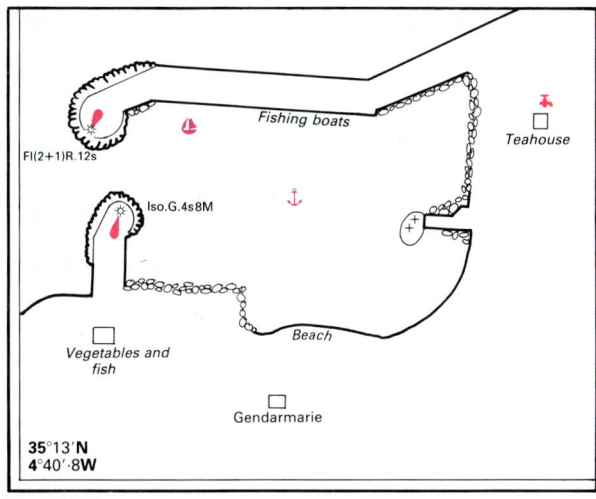

EL JEBHA

El Jebha: One of the quietest harbours in Morocco

Lights
Approach
1. **Punta de Pescadores** 35°13'·2N 4°40'·7W
   Fl(2)10s38m18M 090°-vis-270° Black lantern on white hut

Harbour
2. **Port de Pêche S jetty** Iso.G.4s8M

General
The changing world of the past 100 years has had little effect on life in El Jebha. Just 80M south of Marbella, and what contrasts! Chickens and goats in the streets and at 12 o'clock at night the lights go out when the generator is shut down. The small port does not get many visitors but yachts can usually find room between the fishing boats. Overall protection is good. Jebha is beautifully situated in an isolated, mountainous part of the coast where the cultivation of *kif* is the major activity. W of the port are deserted beaches and the rocks towards Cala Congrejo are good for snorkelling. This is the place to stay for a couple of days to get away from it all; if possible be there for the Tuesday *souk* when the village comes to life. The streets are filled with the donkeys of the mountain people and small boats come and go to pick up families living in isolated parts along the coast. Few places in Morocco offer such an interesting look at the old ways of life.

Approach
The port of El Jebha is situated ¼M SW of Punta de Pescadores which is rocky with an islet close by. It is not as high as the surrounding coast and on its summit is a rock resembling a tower. The entrance to Cala Congrejo, E of Punta de Pescadores, is not clearly visible from seaward.

Berthing
If there is room, go alongside the N quay. A sunken wreck lies half submerged at the end of the quay and it may be possible to lie alongside or just forward of this. Otherwise tie up to a fishing boat which is not on the point of leaving. The fishing fleet leaves at around 6 am, so early disturbances are inevitable, unless you can berth alongside the wreck. It is possible to anchor in the middle of the port but there is not much room to swing and care must be taken to avoid mooring lines. There are plans to build a quay in the S part of the port which will create more room for visiting yachts. In good weather, yachts can anchor very quietly in Cala Congrejo but be sure to inform the authorities beforehand.

Formalities
Although entry in Morocco is possible here, it may give rise to suspicions that you have come to Morocco to buy *kif*. Therefore El Jebha is best visited after first clearing in Marina Smir or Kabila and having informed the authorities there of your intention to visit. Most likely the *caïd*, *marine marchande* and *gendarmerie* will all arrive at the same time. The port authorities offices are on the opposite side of the harbour. Officials are very friendly here and very pleasant to deal with.

North Africa

Facilities
Water and electricity It may be possible to fill water containers in one of the tea houses around the port. There is no electricity on the quay.
Fuel In containers from the village but at times in short supply.
Provisions Only very basic provisions are available from a small market near the SW corner of the port and several little shops in the village. Meat is not always available and chickens may have to be bought off the street. The best supplies can be bought on Tuesday at the weekly *souk*. Fresh bread is always available.
Post office Letters can be sent from the village but there is no post office.

Eating out
There are some very simple eating houses in the village.

Torres de Al Cala (Cala Iris)
A new port is currently under construction. No information is yet available (Dec 1998).

Peñón de Véléz de la Gomera
35°11'N 4°17'·5W

Light
Peñón de Véléz de la Gomera
Fl(3)20s47m12M Grey tower and dwelling

General
A useful good-weather anchorage off the beach between Peñón de Véléz and Cabo Baba and a convenient stop to cut the stretch from Jebha to Al Hoceima into two day-trips. The steep rock is still Spanish territory and it was an island until silting connected it to the Moroccan shore by a narrow strip of sand. The remote setting resembles a miniature Gibraltar. When approaching, the sight of an armed Spanish lookout waving one away from their territory can be intimidating, but at a distance they do not seem to mind the presence of yachts. Moroccan military boats frequently patrol the area and may warn yachts away if close inshore. The surroundings are beautiful with steep barren mountains but it is completely open to the N and protection from the swell is poor. Dolphins are often seen very close to the shore and always accompany passing yachts.

Anchorage
Anchor in 8m or more; gravel and rocks with poor holding.

The rock of Véléz de la Gomera with the Spanish flag flying from the military post on top, viewed from NW. The anchorage is behind the rock

Straits of Gibraltar to Saidia

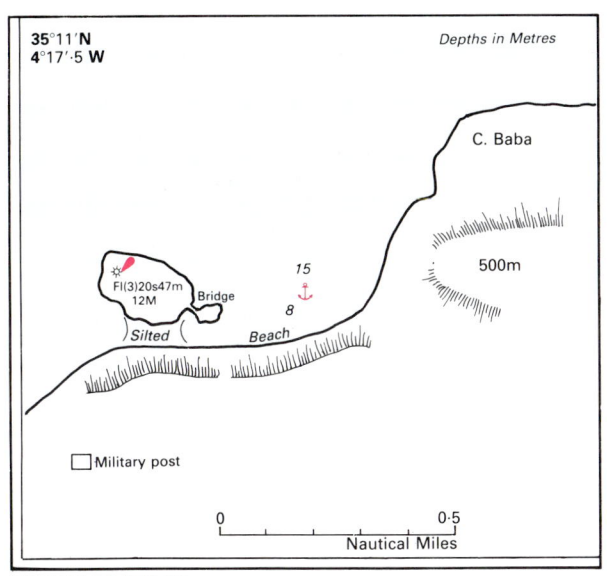

PENON DE VELEZ

Formalities
Be sure to inform the authorities at the port of departure when planning to spend a night here. There is a Moroccan police post among the scattered houses in the valley; they probably will not bother a yacht stopping for the night but do not land. You can be sure to be under surveillance.

Al Hoceima (formerly Villa Sanjurjo)
35°14'·9N 3°55'·1W

Distances
El Jebha 40M – Melilla 60M

Tides
MHWS	MHWN	MLWN	MLWS
0·6m	0·5m	0·3m	0·2m

Charts
	Approach	Port
Admiralty	773	580
French	6570	5864
Spanish	431	431 (inset)
US	52040	52047

Lights
Approach
1. **Cabo Morro Nuevo, Pta de los Frailes** 35°15'·7N 3°55'·7W
   Fl(2)10s151m20M 082°-vis-275° White support, black lantern

Harbour
2. **Dique de Abrigo** Iso.G.4s14m4M White tower, green top
3. **Dique de Los Islotes** Iso.R.4s15m5M White tower, red top.

Functioning of the leading lights is doubtful and not necessary for a yacht and therefore omitted.

The naval and fishing port of Al Hoceima, formerly Villa Sanjurjo set in the Bay of Al Hoceima

85

North Africa

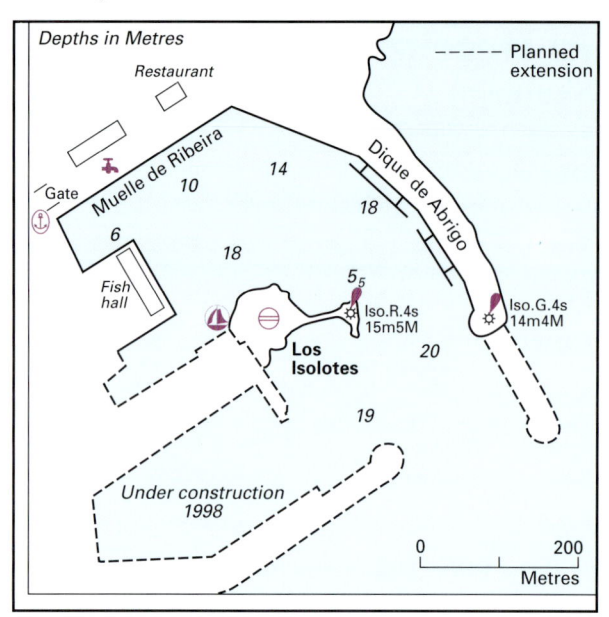

AL HOCEIMA

General
A medium sized fishing and naval port in a beautiful setting, situated in the W corner of the Bay of Al Hoceima. The port is enclosed by steep hills and protected from the S by a breakwater which connects the rocks of Los Islotes with the shore. This is another harbour in Morocco undergoing radical changes which should, when completed, favour yachtsmen. Formally, yachts used to moor in the NW corner among many confiscated and discarded vessels. A new area has been designated, tucked in behind the natural rocky promontory which forms the W breakwater. At present, up to 10 yachts can moor on the quay, with electricity and water available. Pontoons are expected to shortly be in place for the use of pleasure craft. A new harbour is also under construction adjoining and to the S of the old one. This will be the home of the Moroccan Royal Navy and the fishing fleet. Once completed, the yacht area, being in the inner harbour, will be one of the safest and most pleasant in the area. A road and steps lead up to the village of Al Hoceima on top of the hill and the beach in the bay is popular.

Approach
The headland of Cabo Morro Nuevo with the light of Punta de los Frailes is prominent and from the N, the port is not visible until well around the cape. A fairly strong westerly current (between 1–2kts) is common along this part of the coast and between Cabo Morro Nuevo and Punta Bocic it sets towards the coast. One large and two smaller fuel tanks on Los Islotes are conspicuous when approaching the port.

Berthing
The quay at Los Islotes has room for about 10 visitors to lie stern or bows to. Holding is not very good. The quay is not particularly clean so it is advisable to use old warps. Harbour dues are charged on an irregular basis and seem to be expensive for the facilities offered. As stated above, things are changing here for the better. Provided you arrange for a guardian, Al Hoceima can be used as a port to leave the boat to make a trip inland.

Formalities
Port of entry. With the presence of the Moroccan Navy, formalities are taken seriously and besides the usual officials, naval personnel may also visit.

Facilities
Water and electricity Recently laid on the jetty at Los Islotes.
Fuel Can be delivered in drums, although pumps are expected to be in place shortly.
Provisions Bread can be bought in the tea house near the fish hall. For other supplies climb up to the village or take a taxi. At the end of the road leading from the Muelle de Ribera up to the village is an *alimentation général* and butcher. Alternatively take the steps behind Hotel Quemado which lead to the centre of town where there are several small shops. The market is on the other side of town.
Post office In the centre of the village.
Telephone In the post office or Hotel Quemado.
Bank Several banks in the village and a money exchange in Hotel Quemado.
Repairs The coral diving boats employ good mechanics who will be able to take care of most engine problems.

Eating out
Several fish restaurants in the port along Muelle de Ribera. The restaurants in the village seem to cater more to tourists.

Transport
Buses from Al Hoceïma are convenient but its location is isolated and a journey in any direction will take several hours on scenic but narrow winding roads through the Rif mountains.

History
Both the English and French occupied the small islands in the southern part of the Bay of Al Hoceima before the Spanish took over and, in 1673, changed Peñón de Alhucemas into a fortress. It was from this island that the Spanish General Sanjurjo invaded the mainland in 1926. Following the invasion the new town of Alhucemas was built in the barren hills and it retains a definite Andalucian atmosphere.

Tourism
Although a pleasant place, the most interesting things to do are outside of Al Hoceima. The fascinating city of Fes is only a day trip by bus. The road leads up to the highest parts of the Rif mountains with splendid views over wide valleys on one side and the Mediterranean on the other. During the various stops, one gets a good impression of life in the small mountain villages. Of all the cities in North Africa, Fes is the one where traditional life has survived with the least compromise. Walking through the narrow streets, being pushed aside by loaded donkeys, there is a biblical atmosphere. Many of the craftsmen who

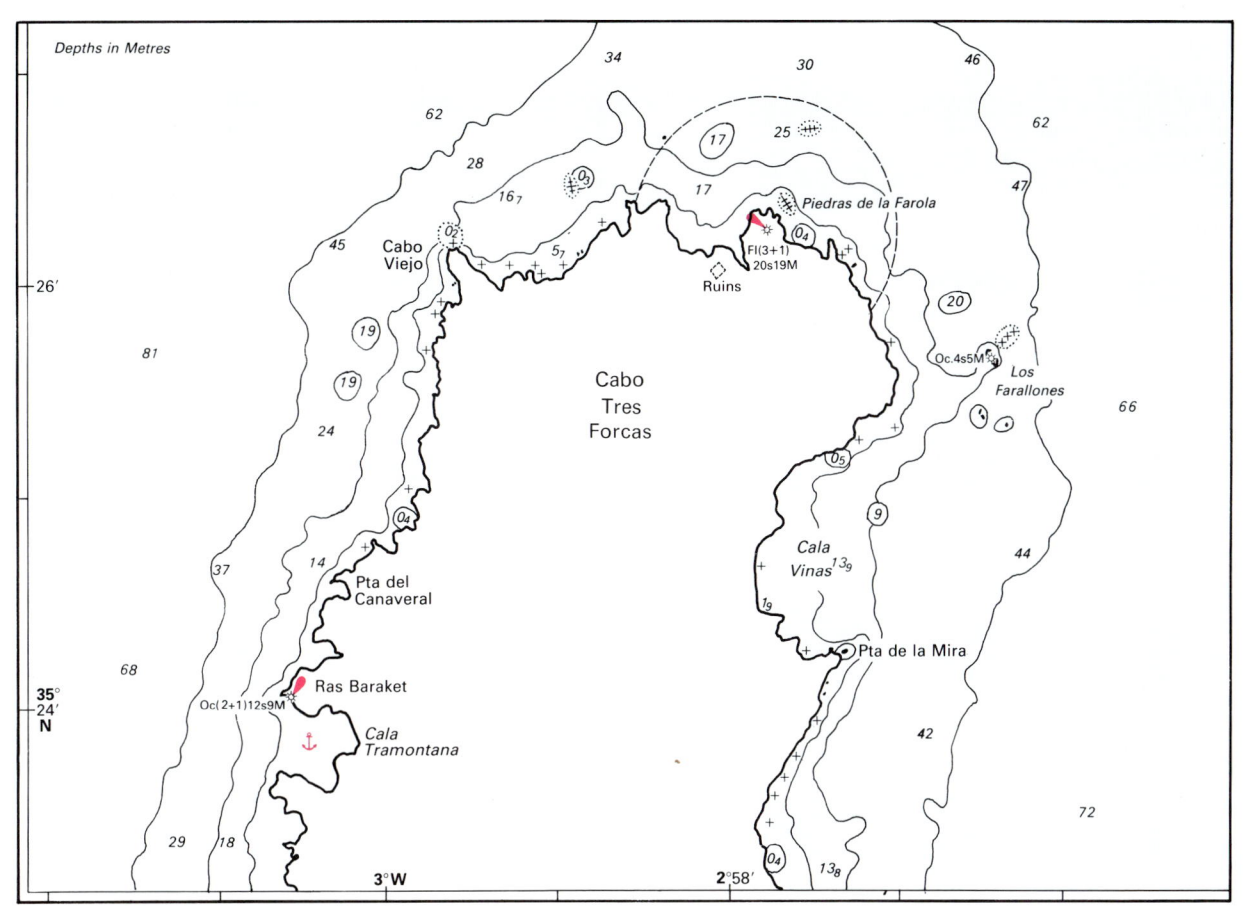

CABO TRES FORCAS

renovated the old Islamic monuments and who built the spectacular mausoleum for Mohammed V in Rabat came from Fes. Another interesting excursion is to Chefchaouen, a formidably remote town in the Rif mountains. The Moors (the mix of Arabs and Berbers that conquered Spain), who were pushed out of Andalucia after the fall of Granada, built mosques, baths and tiled courtyards, planted fruit trees and declared Chefchaouen a sacred city. Until the arrival of Spanish troops in 1920, it had been visited by just four Europeans. As the *Rough Guide* puts it, 'There are few journeys in Morocco as spectacular as that from Al Hoceima to Chefchaouen'.

Cala Tramontana

35°23'·8N 3°00'·5W

Light
Ras Baraket on the N side of the entrance to Cala Tramontana 35°24'·1N 3°00'·6W
Oc(2+1)12s49m9M White round tower

General
A good anchorage on the W side of Ras Tleta Madari (formerly Cabo Tres Forcas) and a useful stop between Al Hoceima and Melilla. Protection in the horseshoe-shaped bay, surrounded by the hills of the Tleta Madari headland, is excellent from NE to S. The only signs of civilisation, on this otherwise deserted part of the coast, are a few boats from the small fishing community near the beach. Conical hills on the N side at Ras Baraket and on the S side make the entrance well visible from seaward.

North Africa

Melilla
35°17'·4N 2°55'·5W

Distances
Al Hoceima 60M – Ras el Ma 26M

Tides
MHWS	MHWN	MLWN	MLWS
0·6m	0·5m	0·3m	0·2m

Charts
	Approach	Port
Admiralty	773, 2437	580
French	6570	5864
Spanish	432	4331
US	52040	52047

Lights
Approach
1. **Cabo Tres Forcas** 35°26'·3N 2°57'·8W Fl(3+1)20s112m19M Siren(3+1)60s 083°-vis-307° (224°) Grey square tower and dwelling plus White bracket on metal hut
2. **Los Farallones** 35°25'·7N 2°56'·4W Oc.4s21m5M White and grey tower
3. **Melilla LtHo** 35°17'·7N 2°56'·1W Oc(2)6s40m14M Brown tower with aluminium dome

Harbour
4. **Main entrance Dique Nordeste** Fl.G.4s22m5M
5. **Main entrance Muelle de Nador** Fl(2)R.6s8m10M
6. **Muelle de Segunda Rama head** Fl(2)G.7s7m3M
7. **Ore loading pier head** Fl(2+1)R.21s8m3M
8. **Small craft basin E pier head** Oc.G.4s6m3M
9. **Small craft basin W pier head** Oc.R.4s8m2M
10. Fl(2)G.7s1m1M
11. Fl(2)R.7s1m1M

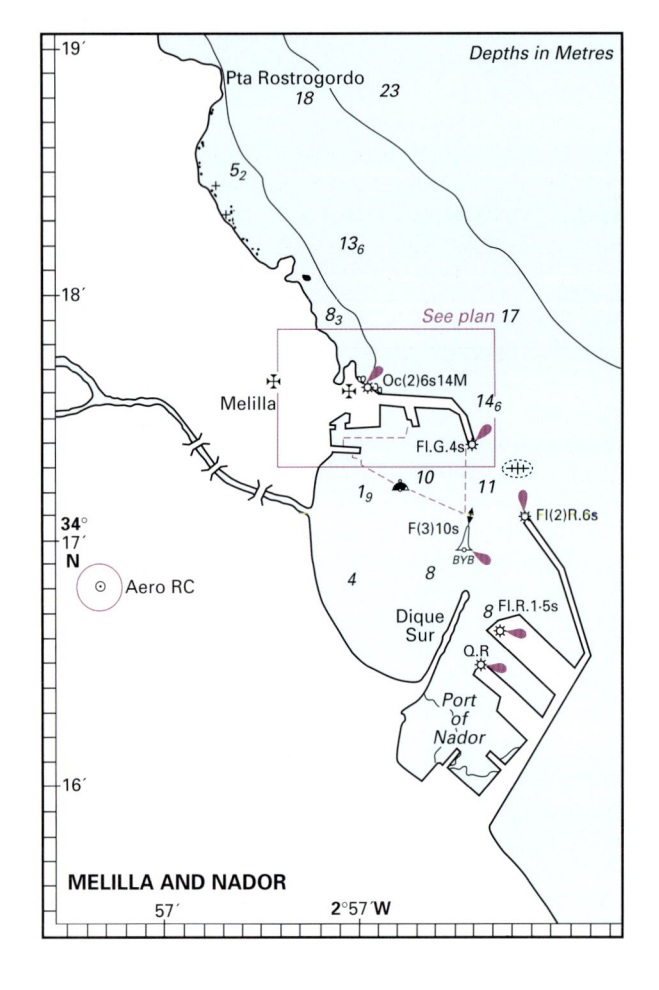

General
Another of the peculiar Spanish possessions on the Moroccan coast, Melilla used to be of commercial importance during the time of the Spanish Protectorate but declined after Moroccan independence. The main outer entrance is shared with the Moroccan port of Nador which has taken over the mineral trade. The ferry terminal sees the most important activity today along with fishing and smuggling.

A new marina has been built in the past year on the south side of the old jetty, Cargedero de Minerales. This is well enclosed providing considerable protection from the swell which enters the main basin. A friendly yacht club is located in the S corner of the Darsena Pesquero basin.

Security has always been a problem in Melilla: the influx of Moroccans, who have come to Melilla for a share of the Spanish affluence, has not produced a happy mix and theft along the public quays was a real problem. This may be resolved with security arrangements in the new marina.

By Moroccan standards supplies are abundant, but they pale in comparison to Ceuta. There is a good *mercado* (covered market) with fresh produce and smaller supermarkets have a good supply of staple articles, beer, wine and spirits. Melilla is quite useful as a base from which to explore Northern Morocco.

Approach
The headland of Cabo Tres Forcas is an unmistakable landmark and makes the approach to Melilla easy from any direction. The starboard entrance pier is Spanish and the port side is part of the Moroccan port of Nador. This is the reason for a unique peculiarity of the entrance.

Both sides are equipped with the usual lights for night entry, but the Nador red light is frequently not functioning.

Entry
Minimum depths of over 7m are found in the outer basin and the new marina entrance has been dredged to 9m. Once inside the outer basin, head east to the outer mole of the new marina. Once rounded, minimum depths of 2·8m are confined to the main pier.

Berthing
On the pontoons, depths are less than 2m at present.

Formalities
In the marina. Formalities are now more relaxed than previously. Port officials may call at the yacht.

Facilities
Water and electricity Being laid at each berth on the pontoons.

MELILLA AND NADOR

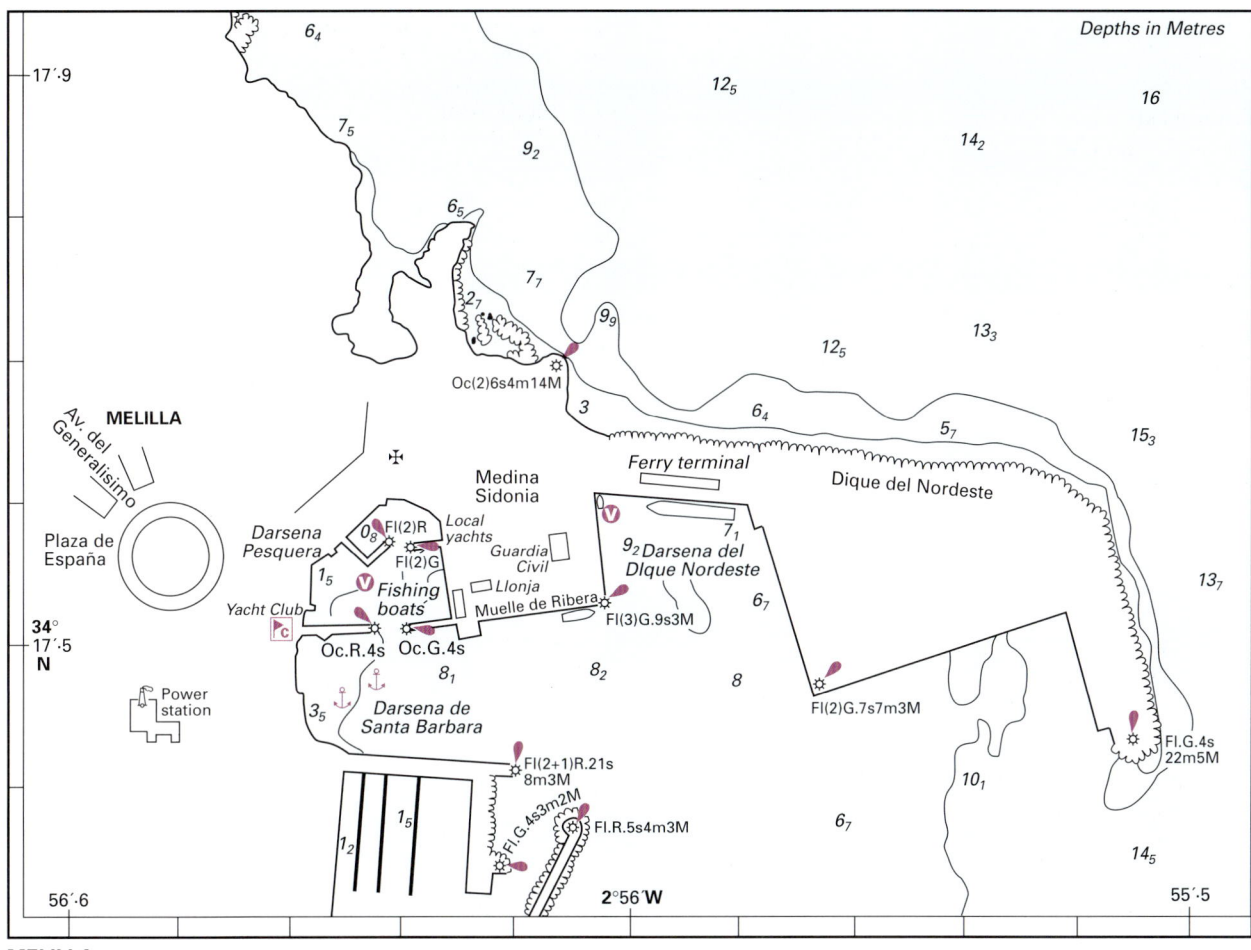

MELILLA

Fuel From a pump, at Ceuta prices.
Provisions The covered *mercado* has a wide assortment of Spanish products. It is 200m past the end of the main street, Avenida del Generalisimo, about 20 minutes walk from the port. Just before the market there is a small but well stocked Moroccan-owned *supermercado*, Hakin. Moroccans also operate many of the stands at the market. All shops sell duty-free electronic equipment, cheap alcoholic beverages and cigarettes.
Showers On request. Visiting yachtsmen can use the showers in the yacht club regardless of where the boat lies.
Post office and telephone Off the N side of the Avenida del Generalisimo.
Bank In the ferry terminal and on the main street. Many money changers on the street corners but be careful of their rates and commission.
Repairs Emergency engine repairs can be carried out.
Charges A new scale of charges will be in place when facilities are completed.

Eating out

Not as many restaurants as one might expect in a city of this size. Good *tapas* (typically Spanish hors d'oeuvre with several courses) available at the yacht club bar.

Tourism

The old fortified town, Medina Sidonia, is worth a visit. In the beginning of the century this was all there was of Melilla. It was built around 1497 after the Moors were defeated in Granada. There is a small museum and several buildings have been well restored. The main business activity in Melilla centres around the ferry terminal and duty-free shopping for mainland Spaniards and Moroccans. A separate, and observable activity, is smuggling. At night, a sizeable fleet of small overpowered motorboats, unlit and fully loaded, leaves the port to drop their cargo in Morocco. The Spanish customs ask no questions and the Moroccan operators obviously have the right contacts to go undisturbed about their business there.

In summer, daily ferries to Malaga, Benalmadena and Almeria. Out of season services drop to 3 times per week. Buses to the border with Morocco, about 3km away, leave from Plaza de España.

Nador

35°17'·2N 2°55'·1W

Nador is the Moroccan commercial and fishing port which shares the entrance with Melilla. The fishing port is crowded and the only place for a yacht is alongside a fishing boat where it may easily be damaged. There are no shops or facilities in the immediate vicinity and there is little reason to visit Nador.

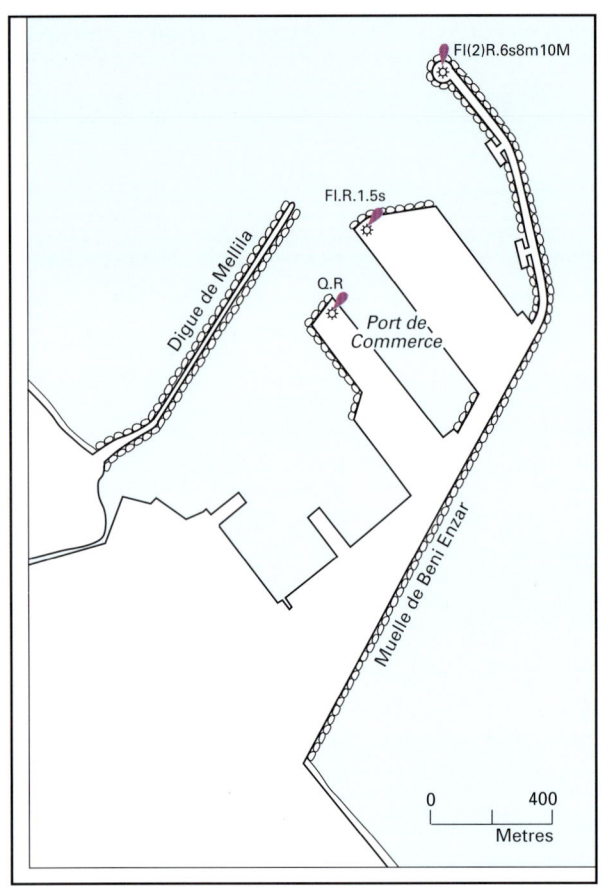

North Africa

PORT DE NADOR

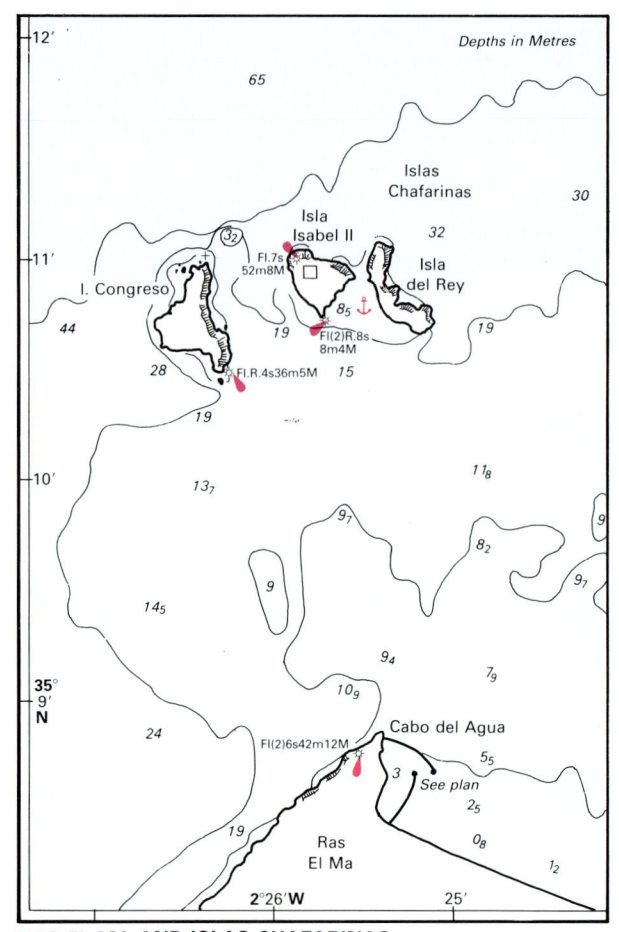

RAS EL MA AND ISLAS CHAFARINAS

Ras el Ma (Ras Kebdana)
35°08'·8N 2°25'·3W

Distances
Melilla 26M – Ghazaouet 27M

Tides
MHWS	MHWN	MLWN	MLWS
0·4m	0·3m	0·2m	0·1m

Charts
	Approach	Port
Admiralty	2437	–
French	6570, 6011	5864
Spanish	434	–
US	52040, 52060	–

Lights
Approach
1. **Cabo del Agua** 35°08'·8N 2°25'·3W
   Fl(2)6s42m8M White tower on 8-sided dwelling
2. **Isla Congreso S point** 35°10'·5N 2°26'·1W
   Fl.R.4s36m5M Grey rounded tower Obscd when bearing less than 110°
3. **Isla Isabel II NW point** 35°11'N 2°25'·7W
   Fl.7s52m8M White tower and dwelling 045°-obscd-080° by Isla Congreso

Harbour
4. Ras Kebdana N breakwater head
   Oc(3)G.12s12m10M White tower
5. East breakwater head Oc(3)R.12s13m10M White tower

General
Ras el Ma is the ultimate sleepy fishing port on the North coast of Morocco. Built by the Romanians in exchange for phosphates in 1985 it has escaped the attention of the chart makers and it does not appear on any British, French or Spanish charts. The port

The quiet fishing port of Ras el Ma with deserted beaches stretching to the Algerian border

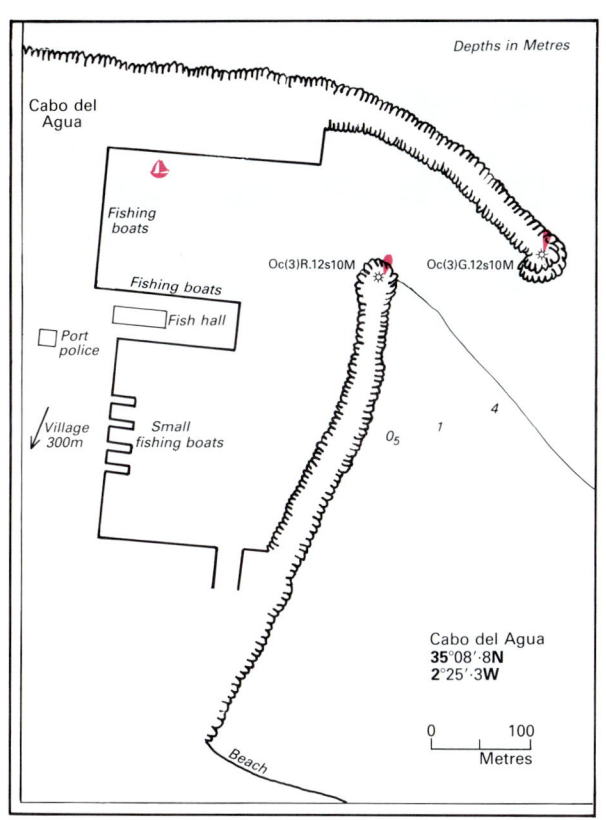

RAS EL MA

is situated on the E side of Pointe de Ras-Kebdana (Cabo del Agua in Spanish), opposite the Spanish Chafarinas Islands. In July and August, Moroccan tourists camp out on the beautiful beaches that stretch for miles towards the Algerian border. The village is a short walk from the port and consists of no more than a dusty main street with tea houses and small shops. The port offers good protection and the fishermen as well as the authorities are friendly. The rocky coast W of the port makes for good snorkelling and aside from the fishing boats the port is visited regularly by a seal who lives in the area.

Approach
In season, fishermen lay nets at night between Ras el Ma and the Chafarinas Islands and their lights can not be seen until fairly close to. Night entry is not recommended.

Entry
When entering, stay close to the starboard breakwater head, because the port side of the entrance shallows abruptly due to silting around the head of the SE breakwater.

Berthing
Tie up alongside in the large basin where yachts will find plenty of room. Leave the fish market quay to the fishermen. The port is far from being full and in view of the dwindling quantities of sardines in the area, is unlikely to change in the near future.

Formalities
Authorities are friendly and yachts are still a novelty. It can be used as a port of first entry but there are no immigration officials to make a formal entry into Morocco.

Facilities
Water and electricity None laid on but it is possible to have water delivered by tractor.
Fuel In containers from the village.
Provisions A good assortment of cheap fresh produce and soft drinks. If en route to Algeria one can stock up reasonably well here (by Moroccan standards).
Post office A short walk outside of the village opposite the police office.
Bank One bank on the main street.
Repairs More likely you will be asked to lend a hand on a fishing boat with its own troubles. There is a new slipway to haul large fishing boats.

Eating out
It is possible to dine for virtually nothing in the most basic of eating houses to be found in Morocco. In the summer time several 'tent restaurants' are installed on the beach.

Tourism
Early morning buses leave daily to Berkane and Oujda. Berkane is in the middle of an extensively irrigated wine growing area and has a good market. Oujda is the provincial capital with a dusty but lively daily market. Several small eating houses around the market serve sheep's head which seems to be a speciality of Oujda; if this is unacceptable, try some other less exotic but well spiced dish from a stall around the market. Both towns can easily be visited in a day trip.

Under normal circumstances it is possible to obtain visas in Oujda from the Algerian Consulate. However, with the land border closed due to the troubles there, this facility is now also closed.

Islas Chafarinas
35°10'·6N 2°26'W

Distances
Ras el Ma 2M

Charts
	Approach	Port
Admiralty	580	–
French	5864, 6011	–
Spanish	4341	–
US	52040	–

Lights
1. **Isla Congreso S Point** 35°10'·5N 2°26'·1W Fl.R.4s36m5M Grey round tower Obscured when bearing less than 110°
2. **Isla Isabel II NW Point** Fl.7s52m8M White tower and dwelling 045°-obscd-080° by Isla Congreso
3. **Isla Isabel, S Point** Fl(2)R.8s8m4M Square truncated pyramidal metal tower

North Africa

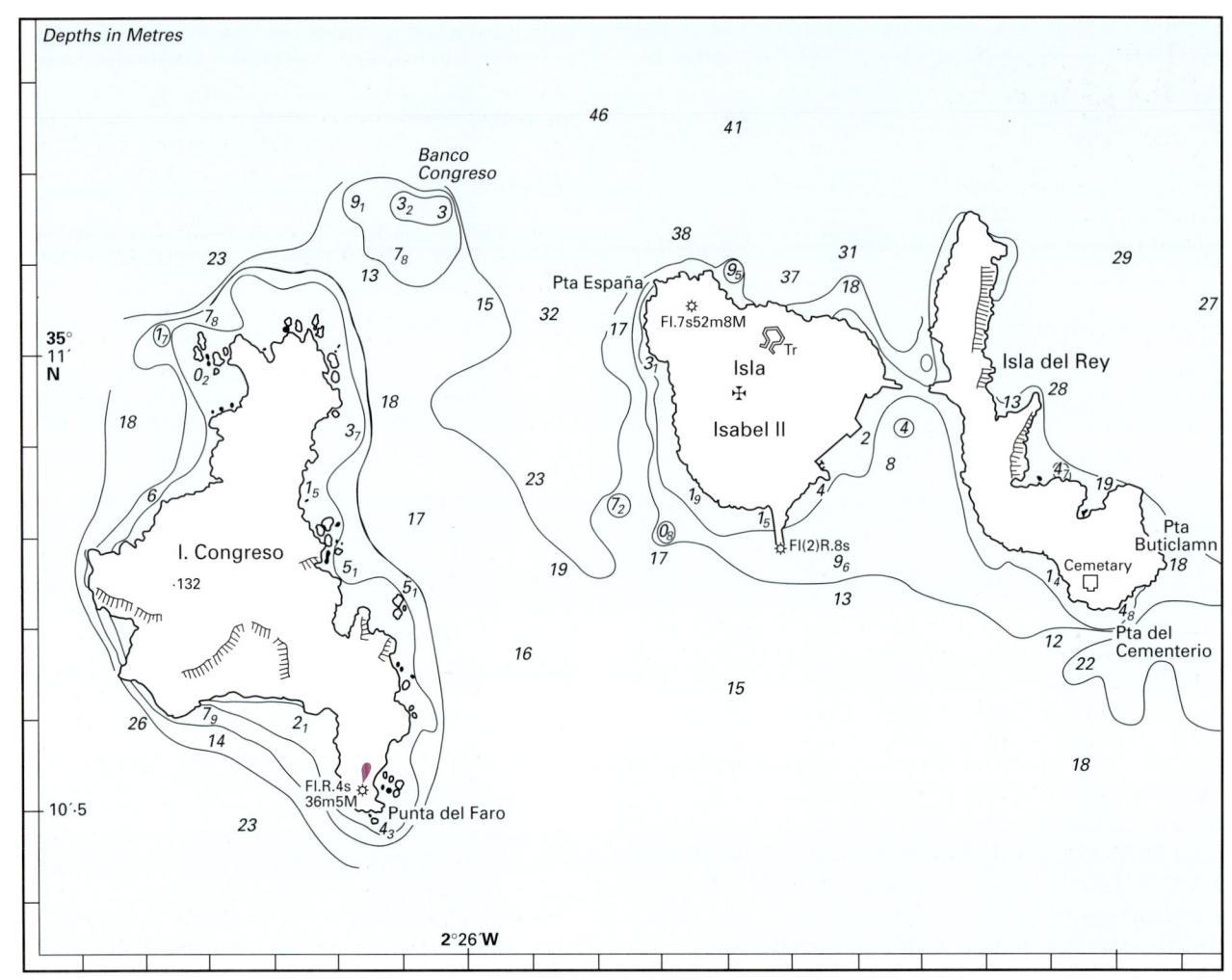

ISLAS CHAFERINAS

Note
A group of 3 small Spanish islands just 2M N of Ras el Ma. The most eastern island, Isla del Rey, and the middle island, Isla Isabel II, are joined by a partially destroyed pier. The bay to the S is the only natural anchorage suitable in N winds along the Mediterranean coast of Morocco. However, the area is a Spanish military zone and the authorities do not seem to like yachts anchoring in the vicinity of the islands, which are rich in fish.

Saidia

35°07'N 2°11'W (approx)

Lights and tides as for Ras el Ma

General

The development of this new pleasure complex located E of Ras el Ma, 42M from Cabo del Agua (Ras Kebadana, 35°08'·8N 2°25'·3W) is near the village of Saidia. Development began in late 1998 and includes a marina to accommodate 180 yachts with a separate fishing harbour. This promises to be a friendly marina with every facility for the yachting community.

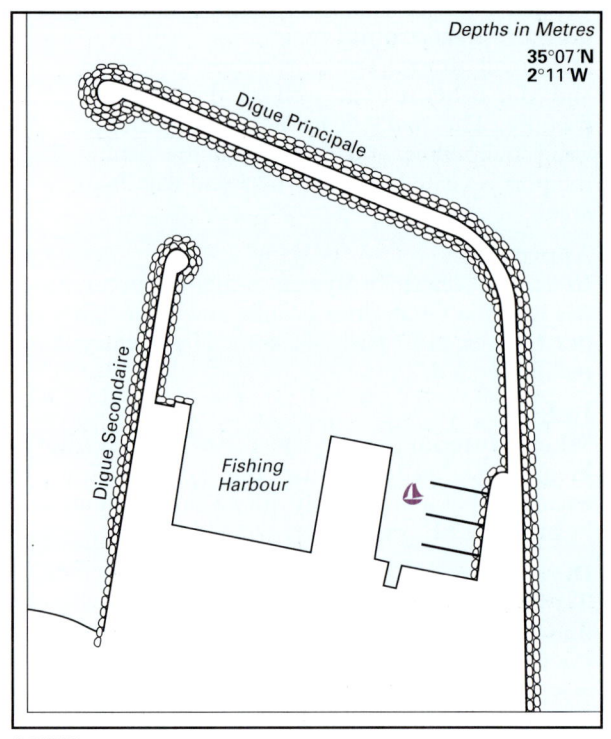

SAIDIA

Algeria

Capital Algiers
Area 2,381,741 sq km
Population Approximately 24 million
GDP per person $2,760 (prior to the civil war)
Average annual population growth 3·2%

Introduction
Algeria is the second largest country in Africa and almost half the size of Europe. Some 85% of its territory lies in the Sahara Desert and the majority of its population lives in the green and fertile land bordering the Mediterranean. Two mountain ranges run parallel to the coast: the Tell Atlas which is a continuation of the Moroccan Middle Atlas and the Sahara Atlas which marks the transition to the Great Desert. Of the three Maghreb countries, Algeria had the highest per capita income before the recent civil war, but this is not reflected in the general welfare of the population.

Although the Mediterranean coastline holds great potential for tourism it remains undeveloped, apart from a very small number of coastal towns which were frequented by French Society tourists.

The present troubles and civil war in the country, the result of an experiment in democratisation, means that at present Algeria is unsafe to visit.

A brief history
Algeria, with its present borders, scarcely appears in European history books until the 16th century. Earlier history is shared with its more powerful neighbours to the east and the west. The Phoenicians were the first to set up trading posts to barter with the Berbers. In Roman times it was a province called Numidia. After the Arab invasions it was part of the Almoravid and Almohad dynasties from Morocco and in the 13th century Algeria was ruled by the Hafsids from Tunisia. Around this time West Algeria around Tlemcen flourished under the influence of Hispano-Moorish culture. After the fall of Grenada in 1492, Spain started to occupy ports on the North African coast. Its authority never extended much beyond garrison towns such as Melilla and Oran, the latter of the two remaining in Spanish hands from 1509 until 1794. With Turkish support and the help of the Barbarossa brothers, (converted Muslim corsairs from Greece based in Jerba) the Spanish were driven out of Algiers by 1529 and it became a province of the Ottoman Empire, ruled by a succession of Deys and Beys. For more than two centuries it also became home port for a notorious pirate fleet. In 1710 the Dey of Algiers broke with Turkey and for the first time Algeria became independent. It did not last long. A famous incident formed the prelude to French intervention. During a discussion about a loan, the Algerian Dey struck the French ambassador in the face with a fly swat. This provided the excuse for the French to intervene and their forces landed in Sidi Fredj (now called Sidi Ferruch) in 1830. Seventeen years of fighting followed before the major parts of the country were under French control but it took until 1871 to pacify the Kabylie region which has been and still is a Berber stronghold. There followed a large influx of French settlers; Algeria was incorporated into metropolitan France and the country was reshaped into a beautiful southern département. Large ports were constructed and French architects converted Oran, Algiers, Bejaïa and Annaba into beautiful cities; nowhere in the Maghreb is the French influence as obvious as in Algeria. Agriculture was developed and Algerian grapes were used to improve the quality of French wines.

Recent history
The Algerians themselves benefited little from the prosperity brought by the French occupation and eventually this led to rebellion. In 1954 the Front de Libération Nationale launched a war for independence which was ruthlessly opposed. As fighting continued over the years the French Government under General de Gaulle was willing to compromise but under pressure from the Algerian French, who were defending the country that their fathers had built, the war continued. By 1961 serious negotiations had begun, leading to Algerian independence in 1962 but by that time more than one million Algerian lives had been lost in the long and bloody struggle.

Independent Algeria opted for a socialist government under a single party, the FLN, led by Ahmed Ben Bella, which nationalised all French property. Locally, reconciliation was impossible; although the rights of the French settlers were guaranteed, practically all of them left the country. This sudden departure, coupled with damage caused by seven years of civil war, left the country in great disarray. In 1965, Colonel Houari Boumédienne overthrew Ben Bella in a military coup, to be succeeded after his death in 1978 by Colonel Chadli Bendjedid. The basic policy of socialism, industrialisation and an anti-western foreign policy was continued but despite this and antipathy to the French, France continued to be Algeria's major trading partner. Algeria did well as large oil, natural gas and phosphate reserves were discovered in the Sahara. Ambitious plans were made for industrial development and housing projects to accommodate the rapidly increasing population and large agricultural co-operatives were set up to utilise the relatively small area of tillable land. With its sizeable export earnings, it could afford large projects and food imports compensated for what the inefficient co-operatives could not produce. When oil prices slumped in 1985–86, plans had to be adjusted and food imports were reduced resulting in increasing unrest among the population culminating in the food riots of September 1988. Other factors behind this large uprising, in which many civilians were killed, were

North Africa

ashore unless permission has been given. If possible inform the authorities of your itinerary.

Money
The Algerian Dinar (DA) may not be imported or exported and can only be exchanged legally within Algeria; it is not listed in the international market. Permission to change back left-over notes on leaving Algeria is not always given. Traveller's cheques and cash are acceptable but credit cards and Eurocheques are not. Changing money on the thriving black market gives a much better rate and even officials will offer to oblige. Do not be tempted; the risks are not worth it.

The real value of the dinar is roughly a quarter of the official rate which is one reason why the cost of living is high for foreign visitors. Prices quoted are based on an official exchange rate of DA57 = $1.00. (Nov 1998).

Provisioning
Basics such as bread, vegetables, fruit, milk, meat, etc. are usually available although often not all together at the same time of the day. Except for subsidised products such as bread and milk, some food prices equate to UK prices but are more often higher. Butter, cheese, cream, tea, coffee, soft drinks, mineral water, canned products, oil, pork, toilet paper, wine, beer and liquor are unavailable or of poor quality. Bring all staple foodstuffs.

Water
Water is available in most ports though scarcer west of Ténès. Quality is generally good, except in Oran, and after acclimatising can be drunk unboiled. With some improvisation, hoses can be hooked up in Oran, Cherchell, Sidi Ferruch, Jijel, Collo and Annaba but supply is variable. Elsewhere containers are necessary. Water is usually free of charge but it is a precious commodity; deck washing is unacceptable for instance, except in Sidi Ferruch and Cherchell.

Electricity
Nominal voltage is 220v, 50Hz. With the exception of Oran, Sidi Ferruch and Annaba electricity is not available in the ports.

Fuel
Good quality diesel and engine oil is available in many of the ports. Prices are basically the same everywhere and probably the lowest in the Mediterranean, even at the official exchange rate. Due to the restrictions, one has to pay in Algerian dinars. It is risky to offer payment in hard currency.

Harbour charges
In commercial and fishing ports no harbour dues are charged. The yacht club in Oran charges a flat rate for visitors and at Sidi Ferruch rates are unrealistically high.

Repairs
Emergency engine repairs can be carried out in the major cities if the engine resembles a truck or tractor engine used in Algeria. As a rule spare parts are not available but the Algerians are masters in repairs 'à la systeme D', that is, improvising. In Sidi Ferruch and Oran where there are a few local pleasure craft simple yacht repairs can be carried out.

Telephone
International calls are best made from a post office. They are all routed through Algiers and consequently may take some time when made from another city. Many local phone boxes prove to be defective.

Health precautions
Medical facilities in Algeria are elementary, drugs are scarce and basic commodities such as lavatory paper and tampons unavailable. Have a good first aid kit. It is essential to have good medical insurance including repatriation as any serious accident or illness will have to be treated in Europe. Except for yellow fever if coming from an infected area, vaccinations are not required but consult your doctor. Clean toilets are rare.

Tourist information
Information on Algeria is hard to come by. The ONAT (Office National Algérien du Tourism) has offices in the big cities in Algeria but their information is limited. The best sources are the travel guides listed under *Books*.

Tipping
For a visiting yachtsman in Algeria there may be few occasions to tip but one may desireto repay some of the hospitality or friendliness that will be encountered. Practically any clothing item can serve this purpose as well as American or European cigarettes, a pencil, etc.

Transportation
At present it is very dangerous for foreigners to move around in Algeria without an armed military escort. However, under normal circumstances the following applies: Buses are the best way to get around the country as the railway system is not well developed. Taxis and *louages* are more expensive. Car rental is expensive as it must be paid with officially exchanged money. Hitching is commonplace for men.

Public holidays
New Year's Day 1 January
Labour Day 1 May
Anniversary of the overthrow of Ben Bella 19 June
Independence Day 5 July
Anniversary of the Revolution 1 November

Business hours
Algeria follows the Islamic week; banks and offices are closed on Thursday afternoons and Fridays.

Opening times vary but most shops and offices open between 0800 and 0900. The afternoon break is from 1200 to 1500 and closing times are between 1700 and 1900. Small shops and markets are often open seven days a week.

Time zone
Algeria follows Central European Time, i.e.

UT+1hr without Daylight Saving Time in the summer.

Photography
The attitude towards visitors taking photographs has relaxed, but photographing ports or industrial sites may cause difficulties and photographing military objects will certainly do so. As most Algerian ports are in bigger cities, objections on religious grounds to taking pictures of people in the vicinity is not as common as it is in the country.

Security
The British Embassy in Algeria warns travellers along the coast about the high incidence of theft from caravans or trailers. The problem is not as serious for yachts as in most of the ports there are many policemen and an Algerian on a foreign yacht would be very conspicuous. However be more careful than in the other Maghreb countries. Never leave valuable articles, which by Algerian standards includes almost anything, lying around loose on deck.

Embassies
United Kingdom 7 Chemin des Glycine, BP 43, Algiers ☎ 605601
United States 4 Chemin Cheikh Bachir Ibrahimi El Biar, Algiers ☎ 601425
Germany 16 Rue Chemin Sfindja, BP 664, Algiers. ☎ 634845

Entry formalities
Yachts are a rarity and entry procedures are geared to merchantmen; this results in much tedious form-filling which must be borne patiently. It is important to fly an Algerian courtesy flag. Officials are correct but unsure and this is sometimes covered up by formal or authoritative behaviour and a yacht, as an unusual visitor, is often suspect. Be open and friendly. It is a good idea to announce your arrival by VHF. *Bakhshish* is not generally necessary and offering it may be interpreted as a bribe.

Merchant ships have sometimes found the authorities sensitive about detail: for instance inspecting medicines in life rafts or fining them for failing to lower their flag at sundown. Yachts generally escape such attention though deratification certificates have been asked for. The only papers yachts are required to have are ownership papers and radio licences. Crew members need valid passports and possibly visas. The best way to deal with awkward questions is to remain friendly and maintain innocence while keeping a low profile. It is best to avoid entering at the commercial ports of Ghazaouet and Annaba: go to Beni-Saf, Oran, Mostaganem, Bejaïa, Jijel, Skikda or one of the fishing ports; nevertheless, the ease with which clearance is obtained varies and depends largely upon the attitude of local officials towards the yacht and her crew.

The authorities encountered will be
The PAF (Police au Frontière) – Border police in civilian clothes or blue uniform. Checks passports and visas (in so far as they are required) of all crew and oddly they sometimes ask for the value of the boat; curiosity seems to be the reason for this question, as for many of the others. As a rule passports stay with the *PAF* and can only be collected just before departure. Technically, the crew of a vessel is not required to have visas as long as individuals stay in the port area, but without them it is difficult to obtain a *permis d'escale*, the permission to leave the port, which is issued in all commercial ports. In small ports and fishing ports this paper is not necessary.

Customs – Almost always wear uniform and come on board with a minimum of two persons and besides their usual functions, they enforce the strict currency regulations. In the first port a thorough inspection can be expected. It is illegal to bring drugs or pornographic material into the country and there are very heavy penalties for those breaking the law. All weapons (particularly important), valuables, alcohol and currency have to be declared. Weapons will be impounded during the stay and large quantities of liquor will be sealed on board. A visiting yacht does not have to pay duty on these articles.

Coastguard – mostly young servicemen – always in uniform. A branch of the Algerian navy and operates coastal patrol boats. Their list of questions varies from port to port but it is always long and is mainly concerned with the boat, safety and radio equipment. Most coastguard personnel are young and may be brash. In case of an emergency at sea the coastguard provides assistance free of charge.

The capitainerie (harbourmaster) – in the commercial ports.

The gendarmerie – only on rare occasions (chiefly out of curiosity).

When entering the ports there is no need to seek out officials; they will most likely be waiting. In the bigger ports the *PAF*, customs and the coastguard will always show up and sometimes the *capitainerie* visit. Generally in the smaller ports, only the *PAF* is interested, unless the stay is longer than a few days; then the others may become involved. Upon departure, yachts are considered to leave Algeria even though they stay in territorial waters on the way to the next port and customs clearance has to be repeated. After a few ports, customs will give up searching the boat, but paperwork for all will still have to be dealt with. If visiting several ports, prepare an inventory of all boat equipment, with serial numbers of electronics, and another list with boat data (see *Introduction*) It shows one cares and may speed up matters slightly.

One yacht reported dealing with over 80 officials while cruising the coast. All behaved correctly and only a few were officious. Bribes were never asked for.

Declaration of gold and foreign currencies
All foreign currencies, travellers cheques and

North Africa

valuables, (which includes weapons) on board at the time of entry into Algeria can be taken in or out of the country without paying any taxes but they have to be declared on the so-called Declaration of Holdings of Gold and Foreign Currencies. Failure to do so or making a false declaration can result in confiscation of all money plus heavy fines and even a prison sentence. All currency exchanges should be done officially at banks or hotels and the amount exchanged will be marked on this paper. Bank slips and forms should be carefully kept as they can be checked on departure although in practice they do not seem too keen on checking yachts. Officially a minimum of DA 1,000 has to be changed for every person on board but in practice this is often not enforced on yachtsmen. Start out changing what you think you will need and take things from there. If the amount seems reasonable in view of the length of the visit, there should not be any difficulty.

Official Ports of Entry
Ghazaouet, Beni-Saf, Oran, Mostaganem, Ténès, Cherchell, Sidi Ferruch, Dellys, Bejaïa, Djen Djen, Skida, and Annaba.

Good all-weather ports
Entry safe by day and night and in bad weather: Ghazaouet, Oran, Mostaganem, Ténès, Bejaïa, Jijel, Skikda (not in strong northerlies) and Annaba.

Visas
British citizens need a visa which is only obtainable from the Algerian Consulate in London. Americans and several European nationalities need visas but check for details beforehand with an Algerian consulate. The most straightforward way to get a visa is to apply to the Consul at the Algerian embassy in the country of residence. If this does not fit travel plans, visas can be issued at other Algerian consulates but it takes more time. Previously, when going from Morocco to Algeria the most convenient Algerian consulate was in Oujda which could easily be visited from the port of Ras el Ma. Unfortunately, this facility is closed at present.

In Tunisia the most logical place to apply for a visa is at the Algerian Embassy in Tunis at 136 Avenue de la Liberté, half a block from the US Embassy. The procedure requires four passport-size photos and 7500 Tunisian Dinars; for Americans a 24 hour wait, and Germans have experienced a much longer delay, up to three weeks. Applicants with stamps of Israel, South Africa, South Korea, Taiwan or Malawi in their passports will be refused visas.

Vessels calling in at Algerian ports for an *escala technique* are treated as yachts in transit and crew members will be allowed ashore for a limited period. An inland pass may also be obtainable, but in the present circumstances, we do not recommend any travel inland.

Inviting Algerian friends on board
One of the pleasant aspects of cruising in Algeria is that it is easy to meet very friendly Algerians who may go far out of their way to please the visitor. Returning the favour by inviting them on board may cause problems with the authorities, as Algerians are officially not allowed to be on board a foreign yacht. This rule is interpreted with varying stringency and it is best to check with the local police before making an invitation. This rule applies through North Africa.

International travel
Algiers Regular flights to several European capitals. No direct flights to the US. Flights from Oran and Annaba go mostly to destinations in France. Ferry to Marseille (the most popular route), Palma de Mallorca and Alicante (irregular).
Oran Ferry to Marseille, Sète and Alicante.
Bejaïa Ferry to Marseille.
Annaba Ferry to Marseille.
Skikda Ferry to Marseille.

Ferries are operated by the Compagnie Nationale Algérienne de Navigation (CNAN) with offices at 29 Blvd des Dames, Marseille 13002, ☎ 91 90 64 70, and in Paris, Palma and Alicante. Summer schedules vary from almost daily to Algiers to three times per month to Skikda. Winter sailings are much less regular.

Note
Due to the problems in Algeria, the following is largely based on information current at the time of the first edition of this pilot. However, it is most probable that little will have changed.

Ghazaouet
35°06'·3N 1°52'·2W

Distances
Ras el Ma 27M – Beni-Saf 28M

Tides
Range does not exceed 0·6m.

Charts
	Approach	Port
Admiralty	2437	178
French	6011	5873
US	52060	52069

Lights
Approach
1. **Main light** 35°05'·9N 1°52'·3W
Fl(3)15s92m24M Tower on dwelling 058°-vis-248° obscd by Plateau de Touent when bearing more than 237°

Harbour
2. **Jetée Nord head** Oc.R.4s17m8M
3. **Rocher Les Deux Frères** Fl(2)G.6s26m5M
4. **Inside of N jetée** F.R.8m6M
5. **S Mole** F.G.8m5M

General
Ghazaouet is a good-sized commercial port protected from the E by the Plateau de Touent which towers above the village and from the N by a long breakwater extending from the plateau. A small bank surmounted by the rocks of Les Deux Frères

Algeria

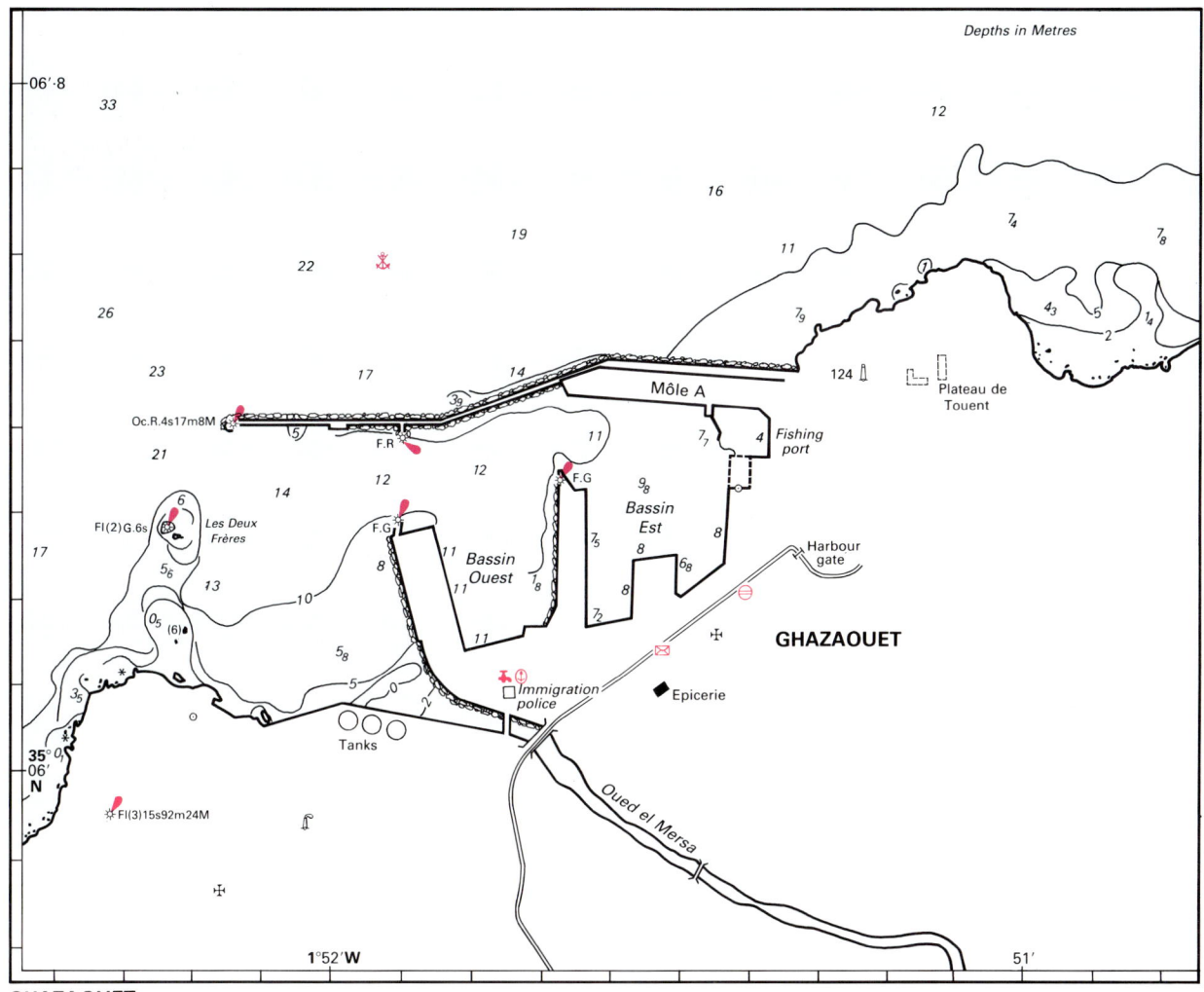

GHAZAOUET

forms the SW extremity of the port entrance. The setting of harbour and village is not unattractive. The port was once important for the export of minerals from Morocco (which does not have any big ports on this part of the coast) but after border disputes, Morocco pulled out. Today's main activities are fishing and repair work.

Berthing
Yachts can tie up in the fishing port in the NE corner of the commercial port or in Bassin Est.

Formalities
All necessary officials will turn up.

Facilities
Water Containers can be filled at a tap near the police office in the SW corner of the port.
Fuel Available in the port.
Provisions There is a small grocery shop outside the harbour gate behind the police office and further supplies are obtainable in the village.
Post office and bank In the village.

Beni-Saf
35°18'·5N 1°23'·3W

Distances
Ras el Ma 54M, Ghazaouet 28M – Oran 54M

Tides
Range does not exceed 0·6m.

Charts

	Approach	Port
Admiralty	2437	178
French	5940	5876
US	52060	52069

Lights
Approach
1. **Ile Rachgoun** 35°19'·5N 1°28'·7W
   Fl(2)R.10s81m16M Yellow square tower on hut

Harbour
2. **Jetée Nord head** Iso.G.4s11m7M 072°-vis-342° Black column on hut
3. **Jetée Est head** Oc(2)R.6s9m8M Red column

General
Beni-Saf is the most active fishing port on the Algerian coast and possibly in this entire part of the Mediterranean. The friendly town, up in the hills, is spread out across a valley which descends down to the harbour. Initially constructed in French colonial times for shipping iron-ore from mines in the

99

North Africa

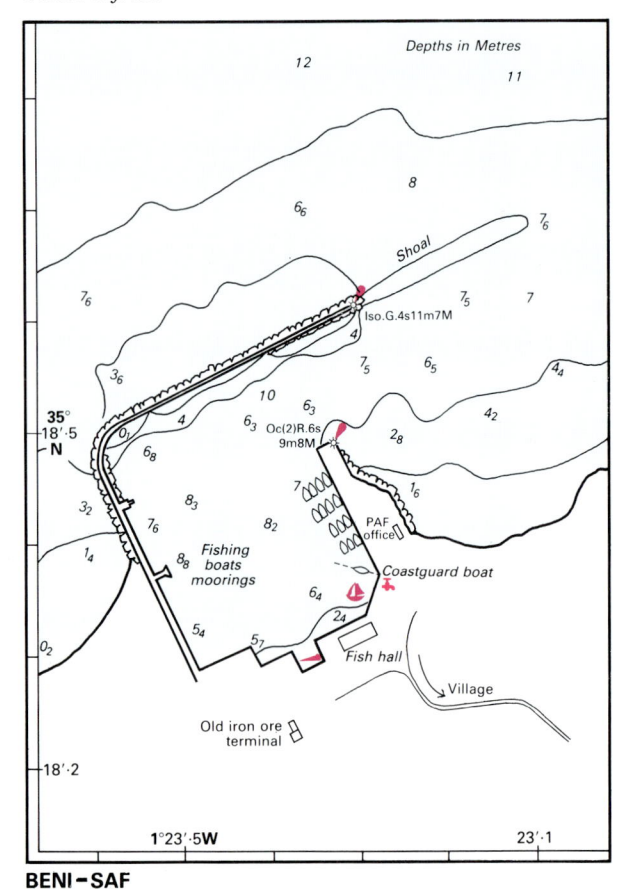

vicinity, fishing became the main activity after the mining company left in 1977.

Approach
From the head of the N breakwater a bank extends 300m in an ENE direction. Entry can be difficult in fresh N and NW winds and dangerous in gales (rare).

Berthing
This medium-sized port is filled by its large fishing fleet. Fishermen may invite yachts to come alongside but most likely room will be made on the short quay in the SE corner next to the coastguard patrol boat. This is more convenient for clearing customs. There is no room to anchor.

Formalities
Port of entry. Officials are friendly and are used to yachts. Passports stay with the *PAF* and have to be picked up shortly before departure.

Facilities
Water From a small tap on the quay at the coast guard boat. Patience is required since most of the time there is no pressure. Early morning or evening seems to be the best time to try. Another option is to carry containers from the fish market.
Provisions Bread from a small shop just outside the port and fresh fish around the fish market. More shops and a well stocked market (by Algerian standards) in the village. For a real 'Eastern-Bloc' feeling walk around the covered market hall where one is 'allowed' to buy oil, a sack of flour or a TV antenna from disinterested government employees.
Showers There is a *hamman* in the village.
Post office Next to the covered market.
Bank In the village.

The fishing port of Beni-Saf viewed from the N. Left of centre are the remnants of the iron ore terminal

Eating out
A few very simple eating houses around the port.

Tourism
From Beni-Saf it is easy to visit Tlemcen, a city rich in history, located 800m high in the Tell Atlas mountains. In the 15th century it was an important trading centre between Europe and Africa. Although much has apparently been demolished over the years, the remaining monuments built in Hispano-Moorish style and the beautiful setting in the mountains make Tlemcen well worth a visit.

Bou-Zadjar
35°34'·5N 1°10'W

General
A fishing port in the SW corner of the bay called Mersa Bou Zadjar (1½M E of Cap Figalo). In 1989, although unfinished, it was used by a large fishing fleet with boats moored and anchored. For yachts it is a useful place to stop in order to make a daytime approach to Iles Habibas. There is nothing in the port and the village of Bou Zadjar is some distance away on the other side of the bay. There are no customs and it is not a port of entry. There is an alternative good weather anchorage between moored fishing boats in front of the village on the other side of the bay.

Mersa Ali Bou Nouar
35°38'N 1°04'W

Charts
French 5886

General
An interesting little bay surrounded by steep hills on a thinly populated part of the coast and a useful stop en route from Beni-Saf to Oran or the Habibas Islands. It is shown without name on British Admiralty charts. Good protection can be found from NE through S to SW. When entering in the middle of the bay, which is only 300m wide, beware of the submerged rocks on the W side. The bottom shoals gradually towards the head of the bay. Anchor in the middle, sand, 5–7m.

Iles Habibas
35°43'·3N 1°08'W

Distances
Beni-Saf 28M – Oran 27M

Tides
Range does not exceed 0·6m.

Charts
	Approach	Port
Admiralty	2437	–
French	5940, 5948	5886
US	52060	–

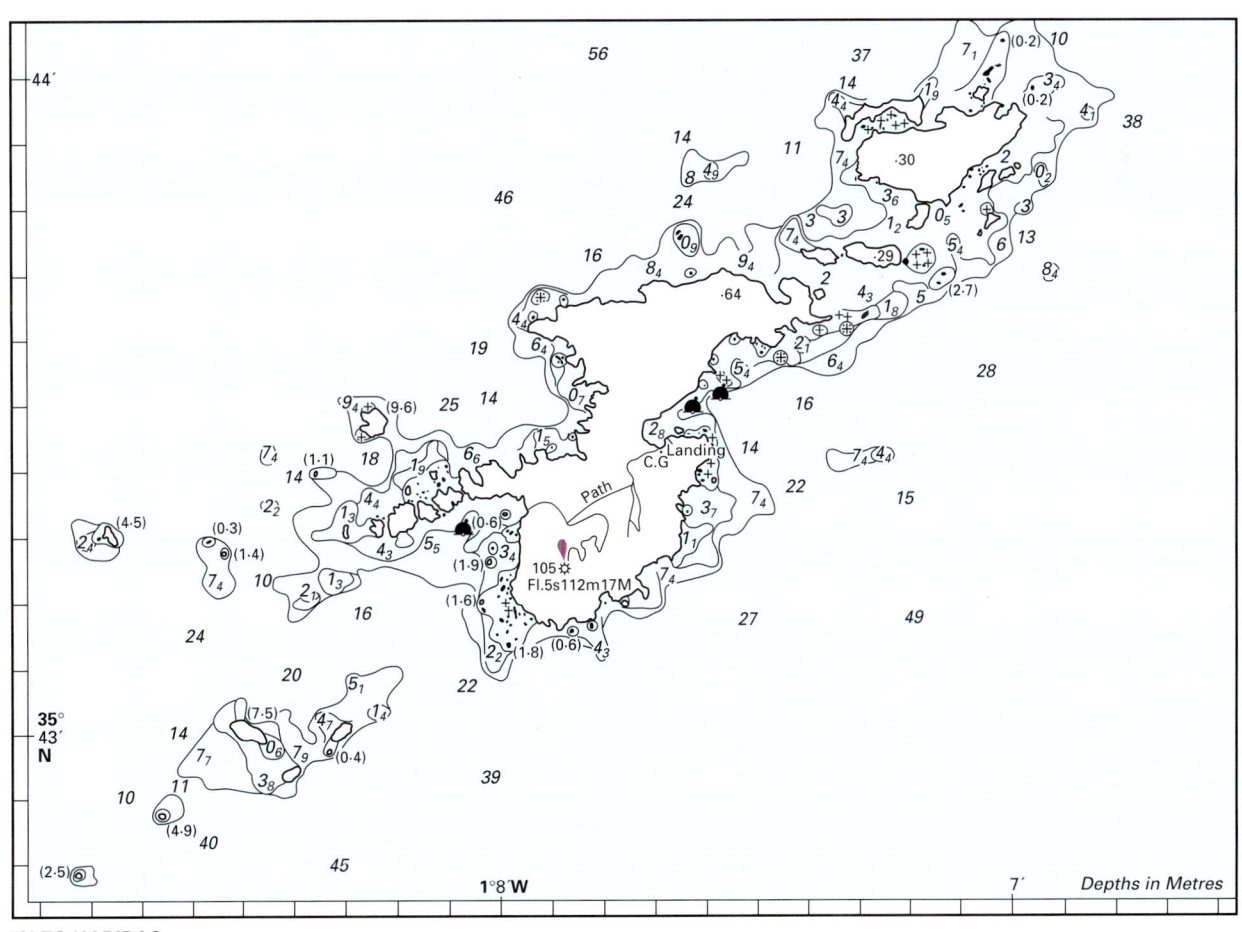

ISLES HABIBAS

North Africa

ORAN

Lights
Approach
1. **Iles Habibas** 35°43'·0N 1°07'·2E
   Fl.5s112m17M Red square tower on dwelling

General
The Iles Habibas, situated 9M NNE of Cap Figalo, are made up of two islands and numerous islets and rocks. Except for the lighthouse keeper and a couple of military guards, they are uninhabited. Two anchorages offer good protection in the prevailing wind directions. For those who like a splendid, natural setting, this is among one of the most attractive places to visit on the entire North African coast. Be sure to bring snorkel/diving gear to explore the unpolluted underwater world. A good path leads up to the lighthouse which offers a spectacular view of the islands and the coast. The visitors book in the lighthouse was started in 1879 and it is closer to a museum piece than anything one will ever find in a real museum in Algeria. The first entries are from French survey lieutenants, followed by naturalists, divers and a few visiting yachts. The bay on the SW side at the foot of the lighthouse, offers good protection from N and E winds and is a good base for diving or fishing expeditions. There is a big mooring buoy which can be used but make sure to throw a kedge. Holding is not good but with enough scope the anchor will eventually set somewhere behind a rock. In W winds, it is best to pick up one of the two mooring buoys on the E side of the island. The coastguard may recommend a little quay in the narrow inlet; it has only 1·5m alongside and is filled with rocks.

Approach
Only by day in good weather. The SW bay can be entered from the S by keeping midway between the SW extremity of the island and 0·4M SW of the lighthouse. With the lighthouse bearing about 070° steer for the big white mooring buoy. This route has depths of 4m or more but keep a good lookout on the bow for rocks.

Formalities
The coastguard has three young men on station, but have no boat. They may arrange to visit by fishing boat and have been known to swim back ashore with notes above their heads! This is obviously not a port of entry.

Facilities
None and more likely the coastguard will ask you for something because they are dropped there for a two week stay with less than abundant provisions.

There is a good supply of rainwater at the lighthouse but slightly impractical at 110m above sea level!

Mers-el-Kébir
35°43'·5N 0°40'·5W

General
A large naval and commercial port 1M WNW of Oran. Entry by yacht is forbidden.

Oran
35°43'·2N 0°37'·5W

Distances
Beni–Saf 54M, Iles Habibas 27M – Mostaganem 42M

Tides
Range does not exceed 0·6m.

Charts
	Approach	*Port*
Admiralty	2437, 1909	812
French	5948	–
US	52281	52282

Lights
Approach
1. **Jetée du Large head** 35°43'·2N 0°37'·5W
   Fl(2+1)15s21m22M Horn 60s 062°-vis-332° White metal framework tower

Harbour
2. **Epi du Large** 35°43'·1N 0°37'·6W
   Iso.G.4s8m7M Black column
3. **Traverse du Large** 35°43'·0N 0°37'·5W
   Iso.R.4s9m8M Red column check
4. **N side Vieux Port, Mole du Centre SE corner**
   Iso.G.4s9m6M
5. **N side Vieux Port, Mole du Centre NE corner**
   F.R.9m7M
6. **S side Vieux Port, Mole St Marie E corner**
   Oc.R.4s9m7M
7. **S side Vieux Port, Mole St Marie E jetty head**
   F.R.6m7M

General
Oran is the second largest city of Algeria with some 650,000 inhabitants. When entering from sea the first impression is of a modern city where the port and industry play an important role. The big commercial harbour has seven basins and yachts can stay in the furthest basin called Vieux Port. A small yacht club with floating pontoons is located on the N side of Vieux Port. Opposite the yacht club are quays for an active fishing fleet. The yacht club is friendly but has no facilities to offer. Authorities are thorough but not unfriendly.

Approach
Tunny nets may be laid between March and November in the area of Baie des Aiguades, SE of Cap Falcon. Entry into the port of Oran is easy in good weather. Fort Santa Cruz (at an elevation of 352m on Jebel Murdjadjo E of the port between Mers-el-Kébir and Oran) is a good landmark. In a rare W gale, a current sets S across the entrance. The Vieux Port is 1½M from the entrance and getting there is a matter of counting piers.

Vieux Port in the W corner of the commercial port of Oran

Berthing
Lie stern-to at the yacht club or, if not possible, tie up alongside a fishing boat in the Vieux Port; Oran is a big city and chances of theft are greater on the public quay. Yachts do not visit every day and it may take the caretaker in the yacht club a while to show up and allocate a free berth with mooring line. The bottom between the pontoons is fouled with moorings and cables.

Formalities
Customs will search your boat whether or not she has been examined in other ports. The *PAF* will ask the skipper to call at their office (a long walk from the yacht club on the other side of the port, near the ferry terminal) and will keep passports there. To save time and effort when leaving Oran, one can best sail to the pier at the Gare Maritime on the way out to pick them up. The yacht club charges Dn 30 per day (based on 1991 rates) regardless of size. When going into town in the evening make sure there is somebody to open the gate on your return.

Facilities
Water A trickle of water in the daytime from several taps on the pontoons. Usually there is some pressure in the evening but make sure not to use the initial stagnant water for drinking.
Electricity Can be arranged at the club.
Fuel In the port.
Provisions Aside from an alimentation général and a fishmonger outside the harbour gate (Oran is one of the few ports where good-size swordfish are brought in daily) there are no shops near the port. There are more shops in the former Jewish quarter in the city which can best be reached by bus.
Showers In the yacht club but they are not salubrious.
Post office and bank In the city.

Eating out
A small restaurant next to the yacht club and two upmarket restaurants near the fishing quay. Outside the gate, opposite the petrol station, you will find Sindbad and further along the road another 100m, Le Dauphin.

Algeria

Tourism
In 1791 Oran, then a Spanish city, was largely destroyed by an earthquake which killed half of the population. The Spanish king left the ruins to the Turks who settled a Jewish community there. When the French arrived in 1831 the city had 4,000 inhabitants. Oran prospered under French rule and grew to the present size and the large commercial port was constructed. After independence the growing population made further expansion of the city necessary and the government decided to build a new, truly Algerian city. In the eastern part of Oran these ambitious plans have been largely realised but the western part, near the Vieux Port, has not been developed and houses have been neglected because they are destined to be torn down as part of the renovation. A walk from the port to the Château Neuf park leads through the former Spanish and Jewish quarters, though there is not much left of them. There is a good view of the city and port from this well-kept park; the impressive Château Neuf was the seat of the Spanish governor until 1701 and today is used by the military. It is not open to the public. Alternatively there is a 4km walk to the Spanish Santa Cruz castle, 350m high on Jebel Murdjadjo (or Mount Aidour by the old name). Most people prefer to take a taxi – the summer heat should not be underestimated. Either way, the view from Santa Cruz is equally rewarding.

Arzew
35°51'N 0°22'·5W

General
Arzew is a small village where in recent years one of the biggest commercial harbours of Algeria has been built for the exportation of liquij131
fied gas and oil.
There is nothing of interest for a yacht.

Mostaganem
35°56'N 0°04'·2E

Distances
Oran 42M – Ténès 75M

Tides
Range does not exceed 0·6m.

Charts
	Approach	*Port*
Admiralty	1909	178
French	5951	5696
US	55260	52263

Lights
Harbour
1. **Jetée du Large** Fl(4)WR.12s17m13/10M
   197°-R-234°-W-197° White tower, red top
2. **Mole Sud Ouest head** Oc(2)G.6s13m5M
   248°-vis-073° White column, green top
3. **Inside of Jetée du Large** Oc(2)G.6s13m5M
4. **Mole de l'Indépendence head** Fl.G.4s11m9M
   351·5°-vis-261·5° White hut, green top

General
A medium-sized commercial port situated in an agricultural area in the NE corner of the Bay of Arzew. At one time Mostaganem was important for exporting wine and cereals but its main activities are now fishing and importing potatoes, sugar and timber. Mostaganem is a modern, European-style city with some 300,000 inhabitants. The dusty port is situated on the northern edge of the town and in the summer heat walking to the centre is tedious. The rather nondescript surroundings of the practically empty port are offset by the friendly officials. Visiting yachts have experienced a hospitable reception. Not a bad port of entry to Algeria.

Approach
Aero RC and radiobeacon on the entrance pier. At night the lights are obscured by street lights until fairly close.

Berthing
Plenty of room. Tie up alongside the NE Quay in the back of the port near the tugboat berth.

Formalities
Port of entry. A *permis d'escale* is issued to leave the port area on foot.

Facilities
Water Containers can be filled.
Fuel No diesel in the port.
Provisions From a couple of small shops a short walk into town.
Post office and bank In the town.

Weather
Forecast available from the harbourmaster's office.

Eating out
Coffee bar at the harbour gate.

North Africa

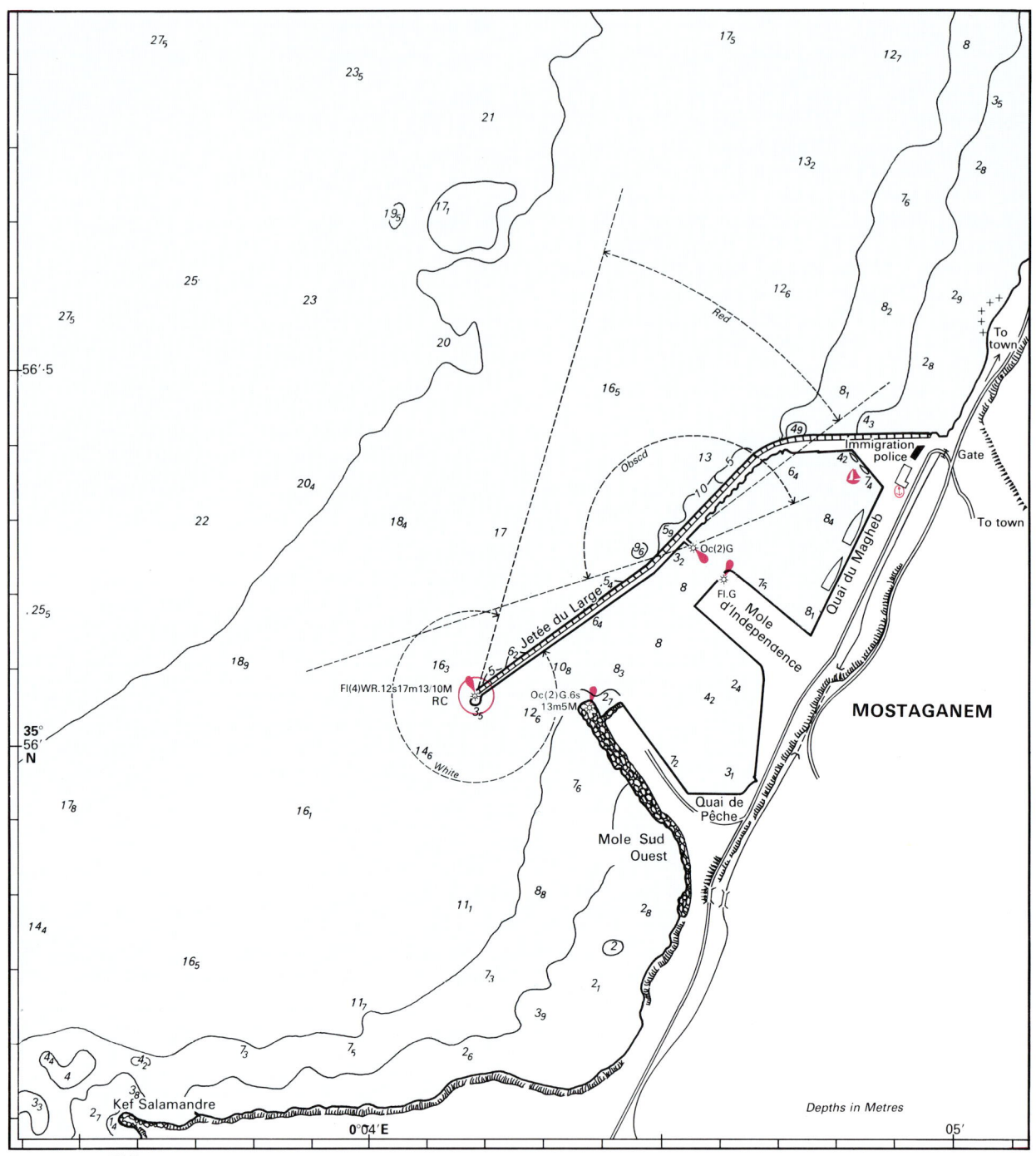

MOSTAGANEM

Ténès

36°31'·8N 1°18'·9E

Distances
Mostaganem 75M – Cherchell 45M

Tides
Range does not exceed 0·6m.

Charts

	Approach	Port
Admiralty	1909	178
French	3234	5708
US	52260	–

Lights
Approach
1. **Cap Ténès** 36°33'·1N 1°20'·6E
   Fl(2)10s89m31M White square tower on dwelling

Harbour
2. **Detached breakwater W head** Q.10m10M
3. **Detached breakwater E Head** Iso.G.4s10m6M
4. **Jetée NW head** Oc(2)G.6s10m7M
5. **Jetée NE head** Oc(2)R.6s10m8M

Lights are reported to be unreliable.

General
A medium-sized commercial port similar to Mostaganem though smaller. Commercial traffic

106

Algeria

entering the port by the W entrance during strong NW winds to avoid being set down on to the SW jetty. In heavy weather entry is dangerous.

Berthing
Follow instructions from the harbour authorities.

Formalities
Port of entry.

Facilities
Water On the SW quay.
Provisions In the village 1·5km from the port.
Post office and bank In the village.

Tourism
The small village of Ténès, with 15,000 inhabitants, lies 1·5km from the port on a hill. The site of Ténès has Phoenician and Roman origins but there are no monuments remaining from those eras. The old Berber village of Vieux Ténès, 2km S of the new town, is worth a visit. Just N of the port is a good beach.

Cherchell
36°36'·8N 2°11'·5E

Distances
Ténès 45M – Sidi Ferruch 34M

Tides
Range of the tide is about 0·5m.

TÉNÈS

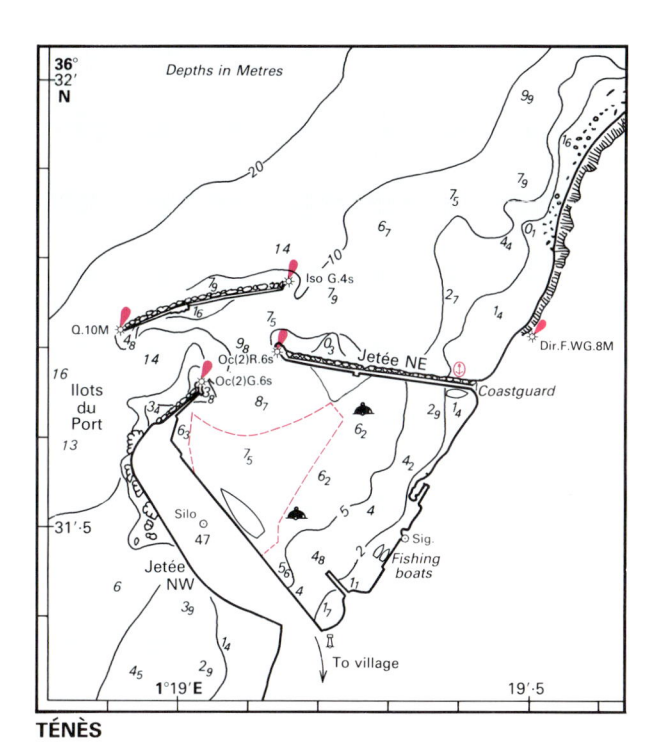

has declined over the years and today's main activity is fishing.

Approach
Radiobeacon on Cap Ténès. Yachts can use either the W or E entrance. Caution is necessary when

The small fishing port of Cherchell. The basin in the foreground is only knee-deep

107

North Africa

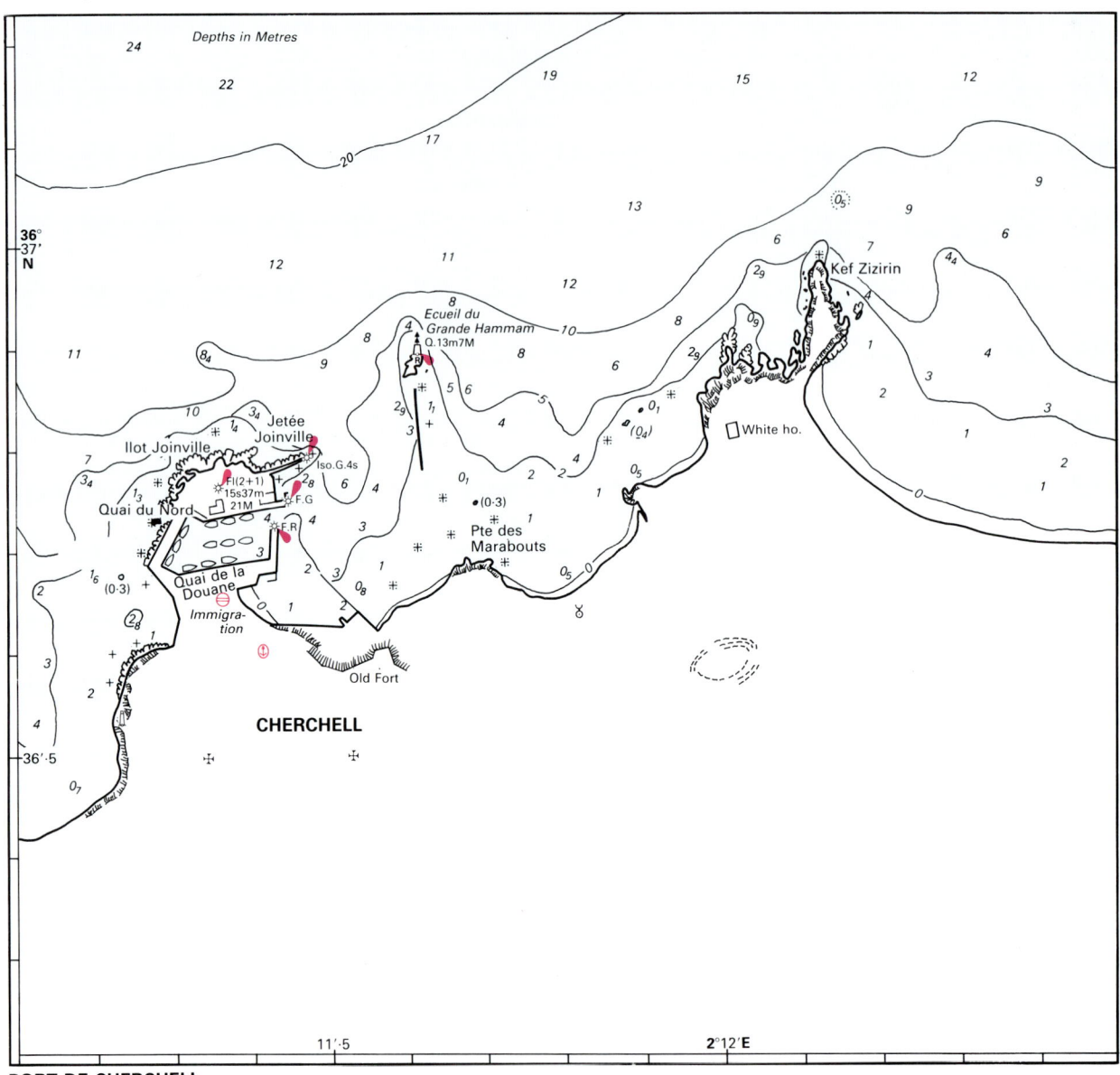

PORT DE CHERCHELL

Charts
	Approach	Port
Admiralty	1909, 1910	1710
French	3202	5699
US	52240	—

Lights
Approach
1. **Forte Joinville** 36°36'·7N 2°11'·4E
   Fl(2+1)15s37m21M 326°-unintens-037·5° White tower, black lantern
2. **Ecueil du Grand Hammam** 36°36'·9N 2°11'·7E
   Q.13m7M ↑ card BY
3. **Jetée Joinville head** 36°36'·8N 2°11'·5E
   Iso.G.4s10m7M White tower

Harbour
4. **Quai Nord E end** F.G.8m6M
5. **Quai Est N end** F.R.8m6M

General
One of the most attractive harbours on the Algerian coast. The small town of Cherchell is set amidst green hills and the fishing port is constructed in a natural setting between the coast and an off-lying rock. There is an active fishing fleet operating in the port and the prawn fishermen seem to be prosperous. The history of Cherchell goes back to the Phoenician trading post of Iol which enjoyed great prosperity. Evidence of this period is found in two small museums and some Roman ruins around the town.

Approach
Aero RC. There is a submerged wall extending S from Ecueil du Grande Hammam. When entering, round the head of Jetée Joinville at a short distance but keep well clear of Ecueil du Grande Hammam. The small-craft harbour S of the port entrance has only knee-deep water. The entrance to the fishing port is narrow with a lively traffic of fishing boats in the early morning and late afternoon. In bad weather the entrance is impassable. The anchorage off Cherchell is very bad; it is entirely exposed and even moderate breezes raise a heavy sea. Night entry is not recommended.

Berthing
There is not much room and several fishing boats are moored in the middle. A yacht can usually find a place alongside a fishing boat.

Formalities
Port of entry. Authorities are friendly.

Facilities
Water Taps all around the port with plenty of good water which is only turned on in the morning.
Fuel Available only from bowser.
Provisions A good assortment of fresh produce can be found at the market and several small shops around it in the pleasant village, a short walk from the port.
Post office and bank In the village.

Eating out
A seafood restaurant near the port and several eating houses in the village.

Tourism
The Numidian King Juba II ruled in Iol (the old name for Cherchell) with Roman protection from 25BC to AD25. In honour of the Roman emperor he renamed the town Caesarea. Juba was educated in Hellenistic style in Rome and being married to the daughter of the Egyptian Queen Cleopatra, he developed a broad interest in the arts of different civilisations. Consequently, he enriched Caesarea with a large art collection from Mediterranean countries. Even though many of these were copies of classic masterpieces, the importance is significant today because the original work has often been lost. Some of the best examples are on display in the Louvre in Paris and a mosaic, picturing a racehorse, decorates the El Djezaïr Hotel in Algiers. Among the collection in the museum of Cherchell are statues of Apollo and the Emperor Augustus. Mosaics are found in the tranquil outdoor museum. Both can easily be visited in one day. Compared to the museums, the Roman ruins are relatively insignificant although they make for a pleasant walk.

Cherchell and the beaches around it are a popular resort area and in summertime Algerian holidaymakers and a few European tourists liven up the streets in the village.

Nearby, Tipasa is a modern summer resort in an idyllic setting with unique remains of the Roman era. If the weather makes anchoring there unsafe, Cherchell is a good base for a visit

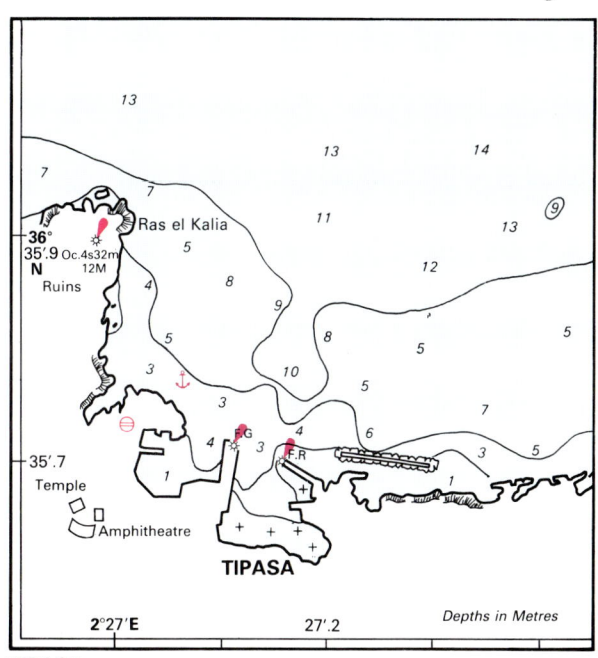

TIPASA

Tipasa
36°35'·8N 2°27'E

Charts
French 5699

Lights
Ras el Kalia Oc.4s32m12M

General
Although Tipasa has two ports, both are too small and shallow for a yacht but the bay is a pleasant good-weather anchorage. It is near the interesting ruins of an old Phoenician and Roman trading post which can be visited in the Parc Archéologique. Even though it has been developed on a small scale for tourism, the site amidst the thickly wooded coast is quite attractive. The *Travel Survival Kit* has a good description of its history and archaeology.

The bay is between Ras el Kalia in the W and the islets of Sidi Saïd to the E and offers some protection from the W but is exposed from NW to E. Anchor in 3–6m. Even light onshore breezes can make landing with the dinghy difficult.

Bou Aroun
36°37'·6N 2°39'·5E

Charts
French 3030

General
A very small fishing port approximately 10M E of Tipasa. The entrance may have depths of 2m or more but the port itself is too shallow for an ordinary yacht.

North Africa

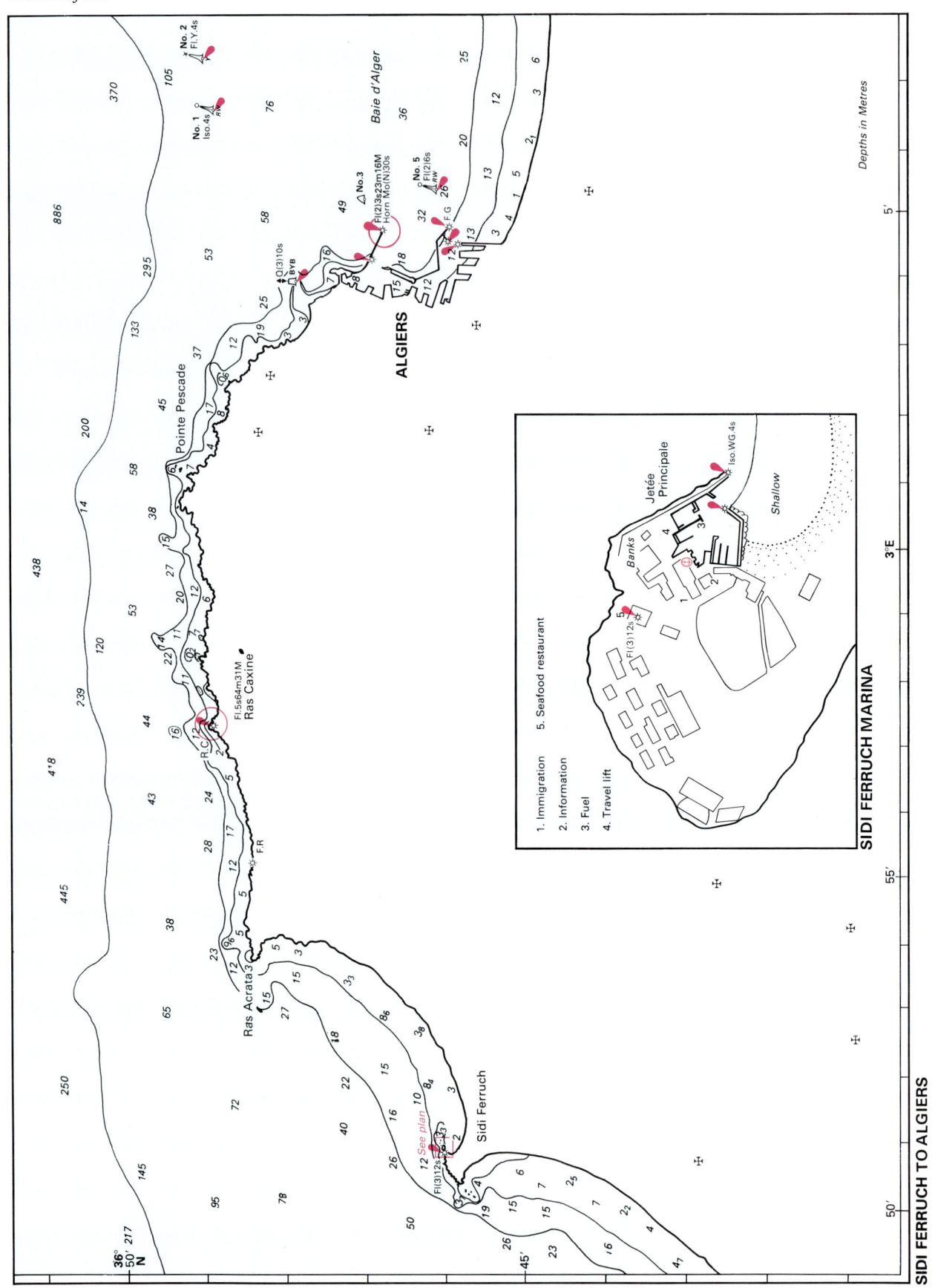

ALGIERS

Baie d'Alger

Pointe Pescade

Ras Caxine
Fl.5s64m31M

Ras Acrata

Sidi Ferruch

SIDI FERRUCH MARINA

1. Immigration
2. Information
3. Fuel
4. Travel lift
5. Seafood restaurant

Jetée Principale
Banks
Shallow

Depths in Metres

SIDI FERRUCH TO ALGIERS

Algeria

BOU AROUN

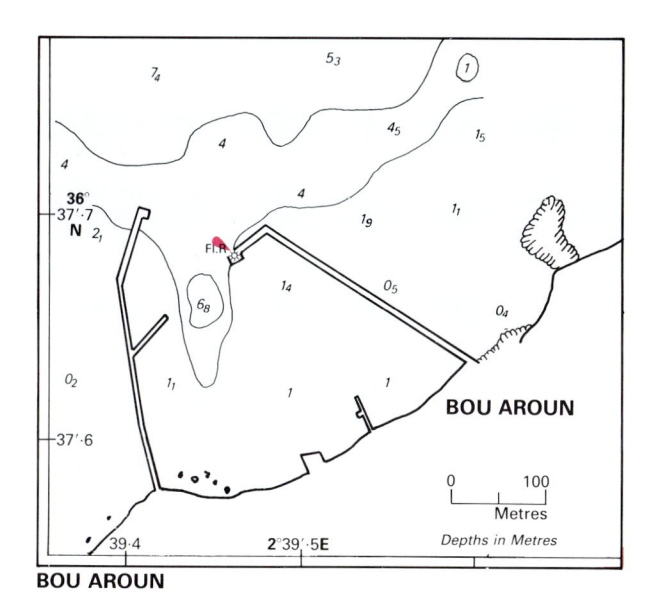

Chiffalo

36°38'·4N 2°40'·4E

Charts
French 3030

General
A tiny harbour 1M NE of Bou Aroun. The depth outside the port is about 2m and inside the water is not much more than knee-deep.

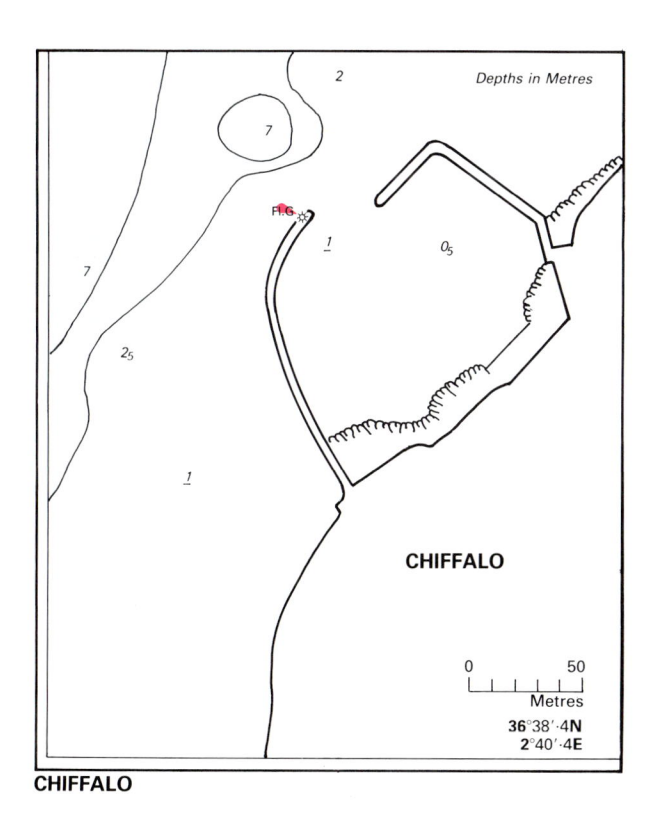

CHIFFALO

Sidi Ferruch (Sidi Fredj)

36°46'N 2°51'E

Distances
Cherchell 34M – Dellys 55M

Tides
Range of the tide is about 0·5m.

Charts

	Approach	*Port*
Admiralty	1910	–
French	3030	–
US	52240	–

Lights
Approach
1. **Ras Caxine** 36°48'·8N 2°57'·4E
   Fl.5s64m31M 075°-vis-300°
   Yellow square tower, green top
2. **Sidi Fredj Marina** 36°46'N 2°50'·9E
   Fl(3)12s42m17M Low tower on hotel

Harbour
3. **Jetée Principale head** Iso.WG.4s14m11/8M
   190°-W-129°-G-190°
4. **Marina entrance starboard side** F.G
5. **Marina entrance port side** F.R

General
Sidi Ferruch, or Sidi Fredj, is a large holiday resort and tourist complex with the only marina in Algeria. It is often used as port of entry even though many other ports serve just as well. It lacks the facilities normally associated with a marina and the artificial surroundings of restaurants, apartments and hotels give a very distorted picture of the country. On the other hand, authorities are used to yachts and it is the port nearest to Algiers, where yachts are not welcome. Other than beaches there are no particular points of interest and the nearest village Stauoéli is 5km away. Harbour charges for visitors are high compared with the services but the first forty-eight hours are free of charge. The few visitors' berths available lack any privacy, with hoards of holidaymakers promenading along the quay and speedboats whizzing in and out. Most of the yachts in the harbour belong to French and other expatriates working in Algiers.

Approach
RC beacon on Ras Caxine. The peninsula of Sidi Ferruch is low and not remarkable except for the buildings around the port. When coming from the NW and rounding the marina complex, beware of shoals 50–100m offshore. One shoal at the root of Jetée Principale is almost totally submerged. The port side of the entrance is silted up, with a depth of barely 2m and entry should be made well to starboard. The harbourmaster did indicate that it was to be dredged.

In NE winds of force 5 or more entry will be difficult, with waves breaking on the banks around the entrance. A night entry should be avoided as the harbour lights are unreliable and there are only a few street lights in the port.

Berthing
There are severely limited spaces but visitors can usually find a berth on the Jetée Principale, either inside the spur or in the inner basin. Most likely a kedge will be needed to lie bows or stern-to. In some parts along this quay a chain has been laid in the middle, so a sinking tripping line should be used without marker buoy to avoid speedboat propellers. If there is no free mooring here, tie up temporarily at the fuel quay. With diplomacy it may be possible to keep the authorities from boarding immediately; if not, there may be oil marks on the deck.

Formalities
Port of entry. The authorities are friendly.

Facilities
Water and electricity The water taps on Jetée Principale are broken and only a few electric sockets function. Water is available on the opposite quay and some visitors had submarine hoses to taps there.
Fuel Diesel, petrol and engine oil at the fuel quay. Good quality and very cheap.
Provisions A very limited supply from a so-called supermarket in the harbour. No fresh vegetables, milk, or meat. Reasonable supplies in Staouéli.
Showers Warm showers available near the harbourmaster's office.
Post office In Staouéli.
Telephone In the hotels.
Foreign exchange In the hotels at bank rates.
Repairs A 16-ton travel-lift. Emergency repairs can be done as long as no parts are required.

Eating out
Several restaurants around the port and a good French-style seafood restaurant with large aquarium at the end of the small channel which cuts across the peninsula.

Transport
Buses every 30 minutes to Algiers. Bus stop outside the harbour and the ride takes about 45 minutes. Trips with excursion buses to Algiers can be arranged at the hotels.

Tourism
The main reason for visiting Sidi Ferruch is its proximity to the beautiful capital. Algiers is built like an amphitheatre in green hills which rise steeply from the port and compared with the other big cities in the Maghreb it is the most cosmopolitan. Many prominent buildings from French colonial times have been well maintained and the Arabic character is still found in the *kasbah* where, incidentally, the food riots in 1988 started. There are several good museums, mosques and an extraordinarily pretty post office. A tour of the city can best be planned with the tourist information office.

Sidi Ferruch was designed by a well-known French architect, Fernand Pouillon, an enthusiastic sailor who spent the last years of his life on board his boat there. After his death in France, his boat was set up as a monument in the port.

Algiers
36°45'·8N 3°05'E

Tides
The tide is hardly noticeable.

Charts
	Approach	Port
Admiralty	1910	855
French	3043, 5638	5617
US	52240	52243

Lights
Approach
1. **Roche M'Tahen** 36°47'·8N 3°04'·1E
   Q(3)10s12m8M ♦ card BYB
2. **Port d'Alger Jetée ED Dinn head** 36°46'·7N 3°04'·8E
   Fl(2)3s23m16M Horn Mo(N)30s Metal tower 154°-vis-055° RC F.R lights on radio masts 2·6M NW

Harbour
3. **Jetée Kheir Eddine spur** Fl.G.4s10m7M
4. **Jetée du Vieux Port N end** Fl.R.4s10m8M
4. **Jetée de Mustapha spur** Iso.G.4s12m8M 295°-vis-104° White tower, green top
5. **Passe Sud Brise-Iames Est head** Oc.R.4s12m9M 005°-vis-312° White tower, red top 5F.R(vert) on each of 2 radio masts 1·07M SSW F.R on Memorial des martyrs 1M SSW

General
The capital of Algeria with 3·7 million inhabitants.

The commercial port of Algiers may only be entered by yachts in case of emergency and entry in other circumstances may be penalised. If entry is necessary, ask permission by VHF. Running out of fuel might qualify as an emergency but entry would be useless as there is no diesel available for yachts. Yachts that do enter are berthed by the military vessels. Personnel there are very unfriendly.

La Pérouse
36°48'·3N 3°13'·9E

Charts
Admiralty 855
French 5617

Lights
1. **Pier head** F.R.10m6M White column, red top, on hut Obscd by Cap Matifou when bearing more than 145°
2. The existence of Ras Matifou buoy (Iso.R.4s) is uncertain.

General
A pleasant anchorage in the NE corner of the Bay of Algiers, just S of Cap Matifou, with good holding and excellent protection from easterlies. A pier juts out SSW from the headland; anchor behind it between local boats or take a free mooring if available. To the S is the small beach resort, Alger Plage, and the ruins of the old Phoenician and Roman city, Rusguniae. A good stop-over between Sidi Ferruch and Dellys. There is a restaurant in the area. Officials are friendly but not accustomed to

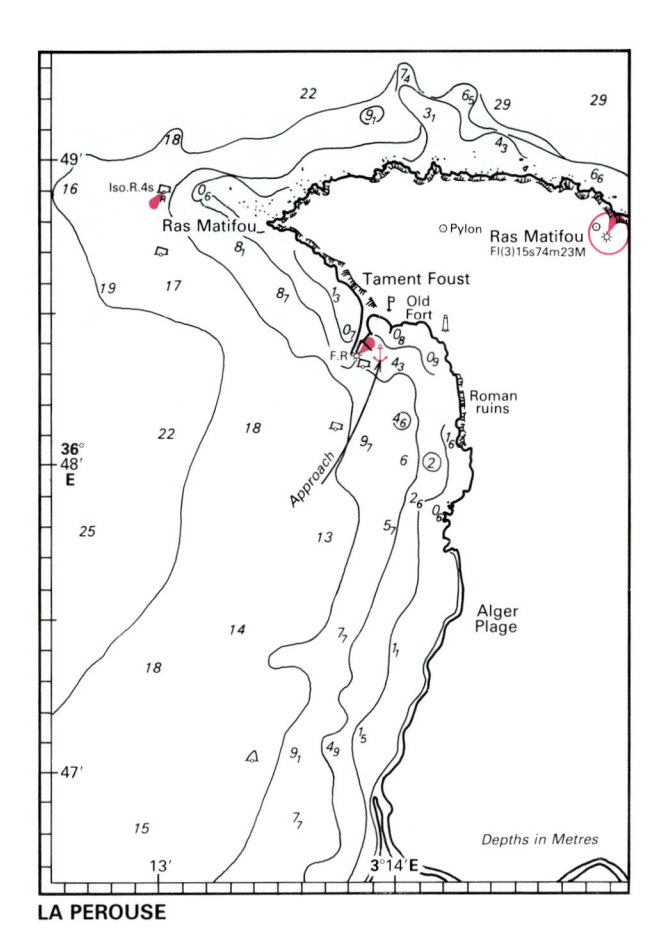

Algeria

LA PEROUSE

General
A small port between Cap Matifou and Dellys. Depth in the entrance is 4–5m but shoals to less than 1·5m towards the west breakwater and the beach in the SE corner of the port. The port silts up and the approach should be made carefully. There are no officials that can deal with the entry formalities.

Dellys
36°54'·9N 3°55'·2E

Distances
Sidi Ferruch 55M – Bejaïa 64M

Tides
Range of the tide is about 0·5m.

Charts
	Approach	Port
Admiralty	1910	1710
French	3043, 3036	5640
US	–	–

Lights
Approach
1. **Cap Bengut** 36°55'·4N 3°53'·7E
   Fl(4)15s63m30M 079°-vis-287° Obscd by Pointe de Dellys when bearing less than 270° White square tower green top
2. **Pointe de Dellys** 36°55'·4N 3°55'·4E
   F.R.41m8M 066°-vis-336° obscd by Cap Bengut when bearing less than 094° Yellow tower, red lantern

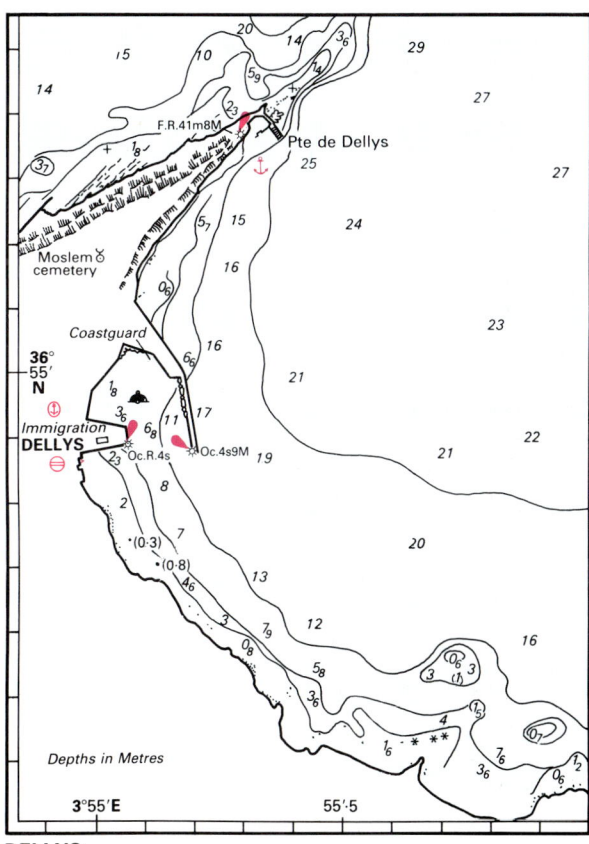

visiting yachts and they may insist that you row ashore with them to do the routine paperwork.

Zemmouri Bahar
(formerly Courbet Marine)
36°48'·3N 3°33'·6E

Lights
1. **Jetée Nord head** 36°48'·3N 3°33'·6E
   Q.12m6M White tower red top

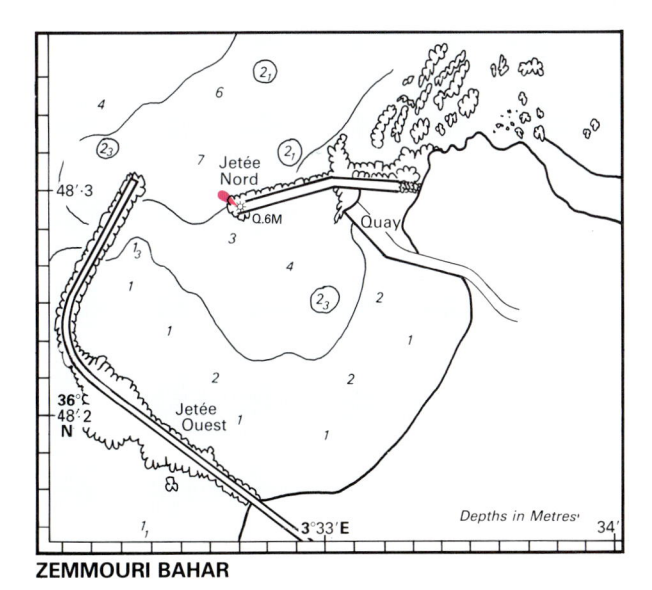

ZEMMOURI BAHAR

DELLYS

113

North Africa

Entrance to Dellys harbour viewed from SE

Harbour
3. **Jetée head** Oc.4s12m9M Obscd by Point de Dellys when bearing less than 193° White tower, green top
4. **Quay Sud SE corner** Oc.R.4s8m7M Obscd by Point de Dellys when bearing less than 203° White tower, red top

General
A small commercial and fishing port, although as with many of the smaller commercial ports in Algeria, not much frequented in recent years by merchantmen. Dellys is a pleasant and lively village set against green wooded hills and is one of the more attractive places along the Algerian coast. There is an active fleet of fishing boats which produce considerable wash in the port and if tied up alongside one of them, good fenders are needed. Protection is mediocre and northerly winds set up a considerable swell. There is not much room for yachts but it may be possible to anchor in the port or temporarily pick up a free mooring. Watch out for petty theft by children.

Approach
From Pointe de Dellys a shallow spit extends 0·3M NE and the remainders of a small jetty extend to the SE. Tunny nets used to be laid off this point but they seem to be a thing of the past. A west-setting counter current may be experienced in the Bay of Dellys, turning N close to the port entrance and bending NE off Pointe de Dellys to join the main E current along the coast. The harbour lights do not work.

Berthing
Beware of the wake from passing fishing boats which can be dangerous when tied up alongside the W quay. It is preferable to go further inside the port near the coastguard boat. Alternatively one may pick up a free mooring or find room to anchor in the port (with tripping line). Holding is not very good; the best place may be SSE of Pointe de Dellys in sand 15–25m deep. Close to the point the bottom is rocky.

Formalities
Port of entry. Authorities are relaxed by Algerian standards.

Facilities
Water Only near the coastguard boat in the N corner.
Provisions A reasonable assortment of fresh produce in the village.
Post office and bank In the village.

Eating out
A few eating houses in the village.

Azzefoun
(formerly Port Gueydon)
36°54·2′N 4°25′·3E

Lights
Jetty head Oc(2)R.6s8m7M Obscd by Cap Corbelin White pedestal, red head on jetty head

General
Azzefoun is a small town S of Cap Corbelin with a port consisting of a single pier. Since 1996 the outer two-thirds of the pier have been removed and the light along with it. Work has started on a new harbour but until this is completed (possibly in a few years) this port is even less sheltered than usual from the strong easterlies, which are common along the coast in the summer. No protection from W to N. Anchor in 4–6m.

114

Algeria

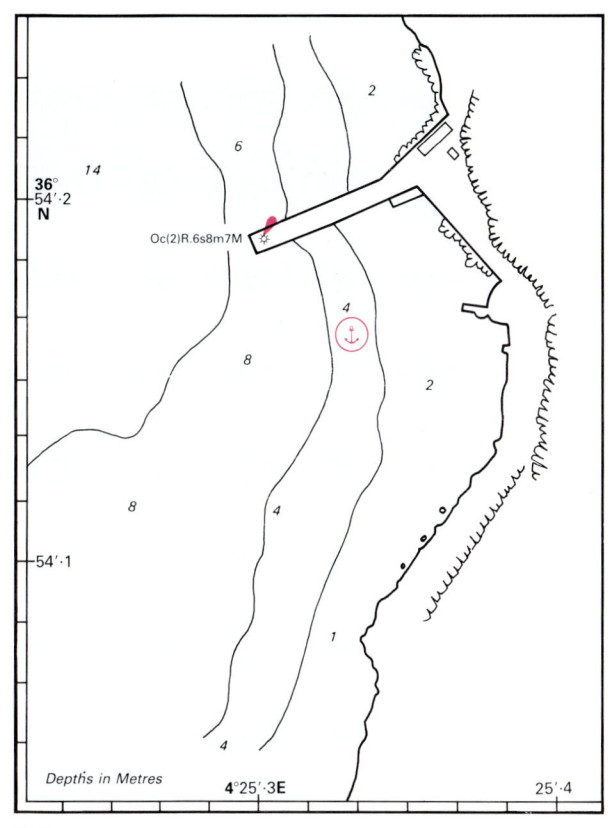

AZZEFOUN

Bejaïa
(formerly Bougie)
36°45'·2N 5°06'·1E

Distances
Dellys 64M – Jijel 34M

Tides
Tidal range is about 0·5m.

Charts
	Approach	Port
Admiralty	1910, 252	1710
French	3029	5641
US	52240, 52220	52221

Lights
Approach
1. **Ras Carbon** 36°46'·6N 5°06'·3E
   Fl(3)15s220m28M Obscd by Cap Noir when bearing more than 333° White round tower on house Auxiliary Fl.WR.1·5s32m10/7M 094°-W-114° obscd by coast, 114°-R-126°-W-295°, 295°-W-316° obscd by coast White round tower, square dwelling

Harbour
2. **Jetée Est head** 36°45'·2N 5°06'·2E
   Oc.4s16m12M Obscd by Cap Bouak when bearing less than 205° RC
3. **Jetée Sud head** 36°45'·2N 5°06'·0E
   Oc(2)R.6s11m10M
4. **Vieux Port entrance** N side F.G
5. **Vieux Port entrance** S side F.R

General
The commercial port of Bejaïa is large and dusty but the town and beautiful surrounding mountains make up for it. If one can put up with the discomforts of the port, Bejaïa is top of the list of interesting places to visit on the Algerian coast. There is plenty of room in the Vieux Port and it is secure in all weather.

Approach
Straightforward with no off-lying dangers. Jebel Arbalou 1317m high, about 20km W of Bejaïa is visible from over 50M in clear weather and Ras Carbon is easy to make out with the lighthouse on top and the remarkable gate at the foot. From the North, Bejaïa is not visible until well around Ras Carbon. In 1989 construction was in progress to enlarge the entrance to Vieux Port by shortening the spur projecting from Jetée du Sud.

Berthing
Yachts are usually accommodated in the W corner of the Vieux Port. This is close to the harbour gate leading into town. If you announce your arrival by VHF, a pilot boat will probably accompany you to a berth.

Formalities
Port of Entry. *PAF* found at the ferry terminal and are friendly.

Facilities
Water Available at a tap 25m from the harbour gate.
Fuel Diesel available in the port.
Provisions A few small shops and good market not far from the port. Once outside the harbour gate walk along the street parallel to the railway tracks in the shade of the trees and turn right at the statue at the end. The market is 50m from the statue.
Post office and bank In the centre of town.
Transport Regular ferry service to Marseille and other Algerian ports. Train and air service to Algiers.

Eating out
Several restaurants in town.

Tourism
From the port it is a short walk into the lively town and to a well-stocked market. Although many buildings have been neglected since independence, the reminiscence of prosperity under French rule is evident from pleasant squares and stylish architecture throughout the town. From Place de Novembre 1 in the town centre, there is a beautiful view of the harbour and the Bay of Bejaïa which, without exaggeration, is one of the prettiest on the North African coast. Once outside the town, a path cut out of the rocks leads to the cape via Les Aiguades, which has a small cosy restaurant where wine and beer are served. Views from the path over the Bay of Bejaïa are splendid and even in mid-summer it is cool and quiet.

The coast north of the port is rough with mountains dropping steeply into the sea and a visit to Bejaïa is not complete without walking up to the lighthouse on Ras Carbon – one of the highest in the Mediterranean. The surrounding shoreline is rich in fish and excellent for snorkelling.

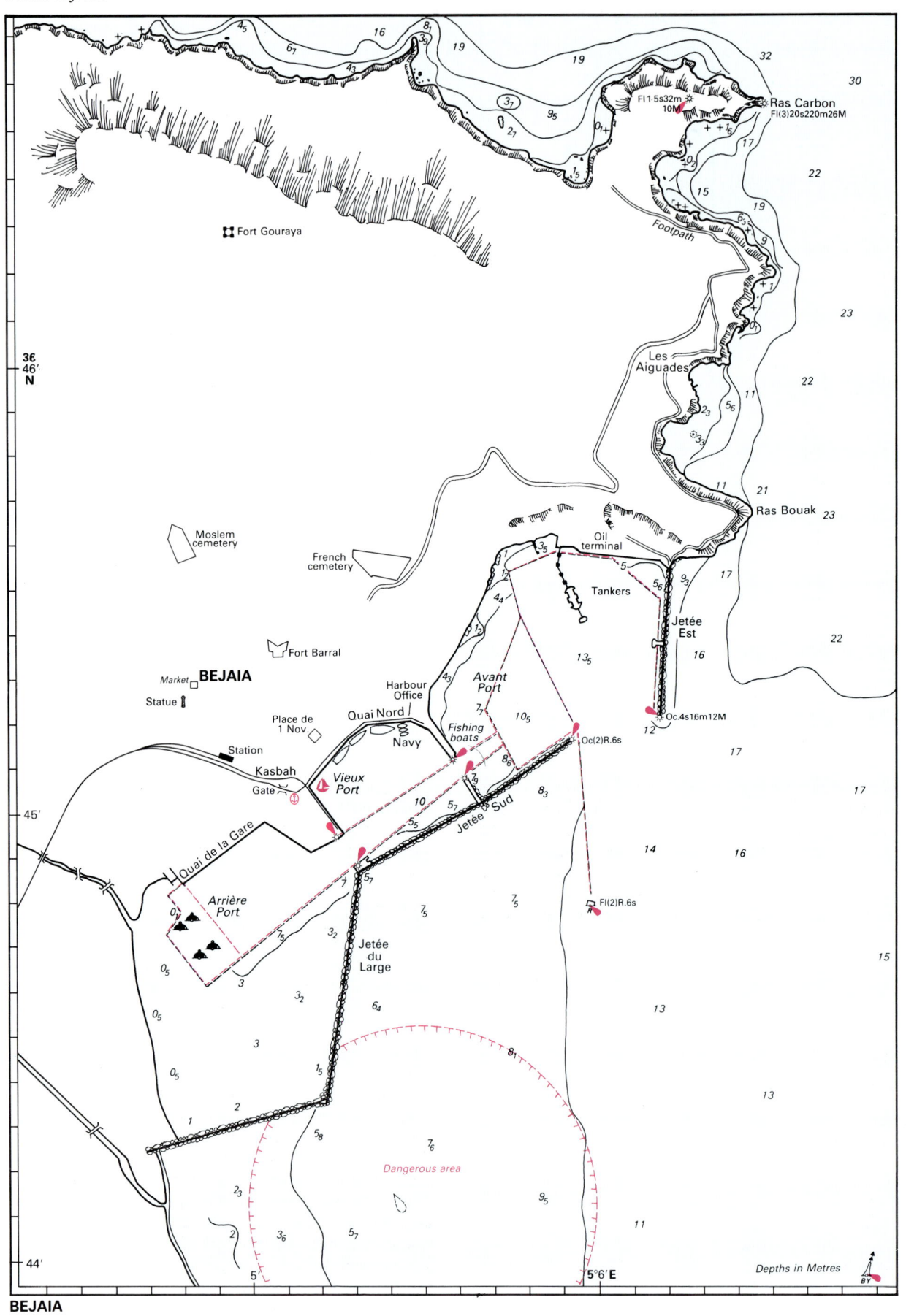

North Africa

BEJAIA

The commercial port of Bejaïa

There are Roman ruins at Djemila. Other worthwhile excursions, a little further away, requiring a taxi, are to Pic des Singes with its wild monkeys and to Fort Gouraya with splendid views across the Kabylie to the high peaks of the Djurdjura Massif. Alternatively, it is worthwhile to hire a car to go further inland and explore the mountainous Kabylie region. The small museum in Bejaïa at Place de Novembre 1 with paintings of people and landscapes of the Kabylie was closed for restoration in 1989.

Jijel
36°49'·5N 5°47'E

Distances
Bejaïa 34M – Collo 48M

Tides
Range of the tide is about 0·5m.

Charts
	Approach	Port
Admiralty	252	1712
French	3029, 3023	–
US	52220	–

Lights
Approach
1. **Ras el Afia** 36°49'·2N 5°41'·5E
   Fl.R.5s43m23M 027°-vis-255° Obscd by Cap Cavallo when bearing less than 064° Yellow 8-sided tower, red top.

Harbour
2. **Jetée Nord** Oc(1+2)WR.12s19m12/9M Yellow square tower, black top 096°-R-101°-W-096° Obscd by the heights of Picouleau when bearing less than 094° F.R lights on masts 4·4M ESE
3. **Jetée Nord head** Iso.G.4s9m Black column
4. **Jetée Sud head** F.R.7m4M Red column
5. **Inner harbour entrance** F.R/F.G

General
The medium-sized commercial port of Jijel is used by a small fishing fleet and freighters regularly call at the recently upgraded SE basin. The NW corner of the port along Jetée Nord is used by the Algerian navy. The coast around Jijel is less spectacular than that to the west or east and the town is flat without any grandeur but not unpleasant and the many tea houses remind one more of Morocco than Algeria. People are friendly. A good assortment of fresh produce can be found in several shops and the market, not far from the port. The long beaches east of Jijel are popular, but not crowded, with Algerian holidaymakers.

North Africa

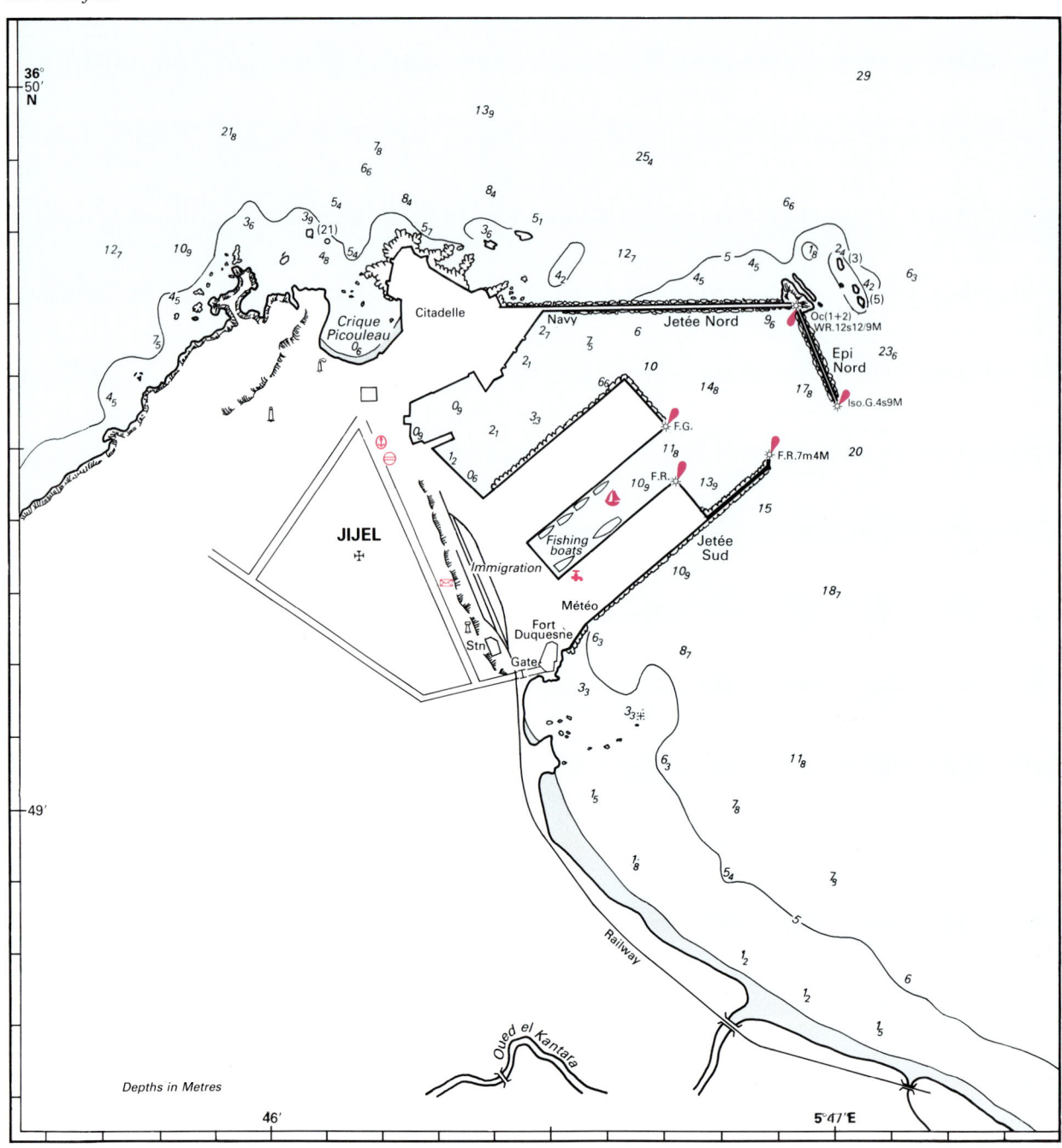

JIJEL

Approach
Beware of rocks 300m NE of the islet in Jetée Nord. Particular care should be taken at night since they are only covered by a narrow red sector of the approach light on the islet.

Berthing
Plenty of room in the SE basin amongst fishermen and the occasional freighter. During strong summer easterlies a considerable swell enters the port.

Formalities
Port of entry.

Facilities
Water In the S corner of Quai Sud.
Provisions A good assortment from several shops and a market in the village.
Post office and bank Along the main street in the village.

Weather forecast
Can be requested from the *Météo* office on the way out of the port.

Eating out
Some simple eating houses in the village.

Djen Djen

36°49'N 5°51'E

General
This large new container and mineral port, 5M east of Jijel, was due to be completed in 1990. The ambitious plans included a railroad to be built by the French and a Russian thermal power plant, while the port was being constructed by an Italian company. No place for yachts.

Mersa Zeitoun

36°57'N 6°16'E

General
An excellent anchorage in E winds in a cove between a shoal spit and an islet with two conical summits at the S entrance point.

Casabianca

36°58'·2N 6°15'·3E

General
Anchorage with shelter from N and E winds 1M North of Mersa Zeitoun. Anchor in sand 10–12m deep off the beach near the house with a red roof.

Collo

37°00'·3N 6°34'·5E

Distances
Jijel 48M – Stora 19M

Tides
Range of the tide is about 0·5m.

Charts

	Approach	Port
Admiralty	252	1712
French	3023	–
US	52223	–

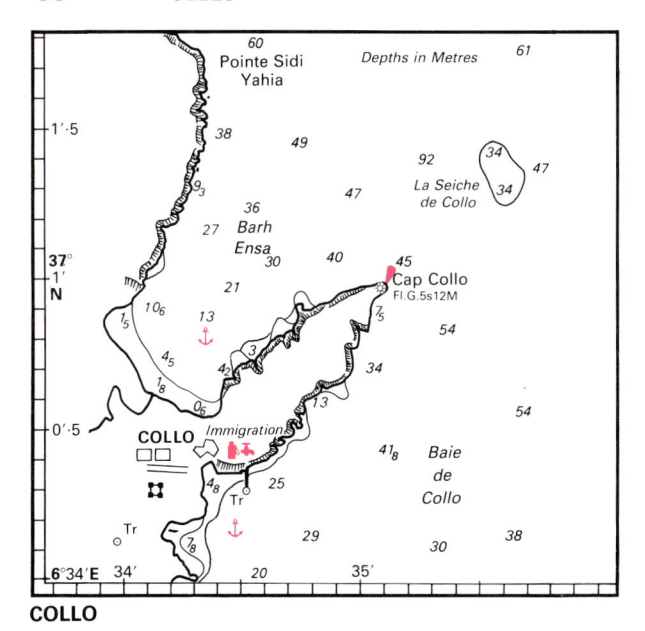

COLLO

Good anchorage off the fishing quay in the open bay of Collo viewed from the S

Lights
Approach
1. **Cap Collo** 37°01·0N 6°35'·1E
   Fl.G.5s26m12M 146°-vis-323° White 8-sided tower, green lantern.

Harbour
2. **Jetée head** F.G Obscd when bearing less than 221° White column, black lantern (out of order 1992)

General
The scenic Bay of Collo is one of the best open anchorages in Algeria with excellent shelter from W and N winds. It is reasonably comfortable in light E winds, but becomes untenable if they reach gale force.

Collo is a little village built amongst green hills in the NE corner of the bay. One breakwater with a single quay forms the port which is crowded with a small fishing fleet. Occasionally cork is exported from the port which has to be loaded by freighter from small barges. The friendly village and untouched countryside around it are well worth a visit.

Approach
Straightforward by day. The light at the end of the breakwater does not work and sometimes the whole village is plunged into darkness. The quay is crowded and fishing boats are moored all around it.

Berthing
Anchor 200–300m S of the quay in sand about 6m deep. Watch out for the mooring lines from boats anchored in the bay and stern lines from fishing boats at the quay. Alternatively one may anchor very quietly in Barh Ensa, the cove N of Collo.

Formalities
Port of Entry. The authorities are relaxed. Do not forget to take paperwork along when rowing ashore.

Facilities
Water From a tap in the middle of the quay.

North Africa

Fuel Diesel pump on the quay but some fishing boats would have to be moved.
Provisions Reasonable supply of fresh produce in the village.
Post office and bank In the village.

Eating out
A few small eating houses.

Pointe Esrah

36°57'·4N 6°50'·9E

Charts
Admiralty 855

One of the several beautiful, peaceful anchorages along this part of the coast. Not very well protected but there is no problem in good weather and it is a paradise for snorkelling. Anchor SW of El Kalaa islet in clearly visible sand patches between the rocks, all in depths of 6–8m (Admiralty charts are not detailed enough to show depths properly). A few fishermen passing by from Stora will probably be the only company. The Bay of Esrah, SE of the anchorage, has a beautiful beach and the area has been destined for future tourist development by a new Algerian/Canadian joint venture.

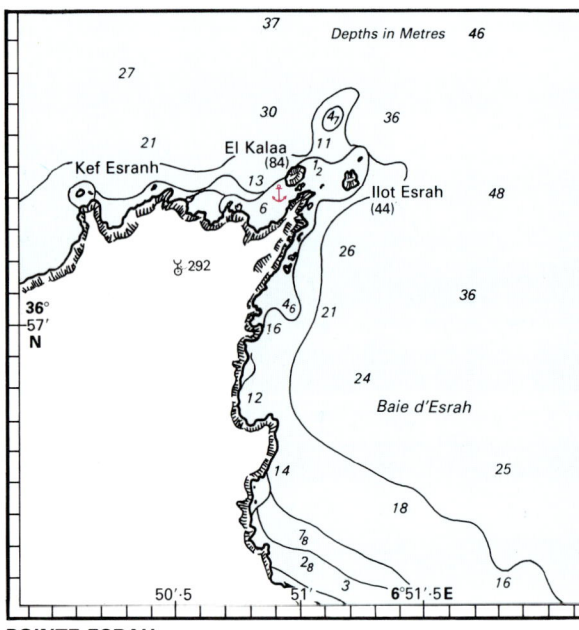

Stora

36°54'·1N 6°52'·9E

Distances
Jijel 62M, Collo 19M – Skikda 1M, Chetaibi 31M, Annaba 55M

Tides
Range of the tide is about 0·5m.

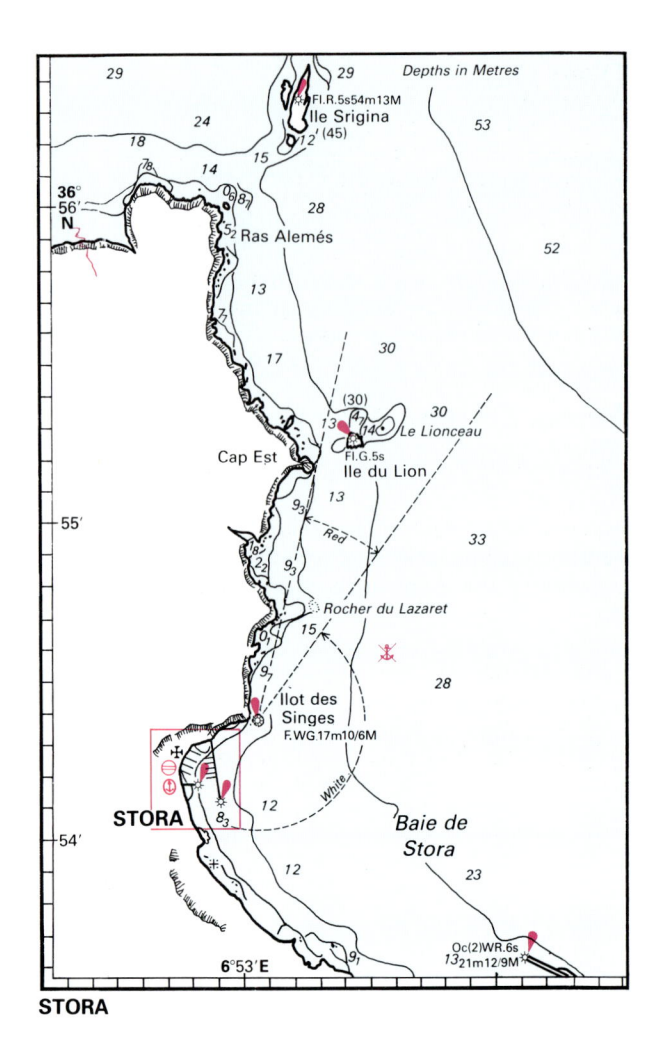

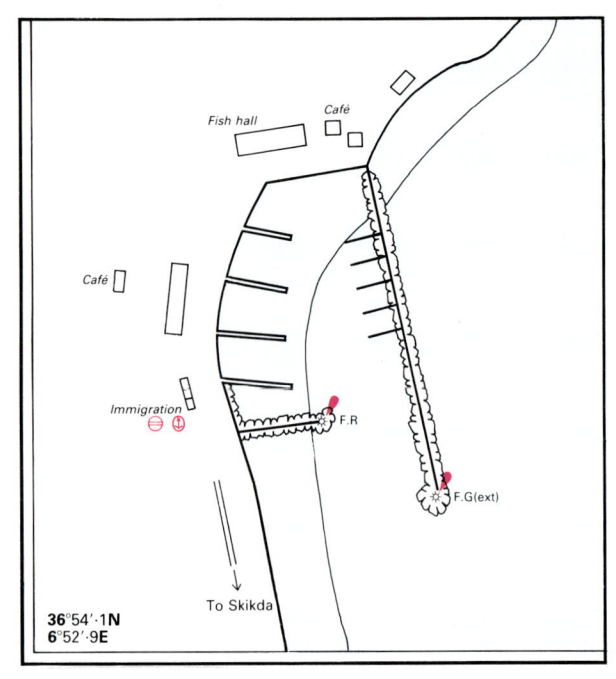

Charts

	Approach	Port
Admiralty	252, 855	–
French	3061	–
US	–	–

Lights

Approach
1. **Ile Srigina** 36°56'·3N 6°53'·3E
   Fl.R.5s54m13M Obscd by Pte Esrah when bearing less than 122° White square tower, red top.
2. **Ilôt des Singes** 36°54'·4N 6°53'·1E
   F.WG.17m10/6M 193·5°-G-216°-W-023°-G-080°. White square tower, green lantern.

Harbour
3. **E Mole head** F.G White tower, green top
4. **Jetée head** F.R Pylon, red top

General
A tiny fishing port on the W side of the Bay of Skikda with a small section reserved for Algerian pleasure boats. The village of Stora, with its steep streets rising directly from the waterfront, is untidy but pretty. The people are very friendly and it is a much more pleasant port than Skikda itself. The port offers reasonable protection but in bad weather, due to the surge and swell, the larger fishing boats move to Skikda, which is better protected. In strong N winds heavy seas roll into the Bay of Skikda; entry into both Stora and Skikda is dangerous under such conditions and a considerable swell enters the port. If necessary check with the fishermen about the weather.

Approach
When entering the Bay of Skikda from NW the commercial port of Skikda and new petrochemical port with refineries to the E are easily recognised, but Stora will not be visible until S of Ilôt des Singes. The gas flares from the refinery behind Port Méthanier are visible from over 20M when in operation. Local fishing boats do not use running lights at night.

Berthing
Tie up on one of the finger piers or alongside a fishing boat. Beware of warps crossing the finger berths when bad weather is expected.

Formalities
Friendly (but very present) authorities, including customs, are to be found at the port. A second visit from the Skikda Customs can be expected.

Facilities
Water Containers can be filled in a coffee bar in the port or at the fishmongers along the N quay.
Fuel Available at the end of the first fishing quay.
Provisions Limited supply of fresh produce from inconspicuous small shops, otherwise an exceptionally good market and other food shops in nearby Skikda. Good general shopping.

The small fishing and pleasure port of Stora with the commercial port of Skikda in the background

North Africa

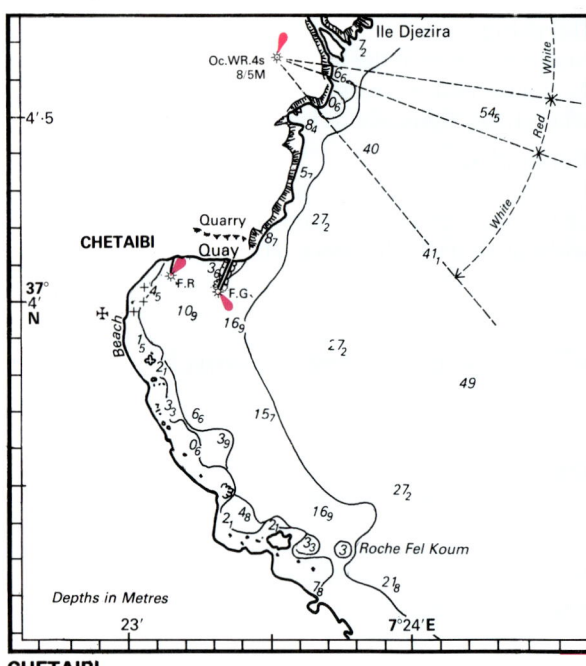

CHETAIBI

General
Another harbour, similar to Collo, nestled in a beautiful part of the coast. This small port, consisting of two jetties with a quay between them, is well protected in N and NW winds but provides no protection in NE and E winds when heavy seas can roll into the Baie of Takouch. There are a few small fishing boats moored and the only activity seems to be at the nearby granite quarry. The village is a short walk from the port and its location, tucked in the corner of the Takouch peninsula, is pretty. A charming place to stay in good weather and do some snorkelling.

Approach
Straightforward – also at night – with enough room to anchor. Both port lights functioned in 1989.

Berthing
In quiet weather tie up alongside the quay but do not leave valuables lying on deck. Otherwise anchor between the piers. Check that the anchor is well dug-in since holding is mediocre.

Formalities
Officials are not too apparent, but take paperwork along when going ashore. Not a port of entry.

Facilities
Water No water in the port.
Provisions A few provisions can be found in the village a short walk up hill.

Annaba
(formerly Bône)
36°54'·3N 7°46'·9E

Distances
Stora 55M, Chetaibi 27M – El Kala 33M, Tabarka 49M

Tides
Range of the tide is about 0·5m.

Charts
	Approach	*Port*
Admiralty	2121	1567
French	5670, 4314, 3024	5669
US	52200	52202

Lights
Approach
1. **Cap de Garde** 36°58'·1N 7°47'·1E
   Fl.5s143m31M Grey square tower, white dwelling
2. **Fort Génois** 36°57'N 7°46'·6E
   Oc(2)6s61m10M 240°-obscd-263° within 0·5M
   White tower on building

Harbour
3. **Jetée du Lion head** 36°54'·3N 7°47'·1E
   Oc(3)G.12s19m8M White tower
4. **Quai Sud head** 36°54'·2N 7°46'·9E
   Oc(2)R.6s16m10M White tower
5. **Quai Sud N corner** 36°54'·2N 7°46'·8E
   F.R
6. **Mole head N side of fishing port** (La Grenouillère)
   F.G.3m2M
7. **Mole head S side of fishing port** (La Grenouillère)
   F.R.3m2M

General
The large and active commercial port of Annaba is one of the best protected in Algeria. The port has several basins but the best place for yachts is in the old fishing port. Yachts are accommodated in a small, friendly yacht club under the watchful eyes of the navy in nearby barracks and when leaving the port one has to pass their gate. The centre of Annaba with its ramblas-like main street is quite pleasant but it is a long walk through a shabby part of the harbour.

If en route to Tunisia, Annaba is a good port at which to fill up with diesel which is easily available in the fishing port. It is cheaper and better quality than in Tunisia.

Approach
Straightforward but keep well to starboard at the entrance and Avant Port. Freighters use tugboats to leave the port and need a large turning circle.

Berthing
Yachts are accommodated in the yacht club in the N corner of the fishing port. Small boats can lie alongside the quay in front of the club but bigger yachts are better off lying bows or stern-to the outside of the small pier. The club charges no fees.

Formalities
Port of entry. Authorities are not particularly friendly.

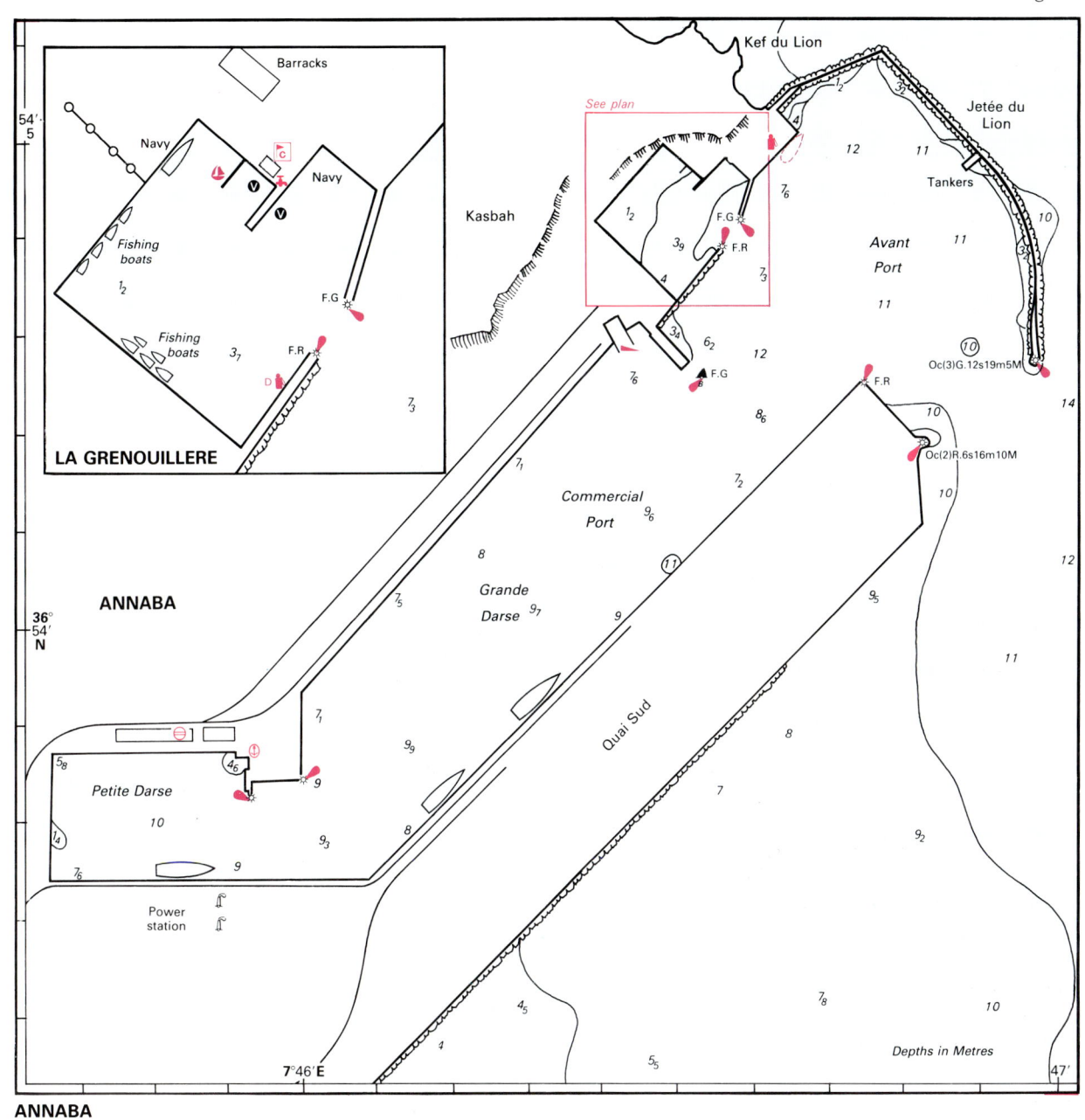

Facilities

Water From a small tap on the quay in front of the yacht club.
Electricity Can possibly be arranged.
Fuel In the fishing port.
Provisions Not very convenient. Bread may be found in two small shops in the *kasbah* not far from the port but for major provisioning take a taxi (about 15 minutes) to the new town.
Post office and bank In the centre of town.

Eating out

Nothing near the port but several restaurants in the centre of town. Tea in the clubhouse.

Tourism

Only 2km south of Annaba are the remains of the Roman city Hippo Regius with an interesting museum. In Annaba itself no monuments have been left of its long history.

North Africa

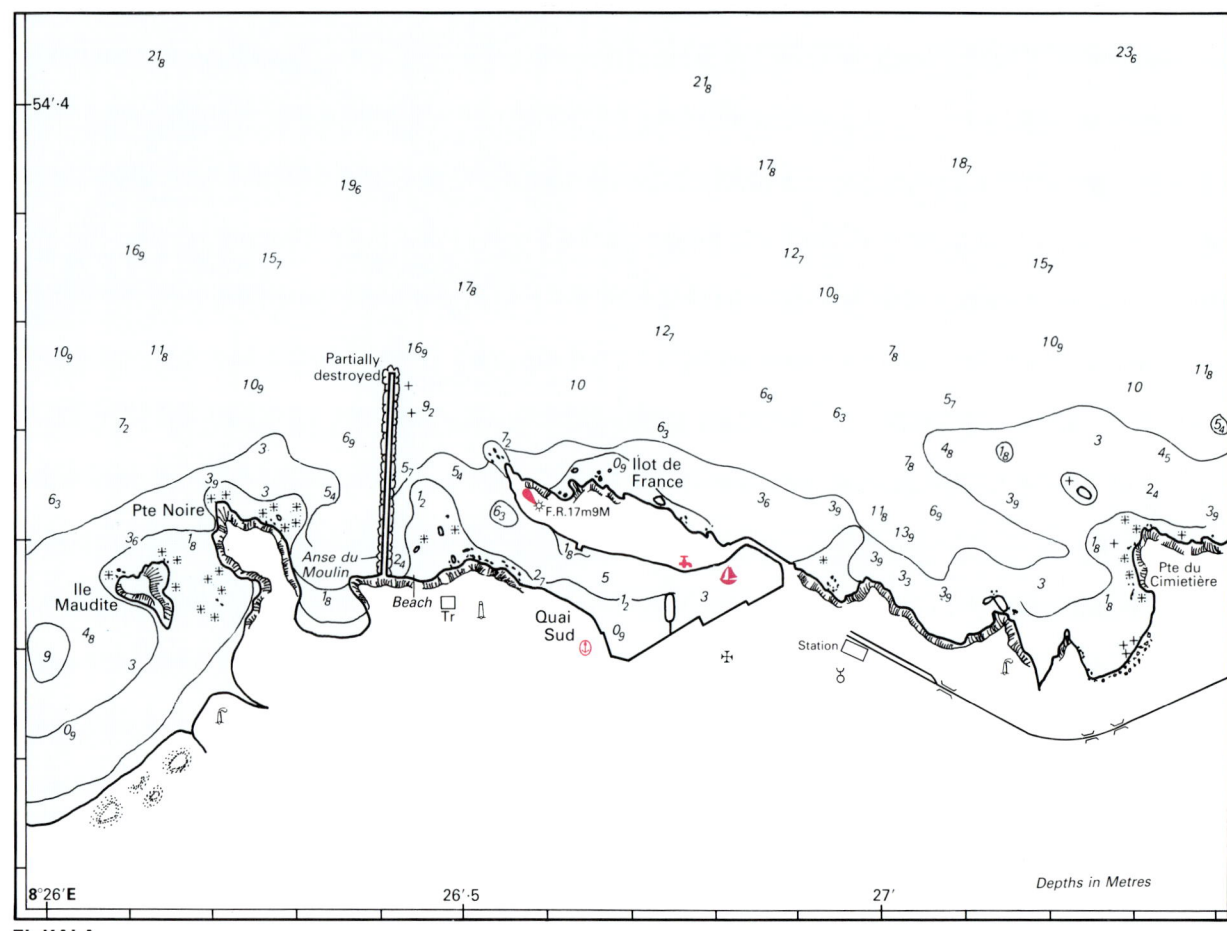

EL KALA

El Kala
(formerly La Calle)
36°54'N 8°26'·5E

Distances
Annaba 34M – Tabarka 17M

Tides
Range of the tide is about 0·5m.

Charts

	Approach	Port
Admiralty	2121	1712
French	4314, 3424	–
US	52200	–

Lights
Harbour
1. **Entrance E side** 36°54'N 8°26'·6E
   F.R.17m9M

General
This small fishing port is formed by an islet, Ilôt de France, which has been connected to shore. Until independence, the island was inhabited by Italian fishermen and the Arab town was on the shore. Unfortunately, the old Mediterranean style houses on Ilôt de France were destroyed in 1985 to make room for a hotel development but the small village has retained a pleasant character and is set in a very wild and secluded part of the coast. In recent years a new breakwater has been constructed which protects the entrance but the harbour is still poorly protected from strong NW winds.

Approach
Approach on a course due S midway between Ilôt de France and the breakwater and enter the port midway between the islet and the shore. The end of the breakwater was partially washed away in a NW storm and some big blocks lie sunk off the E side. The port is dredged but proceed carefully as depths are uncertain.

Berthing
Tie up alongside the quay in the NE corner. Depths in the other parts of the port are not certain.

Formalities
Port of entry.

Facilities
Water There are taps in the NE corner but no water.
Fuel Available in the port.
Provisions, post office and bank A short walk away in the village.

Tunisia

Capital Tunis
Area 163,610 sq km
Population approx 8 million
GDP per person $1,210
Average annual population growth 2·3%

Introduction

Tunisia is the Maghreb's smallest country. It has a varied landscape, of mountains with cork forests and wild boar in the north, rolling farm land in the Tell, market gardens in the Cap Bon peninsula and isolated oases with wheat and vegetables growing under date palms in the south. Olive groves line the coast all the way to Jerba. An enlightened agricultural policy has enabled the country to be practically self-sufficient in feeding its increasing population, now about 8 million. With a warm climate and miles of wide sandy beaches, it has been a popular holiday destination for many years. There are also extensive Punic and Roman ruins all over the country, even in the most isolated corners, and Berber dwellings in the desert.

Tunisia can be divided into four regions. The green, mountainous north from the Algerian border to the Cap Bon peninsula has a sparsely populated coast, apart from near the major cities, which is lined by long stretches of empty beaches. In the centre of the country is the Tell – fertile farm land in rolling hills. The densely populated and essentially flat Sahel coast stretches from Cap Bon to the Kerkennah Islands off Sfax. It is a low coast with long fine beaches backed by farmland and extensive olive groves with tourist centres at Hammamet, Sousse and Monastir. Finally, there is the Chott country south of the Tell and the Sahara regions bordering Algeria and Libya. Chott are large depressions, partly below sea level, covered with a thick layer of salt crystals. The oasis-like island of Jerba close to the Libyan border is an important tourist centre.

The country has phosphates and some small oil reserves which contribute to overseas earnings along with tourism, textile manufacturing and remittances from workers abroad. The European Community, mainly France and Germany, is the most important trading partner although its rich neighbour Libya has been growing in importance since the border was reopened in 1988.

A brief history

Written history begins with accounts of the seafaring Phoenicians trading with the indigenous Berbers, followed by the Carthaginian or Punic era which ended, after earlier Greek assaults, with the destruction of Carthage by the Romans in 146BC. The stability of the Roman Empire resulted in great economic development; the Maghreb supplied two thirds of Rome's grain requirement as well as olive oil, coral, wood and pottery. The spread of Christianity in the 3rd century caused unrest and eventually the 'Roman' Africans revolted, aided by the Vandals. From the fall of Carthage for the second time, in AD439 a new, chaotic, era began under Vandal and later Byzantine rulers, followed by Arab conquest after AD670. Tunisia was then ruled from Damascus and Baghdad for 150 years until Ibn Aghlab established a dynasty and an active Islamic culture which made the country prosperous. The Aghlabites were overthrown by the Fatimids (descendants of Fatima, the daughter of Mohammed) who established a Shi'ite regime rivalling the orthodox Sunni in Baghdad. Fatimid interest in Tunisia declined in favour of Cairo and rule was left to Berber governors. When one tribe rejected Shi'ite for Sunni, the caliph of Cairo banished his troublesome tribes into Tunisia and for two centuries there was anarchy. In the 12th century, the increasing threat from the Normans in Sicily caused the Tunisians to seek help from the Moroccan Almohad dynasty resulting in the founding of the Hafsid dynasty which lasted until the 16th century. Commerce and arts were encouraged, enlivened by Andalucian Muslims expelled from Spain, but control of the country, never firm, slipped and in 1534 Turkish pirates drove out the last Hafsid prince. There followed a turbulent period, warding off Spanish attacks and a struggle between the seafarers and the army for control; this was the notorious period of piracy. Eventually, in 1705, one of the Beys, an army chief, founded the Hosainid dynasty and introduced some order. Efforts to control the country together with courtly extravagance put the regime in debt to Europe and in 1881 the French moved in with the immediate aim of ensuring the security of their Algerian border, pre-empting Italian ambitions and protecting their investment.

Recent history

The country was never entirely happy under French rule and resentment grew during the depression of the 1920s. In 1934 the Neo-Destour party was founded by Habib Bourguiba and became the centre of opposition. After the Second World War the French showed insufficient intention to make radical change and, in 1956 in the face of growing resistance led by Bourguiba and international pressure, they agreed to independence. Nevertheless they retained Bizerte as a naval port and following a short and unnecessary struggle in which 1300 Tunisian lives were lost, the last French left in 1963. The fight for independence was not as violent as in Algeria, partly through Bourguiba's moderation and partly because the French presence was not so firmly rooted.

Bourguiba set the country towards socialism, but in 1969 moved to the right. In 1987 he was replaced in a non-violent coup by the present president, Zine El Abidine Ben Ali. Tunisia today has the most liberal laws in the Arab world regarding religion and women's rights. Although formally a democracy,

North Africa

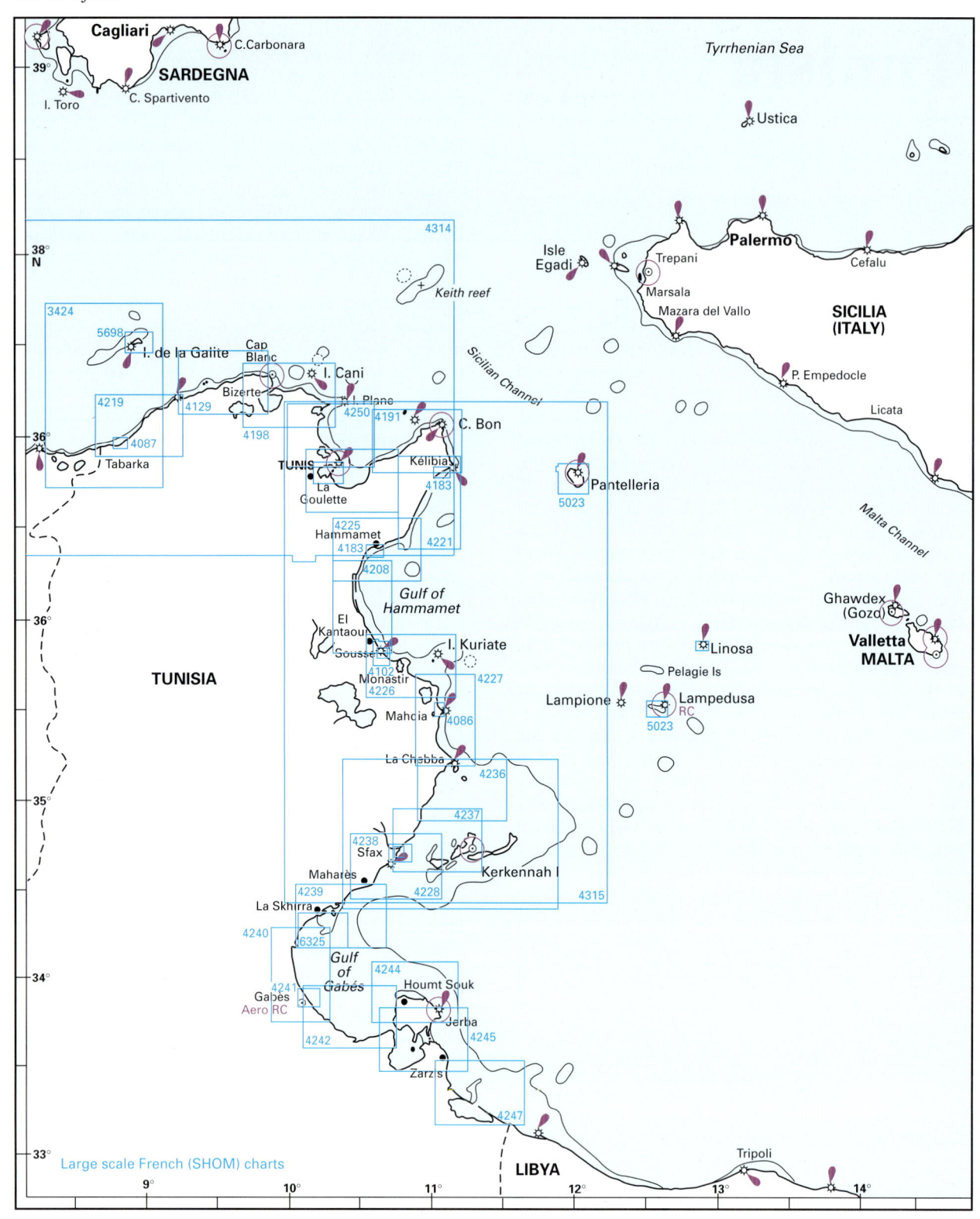

politics are dominated by one party, the Rassemblement Constitutionel Democratique. Within the Arab world, Tunisia has often played a mediating role and it maintains good relations with all Arab nations.

Wintering in Tunisia
An increasing number of yachtsmen are discovering the delights of cruising this coast which welcomes visitors. Around 1,500 yachts of all nationalities visited Tunisia in 1997 and over 500 foreign-owned yachts were either permanently based there or spent the winter in one of the marinas or ports. Monastir and Al Kantoui are the most popular marinas, each with 250 yachts wintering in 1997. The price and facilities at both marinas are similar. Both are reasonably secure to leave a boat unattended in, although the quality of care and supervision cannot

be relied upon. A few foreign yachts winter in Tabarka, Sidi Bou Said, La Goulette, Bizerte and Kelibia. As facilities improve in the new fishing port at Monastir, an alternative will be provided and should reduce the pressure on these marinas, which get very crowded.

Early booking for winter is required at Monastir and Al Kantoui.

General information

Money
The Tunisian Dinar (TD) can only be changed in Tunisia but importing or exporting Tunisian currency is forbidden. A Dinar is confusingly divided into 1,000 millimes and most prices are expressed in millimes, often written as TD 2200 meaning 2,200 millimes.

Traveller's cheques and Eurocheques are accepted at all banks.

Credit cards are accepted in the larger towns and tourist centres.

ATMs are widespread in these areas and cash can be withdrawn on *Visa* universally, *Mastercard* often and *Curias* rarely. The Societe Tunisienne de Banque (STB) will advance cash against *Visa* and *Mastercard*. It can be difficult to get cash in some places against a non-Tunisian card.

There is no limit to the amount of foreign currency that can be taken in or out of Tunisia but keep all exchange receipts as they are needed for rechanging or when applying for a visa. Only 30% of the original amount, to a maximum of TD 100, can be rechanged. The Dinar is relatively stable and prices quoted in this pilot are based on an exchange rate of TD 1·8 = £1.00 (1998).

Provisioning
The best place to buy fresh produce is at the markets which are found even in the smallest villages. Modern storing techniques are not used and imported food products are not common, even in the supermarkets. Consequently supply is largely seasonal, with the best choice in winter, spring and early summer. Prices on the open market are usually well marked – a government requirement. Generally, the quality of fresh produce is very good and prices are low. Two supermarket chains, Monoprix and *magasin général*, are found all over the country. Wine, beer and hard liquor are normally sold only in these supermarkets. Local wines and beer are expensive and of low quality. Yachtsman visiting or wintering in Tunisia prefer to stock up with wine in Lampedusa or Pantelleria. Customs seem to turn a 'blind eye' on large quantities of wine, but are more inquisitive and difficult about an excess of spirits which are exorbitantly expensive in Tunisia. All glass bottles carry a deposit which is marked on the label. Canned products are not common and the choice is limited. Dairy products are of good quality. UHT milk is readily available, fresh milk from vats in the dairies at the market (take your own containers), French and Tunisian butter and a limited choice of bland cheeses. Meat is always fresh but not hung and difficult to get in familiar cuts unless the butcher is shown how. Pork or wild boar can only be found in the capital and other areas where there is a concentration of Europeans. Turkey, chicken and rabbit are of good quality and widely available. Goods like cosmetics, paper towels, toilet paper, etc. are available in the supermarkets and pharmacies and often on the markets as well. Coffee (beans and instant), and tea available in supermarkets.

Women working the fields on the island of Jerba

Some Tunisian Wines

Price in Millimes

Red Wines
Magon, excellent	4500
Pinot, excellent	4500
Chateau Mornay, above average	4000

Rosé wines
Koudiat, adequate	3110
Chateau Mornag, adequate	4000

White wines
Muscat de Kelibia, good if you like muscat grapes	4400
Blanc Crystal, adequate	4000

Water
Good quality water is in abundant supply along the entire Tunisian coast. In the fishing ports containers may be necessary, as rarely is it possible to hook up to a tap; have a long hose and a variety of fittings and hose clips on board. In fishing ports water is charged at TD 1·0 per 1,000 litres. Tanks can easily be filled in Tabarka, Bizerte, Sidi Bou Saïd, La Goulette, Kelibia, Al Kantaoui, Monastir and Mahdia. Ice is available in practically every fishing port and in some of the marinas the harbour attendants will deliver it.

Electricity
Nominal voltage is 220V, 50Hz but it can vary considerably. In Sidi Bou Saïd, for instance, 240V

was the norm most of the time, which can result in overcharged batteries if simple car-type chargers are used. In the three marinas 380/220V is available. With some improvisation electricity can be arranged in several fishing ports but S of La Chebba this will be rare.

Fuel
Diesel has a high sulphur content but causes no problems in yacht engines. When cruising permanently on Tunisian diesel it is advisable to change the engine oil more often as sulphur increases the acid level in the oil. Diesel is available in almost every fishing port. Easy places are Sidi Bou Saïd, Kelibia, Al Kantaoui and Monastir.

Kerosene/paraffin is called 'petrol blue' and available from petrol stations.

Harbour charges
Harbour charges vary depending on the type of port and facilities offered. Small fishing harbours will not normally levy a charge, whereas marinas have standard charges, which are negotiable for longer term stays.

Marina fees have risen recently. Yachts were charged TD 1·0 per gross ton per week in the fishing ports in 1997, payable at the CGP (Commissariat Général de la Pêche). Keep the receipt as remaining days can be used in other fishing ports when visited within the week paid for. Marina fees at the three marinas of Sidi Bou Saïd, Al Kantaoui and Monastir are very reasonable.

Repairs
Most repairs and routine maintenance can be carried out in the three marinas. Possibly Sidi Bou Saïd is better for certain specialised jobs because it is the only marina with a reasonable fleet of Tunisian yachts. Various specialists can be arranged through the yard in Monastir. Hauling out is possible in Monastir, Sidi Bou Saïd and Al Kantaoui. Alternatively, yachts can be hauled in big travel-lifts intended for fishing boats in Tabarka, Bizerte, Kelibia, Monastir, Teboulba and Sfax. High pressure pumps are available in most of those ports. Generally it is advisable to supervise the work and to assume a little knowledge since most of the workers have more goodwill than craftsmanship. The availability of specialised yacht spares such as stainless steel hardware, rigging material, sail cloth, etc. is very limited. Galvanised materials, nylon rope, paints, anti-fouling, etc. as used by fishermen are available in the bigger ports like Bizerte, La Goulette, Sousse and Gabès. Most of these products are manufactured in Tunisia and consequently the prices are low but the quality can vary. Paint and anti-fouling are particularly cheap and also effective (Trans-Ocean antifouling is manufactured under licence) but it may take some time to find out where to buy these products. Engine spares are hard to come by although there are agents for well known brands like Perkins and Yamaha in Tunis. Duty-free import of spares for a 'Yacht in Transit' does not exist, although, duty-free import of personal belongings for yachts wintering in Monastir is possible. For the procedure check with the port captain in advance. Small parts of little value as judged by customs can be sent by mail. Other spares or new equipment are best imported as personal luggage; customs at airports rarely cause Europeans difficulties over such imports. As yachting develops over the years it can be expected that facilities will improve further.

Telephone
Public phones are located in specialist shops known as Taxiphones. (They often have photocopiers and fax as well.)

Taxiphones are very common, but because they are manned only in office hours, making calls at night is a problem. The tariff on calls to UK is approx. TD 1·2 per minute.

GSM – Tunisia does not have a roaming agreement with European networks yet, but the GSM system is in use.

Mail
Postal services are reliable. Letters to and from Europe rarely take more than a week, and two weeks from the USA. Mail can be sent to the marinas if the yacht's name is clearly indicated. Addresses are as follows.

Port de Plaisance Sidi Bou Saïd, 1 Avenue. Jean Kennedy, Sidi Bou Saïd 2026, Tunisia. ☎ 01 741645 *Telex* 14669 SOGRA

Capitainerie, Port Al Kantaoui, Tunisia ☎ 03 30500 *Telex* 30701 PORKAN

Marina Cap Monastir, B.P.60, Monastir 5000, Tunisia ☎ 03 62305 *Telex* 30879

Laundry
Laundry service is available in the marinas of Sidi Bou Saïd, Al Kantaoui and Monastir. Prices vary. La Goulette has one of the few launderettes in Tunisia. Further details under the ports.

Health precautions
Cholera and yellow fever inoculations are required if coming from an infected area. Basic health care is of a reasonable standard; most doctors have been trained in France. The best medical care is available in the private rather than public hospitals and prices are roughly the same as in Europe. It is a good precaution to have insurance covering repatriation to Europe in the case of major surgery. In the marinas of El Kantaoui and Monastir doctors are available in the port.

Animals
Cats and dogs on board need a certificate of good health and valid anti-rabies vaccination papers.

Drugs
The possession of any type of drug is strictly forbidden. Discovery of only a small amount can lead to imprisonment. The water pipes – hubble-bubbles – often seen in the cafés are smoked with a special kind of Egyptian tobacco called *maassal* and not with hashish.

Tourist information
Tourist information offices are found in almost every town. Fine brochures are available free, usually in several languages. They are a good source of information but for serious exploring, the travel guides listed in the *Introduction* will be needed.

Tipping
In everyday life tipping follows the same rules as in Europe although it is not uncommon to have tips refused. In European-style restaurants and tourist areas tipping is expected. It is useful to have some packets of European or American cigarettes on board as a reward for small services.

Public holidays
New Year's Day 1 January
Anniversary of the Revolution 18 January
Independence Day 20 March
Martyr's Day 9 April
Labour Day 1 May
Victory Day 1 June
Republic Day 25 July
Women's Day 13 August
Anniversary of the PSD 3 September
Evacuation of Bizerte 15 October
New Era Day 7 November
Islamic holidays are listed in the Introduction.

Business hours
Banks Mon–Fri (summer), 0800–1100 (winter) and 1400–1600.
Supermarkets Mon–Sat 0830–1200 and 1600–2000.
Markets Roughly the same hours as the supermarkets but every day of the week except Friday afternoons.

Time zone
UT+1hr, summer time UT+2hrs.

Photography
The Islamic rule of not taking pictures of people should be respected. Do not take pictures of military camps, patrol boats and fully armed policemen on guard at government buildings and presidential palaces. Even in the centre of Tunis the police can get very nervous if pictures are taken of the guards in front of the Ministry of Interior.

Security
No problem in the ports. Tunisia is possibly one of the safest places in the Mediterranean for a yacht and her crew. However do not leave valuables or articles like shoes within easy reach on deck along public quays. Increased tourism has left its mark in Tunisia and pick-pocketing does occur in the tourist areas but this is not as severe a problem as in Europe.

Anchoring
Anchoring is permitted in all but military zones provided permission is given in advance. In practice, there is not usually a problem especially during daylight. It is usual for military boats to patrol the coast at night and you may be asked to present ships papers or to move into a port even in bad weather, especially in the area of Bizerte and Tunis.

Good all weather ports
Tabarka, Bizerte (commercial and fishing port), La Goulette, Kelibia, Monastir (marina and fishing port), Mahdia, Sfax, Gabès and Zarzis.

Entry formalities
Yachts can make their first entry into Tunisia at any of the following ports: Tabarka, Bizerte, Sidi Bou Saïd, La Goulette, Kelibia, Al Kantaoui, Sousse, Monastir, Mahdia, Sfax, Gabès and Houmt-Souk. Various authorities will have to be dealt with but the police and customs are the most important. Papers required are official ownership papers issued in the country of registration, passports with any necessary visa, insurance policy, crew list and a list of provisions and equipment. Visitors with Israeli or South African stamps in their passports may be refused entry. Often the officials will be waiting on the quay and it is useful to have the paperwork ready before entering port. On rare occasions the police may want to keep the ship's papers. Passports normally stay on board. In theory clearance has to be obtained once only, at the port of entry, and it should be sufficient elsewhere merely to show the papers. However the reality at small ports may be different; officials are often anxious to come aboard if only to satisfy their curiosity.

Police (immigration police in grey uniform) check all passports and visas of those crew members who need them (see below). The crew list should include the following data: name and surname, maiden name, date and place of birth, nationality, profession, passport number, date of issue and validity, and purpose of the visit. Often the police prefer to use their own forms.

Douane (customs in brown uniform) will normally only make a quick check inside the boat. Officially all provisions and equipment on board have to be declared but in practice the important items as far as customs are concerned are firearms, large quantities of liquor and transmitters. Firearms will be taken into custody. Beer and wine are of no great concern but quantities of spirits, say more than a couple of bottles, will probably be sealed with enough left out for daily use. Finally, customs will write out a *Demande de Permis de Circulation*, also called the *Triptique*, for the temporary import of the boat into Tunisia (see below).

The garde national are the military police in green uniforms. They operate on land and at sea in patrol boats. Their role is supplementary to the clearance procedure. In the marinas of Al Kantaoui and Monastir they are kept informed by the *capitainerie* and if they appear in other ports they will note details on the boat, insurance and equipment, especially transmitters and radios. Insurance is not required by law in Tunisia but it is always asked for and not to have the relevant certificate can cause difficulties.

North Africa

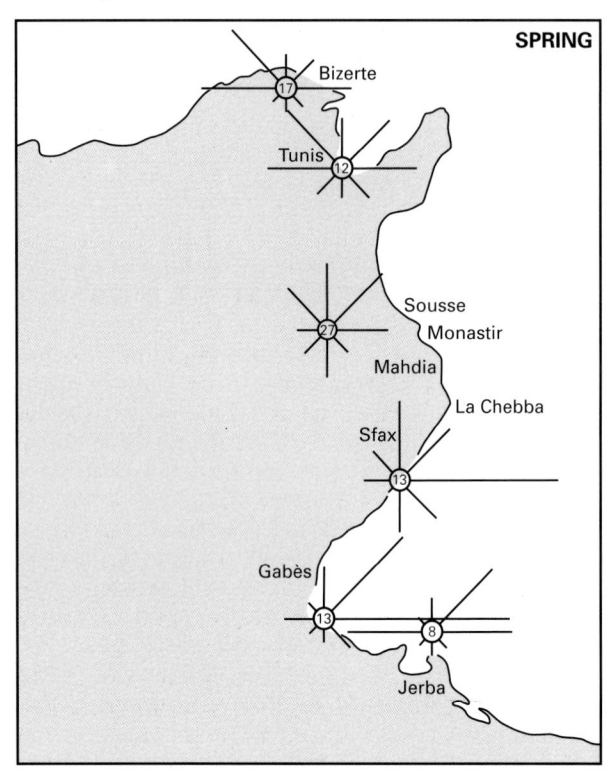

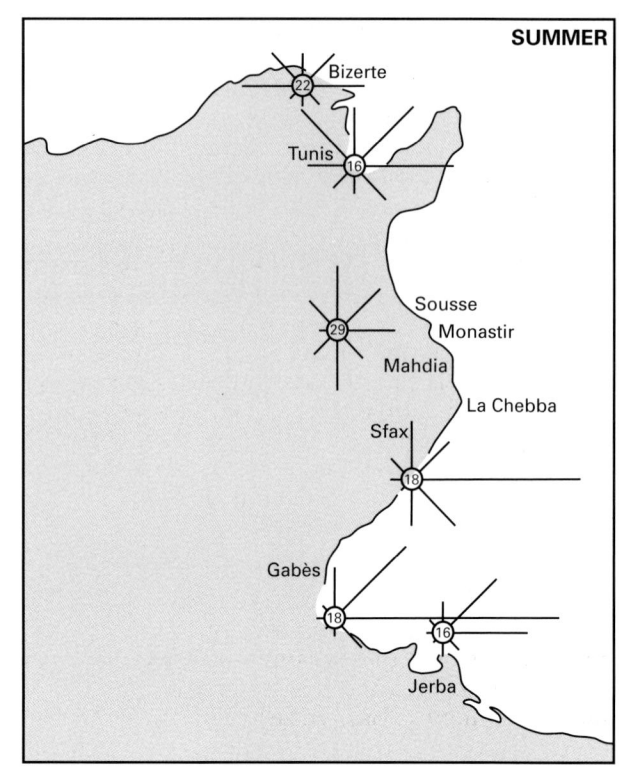

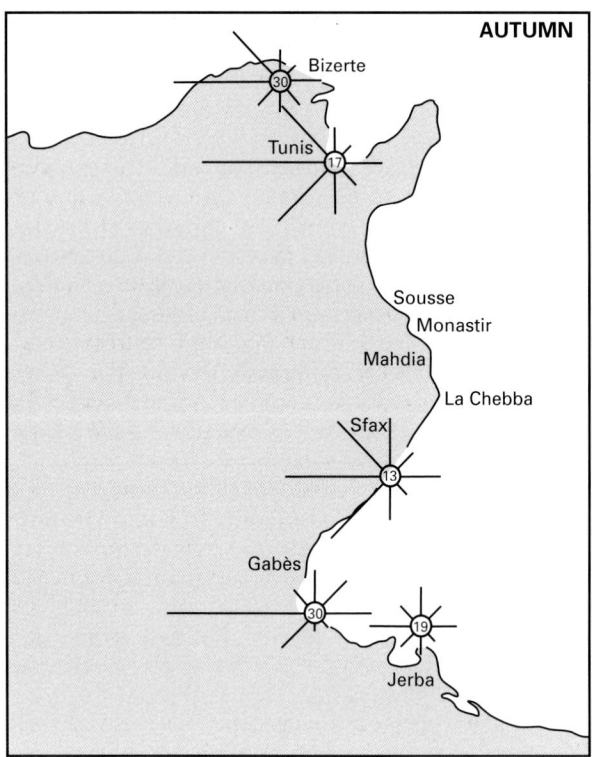

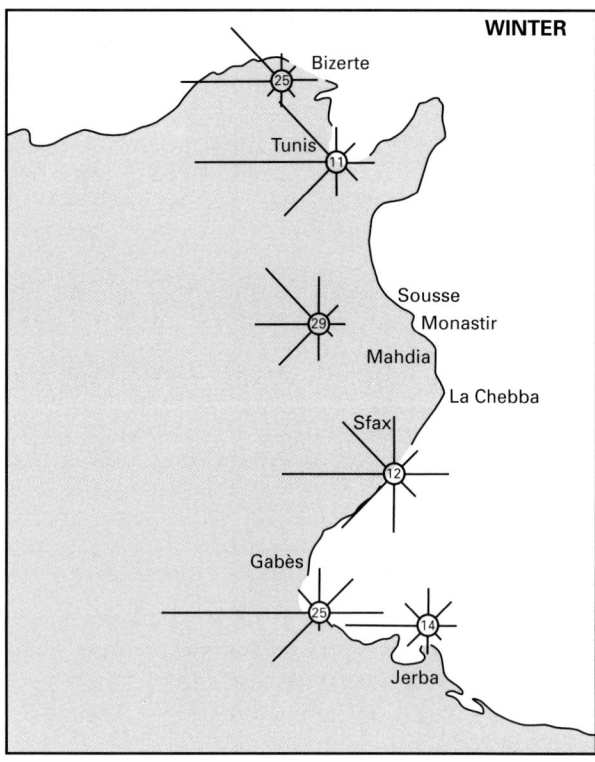

SPRING

SUMMER

AUTUMN

WINTER

Tunisia. Winds - directions and frequencies. Figures at the centres of the roses denote percentage of calm days. Winds blow to the centres of the roses.

Harbour authorities may be represented by the harbourmaster in the marinas, by a representative from *APIP* (*Agence des Ports et des Installations*) in the fishing ports or occasionally by the *marine marchande*.

Notify the port police of any crew change and also if you invite any Tunisian friends on board. If you plan to take Tunisian or European friends out for a day trip, police and customs have to be informed with a complete crew list. If leaving Tunisia, allow enough time to notify the police and customs; they like to know where you are going.

The *Triptique* or *Permis de Circulation*
The *Triptique* is the permit allowing a foreign yacht

to remain in Tunisian waters for one year from the date of entry. Within this year the yacht may cruise Tunisian waters for 6 months. When not sailing the yacht can be put under *plombage* (seal) by leaving the *Triptique* with the customs. The time the yacht remains under *plombage* is not counted as cruising time. When entering the country the customs officer will usually write out a *Triptique* valid for 3 months. An extension can be arranged with a customs office in any port and after it has been extended up to the maximum period of one year a new *Triptique* can be issued. The reason for limiting the *Triptique* is to have a check on the papers of the crew. One copy of the *Triptique* is for the customs officer who writes it out and two remain with the skipper. When leaving Tunisia both copies have to be submitted to customs.

Visas
The following is a guide to the situation which has changed little over the past few years: it is wise to check with a Tunisian embassy and, if necessary, arrange a visa before departure from your base.

German and USA citizens may stay up to four months without a visa; citizens of Canada and all other European countries except the Benelux countries: three months.

Dutch, Belgian, Luxembourg, New Zealand and Australian citizens need visas to enter. If not obtained beforehand, the police at the port of entry can issue a 7-day transit visa and for a longer stay a proper visa may be obtained at the Commissariat de Police in Bizerte, Tunis, Nabeul, Sousse, Monastir, Sfax or Gabès. An extension to a transit visa is normally only for a month. New Zealanders and Australians have for some reason experienced problems getting transit visas extended. Extensions to regular visas, and for non-visa nationals to stay beyond three or four months, have to be arranged at the same offices. Take two black and white passport photos, exchange receipts from the bank, Permis de Circulation and if relevant, a note or, better, a wintering contract from the port captain. Check beforehand with the local police for any changes in the procedure. Be prepared for delays as the procedure is rarely without complications, especially if staying longer than six months.

Embassies
UK 5 Place de la Victoire, Tunis ☎ 245100
USA 144 Avenue de la Liberté, Tunis. ☎ 282566
Germany 1 Rue el Hamra Mutuellevi le, Tunis
  ☎ 281246

Cruising grounds

The Tunisian coast extends 160M eastward from the Algerian border to Cap Bon where it turns S for 330M to the border with Libya. The N coast as far as Cap Bon is for the most part mountainous, interrupted by quiet beaches around Tabarka and the Cap Farina headland, with a few off-lying islands and islets. The area is green and fertile; the Cap Bon peninsula in particular has extensive market gardens, fruit orchards and vineyards. Ras ed Drek just S of Cap Bon marks an abrupt change to the more flat and low coast of the Gulf of Hammamet. The N coast has the marina of Sidi Bou Saïd, 4M N of Tunis, yacht clubs in Bizerte and La Goulette, the combined fishing port and marina of Tabarka, three fishing ports and several anchorages.

The 90M of coast from Cap Bon to Monastir becomes increasingly low with long beaches and hills further inland. Aside from important market gardens and olive groves, the major tourist centres of Tunisia are found here around the fine beaches of Hammamet, Sousse and Monastir. There are enough ports to choose from between Kelibia, as a good port of entry to cruise either N or S, the marinas of Al Kantaoui and Monastir and the small fishing ports of Beni Khiar and Hergla. A peculiar feature of the Tunisian coast S of Cap Bon is the abundant growth of a thick, tough seaweed. During strong winds in the winter this seaweed is torn loose from the bottom and tends to clog the entrance of the smaller fishing ports which consequently have to be dredged regularly to remain in service.

From Monastir, 230M to the Libyan border, the coast becomes even lower with extensive sandy shallows. The tidal range increases to reach a maximum of 1·8m in Gabès. S of Sfax the coast becomes increasingly arid although it is still amazingly green in March with olive groves all the way to Zarzis. A short distance inland the true desert takes over and in Gabès the large oasis of Chenini comes right up to the coast. This area provides a quite different and interesting cruising ground which is worth exploring, especially with a shallow draught yacht, although there are several deep ports as well. Except for the island of Jerba tourism is not obvious and yachts will generally find a warm welcome in some 15 ports. Mahdia and La Chebba are friendly fishing ports and Mahdia is a good and useful port of entry as well.

The Kerkennah Islands are an interesting cruising ground in themselves and with careful navigation even yachts drawing over 2m can explore some of the ports. With the gently sloping sea bottom and the calming effect of the seaweed rough seas do not occur and consequently there are a surprising number of places to anchor in and around the banks.

Sfax is a large commercial and busy fishing port and the other main ports are Gabès, Houmt Souk on the island of Jerba and Zarzis, almost on the border with Libya. The mild winter is a good time to visit this area where the mid-summer temperatures may be too high for north Europeans. With a draught of 1·5m, several of the smaller fishing ports from which lateen-rigged fishing boats still sail, can be visited.

In recent years Tunisia has built many new fishing ports and existing ports have been enlarged in order to exploit its relatively rich fishing grounds. Today

North Africa

View from the Genoese castle on the fishing port/marina of Tabarka and the beautiful beaches to the E

Harbour
2. **Fishing harbour Digue Nord head** Fl(3)G.6s10m8M Tower
3. **Digue Est elbow** Fl(3)R.12s10m6M
4. **Digue Interior** Fl(4)R.13s8m5M

General
Tabarka is set amongst green mountains in the fertile valley of the Oued Kébir. The offshore rock crowned with the Genoese castle made a natural location for a harbour. In 1981 the Tunisian government earmarked the region of Tabarka for major tourist development of which the new port is the beginning. So far, the old S breakwater has been extended NNW, the yacht basin has been dredged, and new quays, a new fish market, an ice factory and a travel-lift have been constructed. Around the yacht basin there is a harbour office with showers and toilets, apartments and restaurants. Yacht facilities have improved and the development of the apartments is ongoing.

The new port lies east of the causeway connecting the rock with the mainland and the old port (mostly silted up) lies to the west. East of the port beautiful beaches stretch for miles towards the anchorage of Cap Negro, but, unfortunately, there has been considerable hotel development. Aside from the fishing fleet there are a few coral-diving boats and a scuba-diving club. Shops in the simple village are a short walk away. There is now an airport nearby.

Approach
Approach from the N is straightforward with no off-lying dangers. W of Tabarka the coast is made up of steep cliffs and to the E are beaches with mountains further inland. Tabarka Island with the Genoese castle and light tower on top provides a good landmark. Watch out for floating fishing nets in the entrance. Fishermen in rowing boats usually lay them between the S breakwater and the beach. In order to avoid them it is best to round the N breakwater fairly closely.

Berthing
There is a large section reserved for visiting yachts in the southern end of the port. Moor bows/stern-to the quay. There should be tailed lines ready, but in 1997 there were areas without lines, so it might be necessary to come alongside the quay and enquire at the helpful *capitainerie*. Using one's own anchor is not recommended. A 2m *seiche* has been reported in the harbour, but in 1997 the *capitainerie* denied any knowledge of this!

Anchoring E or W of the island in mostly sand is possible; however with the predominant NW wind little protection is found and care should be taken of the fishing nets.

Formalities

Capitainerie ☎ 08670599 *Fax* 08643595
VHF Ch 16, 14, 10, 8 (24 hours)
Garde national, police and customs are located in the port. The *capitainerie* in the SE corner of the port charges (TD), for a 12m yacht:

	Day	Week	Month
1/5–30/9	13·5	65	195
1/10–30/4	10·2	45	135

Facilities

Water and electricity Are available at each berth.
Showers Hot showers in the building occupied by the harbourmaster.
Price (TD) for a 10-12 metre yacht each

Day	Week	Month
2·5	18	45

Fuel Diesel available from a pump near the fish hall and petrol from the gas station in the town.
Provisions For groceries and friendly service visit the Mini Market run by Saudi and his wife who lived in England. Wine, beer and the best assortment of cheese in the *magasin général* (wine from the back door). Good fresh produce available from street stalls and a small covered market near the *magasin général*. Every Friday there is a big *souk*, on the Bizerte road just outside the town on the ground under very simple tents.
Showers In the c*apitainerie* building.
Post office and bank A short walk in the town.
Telephone In the post office and will be provided in the new harbour office.
Repairs There is an engine repair shop on the street facing the port. The fishing port has a slip and 250-ton travel-lift. Arrangements for slipping and repairs are made through the *APIP* in the port, who run the boatyard.
Coral shops Red coral has been obtained around Tabarka for ages and today there is still enough left to support a local industry. In the village you will find many shops selling local handmade coral jewellery at better prices than in Tunis.

Diving The Tabarka Diving Club provides complete facilities for scuba diving. In season they make twice daily diving trips to areas close to the port. Training courses are available starting at the elementary level and it is possible to take official CMAS tests. All facilities are available from diving bottles to a decompression chamber.
Laundry In the town, 50m from the port.

Eating out

There are several Tunisian style restaurants and in some a take-away dinner can be bought. European style dining at the Mimosa Hotel, 15 minutes walk from the port. Hotel de France, Ave Bourguiba is also recommended.

History

Tabarka's history goes back to a Phoenician settlement and the name that they gave it roughly translated means 'thickly wooded'. In Roman times marble from nearby mountains was shipped from the ancient port, which then was no more than a causeway to the island. A period of Turkish rule was followed by a short Spanish occupation, until in 1542 King Charles V sold Tabarka Island and the coral fishing rights to a Genoese family. They constructed the castle and managed to stay for two centuries while the Turks controlled the mainland. After the Second World War and during the French occupation of Tunisia, the present causeway and the port on the east side were constructed. A path leads up to the castle from where there is a splendid view of the village and the miles of beaches. There is no access to the castle itself as it is now considered a military zone.

Tourism

The well known Roman ruins at Bulla Regia are about 60km from Tabarka. To visit them it is best to arrange a *louage* for the day. A winding road takes you up into the cool mountains to Aïn Draham, 1,000m up with spectacular views of the Oued Kébir valley. From there the road descends into the valley of the Oued Ghezala towards Bulla Regia. Although there may not be many yachtsmen who combine sailing with hunting, it is worth mentioning that wild boar are still to be found in the area of Tabarka and hunting is actively promoted by the tourist office. Better restaurants in the area have wild boar on their menus during the hunting season.

Cap Negro (Anse Budmah)

37°06'N 8°59'E

Distances

Tabarka 13½M, Galite 26M – Bizerte 53M

Charts

	Approach
Admiralty	2121
French	4314, 4219
US	52200

The weekly market at Tabarka

North Africa

Approach to Cap Negro anchorage viewed from the W

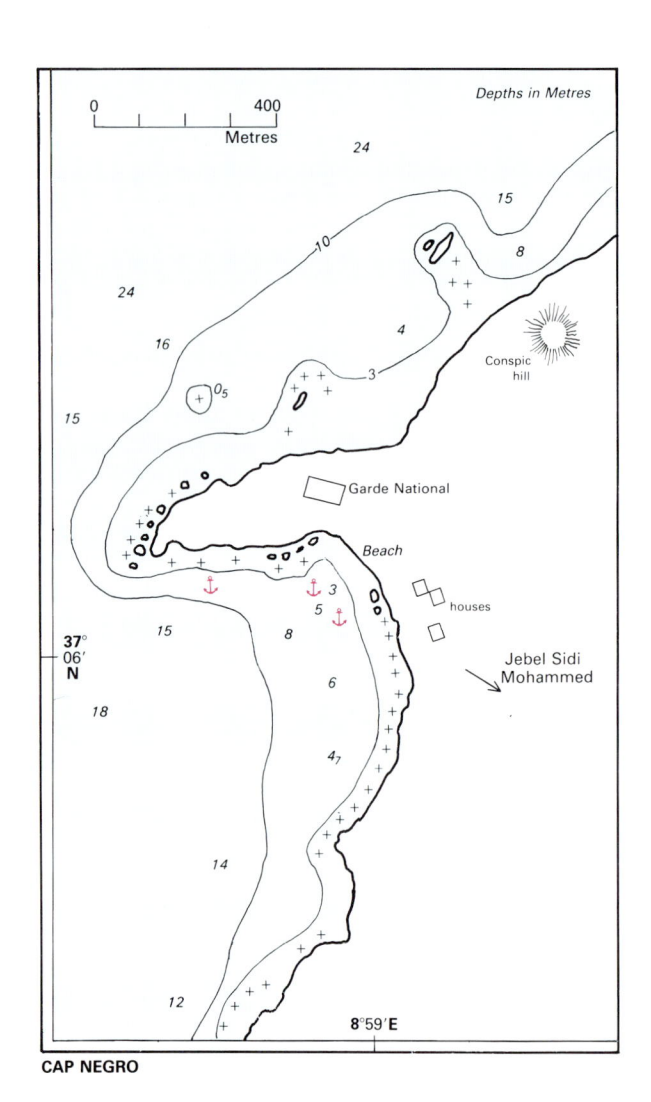

General
Except for a small military settlement and two houses, Cap Negro is uninhabited. There is a small beach with the remains of an old French coral fishing establishment which was chased out by the Bey of Tunis in the 18th century.

Approach
From a distance the point is not very easy to see but when closely following the coastline from Tabarka, the low promontory will be identified. Arriving from Ile de Galite, Jebel Sidi Mohammed, 474m, is a good landmark. Approaching from the E avoid the submerged rocks extending 300m from the point.

Anchorage
The S side of the Cap Negro promontory provides good protection in winds from NE to S but do not hesitate to move if the wind shifts to N or W. Anchor in sand in depths of 5–8m about 200m from the small beach. Residual swell from the W will make the anchorage uncomfortable.

Sidi Mechreg
37°10'·11N 9°07'·56E

General
A new fishing port with all facilities scheduled to be working by the summer of 1998. It is located in the Anse de Sidi Mechreg on the exposed coast between Cap Serrat and Cap Negro.

Distances
Tabarka 22M – Bizerte 44M

Charts
Admiralty approach 2121

Lights
1. **Jetty head N** 37°10'N 09°07'·5E
   Fl.R.4s6M
2. **S** Fl.G.4s6M

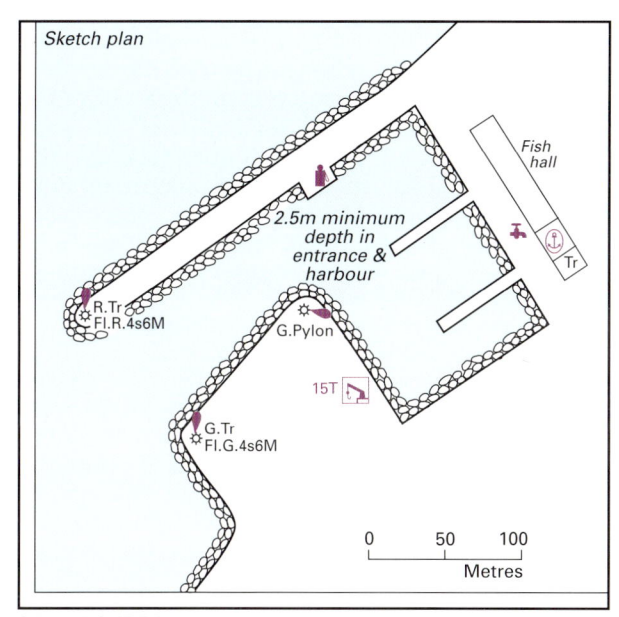

SIDI MECHREG

Position
Midway between crane and green light on pylon.

Approach
The coast W of the port is foul. Make the approach from the NW. The outer breakwater and red light-tower will be seen. The remains of the Roman baths mentioned below, S of the port, make a good landmark. Depths shelve up to the entrance and in onshore winds there is an unpleasant amount of running swell. Depths in the entrance are uncertain. Authorities report a minimum of 2·5m in the port and entrance.

Berthing
In 1997 the port was little used and a yacht could berth wherever there was space alongside.

Formalities
APIP and *garde national* have offices in the port, neither manned 24 hours a day. Telephone (not connected in 1997 so number unknown).

Facilities
Water By the fish market.
Electricity Promised for 1998.
Fuel Pump on fuel quay on the N side of the harbour – not connected in 1997.
Provisions A very small shop and hotel with restaurant 1km from the port.
Telephone APIP not connected in 1997.
Repairs 15-ton crane/travel-hoist.

Tourism
The vaulted remains of a Roman bath house can be seen on the beach 1km south of the port. These are worth a visit – take the road south from the port and 200m past the hotel (1km from the port) follow a track down to the beach. Brushing away the sand over the remains reveals floor mosaics.

Cap Serrat
37°14'N 9°13'·5E

Distances
Tabarka 29M, Galite 22M – Bizerte 37M

Charts
	Approach	Port
Admiralty	2121	–
French	4314, 4219	–
US	52200	–

Lights
Cap Serrat LtHo 37°13'·9N 9°12'·6E
Fl(2)WR.10s199m24/20M Low black tower, white band 238°-R-261°-W-238°

General
Cap Serrat is the most prominent point on the N coast between Tabarka and Bizerte. The anchorage E of the cape is surrounded by rocky coast to the W, deserted beaches to the E and white sand dunes in the background. Protection from WNW to S is good. Solitude is assured in this remote part of the coast. The crystal clear water around the rocks is good for diving.

Approach
The approach is not difficult. From the N, the lighthouse on the cape and further E the high sand dunes of Jebel Blida are easy to identify. On the

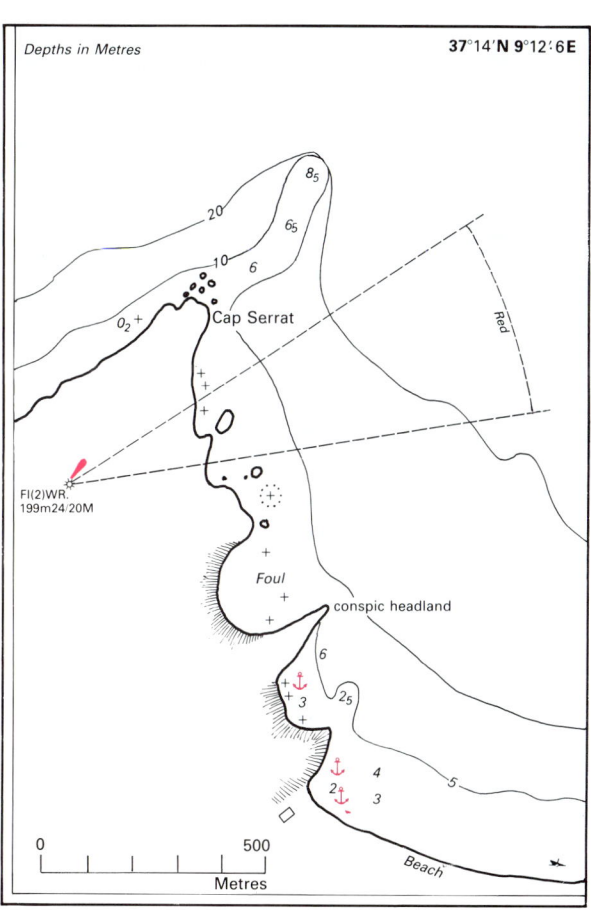

CAP SERRAT

North Africa

beach about ½M from the anchorage are the remains of a stranded tugboat.

Anchorage
The best protection is S of a remarkable projection consisting of large symmetrical blocks piled one on top of the other 0·8M SSE of the cape. Anchor in depths of about 5m in fine sand with a few, well visible, isolated rocky patches. In strong NW winds the anchorage can become uncomfortable with swell rolling in around Cap Serrat.

Ile de Galite
37°31'·5N 8°56'·5E

Distances
Tabarka 35M – Bizerte 50M

Charts
	Approach	Port
Admiralty	2121, 1712	–
French	3424, 5698	–
US	52200	–

Lights
Approach
1. **Galiton de l'Ouest** 37°29'·9N 8°52'·6E
   Fl(4)20s168m24M Black tower, cupola, on grey building 227°-obscd-250° by Ile de la Galite
   May appear as Fl(2)20s at a distance

The light on the buoy in the entrance and the lights in the port are out of action.

General
Ile de Galite, the main island of a small archipelago of volcanic origin, rises steep from the sea bottom to an elevation of 400m. Bizertan sardine and mackerel fishermen work the banks around Galite at night and in season lobster is caught. During the day they use the anchorage and small port on the S side of the island. Except for a small settlement of the *garde national* the island is uninhabited although the original Franco-Italian inhabitants return to their run-down houses in the summertime. The school and church of their small community are now occupied by cows and chickens. The tranquillity, wild vegetation and splendid views are quite addictive.

Approach
Being high and isolated, Ile de Galite and the islets around it are visible from a great distance. In strong winds avoid passing between Galite and the Galitons l'Est and l'Ouest because of breakers on the shallow banks in the channels. A night approach is not difficult with the big light on Galitons de l'Ouest but the lights from the fishermen can be confusing. The large buoy in the entrance to the anchorage is not lit and neither is the little port. There are usually a few fishing boats at anchor in the bay. The buoy that covers the wreck was moved about 50m SW of it by the same storm that damaged the breakwater. The masts of the wreck have been cut and are now about 12m under water. The bay is free of dangers and fairly close inshore good holding ground is found in sand 6–9m deep.

Anchorage
The large bay on the S side provides good protection in NW winds, which are common on this part of the coast. With S winds shelter can be found on the N side of the island which is less steep; care

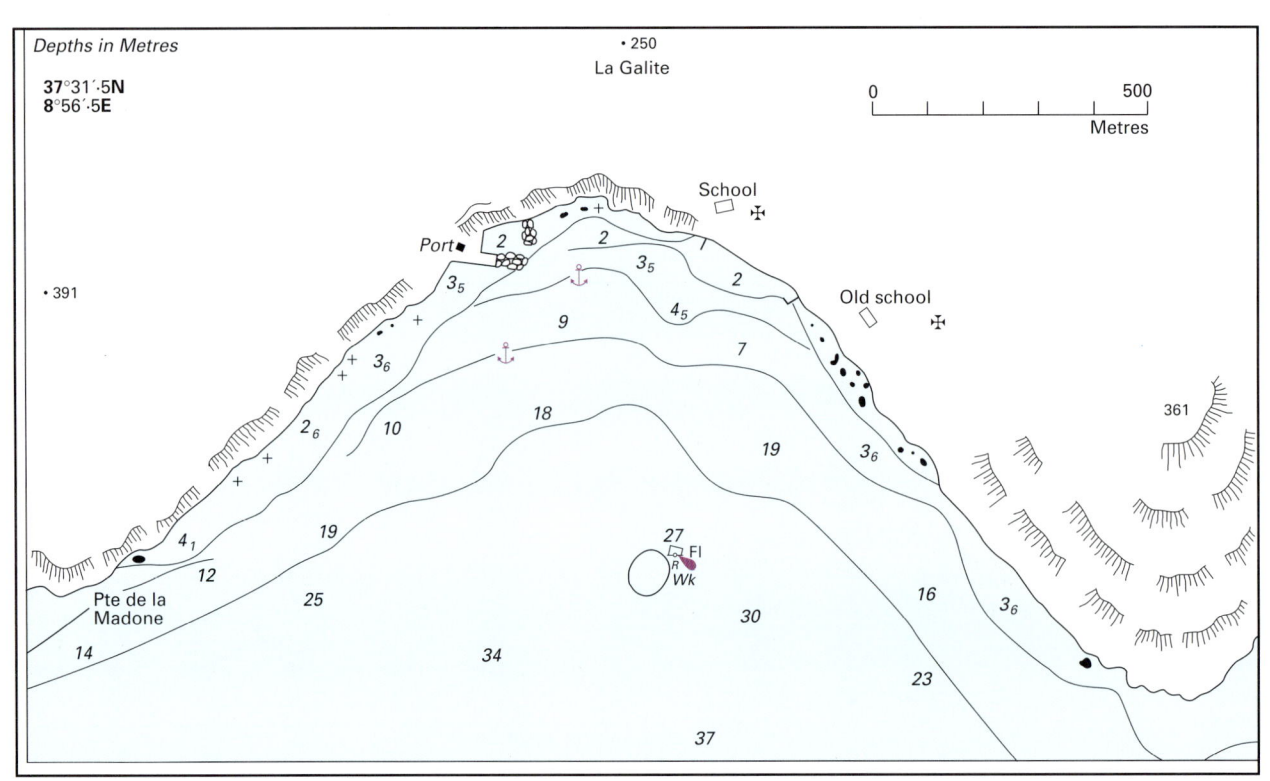

LA GALITE

The very small port in the bay on the S side of Galite

should be taken of isolated rocks along the shore. There is a small harbour in the NW corner but in 1997 it was reported that the breakwater had been considerably damaged and that the harbour was not usable. Plans to rebuild the harbour were underway, with the southern breakwater running E to W and running S from the shore.

Formalities
Ile de Galite is not an official port of entry but yachts calling in on the way from Sardinia to Tabarka found no difficulties. For stays of more than 24 hours, officially a yacht should have cleared into Tunisia. It is advisable to obtain permission from the *garde national*.

Facilities
None, other than fish which you may catch yourself or trade with the fishermen. On the island there are wild figs and cactus fruits. Harpooning is only allowed if you have a licence from the CGP which may be difficult to get because Galite has officially been declared a nature reserve.

History
Galite was inhabited for centuries by Italians from the island of Ponza, near Naples. Fishing was the main source of income for the small community but judging from the fruit trees and spices still found today, they were good farmers too. When Tunisia became independent the islanders had the choice of becoming Tunisian citizens or accepting a French resettlement offer and become French citizens. Everybody went for the last option and gradually moved from the island and the last Italians left around 1975.

Bizerte main harbour – Port de Plaisance
37°16'·9N 9°53'·6E

Distances
Tabarka 65M – Sidi Bou Saïd 42M

Tides
MHWS MHWN MLWN MLWS
0·4m   0·3m   0·2m   0·2m
During February–April Mean Sea Level may fall 0·5m below normal.

Charts
	Approach	Port
Admiralty	2121, 2122	1569
French	4314, 4198 5791	5281
US	52184	52183 (listed under Banzart)

Lights
Approach
1. **Jetée Est N head** 37°16'·4N 9°53'·4E
   Iso.R.4s24m10M Red tower (reported Fl(3+1)R.12s (T) 1998)

Harbour
2. **Jetée Nord head** 37°16'·6N 9°53'·4E
   F.G.15m4M (reported extinguished (T) 1998)
3. **Detached breakwater N head** 37°16'·9N 9°53'·5E
   Fl(2)R.10s10m2M (reported extinguished (T) 1998)
4. **Detached breakwater S head** 37°16'·5N 9°53'·8E
   Iso.G.4s15m3M (reported extinguished (T) 1998)
5. **N breakwater of new fishing port**
   Fl(2)G.10s12m6M (reported extinguished (T) 1998)
6. **S breakwater of new fishing port** Q.R.6M not visible from the N (reported Fl.R.4s (T) 1998)

General
Bizerte is one of the major ports in Tunisia and can be entered in all conditions; it is a good port of entry. Both commercial and naval docks are situated off the channel leading from the Avant Port to the Lake of Bizerte, where the port of Menzel Bourguiba has one of the biggest shipyards of North Africa. The friendly Port de Plaisance is located in the Avant Port, near the entrance to the channel. From this building it is a short walk to the pleasant modern town and small medina. Tourism has not yet touched Bizerte and as the *Rough Guide to Tunisia* puts it 'Bizerte is one of the most underrated of Tunisia's resorts – perhaps because it is not as much a resort as a historic port which happens to have nice beaches'. The picturesque old fishing port, with a fixed bridge at its entrance, is featured on many postcards. There is little of interest to explore on the lake other than the mussel fisheries. This is a friendly, well-run port and not too far from the town.

Note Tunny nets run NNE from Rasez Zebib towards Iles Cani for 3½–4M. It is believed these may be left in place all year. Without local advice it may be best to leave Iles Cani to the south when on passage.

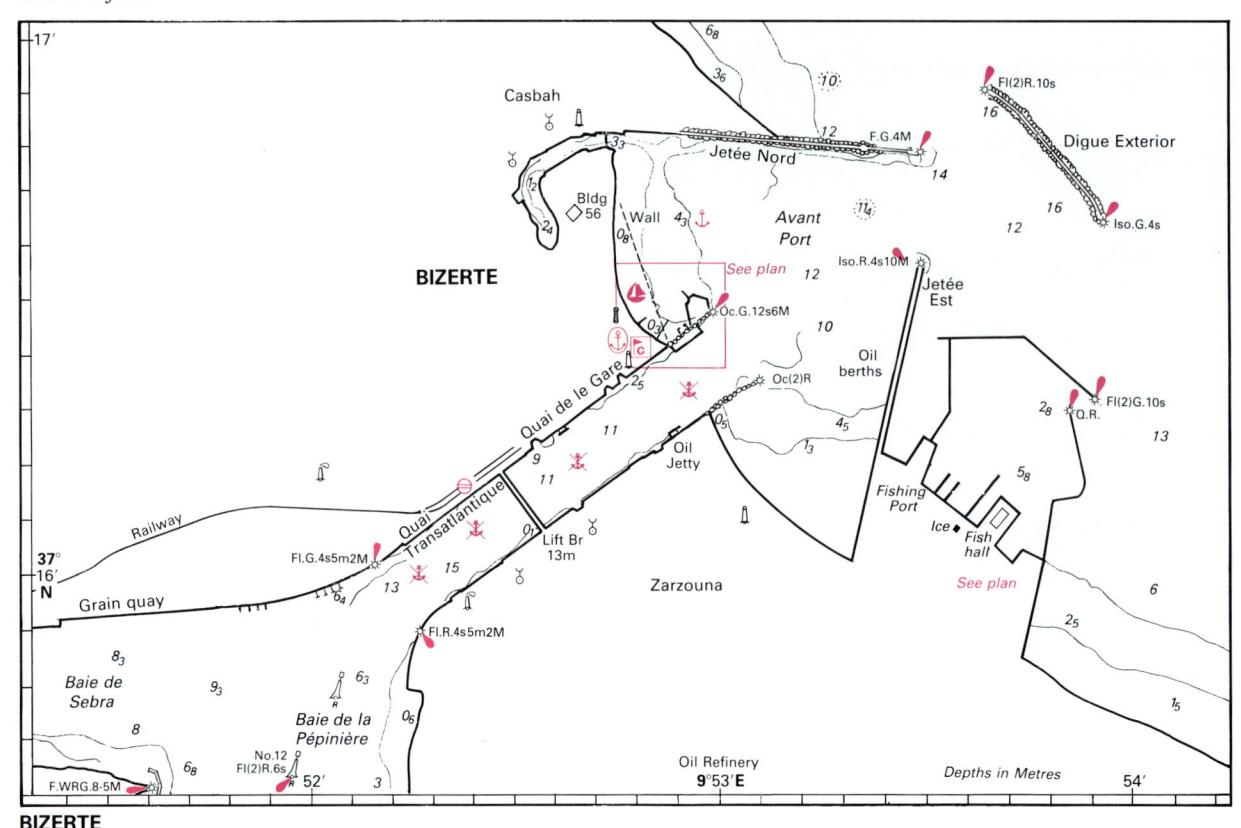

North Africa

Approach
Cap Bizerte is not lit but there are three small but prominent peaks and a conspicuous beacon. The coast between Cap Bizerte and the port is low and well lit from flats and hotels. Stay at least ½M from the shore to avoid Banc de Boberak 2·2M SSE of Cap Bizerte. A night approach to the port can be confusing especially when some of the lights do not work. From the N, No. 1 light will be sighted first although most likely at a much shorter distance than the quoted range of 10M.

Warning At the N entrance to the port there is an E-setting current on the ebb and strong tidal currents are experienced in the channel. Even though the tidal range is small it is sufficient to cause considerable movement due to the large volume of the Lake.

Berthing
Moor where a space is available or as directed by *capitainerie*. The best place is on the quay or alternatively on the floating pontoon but this is more exposed to N winds. In all places moor bow/stern-to; there are tailed lines to the quay. Alternatively when entering at night, one can temporarily tie up alongside the new tugboat quay on the starboard side of the channel to the Lake.

Anchoring in the Avant Port is possible. The best anchorage is N of the yacht club in depths of 5m or more. Closer inshore the bottom is foul and there is an old submerged wall. Close to the entrance of the old fishing port fishermen set floating nets from rowing boats. Use an anchor light because the old fishing port is still in use.

Formalities
Capitainerie ☎ 02 436610 *Fax* 02 435681
Port of entry and formalities are handled efficiently. Harbour dues are charged.
The basic rate (TD) for a 12m vessel in 1997 was as follows.

	Per day	*Per month*
High season	8	180
Low season	4	85
One year	560	

TVA/VAT over 10% for monohulls, +20% catamarans, +30% trimarans.

Facilities
Water and electricity Laid to each berth.
Fuel Diesel at N end of quay.
Gas Camping Gaz and European type bottles can be filled at the *capitainerie*.
Provisions Several small shops in the area and a good market near the old port and another in the new town. A Monoprix (for beer and wine).
Showers Warm showers in the Port de Plaisance building. Several *hammams* in town (addresses on a little map of Bizerte available at tourist office).
Post office On Avenue d'Algérie off the main square
Telephone Taxiphone in *capitainerie*.
Bank In the centre of town near the market. 'Change' in *capitainerie*.
Repairs Small repairs can be arranged through the *capitainerie*. Wood and metal workshops are in town.
Wintering Some boats are left afloat for the winter on the quayed section.
Laundry In *capitainerie*.

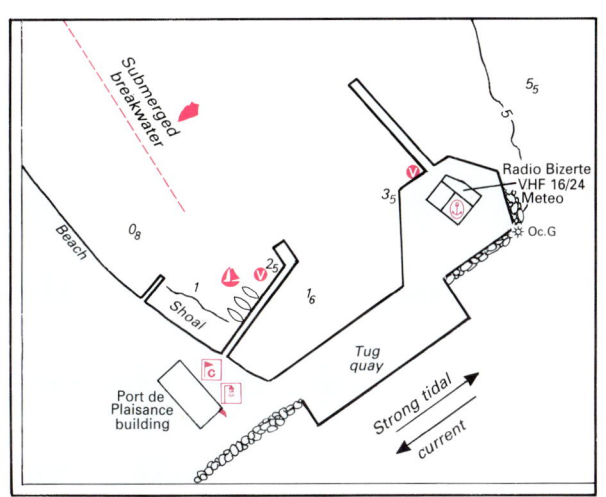

BIZERTE - PORT DE PLAISANCE

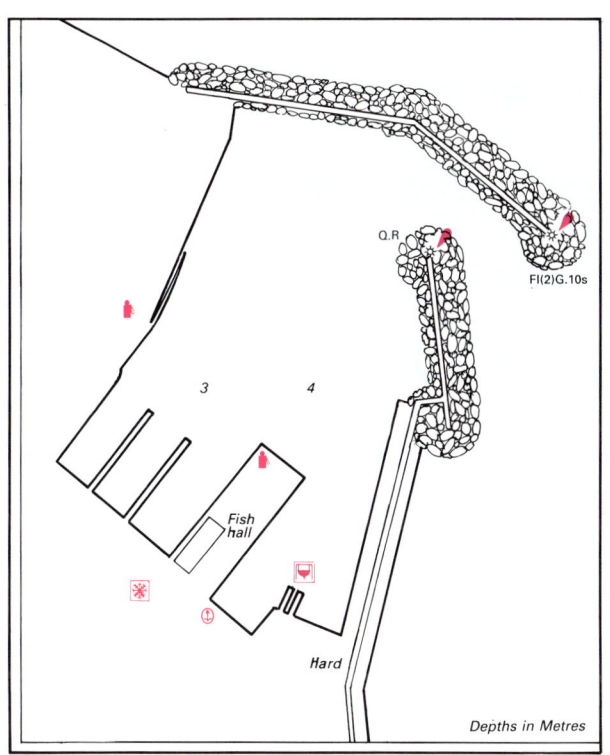

BIZERTE NEW FISHING HARBOUR

Weather forecast
Available from the Bizerte radio station. If the small radio room is unoccupied the operator can often be found outside fishing.

Eating out
Good seafood restaurant above the clubhouse and several Tunisian style restaurants in town where Ave Taieb Mehiri runs into Ave Bourguiba and around Hotel Continental.

Local transport
The main bus station is along the canal past the first bridge and the railway station is a little further on. Hertz car hire in the town.

History
Throughout history Bizerte has been one of the great natural ports of the Mediterranean. The Phoenicians were probably the first to dig a channel between the Lake and the sea. Through the ages it kept its strategic importance under Byzantine, Arab, Spanish and Ottoman rulers. During the French rule the present port was constructed and after the Second World War the French held on to Bizerte (on behalf of NATO) while the rest of Tunisia had already become independent. It took a last effort of Bourguiba's army and many deaths to liberate Bizerte on 15 October 1963 which is now a national holiday.

Bizerte Zarzouna
37°16'·1N 9°53'·8E

Lights
Harbour
1. **Northern breakwater** Fl(2)G.10s12m6M (reported extinguished (T) 1998)
2. **Southern breakwater** Q.R.6M not visible from the N (reported Fl.R.4s (T) 1998)

General
This new fishing port was finished in 1987 and provides good protection in all weather. The surroundings are not very pretty but it is a convenient place to get repairs done.

Facilities
Water Available at the fish market.
Fuel In the NW corner of the port and fish quay.
Provisions Cafés and basic shops in the port. Five fishermen's' chandleries.
Repairs There is a 110-ton and 250-ton travel-lift. 1997 prices 10 Dinars per ton +70 Dinars chocking up fee. Arrangements for this and other repairs through *APIP* Director Homadi Mathlouthi ☎ 02 436190.

Cap Zebib
Position of R light tower
37°15'·96N 10°04'·10E

Distances
Bizerte 9M – Qhar El Melh 14M, Sidi Bou Saïd 31M

Charts
	Approach	Port
Admiralty	2122, 1569	–
French	5791	–
US	–	–

Lights
1. **East Breakwater** Fl.G G tower approx 7m
2. **West Breakwater** Fl.R R tower approx 7m
3. **Beacon** S of west breakwater Fl.R R metal pylon approx 5m.

(Precise characteristics not known.)

General
A brand new port, right on the eastern extremity of Cap Zebib, completed in 1997 with facilities still being installed. Used by small fishing boats but with room for yachts up to 15m. The northern extremity of Cab Zebib is foul and should be given a berth of

North Africa

The quay at the yacht club at Bizerte

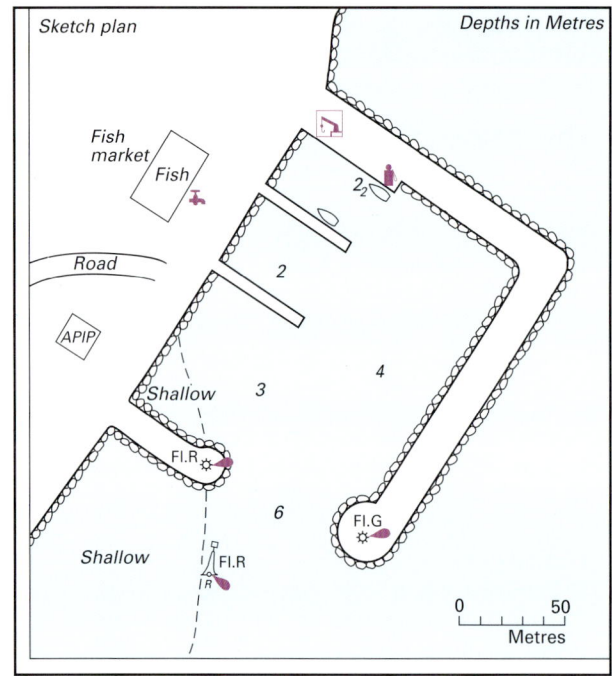

CAP ZEBIB

at least ¼M. Cap Zebib can be identified by its two conical hills, about 90m high. South of the new port are the derelict and very shallow remains of an old port.

Approach
Approach the port from the SE giving the coast a good offing. In the immediate approaches there is shoal water SW of the entrance and a red beacon, which should be left to port, marks this.

Berthing
There are two piers in the centre of the port and a quay at the N end. In 1997 the recommended berths were alongside the N quay or on the N side of the N pier. 2m should be found along most of these positions. As the port becomes used it will probably be necessary to moor bows/stern-to.

Formalities
APIP with charming and helpful *Chef de Port*. Other authorities visit the port occasionally. In 1997 the telephone had not yet been connected.

Facilities
Water At tap by fish market.
Electricity None.
Fuel Diesel obtained from pump on the N quay.
Provisions Shops in village 1·5km from port.
Repairs 15 ton fixed crane/boat hoist on N quay.

ILES CANI AND CAP ZEBIB

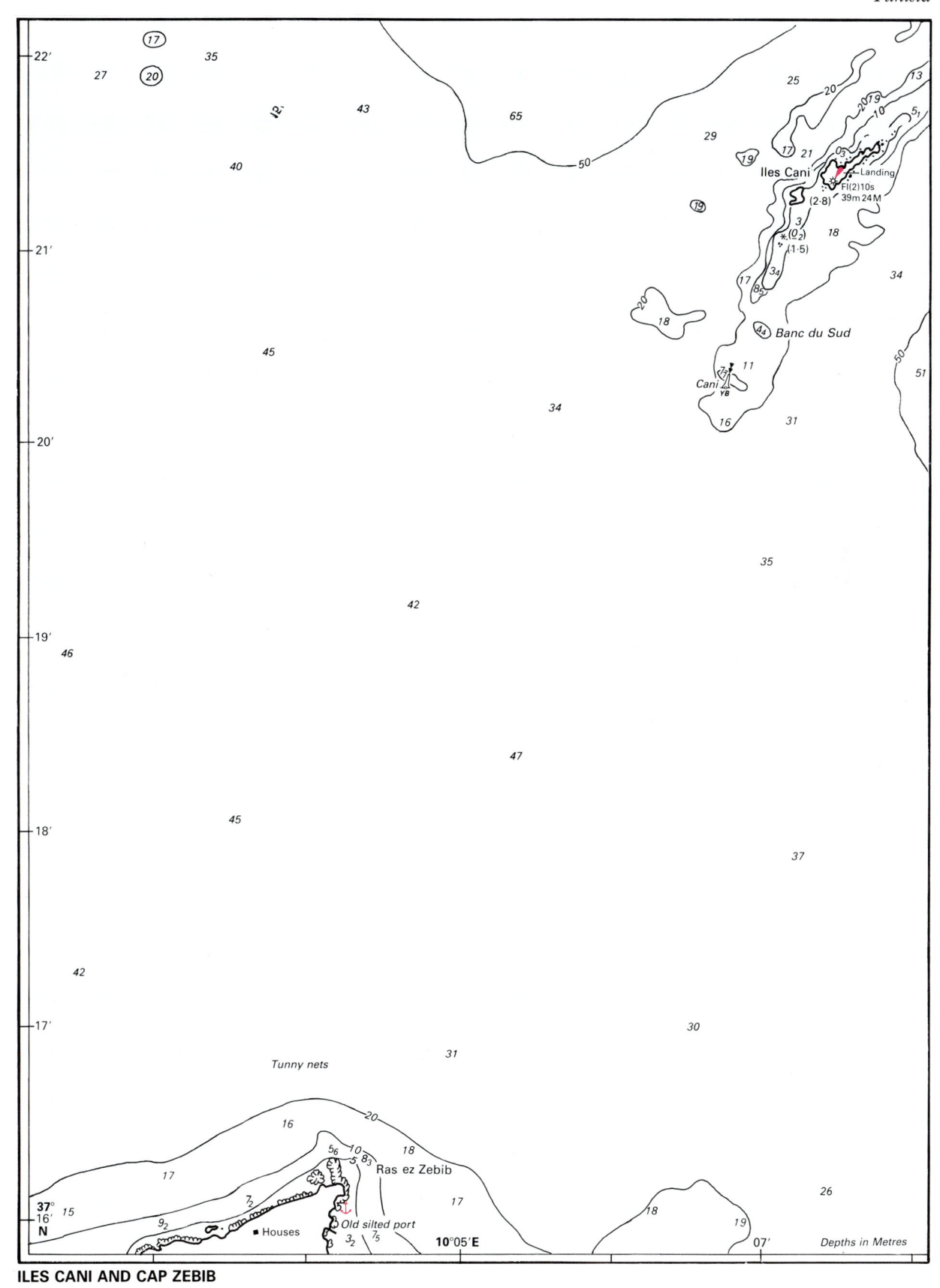

North Africa

Iles Cani
37°21'·2N 10°07'·4E

Distances
Bizerte 12M – Ghar El Melh 17M, Sidi Bou Saïd 33M

Charts
	Approach	Port
Admiralty	2122, 1569	–
French	5791, 5942	–
US	52184	–

Lights
Approach
1. **Iles Canis** 37°21'·2N 10°07'·4E Fl(2)10s39m24M
   White round tower, black bands, on dwelling

General
The Iles Cani consist of two low rocky islets 6M NNE of Cap Zebib, completely exposed to wind and waves with sparse vegetation. Solitude is their main attraction and they can only be visited in good weather. A lighthouse keeper lives with his family on the main islet. The SE side of the largest islet is steep with cliffs.

Anchorage
In good weather it is possible to lie stern-to a small landing close to the lighthouse. The NW side of the islets slopes gently to the sea and is fringed with flat rocks. Either side of the islets provides some protection from the waves. Anchor on the SE side, rocks with patches of sand about 15m deep, less inshore. Admiralty chart No. 1569 gives good detail of Iles Cani and it should be a very interesting place for diving or fishing.

The SE side of wind-swept Ile Cani

Cap Farina
37°10'·4N 10°16'E

Distances
Bizerte 22M – Ghar El Melh 1½M, Sidi Bou Saïd 20M

Charts
	Approach	Port
Admiralty	2122	–
French	4198	–
US	52184	–

Lights
Approach
1. **Ile Plane** 37°10'·8N 10°19'·7E
   Fl(2)WR.10s20m15/11M 067°-R-107°-W- 067°
   White square tower, red bands

General
South of Cap Farina, about 1M from the extremity, is one of the best anchorages between Cap Farina and Cap Bon with good protection in all prevailing wind directions. The bay S of Cap Farina is bordered by miles of untouched beaches formed by the deposits of the Oued Medjerda; this river has shaped the entire area and created the lagoons around Ghar El Melh. If caught in strong head winds on the way N or if draught does not allow entry into Ghar El Melh, this a good place to stop.

Approach
Coming from the N, Cap Farina can be rounded at 1M distance but beware of a small sand spit extending S off the cape. There are several rocky shoals between the cape and Ile Plane which are of no significance in good weather but in strong winds they cause heavy seas and yachts should keep well E of Ile Plane. Watch out for floating nets.

Anchorage
Depths in the anchorage shoal evenly towards the beach and the holding ground is good. Swell or big waves are rare. At night a few fishermen may keep you company in an otherwise deserted surrounding.

Ghar El Melh
37°09'N 10°14'E

Distances
Bizerte 24M – Sidi Bou Saïd 19M

Tides
MHWS	MHWN	MLWN	MLWS
0·4m	0·3m	0·2m	0·2m

Charts
	Approach	Port
Admiralty	2122	–
French	4314, 4250	Livre de Bord suggests 4191
US	52184	–

Lights
Approach
1. **Ile Plane** 37°10'·8N 10°19'·7E
   Fl(2)WR.10s20m15/11M 067°-R-107°-W-067°
   White square tower, red stripes.

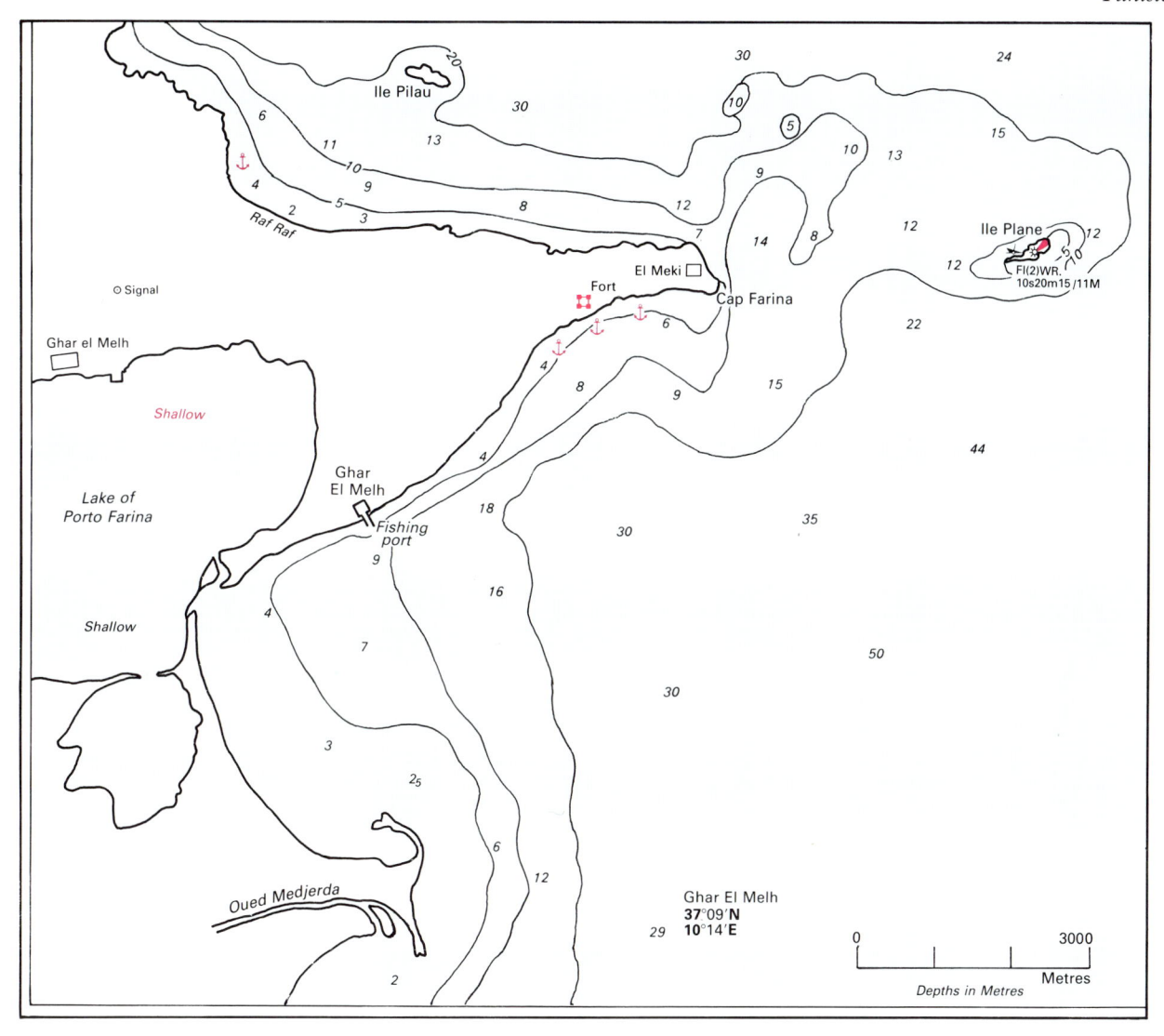

Harbour
2. **Eastern breakwater** Fl.G.2s5m3M
3. **Western breakwater** F.R.5m3M

General
Ghar El Melh is a small fishing port situated 3M WSW of Cap Farina in the delta formed by the Oued Medjerda. The new port is surrounded by miles of deserted beaches and it is a tranquil place. The fish market and a few low buildings are the only signs of civilisation. The village of Ghar El Melh (Porto Farina is the old French name) is 5km away and makes for an interesting walk if one is not picked up by the occasional car passing by. They carry fruit and vegetables from farmers who work the small plots of land and little islands around the lagoon. Small plots of land and little islands around the lagoon produce fruit and vegetables. The Turkish fortress in Ghar El Melh, which overlooks the quaint old port, is used as a school today but its past was less peaceful when it was a notorious pirate's nest. However when the old port silted up it lost its importance and today it is only used by fishermen who work in rowing boats in the Lake of Porto Farina. The lake still has a shallow entrance to the sea. There is a good beach E of the entrance.

Approach
Coming from the N, Cap Farina can be rounded between the cape and Ile Plane in good weather and continuing WSW for 2·8M will bring Ghar El Melh abeam. The port cannot be made out easily because of the lack of buildings. The breakwaters jut out from the beach and they should be given a wide berth because of shifting sand banks. Silting of the entrance has been a problem. Two groynes have been built west of the port and the W breakwater extended to reduce the effects. In 1997 the *APIP* reported 4m in the approach, 3m in the entrance and 2–3m in the port. 2·7m was found at the end of the W pontoon. Once inside the port there are sufficient depths and good protection. Coming from the S, steer roughly for the middle between the village of Ghar El Melh and Cap Farina. A night approach is not recommended.

North Africa

Remarkable natural pyramids on the N coast of the Cap Farina headland near Raf Raf

The new fishing port of Ghar el Melh

148

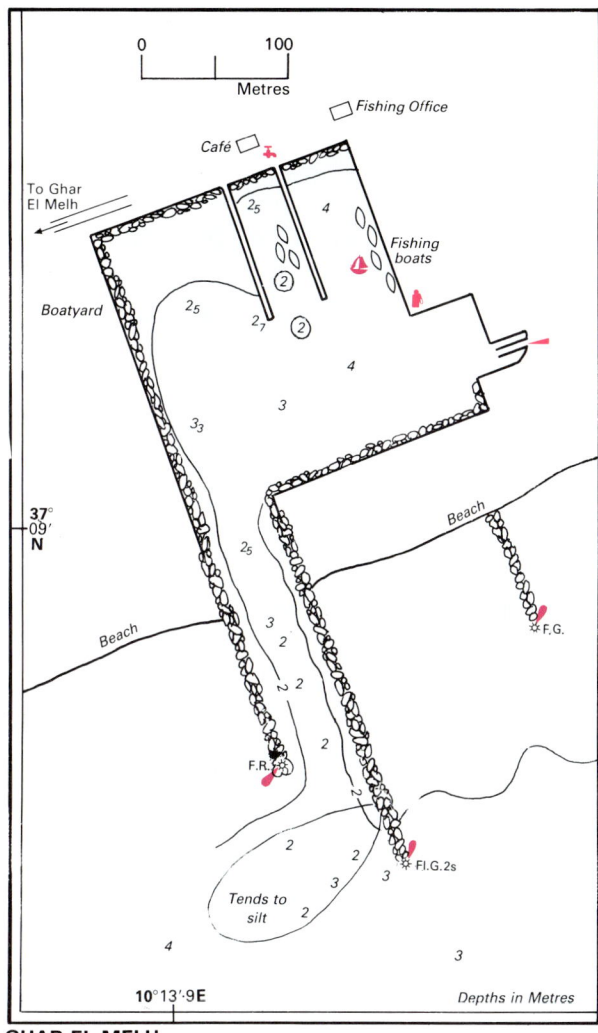

GHAR EL MELH

Berthing
Tie up alongside one of the bigger fishing boats which are usually moored along the quay N of the small slipway or at the ends of the two piers.

Formalities
There is *garde national* post, *APIP* and *Marina Marchander* post. It is not a port of entry.
APIP ☎ 02 448 622 (0800–1300, 1500–1800), VHF Ch 16.

Facilities
Water There is a water tap on the quay.
Fuel Diesel is available on the East Quay.
Provisions Fresh bread and a limited selection of vegetables is available from a small shop behind the restaurant. Fish can be bought at the fish market. A good assortment of fresh produce can be found at the market in the village, 5km from the port. It is often possible to get a lift with some pick-up truck.
Post office In the village.
Telephone Taxiphone in the village.
Repairs There is a small boatyard.

Eating out
One restaurant and a coffee bar in the port.

Transport
A bus to the town runs regularly from the café in the port.

Sidi Bou Saïd
36°52′N 10°22′E

Distances
Bizerte 42M, Ghar El Melh 19M – La Goulette 4M, Sidi Daoud 29M, Kelibia 57M

Tides
MHWS MHWN MLWN MLWS
0·4m 0·4m 0·3m 0·2m

Charts
	Approach	Port
Admiralty	2122	1184
French	4314	*Livre de Bord* 4250
US	52180	–

Lights
Approach
1. **Cap Carthage** 36°52′·3N 10°20′·9E
   Fl.5s146m22M White tower with black top in the village

Harbour
3. **SE breakwater** Fl.G.5·5s6m4M
4. **W breakwater** Fl.R.3s6m4M

General
Sidi Bou Saïd is the oldest marina in Tunisia. It is popular as a port of entry. The authorities are well accustomed to foreign visitors and speak French as well as English. Many Europeans working in Tunis keep boats here and it is a lively place, especially at weekends. There is an active fleet of small fishing boats in a separate corner. The setting of the port at the foot of Cap Carthage is very attractive. A footpath leads from the marina up to the famous village on top of the hill.

Approach
Coming from the N, Cap Gammarth and the village of La Marsa will be sighted first. Cap Carthage with two conspicuous wrecks about 500m from the port entrance provides an unmistakable landmark. Do not get too close to the presidential port 1M SW of Sidi Bou Saïd where navigation is prohibited within a radius of 500m; it is marked off with buoys. The Tunisian navy has a patrol boat permanently at sea which is quick off the mark.

Entrance
The entrance to the marina tends to silt up and is not dredged every year. In 1997 the *capitainerie* reported 5m in the outer approach and 3m in the entrance. It is not buoyed. A sand bar develops from the SW pier head in a NW direction and entry is best made by rounding the SW pier head at 100m and steering for the extreme port side of the entrance. Keep close to the N breakwater head as there is a shoal of 2·5m in the entrance opposite the fuel berth. Entry in NE to S winds of Force 5 is difficult due to breakers on the sandbanks around the SE pier head and with higher winds, entry is not recommended. Under these rare conditions it is better to go to La Goulette.

Night entry is not recommended. The harbour lights are not entirely reliable and once inside there is not much room to manoeuvre.

North Africa

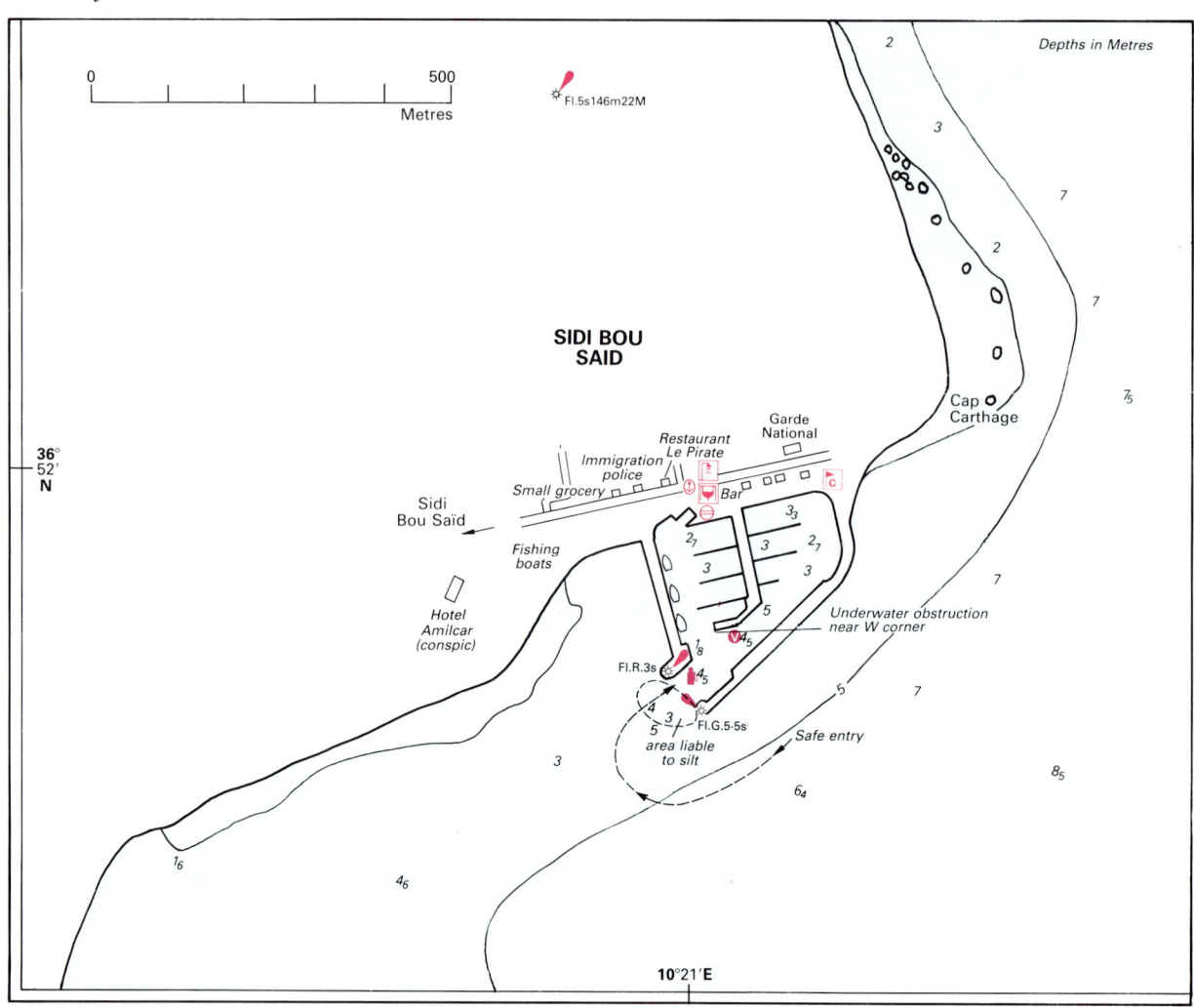

SIDI BOU SAID

Berthing
There are 340 berths, mostly occupied by local motorboats. Tie up alongside the end of the central quay. Beware of two underwater obstructions with minimum depth of 1·8m along this quay: one near the W corner as marked on the port plan, the other is just W of the first bend of the quay. Both are the result of sloppy concrete work when the quays were constructed. The authorities turn up automatically and a yacht may stay here for a short visit, otherwise the port captain will allocate a berth but the harbour does get very crowded in summer. The SE pier is reserved for patrol boats from the *garde national*. In strong winds from the SE, common in the spring, a considerable swell enters the port but overall shelter is good.

Formalities
All officials for custom clearing are available in the port 24 hours a day.
The port captain monitors VHF Ch 9 and 16 during office hours.
Capitainerie ☎ 01 741645
Charges 1998 in Tunisian Dinars

Boat length	High season 1/6–30/9		Low season 1/10–31/5		
	Day	Month	Day	Month	Year
12–13m	26	370	20	260	1700

Water and electricity are not included and vary according to boat length. VAT is added at 17%.

	Day	Month	Year
Water			
12–13m	6	37	180
Electricity			
12–13m	6	37	180

There is a 20% reduction for wintering between 1 October and 30 April.

Facilities
Water and electricity On the pontoons for each berth.
Fuel Diesel and petrol from pumps at the end of the W breakwater.
Gas Difficult to get refills. Ask at the *capitainerie* who will direct you to a shop that may refill *Camping Gaz* cylinders.
Provisions A small shop in the marina and another just outside have fresh bread and a limited assortment of groceries. *Magasin général* in the village and a small covered market next to it. A big *supermarché* in Carthage. A *monoprix* and the best market in La Marsa. Although not the most convenient place to go

Tunisia

Sidi Bou Saïd marina at the foot of Cap Carthage viewed from the SE

Sidi Bou Saïd marina in the Gulf of Tunis

shopping, the colourful central market in Tunis has the best assortment of fruit, vegetable, cheese, meat (including pork and wild boar) and fish that the country produces. Fresh fish can be bought from fishermen in the port – but bargain! Duty-free alcohol, cigarettes, perfumes etc. can be ordered through the harbourmaster. Large orders will be delivered to the boat. Handicrafts can be found in a small market in the village.

Showers In the new harbour buildings. There is a *hammam* in the village.
Post office In the village.
Telephone and Fax In the harbour office.
Bank In the village, 'change' in the *capitainerie*.

151

North Africa

Repairs 22-ton travel-lift with small high pressure pump in the port. Price about TD 200 for 10–12m in and out, excluding the high pressure pump. Maintenance and minor repair work can be carried out. There are two chandleries with limited stock but possibly the best you will find in Tunisia. General Equipment ☎ 01743435. Ask for Narges who is keen to help. A caretaker for wintering afloat can be arranged. Work on the hard has to be carried out within a reasonable time period because of limited space. Perkins has an agent in Tunis.
Laundry Available in the town.

Eating out
European style dining in Le Pirate just outside the marina gate.

Transport
The international airport of Tunis is a 20 min taxi ride from the port (about TD 4). Car hire can be arranged through the harbourmaster but all big agencies have offices at the airport.

Tourism
Sidi Bou Saïd is a place of extraordinary charm and beauty with its narrow streets and white-washed houses with blue studded doors. It was founded in 1888 in one of the pavilions of the Bey's palace. The Bardo museum houses one of the worlds finest collections of antique floor mosaics, which are arranged in six sections, each reflecting a different aspect of history, including Greek, Byzantine and Arab-Moslem. Many famous artists have spent some time here and the Café des Nattes was their favourite meeting place. The location is excellent for visits to Tunis and the ruins of Carthage; once the richest and most desired city in the world. The efficient TGM train goes from Sidi Bou Saïd to the centre of Tunis in 30mins and also stops at the Carthage ruins.

There is not room here to describe the many attractions of Tunis and Carthage but the travel guides in the reference list cover them well. The tourist information office in Tunis is on the Place de l'Afrique, at the beginning of Avenue Bourguiba, about 200m from the TGM station.

Nearby, to the E of Tunis is the new development of Gammarth, which is being built as a special place of beauty to be admired for centuries to come.

La Goulette
36°48'·5N 10°18'·6E

Distances
Sidi Bou Saïd 4M – Sidi Daoud 32M, Kelibia 60M

Tides
MHWS MHWN MLWN MLWS
0·4m 0·4m 0·3m 0·2m

Charts
	Approach	Port
Admiralty	2122	1184
French	4222, 6062	*Livre de bord* suggests 4222
US	52180	52186

Lights
Approach
1. **Jetée Nord SE corner** 36°48'·3N 10°18'·5E Fl(3)12s13m13M partially obscured by the breakwaters 090°-vis-121°, 215°-vis-035°
2. **Chimney 1M SW of entrance** 36°47'·6N 10°17'·0E Fl.R.1·5s(hor)102m8M

Harbour
3. **Digue Nord** 36°48'·3N 10°18'·9E Fl(2)G.10s9m5M
4. **Digue Sud** (channel entrance) 36°48'·4N 10°18'·5E Fl.R.5s9m6M
5. **Jetée Nord NE corner** (entrance to fishing port) 36°48'·3N 10°18'·5E F.R.13m5M
6. **Ro Ro berth** Fl.G.4s7m6M

General
La Goulette is situated at the mouth of a channel which leads through the Lake of Tunis to the capital. It can be entered in all weather conditions and overall shelter is better than in Sidi Bou Saïd. It is a major commercial port without any great charm, but the town, although a long walk away, is attractive. A fishing harbour with yacht club is situated N of the entrance to the channel but since Sidi Bou Saïd was opened foreign visitors have tended to go there. The ferry terminal is situated inside the channel and at its end is the commercial port of Tunis. In 1989 work was in progress on an elevator to haul large fishing vessels, but this is not used for yachts. The corner of the harbour for yachts is quite remote within a large commercial harbour but the club is friendly and prepared to help sort out any problems. Much of the pontoon space is taken up by small motor boats.

Approach
There is an Aero Radiobeacon 1 mile N of the harbour entrance. Day approach is without any particular problem, however keep a good lookout for commercial vessels leaving or entering the port. There are always a few ships anchored in the Bay of Tunis awaiting entry. At night most probably the No. 2 light will be seen first. Enter on a course of 285° and once the green No.3 light is abeam change course to due N and enter the fishing port.

Berthing
The outermost of the 3 pontoons has spaces for visitors; if these are full, take a berth wherever there is space. Moor bows/stern-to, however, the tail lines to the pontoon are getting a bit rickety. If you need to anchor, the holding is good in mud.

Formalities
Port of entry. police, customs and *garde national* will come from the ferry terminal.
☎ Yacht Club 01 637284

Facilities
Water and electricity On the pontoons.
Fuel Diesel available on the fish quay.
Provisions Good market and many shops in the village a short walk from the port. There are many shops around the port too.
Showers Plenty of showers in the clubhouse.
Post office In the town.

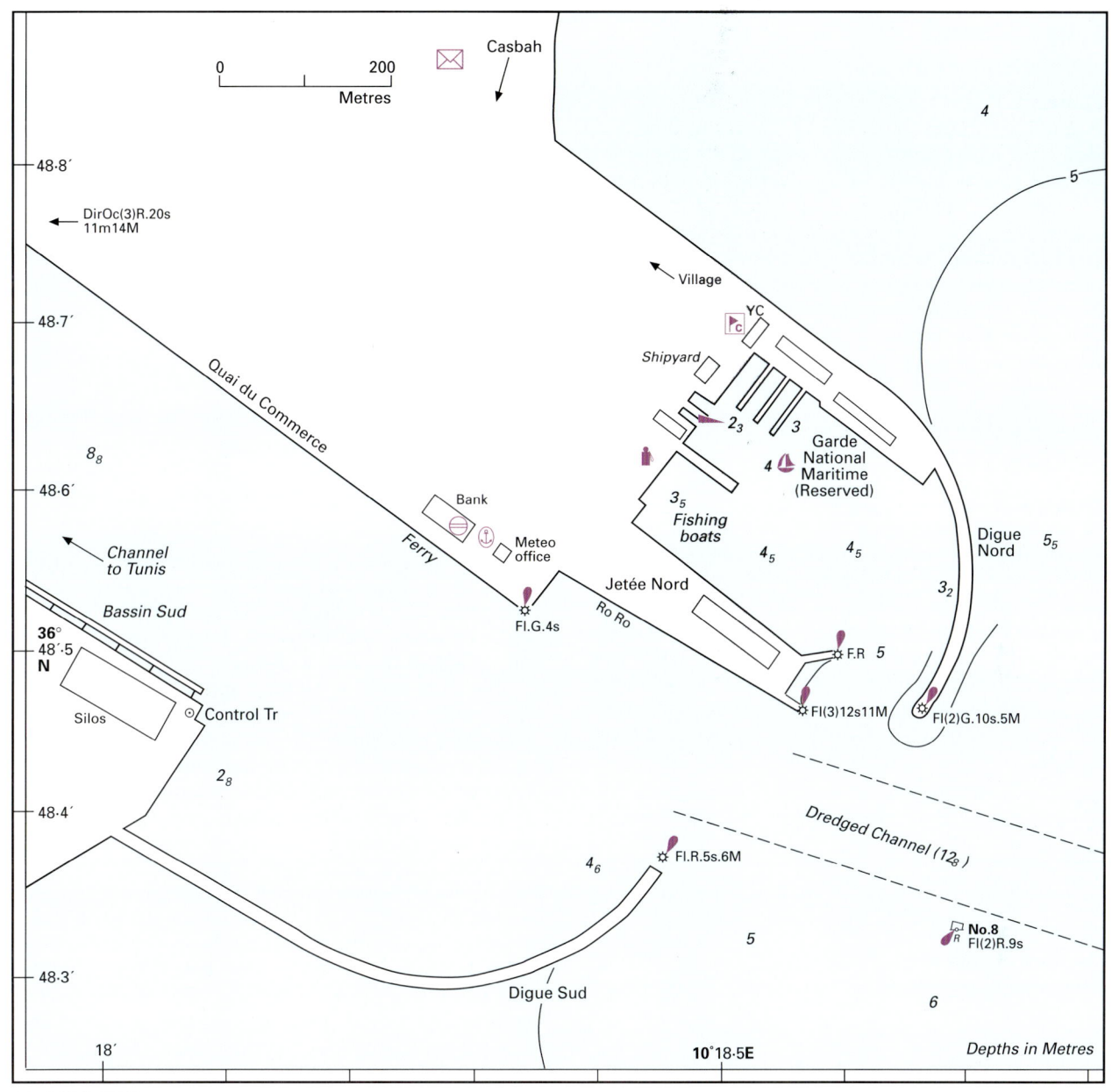

LA GOULETTE

Telephone In the clubhouse.
Bank exchange At the ferry terminal, open 24hrs a day 7 days a week.
Repairs The club haul boats ashore using a mobile crane. La Goulette has all kinds of repair shops. The only problem may be to locate them but with some help from the yacht club you should be able to get any kind of engine repair, welding, etc. taken care of. There is a small crane but for hauling out Sidi Bou Saïd is better. The club can organise a mobile crane easily.
Laundry Probably the only launderette in Tunisia is found in La Goulette, in a key-copying shop at the bottom of the only tall white apartment building. Price roughly TD 4 for 7kg + TD 1 for drying but there is now a washing machine in the yacht club.

Eating out

Beer and other alcoholic drinks are served on the terrace of the yacht club and the atmosphere is relaxed. The town has several good non-touristy fish restaurants.

Transport

The TGM train to Tunis takes about 10 minutes. A taxi to the airport will take about 20 minutes.

Tourism

Apart from the *kasbah* fortress built by the Spanish King Charles V in 1535 and its associated history, there are no particular points of interest in La Goulette but it does have a lively atmosphere. It is a convenient base for visits to Tunis. The channel is without interest for yachts and the commercial port of Tunis, although very close to the city centre, is a dusty and uncomfortable place.

North Africa

L'eau Chaud
36°50'·5N 10°34'·4E

General
A small anchorage in the Bay of Tunis opposite Sidi Bou Saïd where warm water wells up from the sea floor in several places. In the daytime it is popular but in the evening it is a place of absolute tranquillity. The resort of Korbous 2M S serves as a good landmark. Among the few houses around the little bay a blue house is conspicuous. In moderate N winds protection is surprisingly good. Anchor in 7m sand with rocks. A tripping line is a good precaution.

Ras El Fortras
36°52'·6N 10°36'·6E

General
A deserted anchorage in the Bay of Tunis surrounded by barren mountains. A few goats looking for the scarce vegetation may be the only sign of life. Anchor off a short beach with a shipwreck on the N side in 5–6m sand, rocks and sea weed. Protection in E to SE winds which are frequent in the summer, is good but the anchorage is completely open to the NW. The shipwreck shown on Admiralty chart No. 1184 is no longer visible.

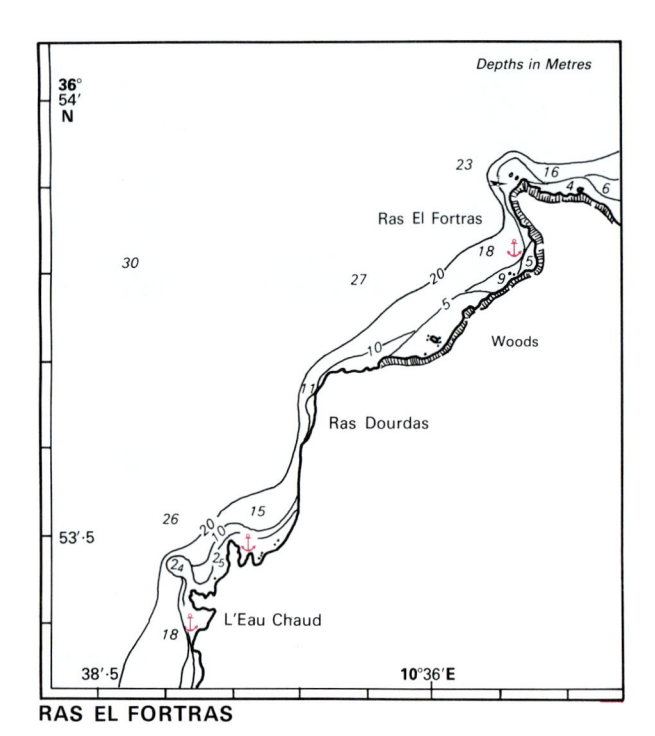

RAS EL FORTRAS

Sidi Daoud
37°01'·1N 10°54'·4E

Distances
Sidi Bou Saïd 29M – Kelibia 29M

Tides
MHWS	MHWN	MLWN	MLWS
0·4m	0·4m	0·3m	0·2m

Charts
	Approach	*Port*
Admiralty	2122	–
French	4314, 4191	–
US	52180	–

Lights
Harbour
1. **N Jetée head** Fl(2)R.10s3m6M
2. **S Jetée head** Fl(2)G.10s3m6M
3. **Directional white light** on white pillar approx 10m at elbow of breakwater (characteristics unknown)

General
Sidi Daoud is surrounded by shallow water and with onshore winds, a sea builds up. The port must be approached from the NW. Depths within the port must be treated with caution. Further dredging will take place in the next 2-3 years.

The port itself is nothing special though during the tunny season from April–June it is quite spectacular to watch the 300 to 400kg blue-fin tuna being caught in the net just outside the port. After they have been brought ashore, a long line of women from the nearby village march into the factory to clean the fish, which are then shipped, fresh on ice, to Japan. A few Japanese are there to make sure that the fish are properly packed. Fish are plentiful in the waters around Cap Bon and occasionally good-sized lobsters are caught. At weekends an excursion boat takes spectators out to the tunny net. These nets run 2M south and north of the port. The fishing port is surrounded by salt marshes and this is one of the few places along the Mediterranean shores where *salicorn* (samphire) grows abundantly. Preserved in

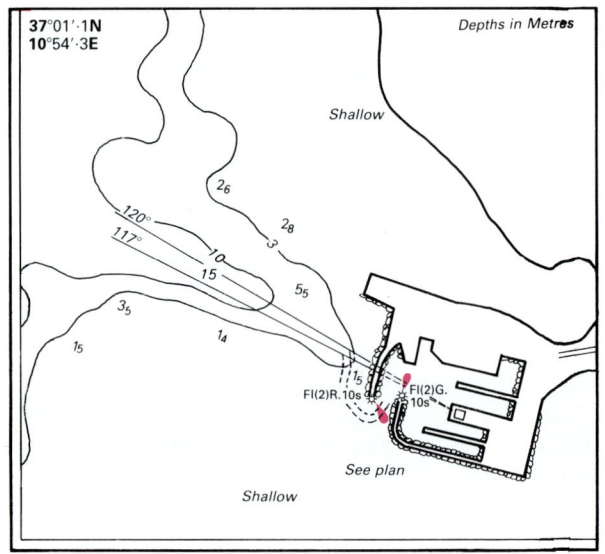

SIDI DAOUD APPROACH

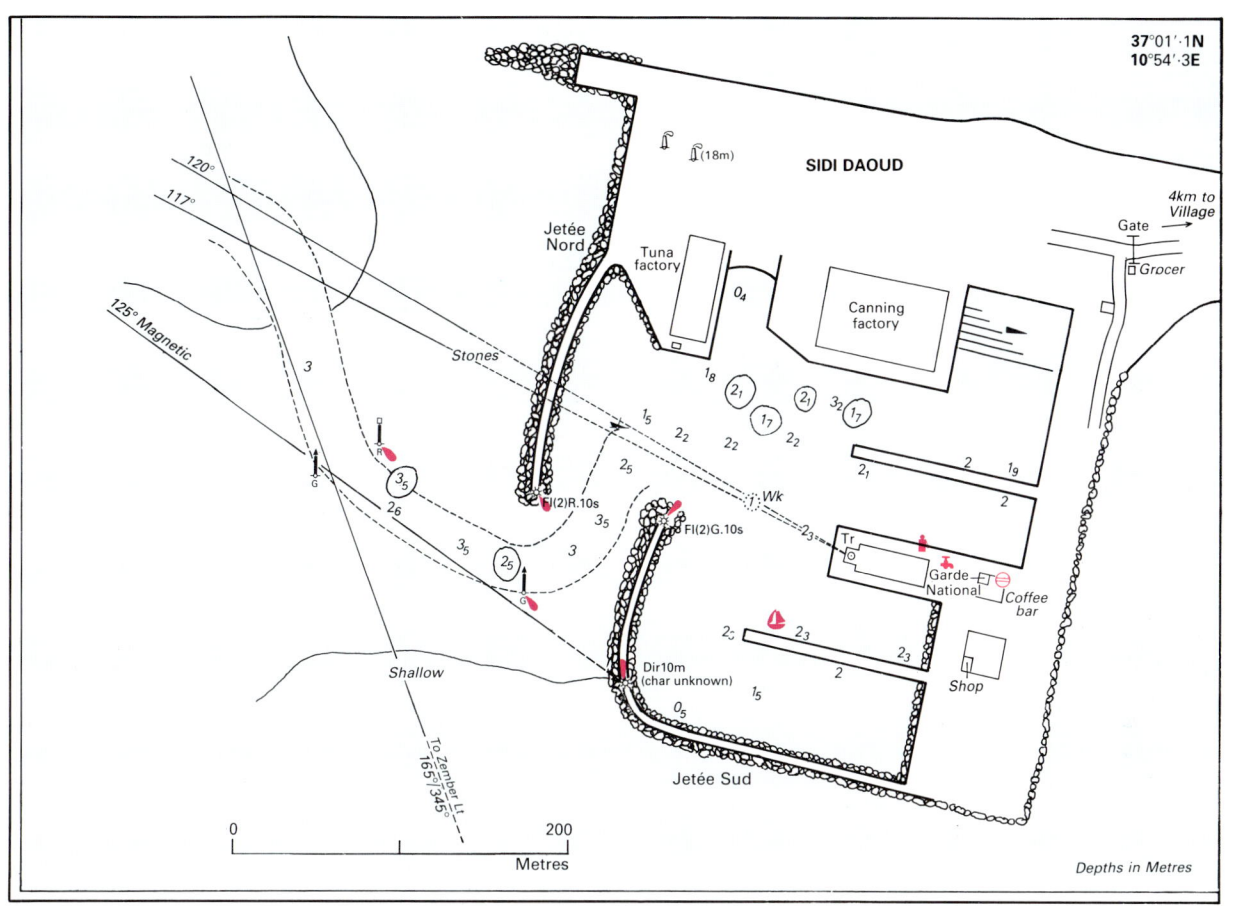

SIDI DAOUD

vinegar this makes a delicious salad ingredient or appetiser.

Approach
The coast within a radius of 0·7M from the port is shallow with patches of sand, weed and rocks with depths between 1–5m. Approach should be from the N during the tunny season as the net extends from the coast in a WNW direction. The outer extremity of the net is marked with a N cardinal buoy. In any onshore wind there is a confused sea in the shallows; approach at night in unsettled weather is not recommended.

Entrance
Considerable improvements have been made to the entrance recently. The dredged channel is marked by a pair of beacons (red and green) and there is a green beacon closer in. There were 5 beacons originally but 2 were washed away in October 1997. Their replacements and the existence of the ones shown cannot be relied upon. There is also a directional white light on the elbow of the S. breakwater. A course of 125°M on this lighthouse leads through the outer beacon. It is believed the approach has been dredged to 5m.

Warning In the middle of the port midway between the green light and fish quay lies a dangerous wreck with less than 1m over it. This should be left to port.

Berthing
Visiting yachts can usually find room on the S pier in minimum depths of 2m. The bottom is covered with thick seaweed and shoals quickly towards the S breakwater. Alternatively, try the N quay. The fish quay has depths of 2m.

Formalities
Garde national and customs in the port but it is not a port of entry.
APIP ☎ 02 294528 VHF Ch 16.

Facilities
Water Water tap near the customs office.
Electricity None available.
Ice Available
Fuel Available in the port.
Provisions A small *épicerie* at the entrance gate to the tunny factory sells bread and some fresh vegetables. There is a small shop SE of the fish hall. The hamlet of Sidi Daoud is about 4km from the port. El Haouaria, 10km, is the nearest town. Taxi TD 1.
Repairs There is a boatyard and slip. Mechanical repairs are possible.
Post office The first house down the road to the village.
Taxi Comes regularly to the port.

North Africa

Anchorages around Cap Bon

Zembra
37°07'N 10°48'·4E

General
An anchorage on the S side of the Island of Zembra near a small port and a few white buildings. The buildings were once used by a sailing club and diving centre. The island is now a military zone and yachts are not allowed to anchor except in emergency. Protection from N and NW winds is good but anchoring is precarious as deep water extends close up to the beach and the holding is mediocre.

Cap Bon
37°04'·9N 11°02'·3E

Chart
Admiralty 2122

General
A remote and useful anchorage with good shelter in NE to S winds in a bay on the W side 1M S of Cap Bon. There is good holding in 4m, close to the shore, in fine sand patches which can be seen in the clear water. The wind will blow steadily down the steep mountain face but the sea will be flat. Between this anchorage and the anchorage of Ras ed Drek good shelter can be found in all prevailing wind directions around Cap Bon. There are no facilities ashore, just good snorkelling around the rocks.

Ras ed Drek
37°02'·3N 11°04'E

General
Ras ed Drek is the dividing point between the mountainous N coast of Tunisia and the low S coast. In 1997 a new harbour was being built, the breakwaters were in place, but there was nothing ashore. Depths in the approaches and port are not yet known. The entrance appeared to be between the wreck and the end of the E breakwater. Until the port is completed the anchorage provides good protection when strong winds from W to N make the trip around Cap Bon uncomfortable. Protection in NE winds is not good as the waves roll around the rocky point on the N side. Anchor between the rocky point and a large wreck, marked either with one mast still above water 400m from the beach or by a metal beacon tower. High up on the cape are the remains of an old fortress. Towards the S wide sandy beaches with scattered houses stretch towards the shore installations of a gas pipeline which is used to export Algerian gas to Italy. Anchor in sand, 4–6m. Good holding.

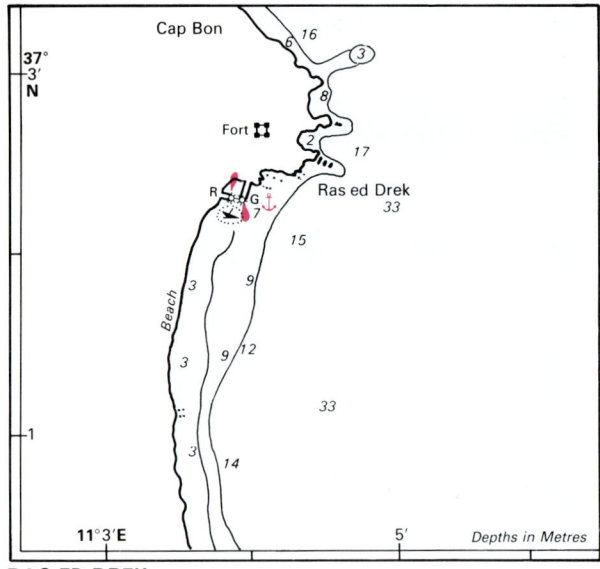

CAP BON

RAS ED DREK

156

Kelibia

36°49'·8N 11°06'·4E

Distances
Sidi Bou Saïd 58M – Beni Khiar 28M, Al Kantaoui 63M

Tides
MHWS	MHWN	MLWN	MLWS
0·5m	0·4m	0·3m	0·2m

Charts

	Approach	Port
Admiralty	2122	
French	4314, 4315	4183
		Livre de Bord suggests 4191
US	52180	–

Lights

Approach
1. **Fortress** 36°50'·2N 11°06'·9E
   Fl(4)20s82m23M White masonry structure with black lantern

Harbour
2. **S Jetée head** Fl.5s5m5M White pylon
3. **Spur of S Jetée head** Fl.G.4s5m2M Green pylon
4. **W Jetée head** Fl.R.2s5m2M Red pylon.

General
Due to its strategic location on the Cap Bon peninsula the fishing port of Kelibia is a common port of entry for boats coming from Malta, Pantelleria or Sicily. The port has undergone extensive reconstruction in recent years and a new quay is reserved for visiting yachts. Facilities are good and protection inside the port is very good. Entry is safe in almost any weather except in strong easterlies which are not uncommon. The main town is some 2km inland but most basic provisions can be found around the port and taxis provide good transportation.

There is a fence around the access to the yacht quay manned by police at the entrance, who are helpful, so security is good. Yachts can winter here.

Approach
The fortress, built on the only hill in the area, provides an excellent landmark from any direction. If coming from the N stay well offshore to avoid the low cape, Ras el Melah, which has a weak light. The approach light (1) is installed in a small tower on the fortress. When rounding the S breakwater do not wander too far N where it shoals towards the beach. The port has depths of 4m and more.

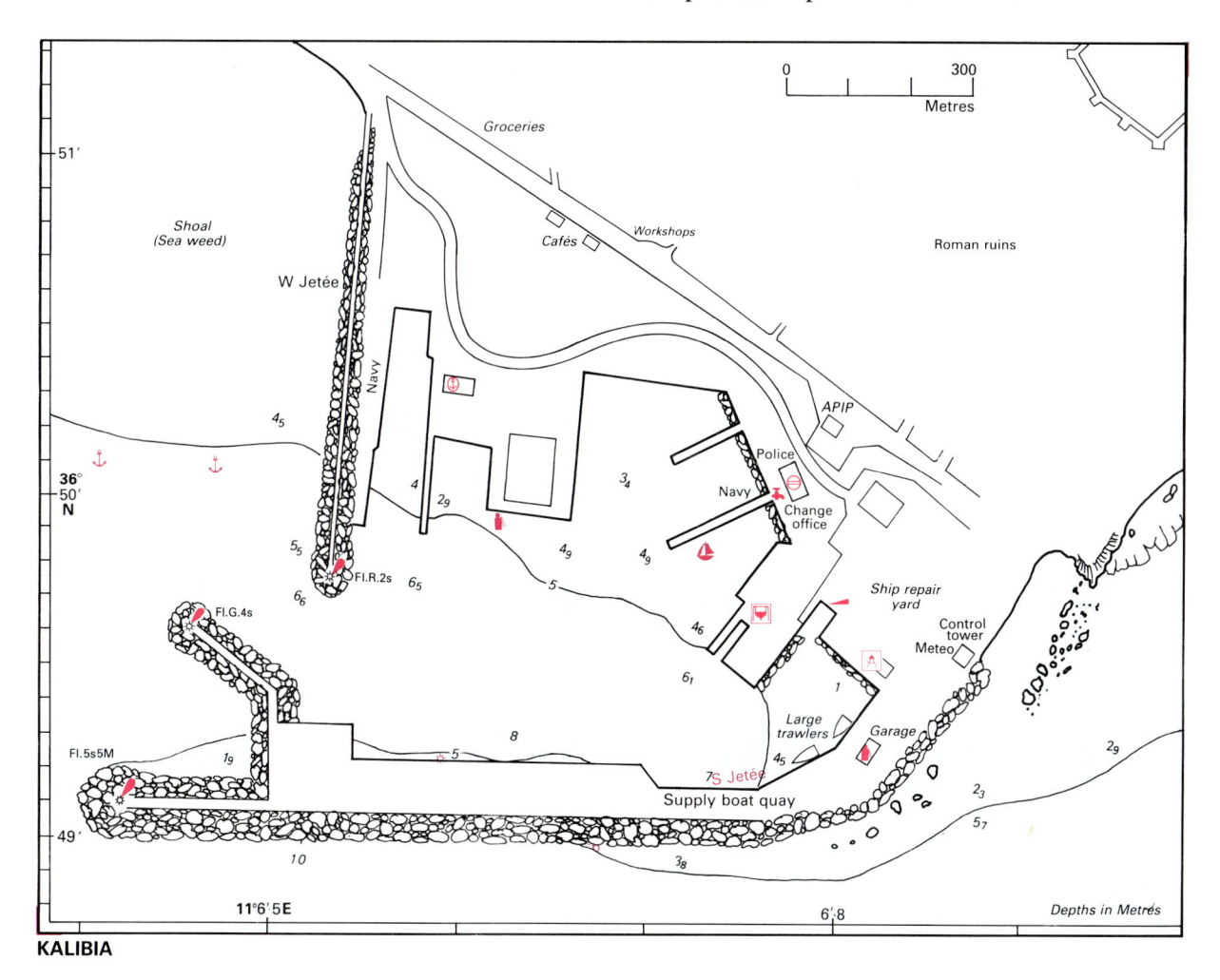

North Africa

View from the fortress on Kelibia port

Entrance
Strong easterlies can produce breakers close to the entrance. The port lights work most of the time and the yacht pier is well-lit. Take care around dusk when the whole fishing fleet, some of them unlit, leaves the port.

Berthing
Lie alongside either side of the reserved quay. A fender board is necessary to keep off the wooden piles mounted on the concrete quay. The quay on the inside of the S breakwater is reserved for the supply tug servicing the Tazerka oil platform and the W breakwater is used by the Tunisian navy. Anchoring W of the harbour entrance is not recommended since easterlies produce considerable waves until fairly close to the harbour entrance. It is shallow with thick weed giving poor holding.

Formalities
APIP ☎ 02 273 639 VHF Ch 16 24hrs.
Port of entry. Authorities are friendly and well used to visiting yachts. Charges are 1 Dinar/tonne/week.
20 TD/week electricity.
30 TD/week water.

Facilities
Water Available from a metered tap at the root of the yacht quay.
Electricity Available from several boxes along the quay.
Fuel Diesel from a pump in the SE corner and another one near the fish hall.
Gas Check if the grocery shops along the road to Kelibia will refill *camping gas* bottles. Other bottles can only be filled if fitted with an open-ended hose.
Provisions Several grocery shops around the port. Fresh produce from the daily market. Monday is the big weekly market.
Ice Available on the fish quay. Do not use in drinks.
Repairs The 250-ton travel-lift can handle any yacht but there are no specialised yacht facilities. Engine trouble can be taken care of by one of the several workshops around the port.
Post office and telephone In the town.
Bank In the town.

Weather forecast
Available at the control tower. VHF Ch 16 then 72. Radio Kelibia for meteology at approx 0600 and 1000 on demand. Also available from Lampedusa.

Eating out
Simple menu and take-away in Le Goeland on the seafront. Two restaurants on the way to Kelibia.

Tourism
Just 15km north of Kelibia is the archaeological site of Kerkouane. This Carthaginian village caused great excitement when it was discovered in 1952. Its

origins have been dated to the 5th century BC and it was abandoned sometime in the 2nd century BC, after the fall of Carthage. Apparently the Romans never reoccupied the site which explains why it is so well preserved. The excavations revealed a complete village and the street plan, drainage systems and even the baths in the houses can still be recognised. The idyllic site on the shore has been enhanced with lovely gardens and a small museum with artefacts found during the excavations, among them some beautiful pieces of jewellery. A taxi from the port reaches Kerkouane in about 20 minutes.

Beni Khiar

36°27'·0N 10°47'·8E

Distances
Kelibia 28M – Al Kantaoui 35M

Tides
MHWS	MHWN	MLWN	MLWS
0·5m	0·4m	0·3m	0·2m

Charts

	Approach	Port
Admiralty	176	–
French	4315	
(*Livre de Bord* suggests 4314, 4183, 4225)		
US	52172	–

Lights
Harbour
1. **SE breakwater** Fl(2)G.10s6M
2. **SW breakwater** Fl.R.5s5m6M

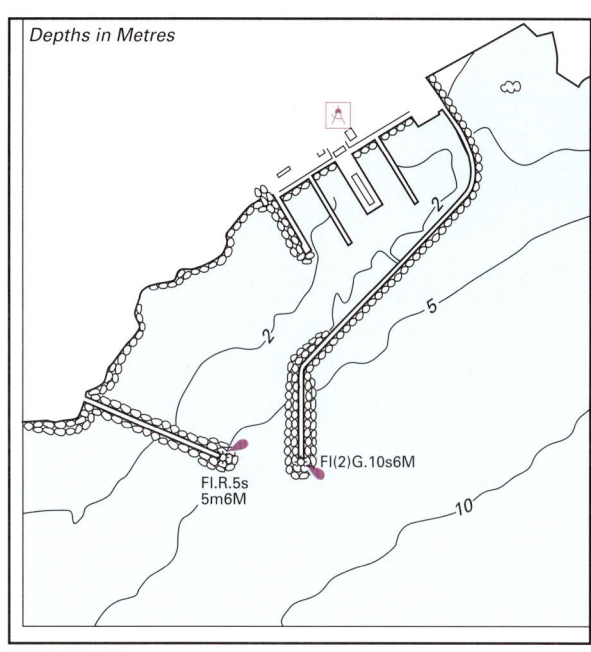

BENI KHIAR

General
A small friendly fishing harbour on the N side of the Gulf of Hammamet completed in 1984. Yachts are welcome and there is sufficient room to tie up. The village of Beni Khiar, 3km further inland, is a weaving centre. The walk from the port leads through fertile land. In summertime an excursion boat makes day trips with tourists from nearby hotels in Nabeul. There is a sandy beach E of the breakwater. In December 1997 major work was being completed.

The fishing port of Beni Khiar viewed from the green entrance light

North Africa

Home-weaver in Beni Khiar

The S breakwater has been extended and a new N breakwater built. The work should be completed by mid 1998, including dredging the entrance and port as shown in the plan. It was not certain if or when the lights would be moved.

Approach
The port is located directly W of Ras Maamoura. A brown minaret in the village of Beni Khiar slightly W of the port and the hotel complexes of Nabeul and Hammamet further to the W are conspicuous. When closer, the ice tower in the port will be spotted behind the breakwater. Keep to the S breakwater side of the entrance to find the deepest water. Until dredging is completed, from the first bend in the S breakwater keep very close to the breakwater. When opposite the first (W) finger pontoon it is safe to cross over to the N side of the harbour and berth. With easterly swell or in strong SE to SW winds the waves break close to the port entrance on the irregular and shallow bottom 300m SW of the entrance and entry is dangerous.

Berthing
Visiting yachts usually lie alongside the first pier which has depths of approximately 2·5m at the end or alongside the fish hall quay.

Formalities
APIP ☎ 02 229376 VHF Ch 16 (0730–1330, 1500–1745).
Garde national, APIP and *marine marchande* in the port. Not a port of entry.

Facilities
Water Available from a tap at the end of the fish hall.
Fuel Diesel from a pump in the port, petrol has to be carried from the village.
Provisions Bread may be obtainable in the port but anything more has to come from the village of Beni Khiar 3km away which is well supplied. 2km E a pleasant walk to Maamowa, for basic shops and beach.
Chandlery There is a fishermen's chandlery run by the Fishermen's Co-operative (☎ 02 2229025) and another chandlery on the road leading to the village approx 1km from the port. Also some small shops.
Post office, telephone and bank In the village.
WCs At end the of the fish market.

Eating out
There is a coffee bar in the port and Beni Khiar has a few simple eating houses. A better selection of restaurants can be found in Nabeul 4·5km from Beni Khiar, which has a few tourist hotels.

Tourism
Weaving bedspreads and carpets is the trade of Beni Khiar. Wandering through the narrow alleys looms will be found in literally every hole in the wall. Nabeul is only a short taxi ride from Beni Khiar and besides being the seat of the provincial governor it is Tunisia's capital for pottery and stonework. The weekly market on Friday has become a sort of tourist attraction but for yachtsmen it may just be a good place to stock up on fresh supplies. Almost all the pork raised in Tunisia and sold around the capital comes from Nabeul.

Hammamet
36°23'·5N 10°36'·5E

Lights
Lantern on *kasbah* wall Fl(2)6s17m15M 255°-vis-165°

General
Just W of the *kasbah* fortress of Hammamet is quite a well-protected anchorage with a bird's-eye view of Tunisia's oldest tourist development. The big hotels, though modest compared with the Spanish Costa del Sol, stretch W along the beautiful beaches of the Gulf of Hammamet. From the sea, the prospect is unexpectedly pleasant and if you take the

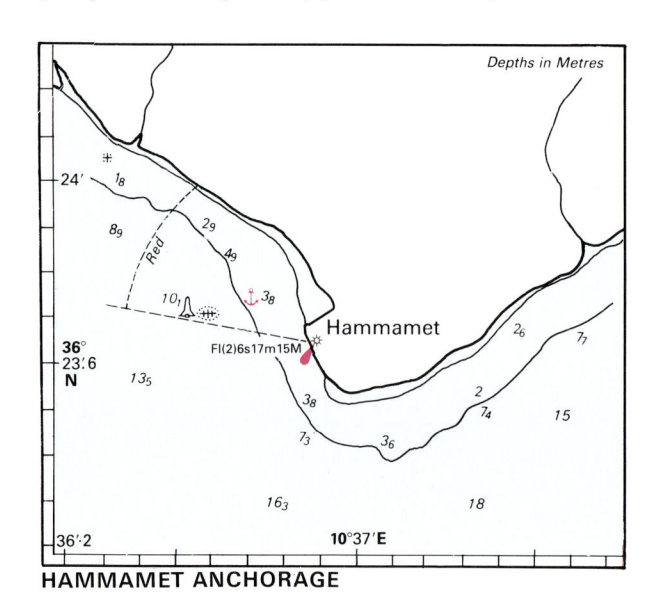

HAMMAMET ANCHORAGE

dinghy to the beach you arrive right in the middle of the old town. The medina around the *kasbah* fortress is filled with shops selling Tunisian handicrafts, but set in their old environment it is quite acceptable. In spite of the all-dominating tourist trade, Hammamet still has local fishermen and they land their boats on the beach.

It has been reported that children like to swim out from the beach to climb on board anchored yachts.

In January 1998, work started on the development of Hammamet Sud, west of the town. A hotel complex and marina is scheduled to be completed by 2001.

Approach
Beware of fishing nets. The wreck on Admiralty chart 372 is no longer marked with a buoy. A night approach is possible if the *kasbah* light is working.

Anchorage
Protection is good even in NE winds, if they are not too strong and as long as you anchor well tucked into the corner. Anchor in sand, 3–4m.

Hergla
36°01'·9N 10°30'·7E

Distances
Beni Khiar 29M – Al Kantaoui 11M

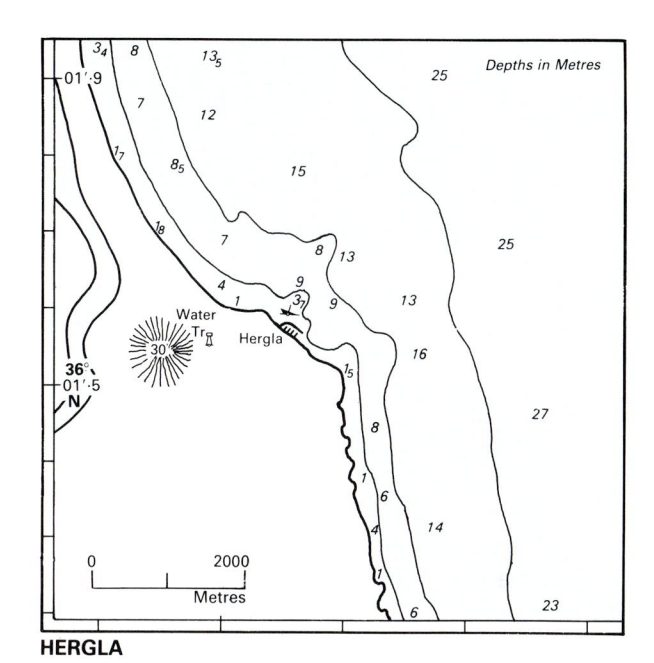

HERGLA

Hergla port and war cemetery viewed from the breakwater

North Africa

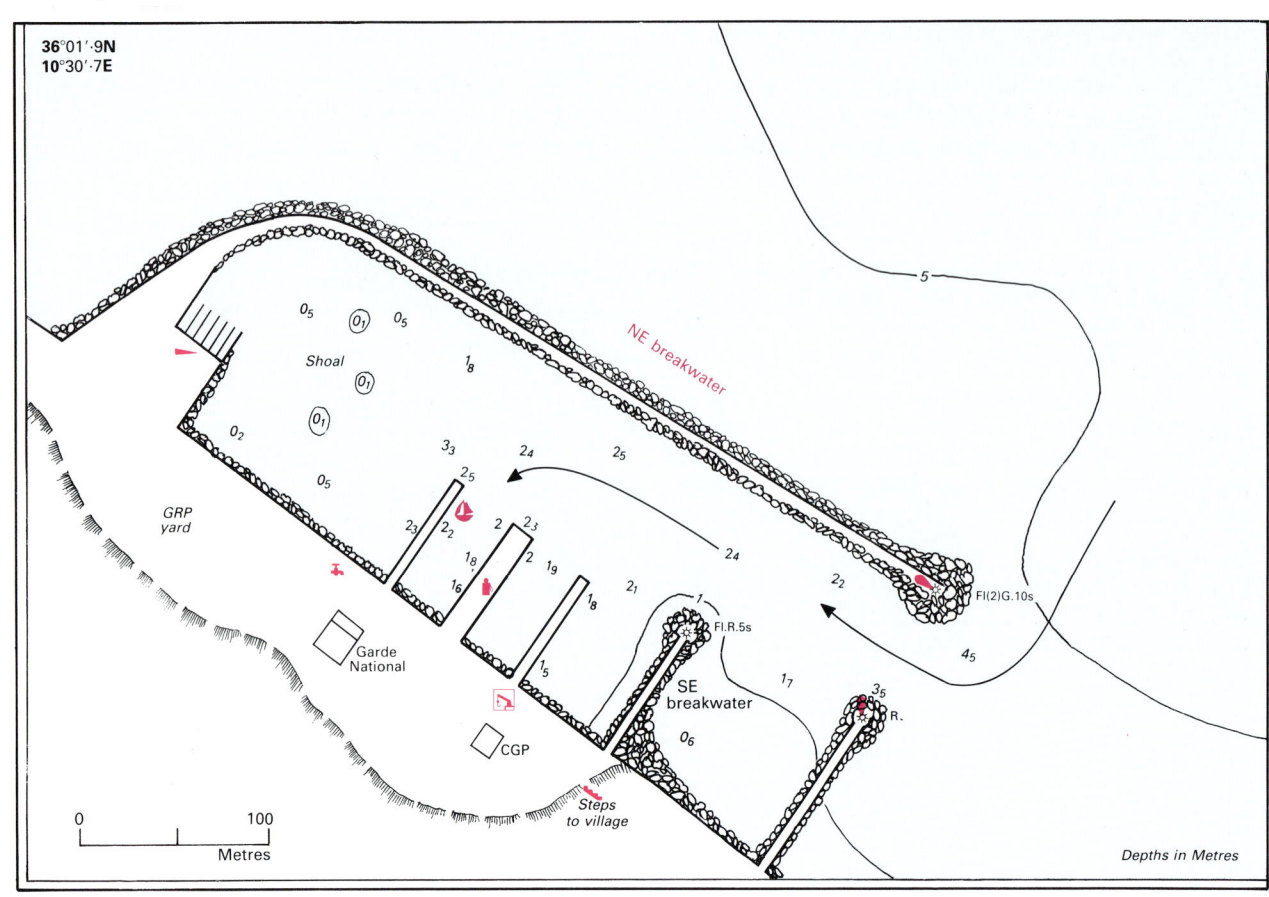

HERGLA

Tides
MHWS	MHWN	MLWN	MLWS
0·5m	0·4m	0·3m	0·2m

Charts
	Approach	Port
Admiralty	176	–
French	4315, 4208	–
US	52172	–

Lights
Harbour
1. **NE breakwater head** Fl(2)G.10s5m6M
2. **SE inner breakwater head** Fl.R.5s5m6M
3. **Nouvelle Jetée Sud head** Fl.R.5s9m6M

General
A small fishing port just N of Al Kantaoui; very similar in layout to Beni Khiar but with less activity. The village lies on a low hill a short walk from the port and amazingly, in view of the large tourist development at Al Kantaoui so close by, it is still relatively untouched. The village is a local centre for the weaving of alfalfa mats which are used in traditional olive presses.

Approach
The coast around Hergla is low but the port is not hard to find because the village is located on the only hill around. Navigation is further assisted by a tall water tower NW of the port and the ubiquitous minaret in the village. Approach the end of the NE breakwater on a course of 250° in order to avoid rocky ledges N and S of the port. The entrance and port itself tend to silt up with seaweed but it is dredged and in 1996 the outer SE breakwater was built to reduce silting in the port. In 1997 the *APIP* reported a minimum depth of 3m in the entrance and 2·5m were found at the ends of the second and third piers respectively. Prudence remains necessary however as the situation can change from year to year. Approximately 300m N of the root of the NE breakwater the remains of an Italian or German naval ship which sank during the Second World War, are just visible awash. Beware of fishing nets around the port.

Berthing
Deepest water is found along the third finger pier. The port is filling up with fishing boats but yachts should have no trouble finding a berth alongside or moor bows/stern-to one of the quays.

Formalities
APIP ☎ 03 251464 VHF Ch 16 (0730–1330, 1500–1745).
The port is operated by the *APIP*. There is only a *garde national* post.

Facilities
Water Tap on the quay.
Electricity None.
Fuel Diesel on the second quay. No petrol in port or village.

Provisions Shops can be found in the village. Market on Thursdays.
Post office and bank In the village
Repairs There is a ship and small-boat yard which will organise emergency repairs.

Eating out
Cafés in the village.

El Kantaoui
35°53'·6N 10°36'·2E

Distances
Kelibia 63M – Monastir 14M

Tides
MHWS	MHWN	MLWN	MLWS
0·5m	0·4m	0·3m	0·2m

Charts
	Approach	Port
Admiralty	176, 1162	–
French	4315, 4208	–
US	52172	–

Lights
Approach
1. **Sousse *kasbah*** 35°49'·4N 10°38'·3E
   Fl.4s70m22M Metal pylon on white square stone tower

Harbour
Buoys in entrance channel are sometimes lit with green on starboard and red on port side.
2. **NE breakwater** Fl.G.6s9m6M
3. **S breakwater** Fl.R.6s9m6M

General
The marina of El Kantaoui is located in the centre of a large holiday resort in Andalucian style 5M north of Sousse. Tourists from nearby hotels and apartments stroll along the quays all year round but because of the spacious layout, yachts can still enjoy reasonable privacy. The port is well styled with cobblestoned pavements, flower gardens and palm trees. The quays are lined with shops, restaurants and terraces and in the evening it is a lively place. An increasing number of yachts spend the winter here and it is also a good and secure place to leave a boat. Yachtsmen can use the swimming pools and participate in the nightly entertainment of the nearby hotels. The location is a good one for joining excursions inland, which leave from the hotels and

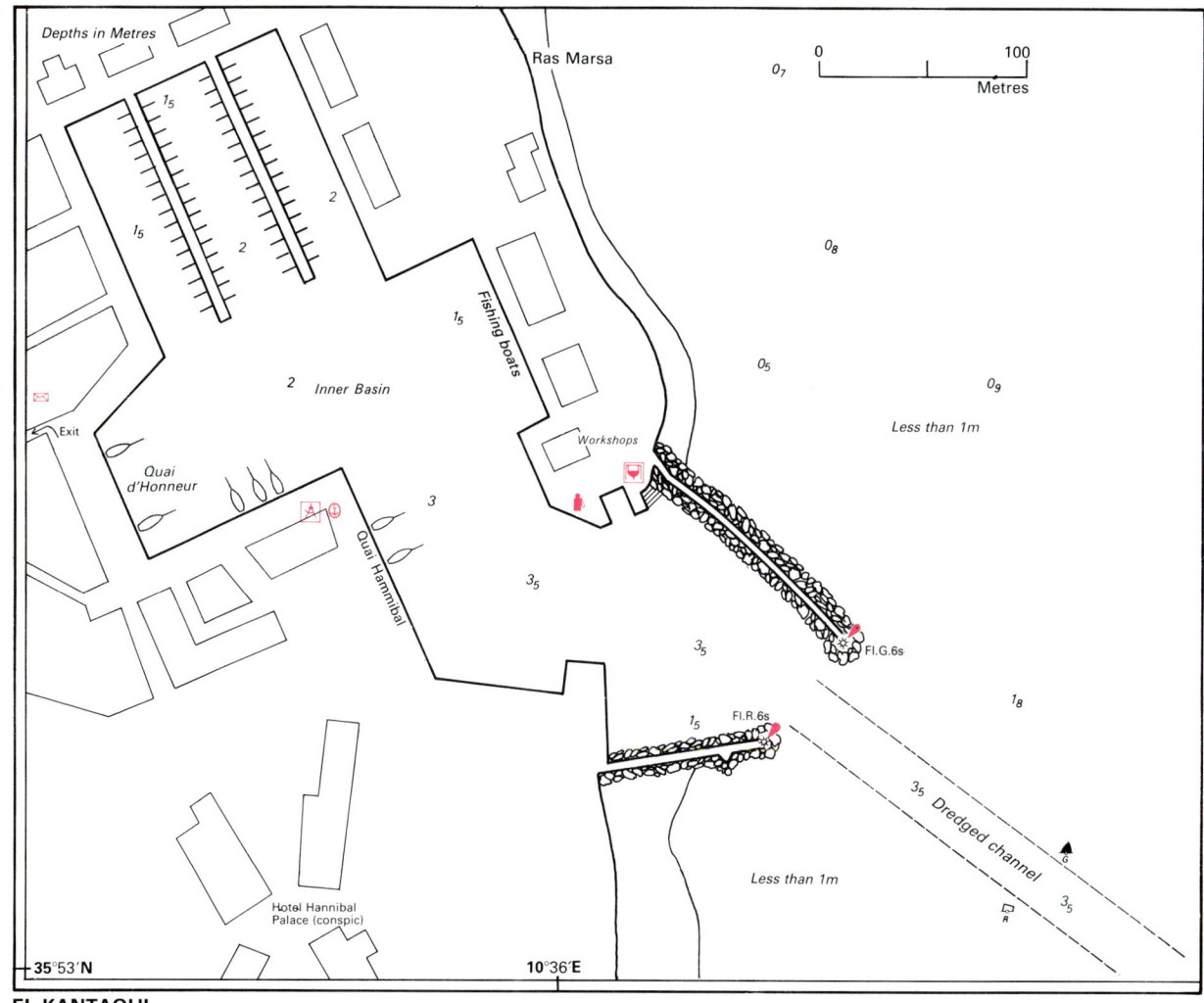

EL KANTAOUI

North Africa

The inner basin of El Kantaoui viewed from the *capitainerie*

there is good transport to the centre of Sousse. English is widely spoken around the port.

Approach
The port is situated immediately S of Cap Ras Marsa, which is hard to distinguish. By day two large pyramid-shaped hotels in the complex make the landfall fairly easy. Entrance is through a short buoyed channel on 305° and entrance to the port is just to the east of the southernmost hotel. In order to avoid the shallows around the entrance, Ras Marsa should be given a berth of at least ½M. Yachts drawing more than 3m should approach carefully as the entrance channel tends to silt up and in the past seaweed has been a problem.

At night the Sousse light on the *kasbah* gives good guidance until the red marina light can be picked up, normally at about 5M. Two large floodlit hotels are conspicuous. The breakwater lights are reasonably visible, in spite of the many lights around the port, because of their isolated position. Hazards in the entrance are the two large buoys marking the entrance channel which are often unlit and, occasionally, nets. On radar Ras Marsa will be noticed as the second promontory to the north of Sousse.

Entry
Entry in most weather conditions is straightforward but strong NE to E winds can cause waves to break around the entrance channel when entry is impossible. Note there are rocks to the SW of the dredged channel near the entrance.

Berthing
Overall protection inside the port is good although the berths on Quai Hannibal are more exposed to wind and waves. Yachts up to about 20m and a draught of 3m are accommodated here. Yachts berth bows/stern-to the quay all round the port and alongside finger pontoons in the northern basin where there are 2 new pontoons. These run SSE from the N wall. They are for boats of up to 12m and will take up to 2·3m draught at the seaward end. Access to these pontoons is by locked gates so they form a secure berth.

Formalities
Capitainerie ☎ 03 348799/348600 *Fax* 03 348757/348506 *Chef de Port* Mr. Hamed Ben Nijma. Entry formalities are dealt with efficiently. Officials are on duty 24 hours a day. The harbour office monitors VHF Ch 16 and 6, 24 hours a day

and is open 0700–2100. Despite the neat and tidy upmarket atmosphere the charges are very reasonable.

Rates in Tunisian Dinars per m² (greatest length x width) in 1997/8

length of stay	high season	min charge	low season	min charge
per day	0·35	4·0	0·25	3·0
per month	5·0	80·0	3·5	50·0
per year		22·0		300·0

In a 10–12m yacht: TD 2·0/day, TD 22/month, TD 900/year.

Water and electricity extra In a 10–12m yacht 2·0 per day, 22·0 per month, 90 per year plus 17% TVA.

Facilities
Water and electricity Laid on the quays for each individual berth.
Fuel Diesel and petrol available from pumps on the service quay next to the travel-lift. Kerosene from a service station outside the port.
Gas Available at the boatyard.
Provisions A good assortment of groceries, wine and beer is available from two supermarkets (including a *magasin général*). Not a great choice of fresh vegetables but the market in Sousse is not too far away. Duty-free delivery of alcoholic beverages is available.
Showers On the S side of the inner basin. Clean and reserved for yachts.
Post office and banks In the marina.
Telephone Coin telephones in the post office but they are also used by many hotel guests.
Repairs A 40-ton travel-lift; hauling out is done in a professional manner. Rates are competitive by Mediterranean standards. Price about TD 120 for 10–12m in and out excluding high pressure pump. Winter guests get a considerable discount on hauling out. There is room for a few boats to winter on the hard but the location is not very secure. The ship chandler has a better assortment of air mattresses than yacht spares.
Laundry Reasonably priced washing and dry cleaning in the marina.
Phone and TV Soon available to each berth.

Weather forecast
From the capitainerie.

Eating out
An abundance of restaurants and cafés around the marina cater to the needs of vacationers and yachtsmen.

Transport
International flights at Monastir (25km) or Tunis (150km). Buses (hourly service to Sousse) and taxis leave just outside the marina. Rent-a-Car has an office with cars opposite the *magasin général*.

Tourism
There is a tourist information office in the marina which can be helpful in planning excursions which in winter time can be made at quite attractive prices. The 18-hole golf course has an international reputation. A sports centre with tennis courts and horseback riding.

Sousse
35°49'·5N 10°39'·1E

Distances
Al Kantaoui 5M – Monastir 10M

Tides
MHWS MHWN MLWN MLWS
0·5m 0·4m 0·3m 0·2m

Charts
	Approach	Port
Admiralty	176	1162
French	4315, 4226	4102
US	52172	52172

Lights
Approach
1. **Kasbah** 35°49'·4N 10°38'·3E
   Fl.4s70m22M Metal pylon on white square stone tower

Harbour
2. **Jetée Abri head** Oc.WR.4s12m10/6M 135°-R-180°-W-045° Red pylon, white base
   Emergency light Fl.WR
3. **Epi Nord head** Iso.G.4s10m8M 258°-vis-112° Green conical tower
4. **Epi Sud head** Fl.R.5s10m8M 079°-vis-277° Red conical tower

General
With the marinas of El Kantaoui and Monastir operational there is very little reason to visit Sousse unless for engine repairs which cannot be done elsewhere, though there are now good mechanics in Monastir. The small basin in the NW corner of the commercial port is dusty and easterly winds, which are common in spring and summer, blow straight in, making it very uncomfortable. The fishing port S of the commercial basin offers good protection but it is full to the brim and not very clean. The street opposite the fishing port is lined with hardware, spare parts and engine repair shops. It has been reported that yachts were charged very high harbour dues in the commercial port. In 1997 there were plans to turn the small basin and fishing harbour into a marina with work scheduled to start in 2–3 years' time. The north section is used by patrol boats.

Approach
Straightforward by day and night. The slightly elevated *kasbah* fortress with tower dominates the Sousse skyline and is well visible from seaward. A thermal power station with red and white striped chimney, 2½M SE of Sousse is another good landmark. At night the 22M range light on the tower of the *kasbah* provides very good guidance. The entrance, without any hazards, is by a dredged and buoyed channel on a course due W.

Berthing
Yachts may find a berth alongside a fishing boat on the E pier of the fishing port. Here the normal CGP harbour charges have to be paid. In case of an emergency the small basin can also be used with the discomforts mentioned before. Yachts are not expected or welcomed in the port.

North Africa

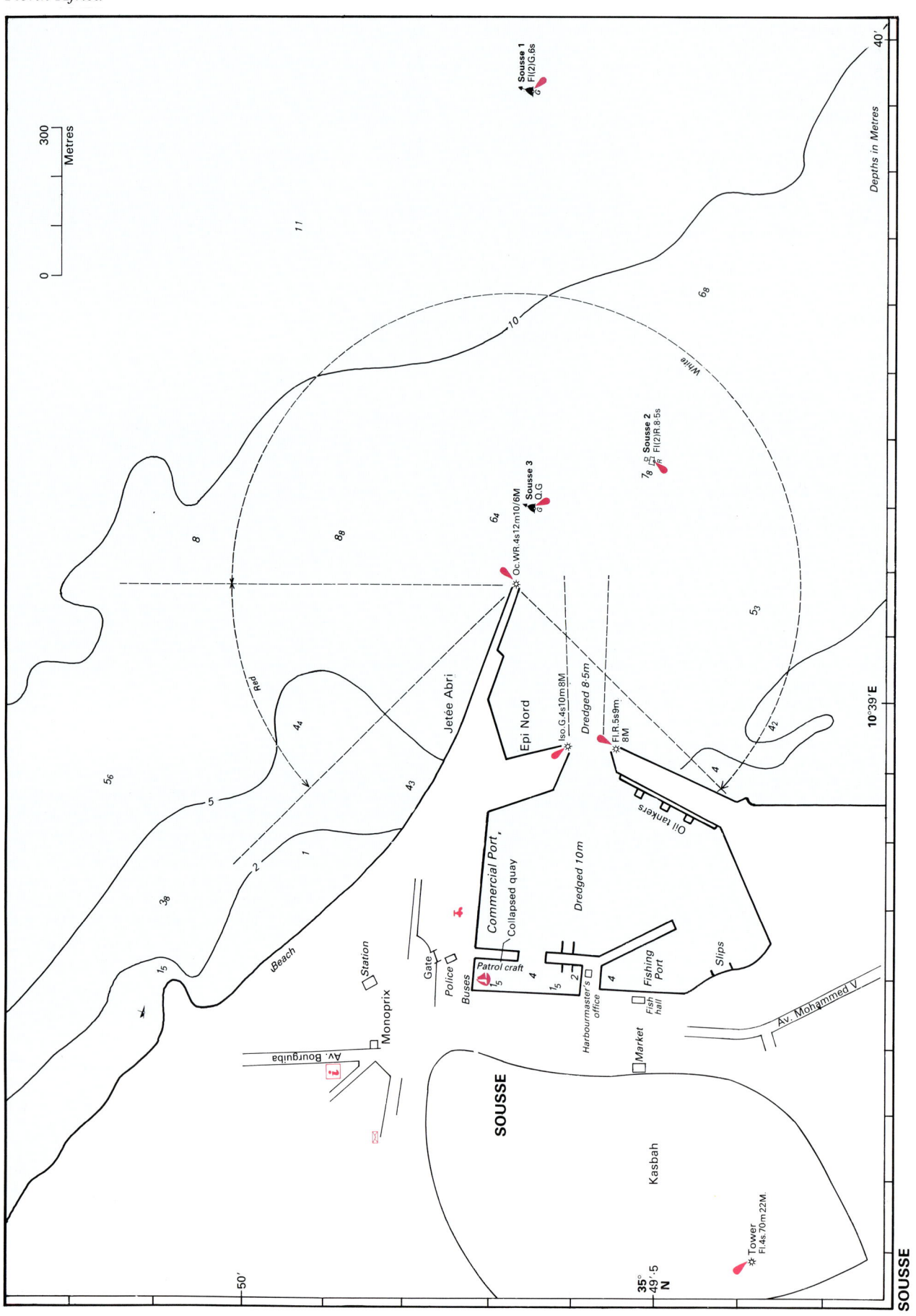

SOUSSE

Formalities
☎ 03 225755 VHF 16 24hrs.
All officials for entry formalities are in the port.

Facilities
Water Containers can be filled in the fish hall of the fishing port.
Fuel On the quay.
Provisions Good provisions are available, all within a short distance from the port. *Monoprix* on Avenue Bourguiba and two markets in the *kasbah*.
Charts French charts may be available from the office of the Service Topography on Avenue Bourguiba opposite the *monoprix*.
Post office and telephone Close to the port on Avenue de la Republique.
Banks Take your pick.
Repairs Good engine repair facilities can be found around the port along Avenue Mohammed V and in the street behind it. Roto diesel on the road to Monastir near the southern railway station undertakes good quality fuel system repair work.

Eating out
Sousse is the city in Tunisia where tourism has been around for the longest time with the advantage that many good and reasonably priced restaurants can be found. Good listing in the *Rough Guide*.

Tourism
Sousse has been an important city to every civilisation that has occupied this part of North Africa because of the fertile land of the Sahel region around it. After independence, Susa, the old Arabic name still used today, became the third city of Tunisia with textiles and tourism as the key economic activities. Several monuments illustrate the rich history and the museum in the *kasbah* has an excellent collection of mosaics. The weekly market is on Sundays, but for a real camel market, as the brochures describe it, one has to go further south.

Monastir
35°46'·6N 10°50'·2E

Distances
Kelibia 65M, Al Kantaoui 14M – Mahdia 25M (via Conigliera Channel)

Tides
MHWS MHWN MLWN MLWS
0·5m 0·4m 0·3m 0·2m

Charts
	Approach	Port
Admiralty	176, 1162	–
French	4315, 4226	–
US	52170	–

Lights
Approach
1. **Ile Kuriat** 35°47'·9N 11°02'·0E
   Oc(1+2)WR.12s30m18/14M 053°-W-348°-R-053°
   Emergency light F.WR

Harbour
2. **Bordj el Kelb** Fl(2)R.6s26m10M 197°-vis-355°
3. **Old Fishing Hbr shelter mole head**
   Fl.R.1·5s6m3M

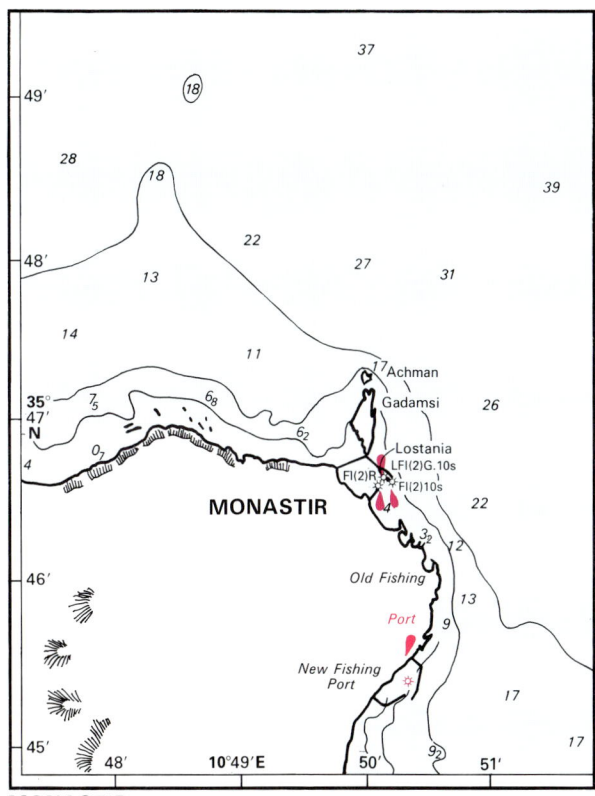

MONASTIR

4. **New Fishing Hbr Entrance** LFl.G.10s12m5M and Fl(4)R.15s12m5M
5. **Marina E side** LFl(2)G.10s8m6M
6. **S breakwater W side** Fl(2)R.10s8m6M
7. **E breakwater head** Fl(2)10s11m7M

General
Monastir is the largest marina in Tunisia and, like Al Kantaoui, it is a most popular place to winter afloat. It is necessary to book a space. More and more yachts call in on passage. The marina complex has shops, apartments and several restaurants. Except for the summer months the atmosphere is relaxed and quiet, though the marina is full by the end of October. The port has been formed by joining two islands with the shore and protection is good. Entry can be made in all weather conditions and the double breakwaters with good depths in the port prevent swell from entering. Apart from the semi-derelict tennis courts, the islands are still in their natural state and the pleasant town centre of Monastir is only five minutes from the marina. Services in the port, led by an obliging port captain, are the best in Tunisia. It is a good port of entry for yachts coming from the East Mediterranean and a practical stop before going on to the south or heading off for the north of Tunisia. Excursions inland can easily be arranged. Transport to Sousse is good and the international airport at Skanes is only 8km from the port.

Approach
Coming from the E, stay far enough N to avoid the tunny net N of Kuriat Island and the shallows between it and the mainland. The tunny net is put

North Africa

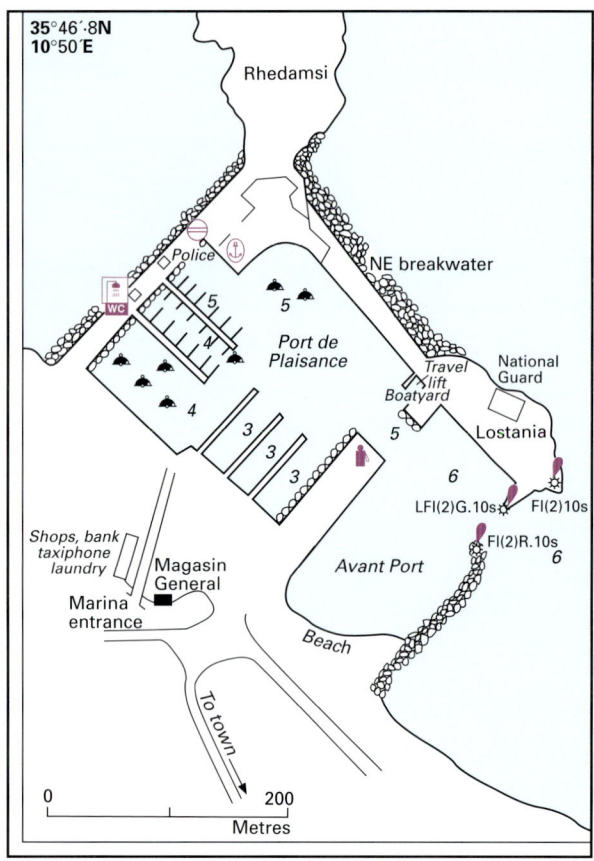

MONASTIR

out every year from April–July. The light on the N cardinal buoy marking its N end is not reliable. During day time and in good weather yachts can take the buoyed channel approximately 1½M SW of Ile Conigliera which has minimum depths of 3m (but don't rely on the buoys being there). When approaching from seawards the remaining unlit buoys are difficult to see. The lighthouse on Kuriat and the ruins of an old fish factory on Conigliera are the only landmarks in this low-lying area which has a hazy atmosphere in summer. Once past Kuriat the approach is straightforward with several minarets and the Ribat serving as good landmarks.

The tunny nets directly N of Monastir and marked on Admiralty chart 1162 are no longer laid but bottom nets with marker buoys are laid in the area. In the bay enclosed by Ile Rhedamsi, N of the marina, floating fishing nets are laid at night.

Entrance
The entrance to the marina although narrow is without hazard and it is possible to come in at night. The harbour lights function reliably but are obscured from N to W by the two islands; a lit buoy should be in position 1M NNE of the marina entrance, but was not on station in 1997.

Berthing
The outer basin is used by a few small fishing boats but is otherwise empty. Yachts over 12m are normally directed to berth bows/stern-to to the NE breakwater where there are buoys to attach to. There is space for very large yachts at the western end of this quay. For yachts less than 12m the 3 piers in the south of the port and the west quay have tailed lines for fore-and-aft mooring.

The two piers in the NW of the harbour have short finger pontoons and lines to sinkers. Smaller visiting yachts are most likely to be directed to these 2 piers. The north side of the N pier is most affected by any swell that enters the harbour. If in doubt as to where to berth, or at night, go to the NW or NE side of the fuel quay.

Formalities
Cap Marina, BP–60, 5000 Monastir
☎ 03 460 951/953 *Fax* 03 462066
Port of entry with 24hrs service. Formalities are handled efficiently. The harbour office monitors VHF Ch 16 during office hours.
Charges in Tunisian Dollars (1998)

Boat length	High season 1/6–30/9		Low season 1/10–31/5	
	month	day	month	day
Up to 12m	9·4	188·0	5·6	112·0

Annual 940·0
1% FDCST and 10% TVA must be added plus an additional 30% for multihulls.
A 12–15m yacht would be charged 1·15 water and 1·25 electricity per day plus 1% FDCST and 10% TVA.

Facilities
Water and electricity Laid on the quays for each individual berth.
Fuel Diesel and petrol from pumps on the service quay. Paraffin available from the Mobil station in town.
Gas Boatyard takes care of filling gas bottles.
Provisions Between the *monoprix*, *magasin général* and the market, all within 10 minutes walking distance from the marina, very good provisions are easily available. There is a smaller *magasin général* at the entrance to the port. Alcoholic beverages can be ordered. Allow 5 days for delivery.
Ice Can be arranged by marina personnel
Showers Proper showers and even a bath tub are on the N side of the marina; due for renovation.

Monastir, the mausoleum for former president Bourguiba

Tunisia

Monastir marina viewed from the SE

Monastir marina viewed from the NE

North Africa

Post office Main office next to the *Monoprix*.
Bank There is a very helpful one in the Marina's shopping arcade and several in the town centre.
Telephone Taxiphone at entrance to port.
Repairs Boatyard with 30-ton travel-lift which can undertake most repairs; limited space for wintering ashore but it is now possible to haul-out for extended periods. The yard is situated on and around the NE mole of the entrance to the Port de Plaisance Marine Service – Cap marina 5000 Monastir ☎ 03 467451 *Fax* 03 468109 – Mohamed Ben Mrad, speaks good English and previously worked in Italian boatyards.

Elite Services have an office in the N corner of the marina and can undertake electrical and electronic repairs and installations: Cap Marina Local 11BP 5000 Monastir ☎ 03 449037 *Fax* 03 461211. Fritz Demmer. See also Monastir New Fishing Port.
Laundry Arranged by marina personnel. Dry cleaning available in the town about 200m past the *magasin général*.
Transport The international airport at Skanes is 8km from the marina. The train to Tunis takes approximately 2¾ hours and from there to its international airport is another 30 minutes. Buses, train and *louages* to Sousse take between 20–30 minutes.

Weather forecast
A daily bulletin is posted in the the *capitainerie*.

Eating out
Several restaurants with seafront atmosphere/prices in the marina. Le Roi de Couscous in the centre opposite Bourguiba statue is good value. Hotel Yasmin 3km N of the port has good European and Tunisian cooking.

Transport
Car hire can be arranged through *capitainerie*. There is also a car hire office in the port. Major car hire companies have offices in the airport and will deliver and collect cars from the marina.

Tourism
The fact that Monastir is the birthplace of former President Bourguiba does not pass unnoticed. His mausoleum with twin gold domed minarets is without doubt the most spectacular of all new architecture in Tunisia and well worth a visit. From the perspective of the port the other obvious monument is the Ribat. Its style is peculiar to a period in North African history when the Muslims were under regular attack from Christians based in Sicily. It served a religious as well as military purpose. In times of war it was a fortress and in peace the fighters studied the Koran in bare cells around the central court, not unlike the *medressas* in Morocco. There is a small museum inside with Cufic script on parchment and some Fatimid glassware. Monastir International Films uses the Ribat as a set and some well known films with biblical connections have been shot here. Large parts of the old town have been taken down to show off the new monuments and the result is a pleasant, open, town centre with lots of greenery. Tennis courts for marina clients are available on Rhedamsi island and Monastir has an 18-hole golf course.

Excursions inland can easily be arranged. The tourist information office is located opposite *magasin général*.

Monastir, old fishing port

A very small basin situated ½M SE of the marina. It is poorly protected and depths in the entrance are uncertain. Consequently of no use to yachts.

Monastir, new fishing port
35°45'·3N 10°50'·4E

Charts
	Approach	Port
Admiralty	176	1162

Lights
Approach
1. **Bordj el Kelb** 35°45'·6N 10°50'·3E Fl(2)R.6s26m10M White tower black bands 197°-vis-355°

Harbour
2. **E breakwater** LFl.G.10s12m5M
3. **W breakwater** Fl(4)R.15s12m5M

General
In 1988 a new large fishing port situated between Bordj el Kelb and the old customs pier to the S was finished. The port is large for today's needs and despite Tunisia's growing fishing fleet there is still room for visiting yachts though there is very little of interest other than excellent protection and boatyards with full repair facilities. Although not as well set up for yachts as Monastir, it is a useful alternative if space or facilities at Monastir are fully booked. There is plenty of space afloat and ashore

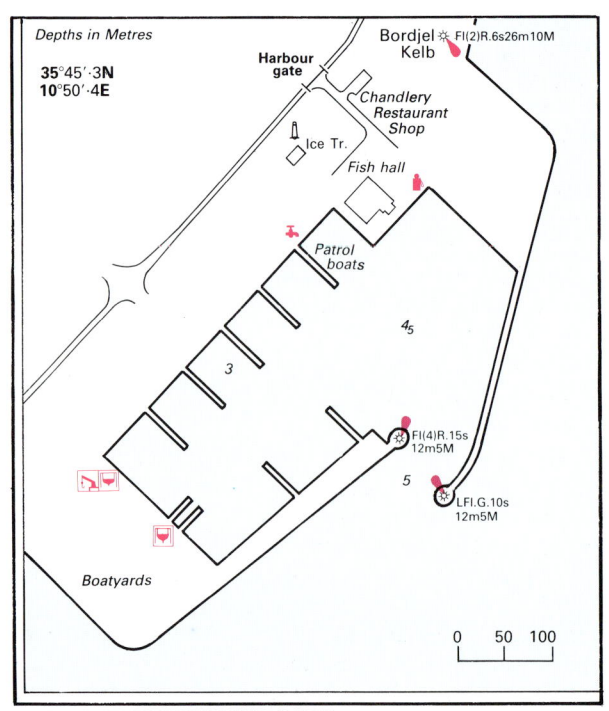

MONASTIR NEW FISHING PORT

Tunisia

and in 1997 about 12 boats were hauled out for the winter. Both yards are keen to attract more work and seem competent at mechanical repairs, welding, painting etc. Sand and grit blasting can be arranged here.

Facilities
Water and electricity Available.
Fuel On the quay.
Provisions There is a chandlery, shop (basic provisions) café and restaurant in the port. All facilities in Monastir, 3km away.
Repairs A 250-ton travel-lift, and high pressure pump. Prices a little lower than Monastir.
Yards Chantier Yasamine ☎ 03 447510, Mr. Montacer. Chantier Naval ☎/*Fax* 03 467122, Mr Ali Bedoui. (Home ☎ 03 461820.)

In 1998 Chantier Naval and Elite Yacht Services had joined together to create full services for visiting and wintering yachts. They have a WC and shower block and run a minibus service regularly into town. Elite is run by a German, Fritz Demmer who speaks good English. Elite ☎ 03 449037 *Fax* 03 461211.

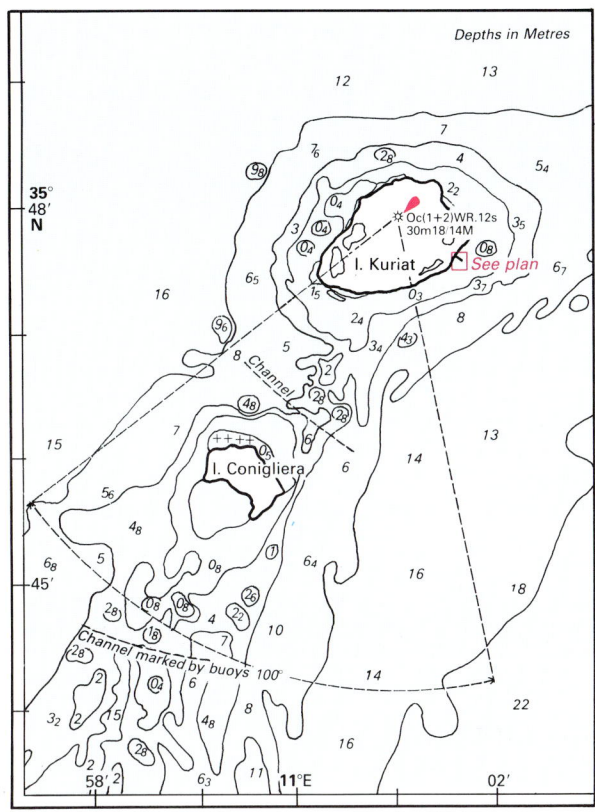

Ile Kuriat and Ile Conigliera

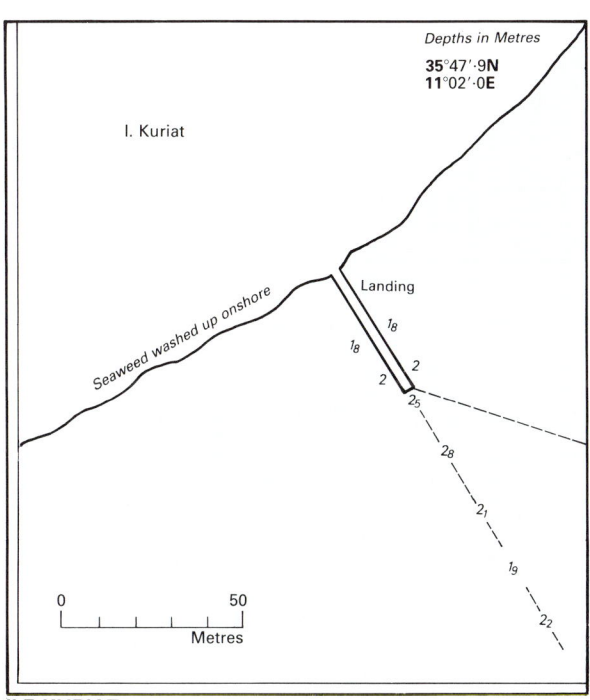

Light
Ile Kuriat lighthouse 35°47'·9N 11°02'·0E
  Oc(1+2)WR.12s30m18/14M 053°-W-348°-R-053°
  Emergency light F.WR

These low-lying islands are part of the extensive shallows which form the SE extremity of the Bay of Monastir. They are a practice ground for navigation in the waters typical of the coastal areas further S. Except for the lighthouse keeper on Kuriat island and a few fishermen during the tunny season, both islands are uninhabited. Their solitude makes for a pleasant day trip from Monastir.

In good weather the wind direction is quite predictable. In the morning the sea breeze starts from the NE and changes to SSE in the course of the day. Slightly hazy conditions, with a visibility of 6M, are normal in the summer.

Approach
There are 3 passages across the shallows
- A newly dredged channel close to the fishing port of Teboulba.
- An unmarked passage between Kuriat and Conigliera which should only be attempted with French chart 4226.
- A buoyed natural channel 1½M SW of Conigliera.

The dredged channel close to Teboulba is described under that port.

The unmarked passage has depths of no less than 4m when keeping 1M from Kuriat and ½M from Conigliera. (Buoys reported missing in October 1997.)

Navigation in this area is complicated by the fact that, aside from the lighthouse on Kuriat and the remains of an old fish factory on Conigliera, there are few landmarks.

The passage S of Conigliera is easier, especially when coming from Monastir. In normal visibility the four large buoys marking the channel (if present) will be picked up from a distance of about 3M. The minimum depth in this channel is about 4m between the buoys but further E it is only 3m which is discomforting as the least depths are expected in the buoyed section.

ILE KURIAT

ILE KURIAT

171

North Africa

A tunny net is laid N of Kuriat from April–July and comes close to the N shore of the island. The net is more than 3M long and well visible with blue floating balls along its full length. Four boats with short masts are permanently moored in the middle to haul the tunny from the 'death chamber'. The N extremity is marked by a N cardinal buoy with an unreliable light. Passage between the net and the island is uncertain.

Anchorage
In good weather anchor, as convenient with the wind direction, in depths of 5m about ½M from the shore. Closer to shore the bottom of sand, limestone and seaweed is irregular and it is easy to run aground – depths can change abruptly from 3m to 1·7m.

A wooden landing on the SE side of Kuriat is used to discharge supplies for the lighthouse and smaller yachts can tie up here. Depths along the landing vary from 2·5m to 1·8m but there are a few shallow patches in the unmarked approach with less than 1·8m.

Ksibet El Mdeiouni
35°41'·5N 10°51'·0E

Distances
Monastir 6M Mahdia 19M

Tides
MHWS	MHWN	MLWN	MLWS
0·5m	0·4m	0·3m	0·2m.

Charts
	Approach	Close approach
Admiralty	176	1162

Lights
Breakwater G. light on white column (characteristics unknown)

General
A very small fishing harbour protected by a single short breakwater. It is crowded and shallow and there is nothing of much merit or interest ashore.

Approach
Through channel marked by 4 pairs of red and green beacons. Depths in the channel are not known. The characteristics of the green breakwater light are not known, so approach is only recommended by day. Note that the coast is very shallow for 1½M offshore in all directions.

Berth
Stern/bows-to where there is space.

Formalities
Port officials at entrance to port.

Facilities
Water and fuel Believed to be available on the quay as indicated.
Repairs Crane/small boat hoist.

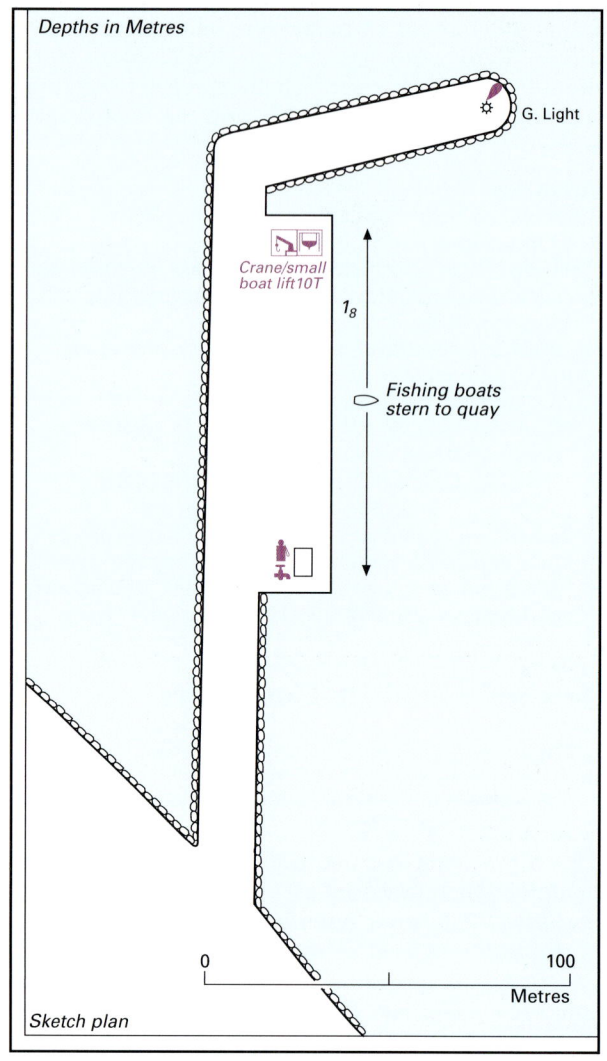

KSIBET EL MDEIOUNI

Sayada
35°40'·5N 10°53'·6E

Distances
Monastir 7M – Teboulba 3M

Tides
MHWS	MHWN	MLWN	MLWS
0·5m	0·4m	0·3m	0·2m

Charts
	Approach	Port
Admiralty	1162	–
French	4226	–
US	–	–

Lights
1. **NW jetty head** Fl.G.4s7m5M green stone tower
2. **NE jetty head** Fl(3)R.12s7m6M red stone tower
3. 2 pairs of R and G buoys, unlit, mark dredged channel

General
A small but busy fishing port in the Bay of Monastir which provides some income for local fishermen. In spite of its insignificance, there is more activity here than in the new fishing port of Monastir; octopus, prawns and sardines are caught in season. The port

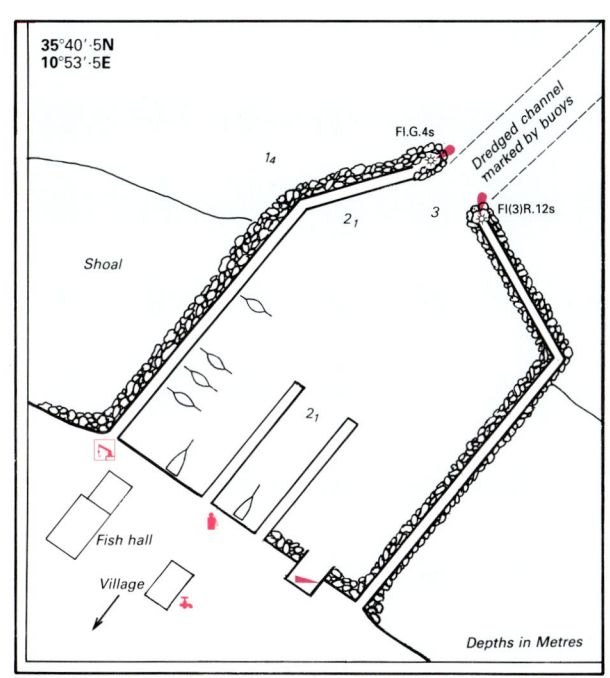

SAYADA

is crowded with small fishing boats, which, in 1997, did not appear to welcome yachts.

Approach
The surrounding coast is very shallow and the dredged channel leading to the entrance is not marked and of uncertain depths.

Berthing
All the best space is taken by fishing boats. There may be space at the outer end of the west breakwater.

Formalities
Garde national and *marine marchande* are situated just outside the port.

Facilities
Water and diesel In the port.
Banks, PTT and shops In the town.

Teboulba
35°39'·6N 10°57'·5E

Distances
Monastir 9½M – Mahdia 16M (via dredged channel)

Tides
MHWS	MHWN	MLWN	MLWS
0·5m	0·4m	0·3m	0·2m

Charts
	Approach	*Port*
Admiralty	1162	–
French	4226	–
US	52170	–

Lights
Approach
1. **Secondary channel No.1** 35°40'·6N 10°59'·1E Fl.G.6s3m2M on green column
2. **Secondary channel No.2** 35°40'·6N 10°59'·2E Fl.R.6s3m2M on red column

Harbour
3. **W breakwater head** LFl.G.10s7m5M on green stone tower
4. **E breakwater head** LFl.R.10s7m5M on red stone tower

General
This is an old fishing port, used by an active fleet of fishing boats, which has been enlarged with new breakwaters and quays. Construction of new port buildings and dredging of the entrance channel was finished in 1989. The port offers a nice change of scenery from the marina in Monastir and it is a good base to explore the shallows on the SE side of the Bay of Monastir. The port offers excellent protection but there is little room for visiting yachts. The town some 3km inland is worth a visit, if only to get a taste of everyday life unchanged by tourism. It is dominated by a huge mosque with lively market around it and the minaret is the tallest in the entire area. Soukrine, the village between the port and Teboulba town, is of little interest and has one small shop.

Approach
The dredged channel is marked by 2 pairs of buoys. The channel has a width of 65m and runs 175°/355° for a length of 0·7M. Minimum depth in the channel is 3·5m and only in the last 500m depths of less than 2m are found outside the channel. The edge is soft sand and mud. A course of 150° for 2·6M from buoy No. 4 in the group of buoys marking the Fosse de Teboulba leads to the beginning of the dredged channel. From this position steer to the port entrance on a course of 175°. From this same position a newly dredged and buoyed channel branches off to Ras Dimas across the shallows.

Berthing
Berth where possible, but there is little space. It was slightly less crowded in the NW corner in 1997.

Formalities
Garde national and CGP. Not a port of entry.
☎ 03 479495 VHF Ch 16 (0730–1330, 1500–1745).

Facilities
Water and ice In the fish market.
Fuel On the W and E quays.
Repairs Boatyard with 130-ton travel-lift, and engineers at port entrance.
Provisions Lively market in the town 3km from the port. It is a busy place with many shops, garage and hardware stores. One may be able to catch a ride with a fishmonger or taxi. There is a chandlery and café in the port.
Post office and bank In the town.

North Africa

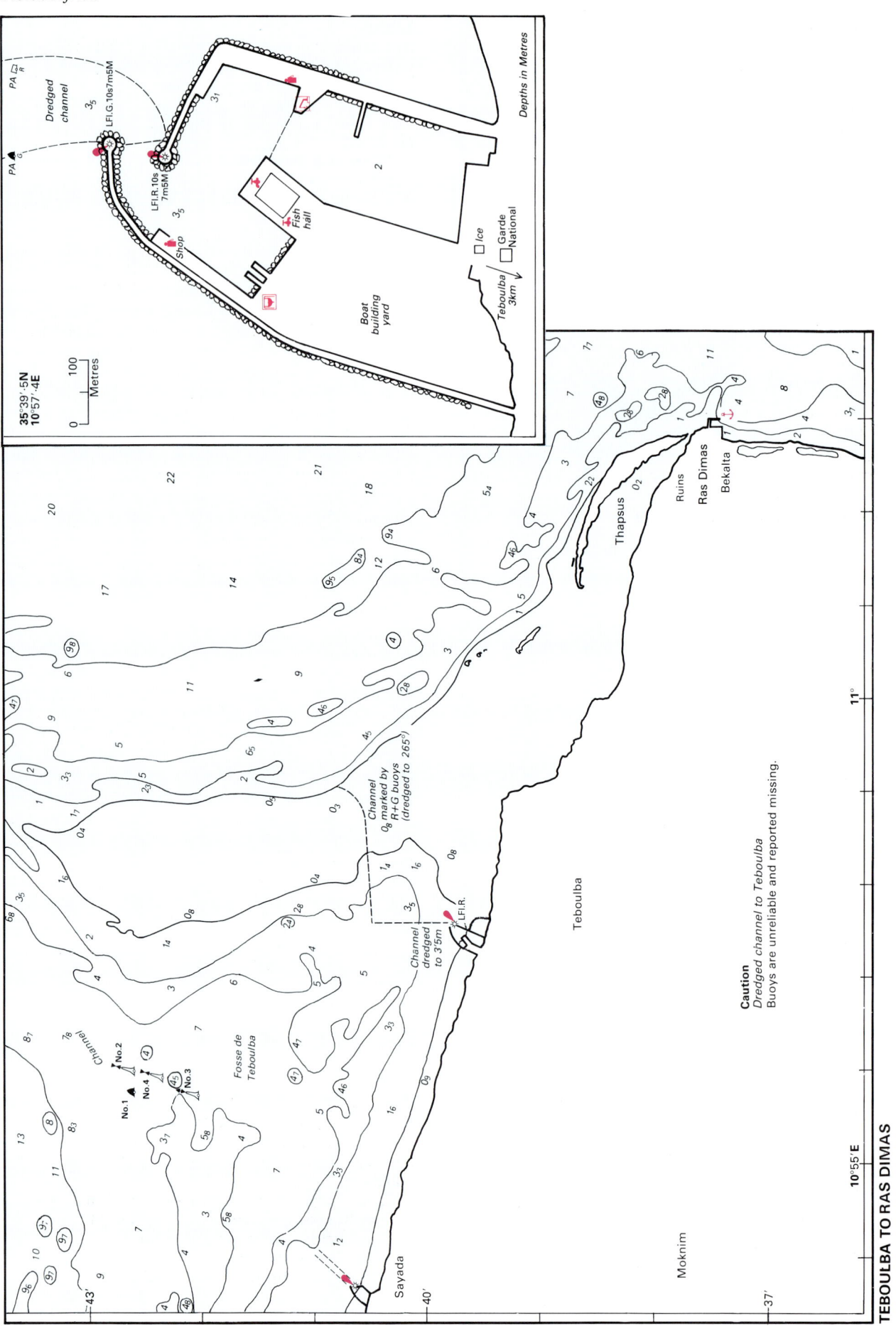

TEBOULBA TO RAS DIMAS

Eating out
Restaurant du Plaisir and Restaurant Populair in Teboulba are not the restaurants many would expect but if you like to experiment and eat whatever the chef offers, it is possible to have a great and original meal.

The channel from Teboulba to Ras Dimas

This channel has been dredged for the Teboulba fishermen who work around Ras Dimas and provides a big short-cut compared to the Conigliera channel. It branches off from the entrance channel to Teboulba at 90° and the course to steer is 85°/265°. Depths vary from 2·5m to 2·75m and the width is about 40m. It is marked by green and red perches. With careful navigation yachts can safely pass through it as the sides are well visible. In the middle section depths outside the channel are about 0·5m. Late in the afternoon the channel is marked by the lively traffic of fishing boats on their way out from Teboulba. Be careful in the narrow parts where there is little room to pass. Special care has to be exercised at the eastern end where the channel bends about 45° to the N for the last 600m. In the last 200m, where the edges are not well visible, follow the light green path.

Warning Sailing fishing boats work on the shallows around the channel and from a distance in the mirage their masts can be mistaken for the perches of the channel.

Bekalta
35°37'·4N 11°03'E

Distances
Monastir 8M – Mahdia 8M

Lights
1. **W breakwater** R light on red tower approx 7m
2. **E breakwater** G light on green tower approx 7m
   Characteristics unknown.

General
This is a small fishing port on the S side of Ras Dimas. Shortly after construction was finished, large amounts of seaweed drifted in rendering it useless. The port was dredged in 1989, but depths are uncertain. Ras Dimas, a low rocky promontory, is the site of the old Roman settlement, Thapsus, of which a few traces can still be found. The tranquil surroundings are attractive with sandy beaches lined with a few palm trees and a few scattered houses. In spring time the area around the port is particularly beautiful with many wild flowers in full bloom and the tide flowing gently through the narrow channel separating Ile de Thapsus from the mainland.

Approach and anchorage
Ras Dimas extends submerged ESE for some distance offshore. In fair weather anchor S of this ridge in front of the port entrance. When approaching from the N the shallow extension of the cape should be given a berth of 0·7M. In 1997 the N pier was crowded with fishing boats but there was a space for a small yacht on the S pier in depths as indicated.

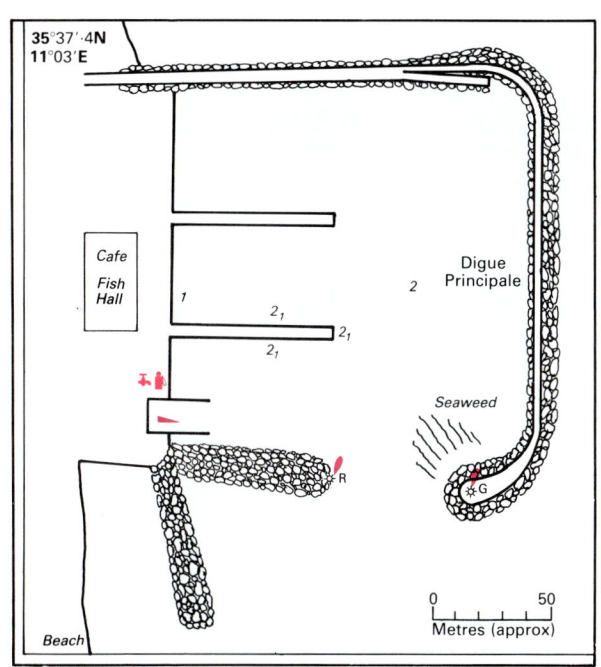

Formalities
None in port.

Facilities
Fuel, water and café In the port.
Provisions The village 2km away has a shop. Bekalth, 5km away, has a garage, shops, telephone and station.

Mahdia
35°29'·8N 11°04'·2E

Distances
Monastir 25M – La Chebba 17M, Lampedusa 75M

Tides
MHWS	MHWN	MLWN	MLWS
0·5m	0·4m	0·3m	0·2m

Charts
	Approach	Port
Admiralty	3403	–
French	4315, 4227	4086
US	52170	–

Lights
Approach
1. **Cap Afrique** 35°30'·4N 11°04'·8E
   Fl.R.5s26m17M White pylon, red top, on dwelling
2. ♦ card buoy off Cap Afrique 35°30'·1N 11°05'·8E Fl

Harbour
3. **E breakwater outer spur head** Fl(2)G.6s6m6M
4. **New breakwater head** Fl(2)R.10s4m6M
5. **E breakwater S head** Fl.2s9m4M
6. **E breakwater inner spur** F.G.6m3M
7. **Terre-plein Ouest, corner** F.R.5m3M

North Africa

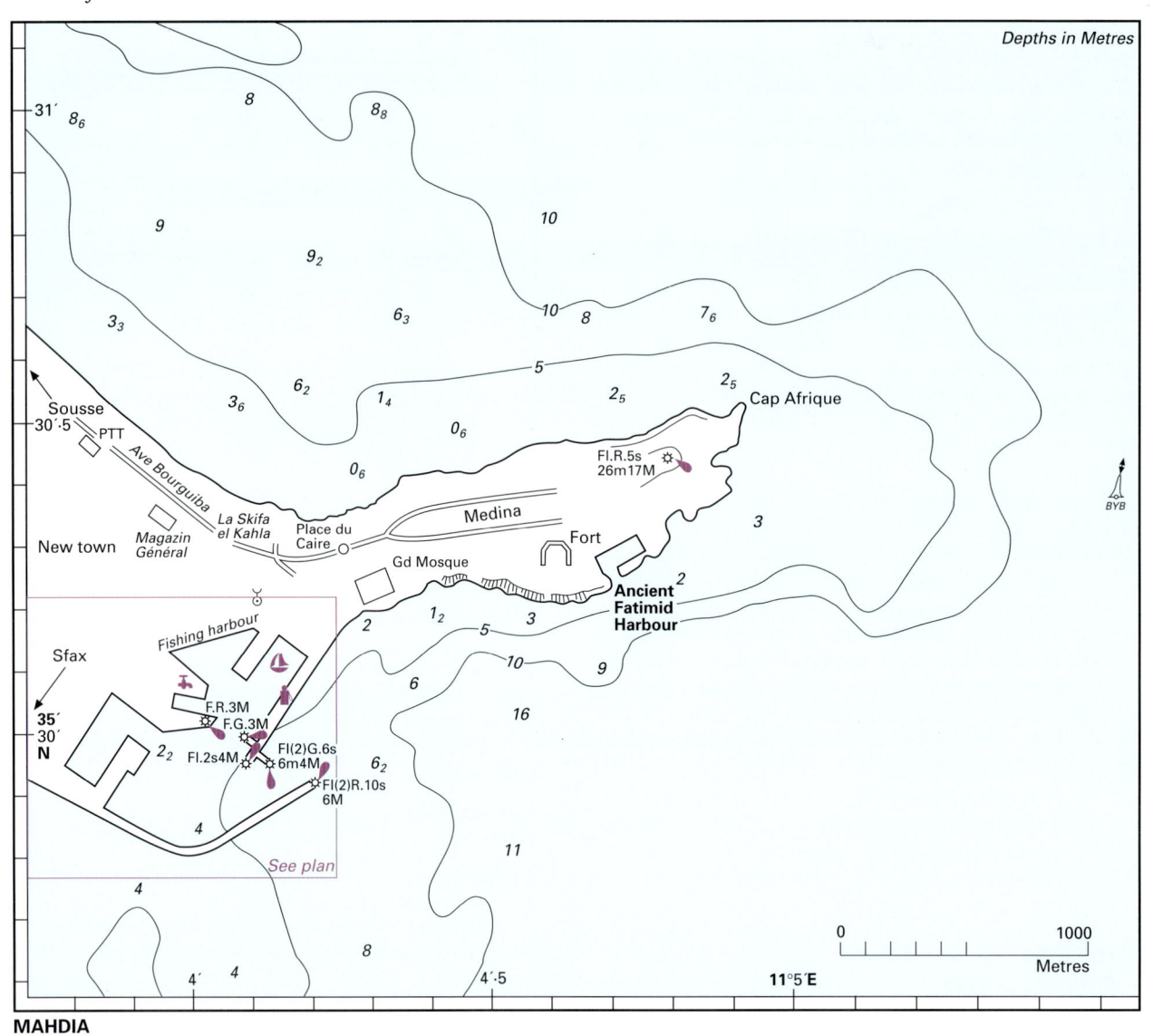

MAHDIA

General
Mahdia is the second largest fishing port of Tunisia and a historic town as well. The significance of fishing is evident from the fact that some 3500 families live off its activities. Recently the port has been enlarged with a new breakwater to accommodate the growing fishing fleet. The picturesque medina on the narrow peninsula is directly adjacent to the port and the market is close by as well. Entry is safe in any weather, protection inside is good and, as it is one of the nearest ports to Lampedusa, it is a good port of entry. The quay reserved for yachts at the fish hall is not quiet but is interesting as it is in the middle of all activity. Mahdia is the most accommodating harbour to yachts south of Monastir. It is primarily a fishing port: however it is well worth visiting. There are possible plans to build a marina here within the next 5 years. It is well located for a visit to the spectacular Roman amphitheatre in El Djem, 42km inland.

Approach
Straightforward without any off-lying dangers. Cap Afrique with the lighthouse and ruins at the end is a good landmark. Beware of the shallow and irregular bottom between the cape and the E cardinal buoy. The seas break here. A factory complex S of the port is for the processing of ground olive pips. In strong SE winds the entrance can be rough. Night entry is possible as the harbour lights function reliably and the port is reasonably well lit.

Berthing
The quay at the SW end of the fish hall is reserved for visiting yachts. Keep fenders low because there is a protruding ledge just on the water line. In strong SE winds a holding-off anchor is useful. The daily movements of fishing vessels produce some wash along this quay. There is an underwater projection in the middle of this quay, where boulders have slipped. A painted warning, 'Don't stop here' marks the hazard. Depth alongside this quay is 2·6–3·0m.

Tunisia

Formalities
APIP ☎ 03 681595 VHF Ch 16 24hrs.
Port of entry. Offices of police and *capitainerie* at the reserved yacht quay. Customs in town.

Facilities
Water From a tap on the W side of the fish hall.
Fuel Diesel from pump on the E breakwater opposite the yacht quay. Petrol from Shell station at the mosque.
Provisions Good daily market next to the port and an interesting and excellent weekly market on Fridays. Wine can be found in a inconspicuous store next to Restaurant Le Lido on the main road along the water front. A *magasin général* is on Avenue Bourguiba.
Post office On Avenue Bourguiba 600m from the port.
Bank Several directly outside the port.
Telephone International calls can be made from a booth next to the Shell service station.
Repairs Emergency engine repairs can be carried out but no specific yacht facilities.
Chandlery Equipment Maritime in the Ave Fashat Hached (☎ 03 695237) on the Sfax Road west of the port, has basic chandlery, but can undertake electronic repairs and is a Furuno agent. Contact Abdallah Jomaa.

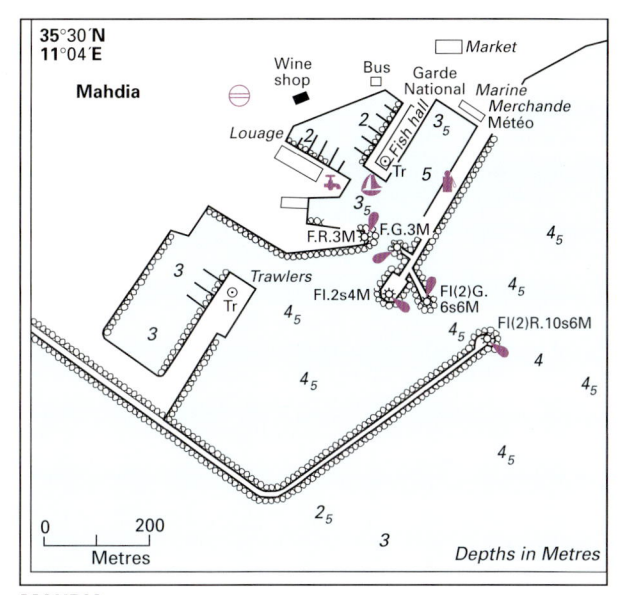

MAHDIA

Horse-drawn carriages are the main means of transport around the busy fishing port of Mahdia, Tunisia

North Africa

Weather forecast
Daily bulletin available from the *Météo* office next to the *marine marchande*.

Eating out
A *pizzeria* and several European-style restaurants (serving wine) along the water front. Restaurant Le Medina next to the market serves reasonably priced typical Tunisian dishes.

History
The strategic location of Mahdia on the narrow peninsula accounts for a long history which goes back to a Phoenician trading post. The remains of the present fortifications were built by the Fatimid ruler Mahdi around 915. He rebuilt the city into one of the most formidable fortresses of the Mediterranean with a massive wall enclosing a Grand Mosque, a palace with military installations and the harbour. After the Fatimids left, the fortified city was taken by Christians from Sicily, reconquered by Islamic forces and later, after unsuccessful sieges by French, English and Genoese, taken by the Turkish corsair Dragut in 1547. Dragut was defeated three years later by the Spanish and to avoid another corsair from threatening their ships again, they blew up the walls. Since then Mahdia has been a peaceful fishing port.

Tourism
Take a walk through the old city, starting at the *Skifa El Kahla* (Tunnel of Darkness) the entrance to the medina, to feel what it once must have been like. The tourist office is located in the restored house of a local Marabout directly behind it. Place du Caire is a delightful little square which is best enjoyed in the shade of a tree with a cup of tea. Around it, several small jewellery shops line the narrow covered alleys. Farther out on the peninsula is the big fortress and old Fatimid port with a graveyard; it is a very tranquil setting. Mahdians like to come out here to find peace of mind.

Salakta
35°23'·3N 11°02'·8E

Distances
Mahdia 7M – La Chebba 11M

Tides
MHWS	MHWN	MLWN	MLWS
0·4m	0·3m	0·2m	0·1m

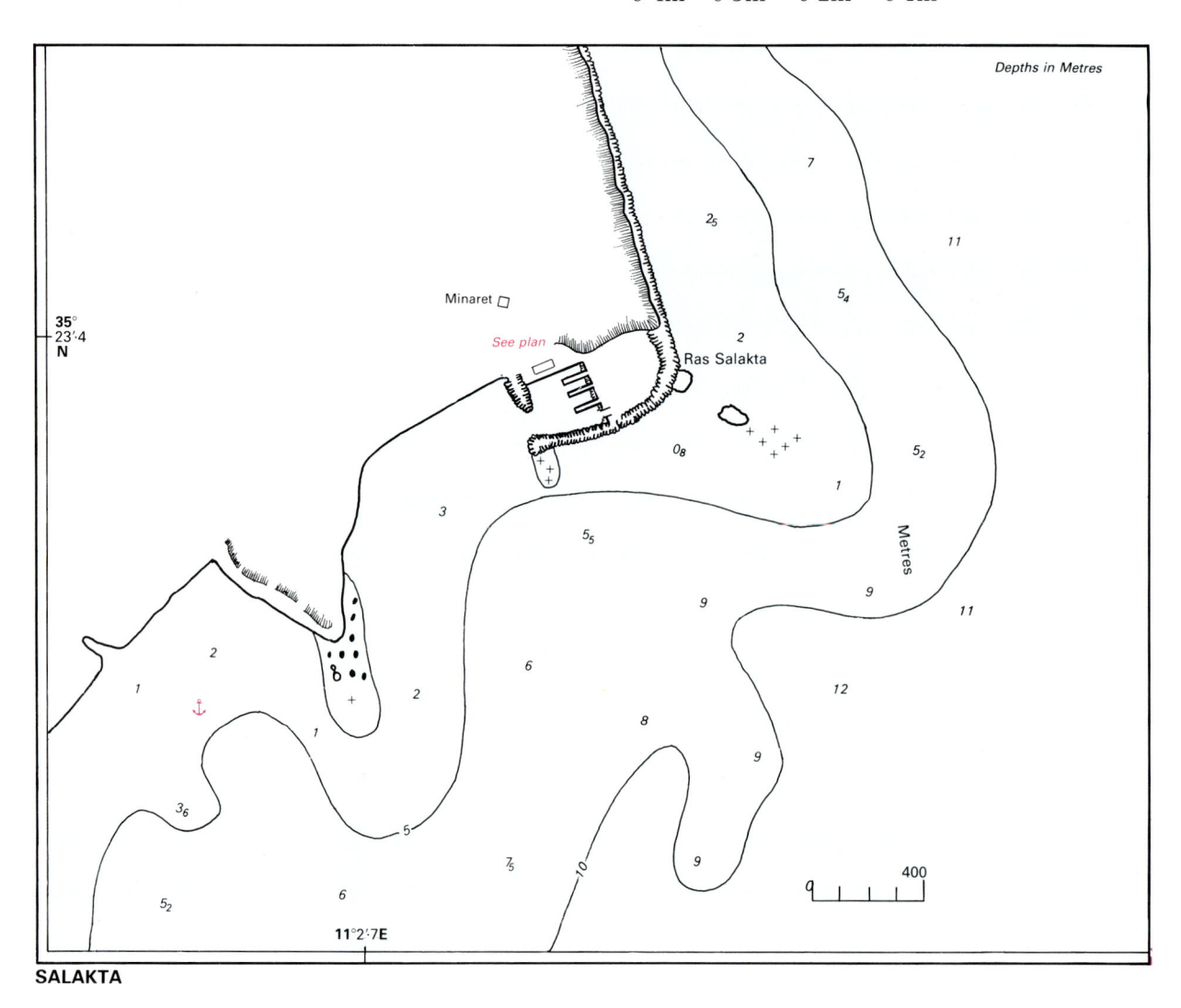

SALAKTA

Charts

	Approach	Port
Admiralty	3403	–
French	4315, 4227	–
US	52170	–

Lights
Harbour
1. **S breakwater** Green light believed to be Iso.4s
2. **W breakwater** Red light believed to be Iso. Both on short round metal poles

General
A small fishing port completed in 1983 situated on the southern side of Ras Salakta. Depths in the entrance vary from year to year and can be less than 2m but it does get dredged. The soundings in the plan were taken in the summer of 1989. In 1997 the *garde maritime* reported depths of at least 1·7m in the port. The village, adjoining the port, is located on the site of Roman Sullecthum but the ruins are hardly worth mentioning. There is a little museum in the port with local finds and the Christian catacombs of Arch Zara, although not spectacular, are interesting. They are located inconspicuously in the middle of a field some 3km from the port and a guide is necessary; take a torch. The harbour is very full of fishing boats and is not used to visiting yachts.

Approach
When approaching from the N give Ras Salakta a wide berth to clear the partially submerged rocks extending from the E corner and the end of the S breakwater. Safe entry is then made from the S. Keep an eye out for fishing nets. The ruins of an old breakwater extend from the coast 500m SW of the entrance. When entering, stay close to the starboard breakwater to avoid shallow seaweed patches. Entry in rough weather is not recommended.

Berthing
Tie up alongside or with a stern anchor to the first or second pier as convenient. Further inside the port depths are uncertain. The basin is not big but there is room for a few visiting yachts with a maximum length of 12m.

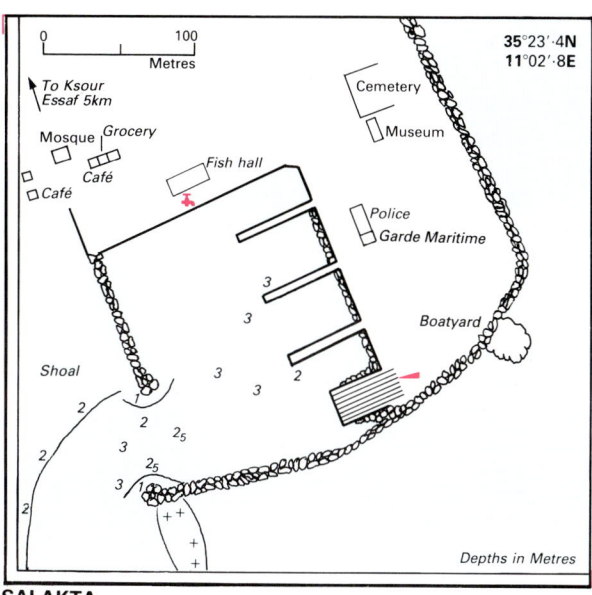

An alternative is to anchor W of the entrance in front of the beach in fine sand with reasonable protection from waves.

Formalities
☎ 03 684415 VHF Ch 16 (0830–1330, 1500–1745).
Police and *garde maritime*.

Facilities
Water and ice In the port.
Provisions Limited provisions from a shop in the port. PTT and a few basic shops in the village. A better assortment in Ksour Essaf 5km from Salakta.
Post office and bank In Ksour Essaf.
Repairs A boatyard building traditional wooden fishing boats has a 17-ton slip and 1-ton crane. Some mechanical repairs can be undertaken.

Eating out
No restaurants in Salakta except for a coffee bar.

SALAKTA

Salakta fishing port

La Chebba
35°13'·7N 11°09'·8E

Distances
Mahdia 17M – Sfax 46M

Tides
MHWS	MHWN	MLWN	MLWS
0·4m	0·3m	0·2m	0·1m

Charts

	Approach	Port
Admiralty	3403	–
French	4315, 4227	–
US	52170	–

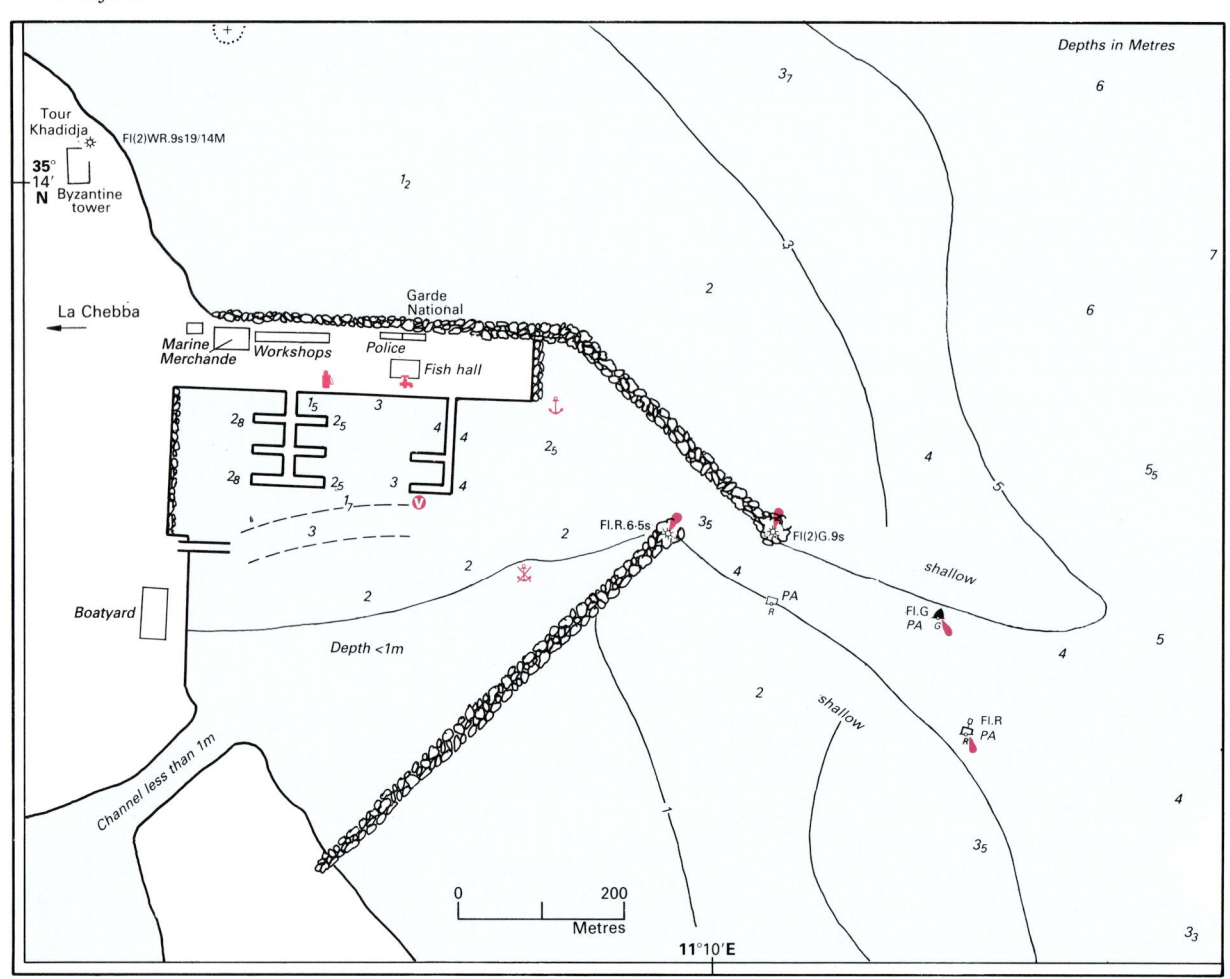

LA CHEBBA

Lights
Approach
1. **Tour Khadidja** 35°14'·0N 11°09'·4E
   Fl(2)WR.9s28m19/14M 135°-W-325°-R-135°
   White metal tower with red bands and inverted triangular topmark
2. **Starboard buoy entrance channel** F.G
3. **Port buoy entrance channel** F.R

Harbour
4. **NE breakwater** Fl(2)G.9s8m6M Green tower
5. **SE breakwater** Fl.R.6·5s8m6M Red tower

General
The fishing port of La Chebba consists of a large basin protected by breakwaters, dredged in the shallows of Ras Kapoudia. The surrounding coast is low-lying with miles of sandy beaches and scattered vacation homes; La Chebba is a popular retreat for affluent Tunisians. The friendliness of the people in this port is perhaps explained by its remoteness, situated 4km from the village. Many of the fishermen return to their boats after taking their catch to the fishmongers, grilling fish on simple barbecues with the tea pot in the middle. There is a canning factory for sardines and octopus; giant prawns are caught during the summer and prepared for shipment to Europe. La Chebba is the last port before the Kerkennah Islands and as such a good jumping off point. The sea here is called Baher Maïte in Arabic, meaning 'dead sea' because even strong winds do not cause big waves. These are the fishing grounds of the traditional sailing fishing boats. Most of them operate from the Kerkennah Islands and La Louza, but a few of them, mostly octopus fishermen, work from La Chebba. In 1997 the harbour was full of large and medium sized fishing boats. The harbour is not used to visiting yachts and one would have to find a berth as best one could, but the *marine marchande* are helpful.

Approach
The red and white bands of the metal tower of Tour Khadidja with its remarkable topmark, the Byzantine tower next to it and the harbour buildings are good landmarks in an otherwise featureless low coast. N of the harbour low houses line the beach. The two buoys marking the entrance channel have moved slightly S during a storm, but 3·5–4m is still found in the centre. The bottom is irregular near the entrance of the channel which makes it rough in strong winds. Although the tidal range is not very noticeable it causes some current in the port, particularly at the entrance, as the SW corner of the basin is open. This helps maintain depths but nevertheless the port has to be dredged. Accurate

tidal predictions are difficult to make as they seem to be irregular. Night entry is possible but there are only a few public lights.

Berthing
Visiting yachts are usually accommodated on the outside of the first pier lying either alongside or stern-to. Beware of the cross-current which flows underneath the open bottomed quays. There is room for about 10 yachts. In an emergency anchor directly E of the first pier.

Formalities
☎ 03 683044 VHF Ch 10 and 16 (0830–1745). Police, *garde national* and *marine marchande*.

Facilities
Water Available from a tap at the ice tower.
Electricity None.
Ice Available on the quay.
Fuel Diesel from a pump. Depth at this section of the quay is approximately 2m. Petrol has to be carried in jerry cans from La Chebba.
Provisions Basic provisions available from 2 small shops in the port. Frequent *louages* to the village, where all provisions and facilities can be found.
Post office and bank In the village.
Repairs Engine repairs can be made by a competent mechanic with workshop in the port and there is a welder, a blacksmith and a hardware shop. Boatyard with 50-ton slip and 1-ton crane repairing timber fishing boats.

Weather forecast
The friendly *marine marchande* official is happy to have customers for his daily report and he even may come around with an express delivery on his Mobylette.

Eating out
In 1989 Restaurant La Sirène opened in the port. Fishermen eat at the counter of a food stall.

Port de Loueta (formally La Louza)
35°02'·5N 11°02'·1E

Distances
La Chebba 23M, Sfax 32M

Tides
No data available.

Charts
	Approach	Port
Admiralty	3403	–
French		4236–

Lights
Harbour
1. VQ(3)R.6s5M
2. Fl(2)G.10s5M

General
This small fishing port in the very shallow coastal waters S of La Chebba was completed in 1985. It has the largest fleet of the traditional sailing fishing boats operating on the Tunisian mainland. Entry is restricted to yachts drawing not much more than 1m. The port itself is ½M offshore, at the end of a long dike in deeper water which has low breakwaters to protect it: big waves cannot build up in the shallow sea around it. The primary attraction of La Louza are the lateen-rigged fishing boats sailing in and out of the port during the busy octopus season (March and April). Apart from a fishing port it is an abattoir as well with sheep being slaughtered on the quay as demand from hungry fishermen requires. This practice may not be legal but the port is remote and nobody cares. An old pier head 1·3M S of the new port, near the hamlet of La Louza, is still used by a few fishermen who wade through the water to get to their anchored boats.

This port has not recently been visited by yacht and most likely never has been. In a leaflet from the Tunisian Tourism Bureau it is listed as a port with room for 10 visiting yachts which seems slightly optimistic.

Approach
The port is situated midway between Ras Batria and Ras El Luza. The ice tower and fish hall are conspicuous as they are the only buildings in the low area. A sandbank about ½M from the entrance has to be rounded at the northern extremity. Four small white buoys about ENE of the entrance possibly mark a passage across the sandbar. French chart No. 4236 is essential even though it does not mark the port but note that it dates back to 1884 with some corrections in 1928. The low breakwaters have the usual green and red light structures. Depths inside the port are not known exactly but around the fish hall there is about 1·5m. Obviously this port should only be entered by suitable boats in good weather during daylight hours. If uncertain about how to come in, anchor in the shallow water surrounding the port.

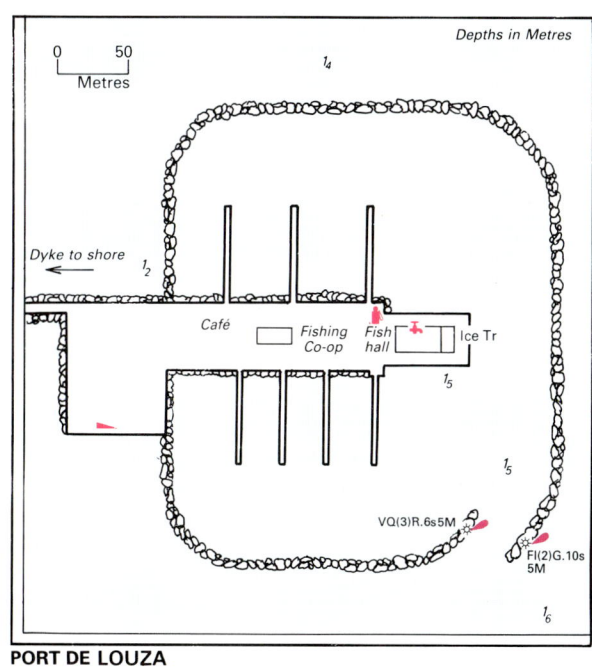

PORT DE LOUZA

North Africa

Octopus fishermen entering the small Port de Loueta

Berthing
The quay around the fish hall can accommodate a few yachts with a maximum length of 12m.

Formalities
☎ 04 270091 VHF Ch 16 (0730–1330, 1500–1745).
Garde maritime and *marine marchande* in the port.

Facilities
Water and ice Available in the port.
Provisions There are two shops for basic provisions in the port and freshly butchered, grilled lamb, is available on the quay out of paper bags. There is a small chandlery for fishermen in the port. The nearest town is Jebiniana some 10km inland. PTT, 2 shops and a petrol station in La Louza. Hezeg has basic shops.
Fuel On the quay as indicated on port plan.
Repairs There is a small crane on the quay north of the fish market.

Sfax
34°43'·2N 10°46'·6E

Distances
La Chebba 46M – Maharès 23M, Gabès 75M, Houmt Souk 62M

Tides
MHWS	MHWN	MLWN	MLWS
1·7m	1·1m	0·8m	0·3m

Charts
	Approach	Port
Admiralty	3403	1162
French	4315, 4237	4238
US	52160	52161

Lights
Commercial Port
Approach
1. **Ras Tina** 34°39'·0N 10°41'·1E
   Fl(2)10s55m24M White tower, red bands, white dwelling
2. **Six pairs of lit buoys** marking the dredged deep water channel leading to the commercial harbour.

Commercial Harbour
3. **Quai du Commerce** DirOc(2)8s18m13M 319°-intens-325°

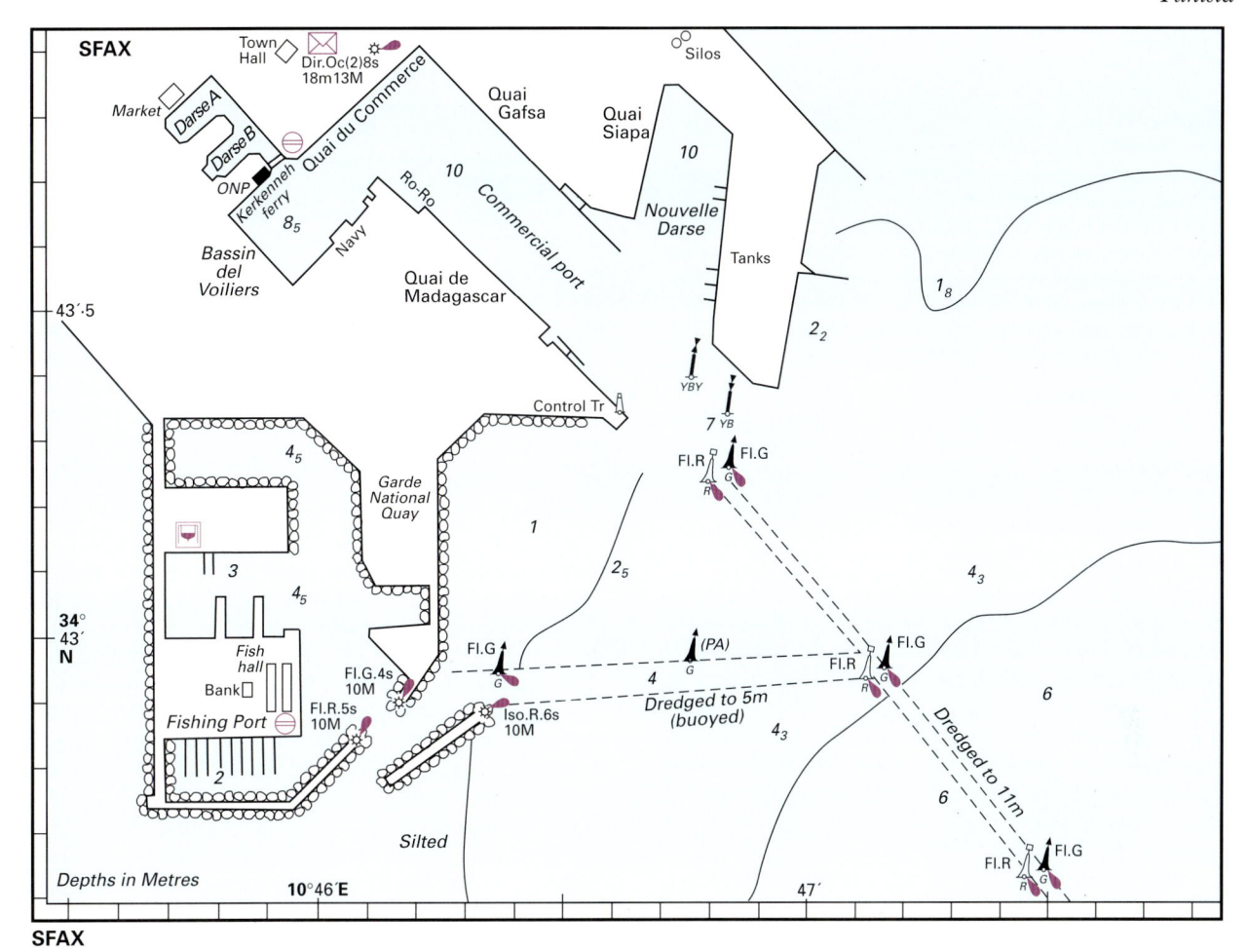

Fishing port
4. **Buoy N of detached breakwater** Fl(2)G.7s
5. **Detached breakwater NE head** Iso.R.6s4m10M Red tower
6. **N breakwater head** Fl.G.4s4m10M Green tower
7. **S breakwater head** Fl.R.5s4m10M Red tower

General
Sfax is the second city of Tunisia and the major industrial centre of the country. The large commercial port is not suitable for yachts and it should only be entered for clearing customs. In bad weather it offers little shelter as it is very open. What is called 'Bassin des Voiliers' on the French and British Admiralty charts is reserved for the Tunisian navy and ferries to the Kerkennah Islands.

The fishing port SW of the commercial port affords excellent protection and is slightly more accommodating to yachts although there is not much room for visitors. It is the largest fishing port on this side of the Mediterranean, and that in itself is spectacular, but it is not very clean and in southerly winds a somewhat malodorous smog from nearby industry blows over it. The city of Sfax is 3km from the port and the road to it passes through dismal surroundings – but it is not necessary to leave the port as it is a town in itself, with grocery shops, eating houses, stores with ship's supplies, a bank and even a mosque as well as repair shops, shipyards and three big travel-lifts. In spite of its disadvantages, Sfax is an interesting place to spend a few days, but it is not used to visiting yachts.

Approach
Entry is easy by day and night. The buildings and factories in the commercial harbour and the tall white control tower at the entrance are conspicuous in an otherwise flat coast. Entrance is by a dredged deep water channel which is marked with six pairs of lit buoys. Beware of current up to 2kts across the channel. From the fifth pair of buoys, marked Sfax 7 and Sfax 8 a dredged channel branches off to the fishing port. A detached breakwater protects the fishing port which should be entered from the E as a sandbar has formed around the SW end.

Berthing
To clear customs, tie up at the quay below the direction light in the commercial harbour. After clearing, move to the fishing port to avoid high harbour dues. Here the best place is amidst the smaller fishing boats on one of the finger piers.

Formalities
☎ 04 296888 *Fax* 04 296816 VHF Ch 16 24hrs.
Port of entry. Clear customs in the commercial harbour. Customs, police, *garde national* and *marine marchande* in the fishing harbour.

North Africa

Facilities
Water Has to be carried in jerry cans from various taps around the fish hall and restaurants.
Electricity None.
Fuel From a pump in the fishing port.
Provisions Fresh produce available in the fishing port and a weekly market on Fridays.
Post office and bank In the fishing port.
Repairs Welders, blacksmiths, engine repair shops, paint, antifouling and hardware available in the fishing port. Two 250-ton and one 150-ton travel-lift and several shipyards for repairs of steel fishing vessels and construction of large wooden fishing boats.

Weather forecast
From the *Météo* office on the N side of the fish hall.

Eating out
Several eating houses along the quay. Good and high class restaurants in town.

Tourism
Compared with the other big cities in Tunisia, Sfax has not been affected much by tourism. Sfaxians are renowned for their entrepreneurial skill and probably never needed the revenues from tourism. The modern town, rebuilt after heavy bombardments in the Second World War, is attractive and quite sophisticated but at the same time it has a large medina which is not overrun by tourist shops. There is a good Archaeological and a Popular Arts Museum of which the *Rough Guide* gives an enthusiastic and detailed account. Whether all of this is enough to overcome the inconveniences of visiting by boat is a personal matter.

The Kerkennah Islands

Charts

	Approach	Port
Admiralty	3403, 1162	–
French	4315, 4235, 4237	–
US	–	–

General
A group of sandy islands 10M from the mainland coast. Vegetation is sparse, mainly wind-blown palm trees, some scattered fig trees and small vegetable gardens. Their greatest attraction is their solitude and the simple, unchanged way of life of hospitable people. But for a long time they have also been a place of exile. During the recent struggle for independence Bourguiba was interned here until he escaped to Libya from Kraten on the NW corner of Ile Chergui.

The group consists of two main islands, Ile Rharbi and Ile Chergui, separated by a narrow channel, and two small uninhabited islets off the E coast. Much of the land is less than 3m above sea level and the highest point is 20m. They sit among the Kerkennah Banks, of sand, mud and weed, which extend 35M from the coast between Ras Kapoudia and Sfax, and are separated from the mainland by the Canal des Kerkennah.

The main activity is fishing on the banks which are easy to work. Traditionally the fish are caught in *charfias*, traps made of palm tree fronds permanently planted in the sea bed. Long lines of these palm fronds stretch from the beach out to sea and serve to divert the fish to a chamber with fishing nets around its circumference. Typically one *charfia* brings in 1,000kg of fish per month. Small rowing or lateen rigged sailing boats are used to empty the nets daily. Two thousand sailing and rowing boats are still in use around the islands together with a slowly increasing number of powered boats. The sailing boats are mostly used from the beaches whereas the powered boats operate mainly from the new fishing port of Ennajet at Kraten.

Approaches
Navigation around the islands is tricky, but less exacting for yachts drawing less than 1·5m which do not mind going aground. Landmarks are few and far apart in the Kerkennah region and accuracy of the French charts is debatable as no proper surveys have been made recently – some no more recently than a 100 years ago – and land features such as buildings, new ports and antennae which could provide useful navigational aids are missing. On the other hand, serious grounding can be avoided by proper timing of the tides.

The seaward edges of the Kerkennah Banks are fringed with shoals and marked by light buoys and beacons. The shallower parts are intersected by numerous steep-sided channels called *oued* (river) in Arabic. The banks, in common with similar shoals off the Tunisian coast, possess the remarkable characteristic of reducing swell. This is due to the gradual slope of the bottom and thick seaweed which covers it. In many of the *oueds* a yacht can anchor safely providing it is has proper ground tackle. The area does not require special anchor gear other than mentioned under 'Yacht and equipment'.

The main shipping route leads around the banks which are well marked with large buoys and beacons though their lights are unreliable and it is worth checking the situation at the *marine marchande*. The alternative route to the S is through the Kerkennah Channel, between the islands and the mainland. This channel is reasonably well buoyed and is used by small coastal ships. Care is required around some beacons which are planted on the shallow sea bed just outside the channel.

South from La Chebba the tidal range increases rapidly and current in the channel has to be taken into account.

Tidal streams
There is no tidal flow chart of the area but the flood comes across the banks from NE or E and enters the Kerkennah Channel from either end. The ebb stream sets in the reverse direction. Thus, when proceeding on the edge of the banks or in the Kerkennah Channel, caution must be exercised as the tidal stream may set directly on to the banks.

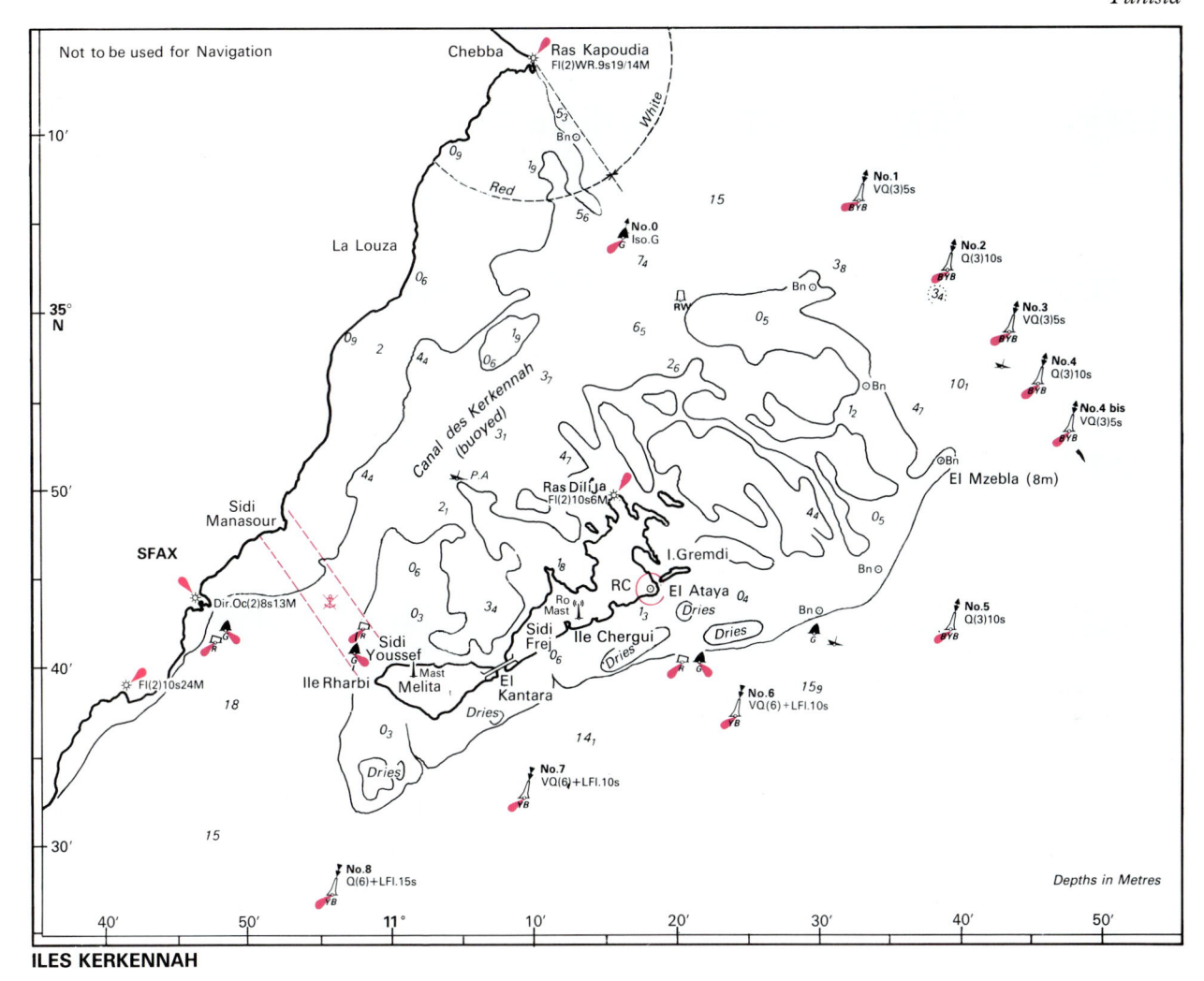

On the eastern extremity of the banks the tidal streams turn about at the time of local high and low water and the maximum rate, at about half tide, does not exceed 1kt. In the Kerkennah Channel the tidal streams are stronger and may attain a rate of 1·5kts. They turn 2–3 hours after local high and low water and attain their maximum rate shortly before the time of high or low water. They set fairly through the channel and meet at about the middle of it, where they are irregular.

The tides (taken from the *British Admiralty Tide Tables*) for the ports in the Kerkennah Islands are as follows

Time based on HW Gibraltar:

	MHWS	MHWN	MLWN	MLWS	HW	LW
Kerkennah Banks, E point	0·8m	0·4m	0·4m	0·2m	−1:05	−0:55
Kraten (estimated)	1·1m	0·7m	0·5m	0·2m		
Bordj el Hassar/ Sidi Frej	1·2m	0·8m	0·6m	0·2m	+2:10	+3:15
Sidi Youssef (estimated)	1·3m	0·9m	0·7m	0·3m		
Kerkennah Banks, S point	1·4m	0·9m	0·7m	0·3m	+0:35	−0:10
El Abassia (near Ataya)	1·1m	0·7m	0·5m	0·3m	+0:43	+1:52
Sfax	1·7m	1·1m	0·8m	0·3m	+0:50	+1:15

The French charts taken together with the general information available on tidal streams, for instance the *Admiralty Tide Tables*, may provide more clues.

Anchorages

There are three small fishing ports in the Kerkennah Islands but with the exception of Sidi Youssef none of them has a properly buoyed approach. Basically it is possible to anchor in many places in and around the banks as the seas will be calm in almost any weather. The prevailing easterly winds will generally favour anchoring on the NW side of the islands.

Sidi Youssef

34°39'·3N 10°58'·0E

Distances

Sfax 10M, La Chebba 45M – Maharès 30M

Tides

MHWS	MHWN	MLWN	MLWS
1·3m	0·9m	0·7m	0·3m

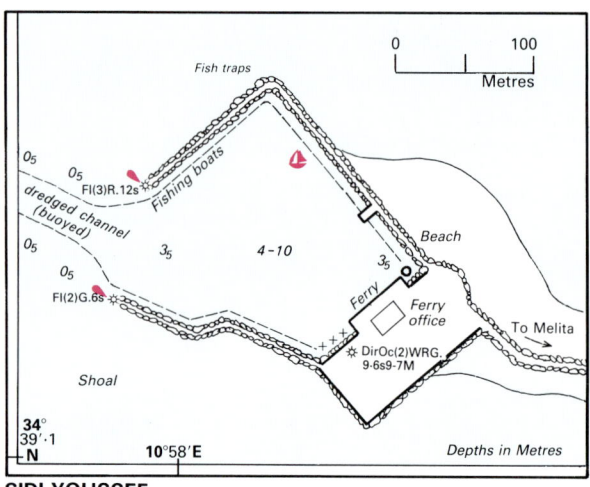

North Africa

SIDI YOUSSEF

Lights
Approach
No.1 34°39'·7N 10°56'·8E Iso.G.4s7m5M Green and white bands
No.2 (close to No.1) Iso.R.4s Red and white bands.
No.3 Not known Green & White bands.
No.4 Not known Red & White horizontal stripes.
1. **Entrance channel E** Fl(2)G.6s8m5M
2. **Entrance channel E** Fl(3)R.12s8m5M

Harbour
3. **N breakwater** Fl(3)R.12s8m5M
4. **S breakwater** Fl(2)G.6s8m5M
5. **Dir Lt** DirOc(2)WRG.9·6s9/7M

General
A small harbour on the W point of the Kerkennah Islands which only comes to life when the ferry from Sfax arrives. It is the only port in the Kerkennah Islands which is relatively easy to enter for normal draught yachts.

There is now a concrete block wall about 4m high the entire length of both breakwaters (not shown on the photograph). This provides good shelter in strong winds. The basin is not very large and has no quays. With some improvising smaller yachts can lie bow-to the N breakwater if sufficient room is left for the ferry.

There are no facilities other than a little stall in the summer season which caters for the needs of passing ferry passengers. The nearest village where some provisions are available is Melita, 5km from the port. Buses are available after the arrival of the ferry six times a day. Taxis are practically non-existent.

Approach
The palm trees on the island will be spotted first and the port not until fairly close by, as the few buildings are low. The waypoint for the first pair of entrance buoys is 34°39'·858N 10°56'·827E.

Entrance
Entrance is through a narrow dredged channel about 1½M long on a course of 112°. The channel is marked by a green and a red buoy at the entrance and 2 more buoys. Yachts should stay well in the centre and it is advisable not to share the channel with the ferry. Be aware of cross-tidal currents.

Berthing
The N breakwater is not quayed but there is a dilapidated wooden landing and the remains of another to take a bow line; use the dinghy to get ashore. The ferry produces considerable wash. When laying the kedge keep in mind that the ferry needs a large turning circle to leave the port. There is no ideal place to avoid obstructing the ferry. Tucked in as close to the breakwater as possible in the N or E corner may be best.

Formalities
☎ 04 239953 VHF Ch 16 24hrs.
A small *garde national* post.

Facilities
Water (and WC) At Café du Port.
Provisions Melita has basic shops, hardware store, café and PTT.

Sidi Frej Anchorage
34°41'·372N 11°08'·046E
Root of pier/breakwater

Tides
MHWS	MHWN	MLWN	MLWS
1·2m	0·8m	0·6m	0·2m

General
Sidi Frej, on the NW coast of Ile Chergui, is the only part of the Kerkennah Islands with some modest tourist development. A few low-key hotels line the beach, from which a recently repaired pier extends from Hotel Cerana 550m into deeper water. It is only accessible to shallow draught yachts.

Approach
Approach is best started from buoy 12 in the Kerkennah Channel. Steer for the small fortress at Bordj el Hassar until 2–3M from the shore whence

The small ferry port of Sidi Youssef viewed from the entrance channel

More dromedaries than cars on the Kerkennah Islands near El Ataya

the course can be set for the pier. Beware of tidal streams which set across the banks. Either way the approach is not too difficult for shallow draught yachts and it is a good way to learn about shallow water navigation around the Kerkennah Islands.

Berthing
The pier used to be frequented by small boats that supplied the islands before the ferry port of Sidi Youssef was built. It is now being used by tenders supplying the oil platform approximately 3M offshore. Tie up at the end bows-to in approximately 1·5m at low water. Alternatively anchor farther out in minimum depths of 2–2·5m with good holding. Beware of uncharted shallow patches in the N part of the anchorage. According to local information there is a channel in the extension of the pier. Protection during the common E to SE summer winds is good.

Facilities
Basic provisions Are available in Ouled el Kassem, a hamlet on the main road to Remla, about 4km from Sidi Frej.
Fishing In the summer some fishing boats make excursions to see the traditional fishing method with *charfias*.

Transport
Bicycles can be hired at Hotel Cercina which also serves good meals.

Ramla
Ramla is the capital of the islands. There is a pier running approximately 250m out to sea, but with only 0·5m depth at its end.

Facilities
Water and diesel Are available at the root of the pier.
PTT, pharmacy, bank, garage and shops Found in Ramla.

Ennajet/Kraten
34°49'·8N 11°15'·4E

Distances
La Chebba 27M – Sidi Youssef 24M

Tides (approx)
MHWS	MHWN	MLWN	MLWS
1·1m	0·7m	0·5m	0·2m

Lights
Approach
1. **Ras Djila** (NW point of Ile Chergui) 34°49'·7N 11°14'·8E Fl(2)10s10m6M

Harbour
2. Green and Red light structures on the breakwater head, periods unknown
3. **East jetty head** Fl(2)R.5s7m5M

General
The main fishing port of the Kerkennah Islands, finished in 1987 and located close to the NW corner of Ile Chergui. Yachts are certainly welcome in the friendly port but approach is restricted to shallow draught yachts. The port and entrance were dredged to depths varying from 1·5 to 2m. A barge used during the construction of the port has been abandoned well above the water E of the port. In 1997 it was reported that the harbour and approach would be dredged to 2·5m in the next 2 years.

Approach
If French chart No. 4237 is to be trusted the approach is from buoy K4 in the Kerkennah Channel. A track of 141° for 6½M will bring the

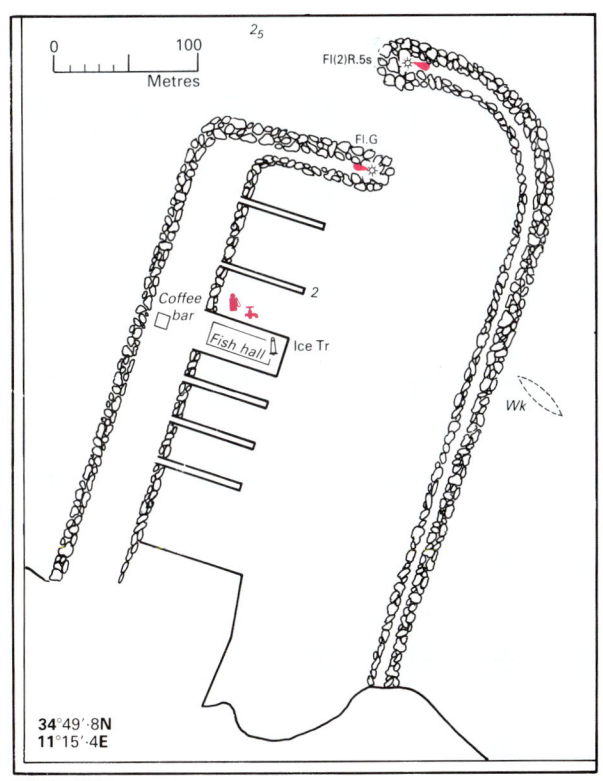

ENNAJET

North Africa

The main fishing port of the Kerkennah Islands, the new port of Ennajet, in octopus season with plenty of clay pots lying around

port abeam; but the survey is old. Avoid the bank which extends approximately 1M N of Ras Djila. There are no buoys and apart from the minaret of Kraten which is not marked on the chart and the ice tower in the port, there are no landmarks. Beware of small banks of sand and seaweed on this part of the coast; octopus fishermen lay their pots in them.

Berthing
There is room for a few visiting yachts (maximum length 12m) which can tie up wherever convenient.

Formalities
APIP ☎ 04 281295 VHF Ch 10 (0800–1800).
APIP in port. Will provide weather forecasts on request – very helpful.

Facilities
Water Available from a tap near the fish market.
Fuel Diesel from a pump.
Provisions Limited provisions available in the small village approximately 3km from the port. There is a coffee bar and small shop in the port.
Repairs A boatyard and slip in the S corner of the port.

El Ataya
34°43'·4N 11°17'·7E

Distances
Sidi Youssef 37M – Sfax 40M

Tides
MHWS	MHWN	MLWN	MLWS
1·1m	0·7m	0·5m	0·3m

Lights
Harbour
1. Red and green lights on outer breakwaters.
2. Red light on inner breakwater (characteristics unknown).

General
El Ataya is a small thriving fishing port in a forgotten corner of Ile Chergui. It has a large fleet of sailing and motor fishing boats, but they are rare visitors. The picturesque setting of the old fishing anchorage makes a nice afternoon walk. The tranquil road from the new port to the simple village is lined with olive and palm trees.

Approach
Entrance to the port is via a 4M long natural channel, Oued Mimoun, of which the last part has been dredged. Two sets of buoys mark the entrance to the channel and palm fronds are planted at random farther on. Once the entrance buoys are located it is best to rely on 'eyeball' navigation as the channel is visible though in rough seas the visibility of the sea water is reduced and the *oued* is difficult to make out. Entry is best started at low water when the drying parts of the banks around the oued are visible. Depths vary from a minimum of 4·5m to a maximum of 12m and the sides are steep-to. The breakwaters protecting the port are low. The antenna from the radiobeacon N of the port and a large factory hall near the port are conspicuous. Once in the *oued*, between the banks, there are plenty of good places to anchor.

Berthing
Tie up anywhere as convenient.

Formalities
APIP ☎ 04 281154 (24 hr)
APIP are helpful and will supply weather forecasts daily.

Facilities
Water Available at SE end of the fish hall.
Fuel From the fuel quay as indicated on the port plan.
Provisions One shop in the port. Basic shops and PTT in El Alaya 2km away.
Repairs A boatyard with 100-ton travel-lift and 10-ton crane, building and repairing fishing boats.

Tourism
Just outside the village on the road to Remla, there is said to be a small museum dedicated to

The shallow anchorage for the fishing boats of El Ataya

EL ATTAYA

North Africa

Bourguiba's escape from the island to Libya. The museum contains several letters Bourguiba wrote while he was exiled, the house he sheltered in and the boat he used for his escape from the French occupation forces.

Maharès
34°30'·5N 10°29'·8E

Distances
Sfax 21M – Gabès 50M

Tides
No exact data available but max. range about 1·5m.

Charts
	Approach	Port
Admiralty	3403	–
French	4315, 4239	–
US	–	–

Lights
Harbour
1. **Maharès** 34°30'·8N 10°29'·9E DirF.WRG.9m3M Lit Bns mark entrance channel
2. **No.1** 34°30'·7N 10°29'·8E Q.G.8m3M (green pylon)
3. **No.2** Q.R

General
A new, small fishing port finished in 1987, in the shallow coast S of Sfax. In order to reach deeper water the port is built at the end of a short dike and the entrance is through a dredged channel which ends between low, partially submerged breakwaters. Good provisions are available in the town which is on the main coast road close to the port. The fishing port is active with little room for visiting yachts. It is a good jumping off point for Gabès or the island of Jerba. Maharès has benefited considerably from the opening of the Libyan border and as it is on the main road to Sfax many Libyans stop here to shop.

Approach
The dredged channel to the port is not buoyed but the minaret in the village and two antenna towers NE of the port provide good guidance to enter safely. The critical part is at the beginning of the channel, where time has to be allowed to take accurate bearings – 356° through the centre line of the entrance channel to the minaret and 16° to the radio mast. Beware of the low breakwaters which are partially submerged at HW. In 1989 the structures for the port lights were ready to be installed but it was not clear whether they would be placed at the end of the low breakwaters or at the entrance to the basin. Minimum depth is 1·8m at LW in the channel and 1·5m in the port itself.

Berthing
Tie up anywhere as convenient in the first part of the port. In 1997 port officials considered the port primarily for fishing boats and neither expected nor particularly welcomed yachts; no yachts visited.

Formalities
☎ 04 290543 VHF Ch 16 (0800–1300, 1500–1745).

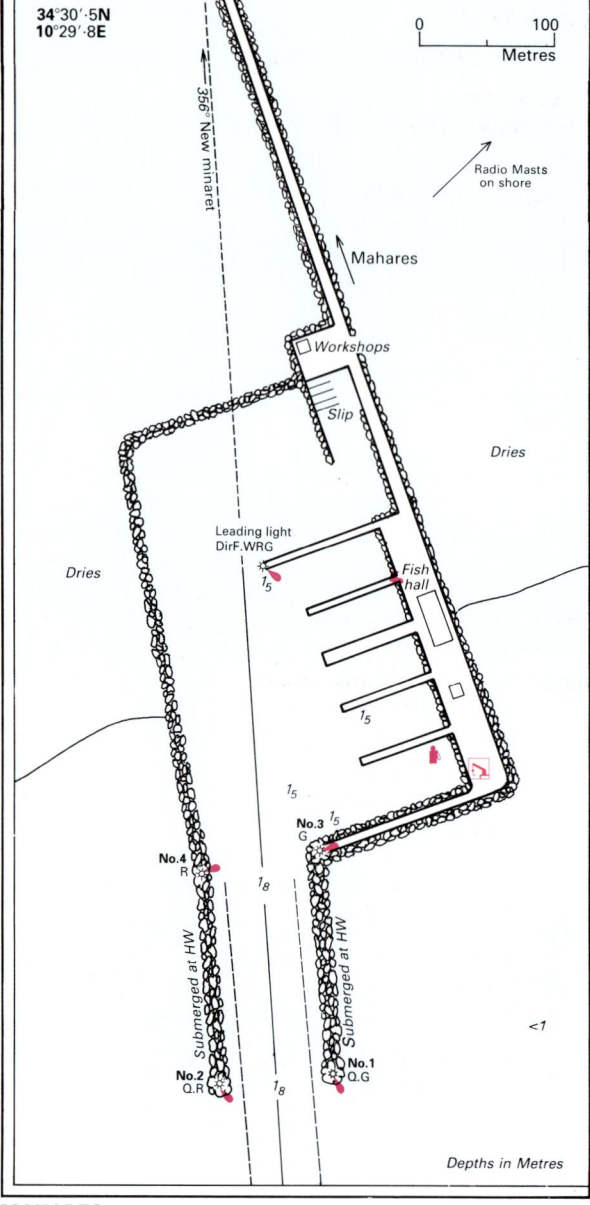

MAHARES

Garde national and *marine marchande*. Not a port of entry.

Facilities
Water From a tap on the quay.
Fuel Diesel pump on the first pier. Petrol from a service station on the main road close to the port.
Provisions Good assortment from several shops close to the port. One small shop in the port.
Post office and telephone In the town past the railway tracks.
Bank Several along the main road.
Repairs There is a yard for small wooden fishing boats and the village has several hardware stores.

Eating out
A good choice of restaurants and cafés along the main road from Sfax to Gabès.

La Skhira

34°17'·0N 10°05'·7E

Distances
Sfax 50M – Gabès 25M

Tides
MHWS MHWN MLWN MLWS
2·1m 1·4m 1·0m 0·5m

Charts
	Approach	Port
Admiralty	3403	9
French	4239	6325
US	–	–

Lights
Harbour
Red and green lights, on metal pylons at the ends of the two breakwaters mark the harbour entrance. Characteristics are unknown.

General
A small fishing port in an unattractive part of the coast, 3M SW of the phosphoric acid terminal at La Skhira-Khedima. The port is well used by small and medium sized fishing boats. Yachts are neither expected or particularly welcome. None had visited in 1997. Exact depths are not known but port officials claimed in 1997 that there was 2m in the port at LW. Most available quay space is taken by fishing boats.

The town of La Skhira has all facilities including a station and is on the main Sfax-Gabès road. It is 1km from the port, past a development of luxury apartments built for the foreign engineers working at the phosphoric acid plant. There is much new building going on.

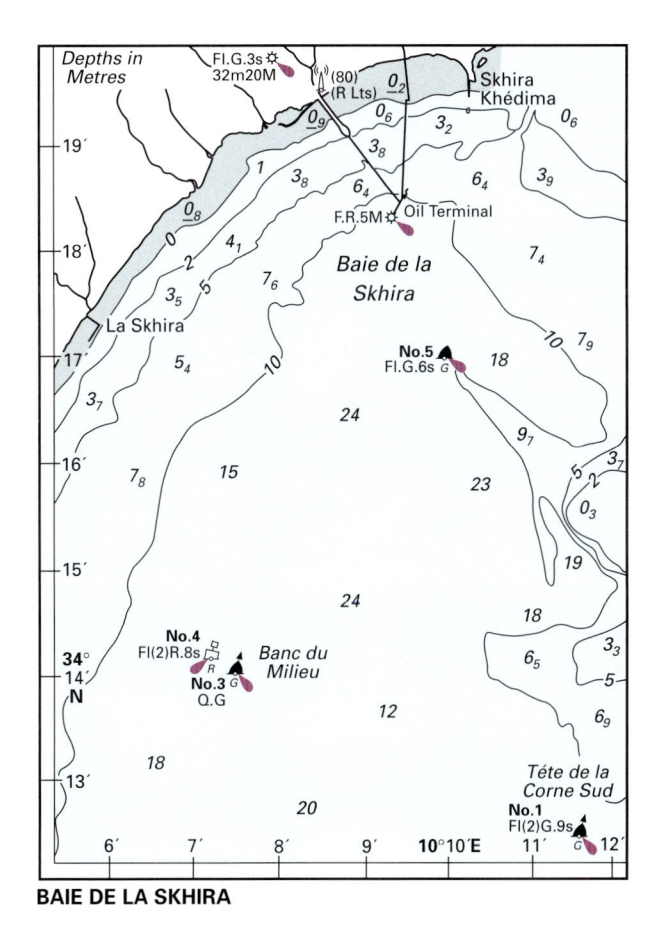

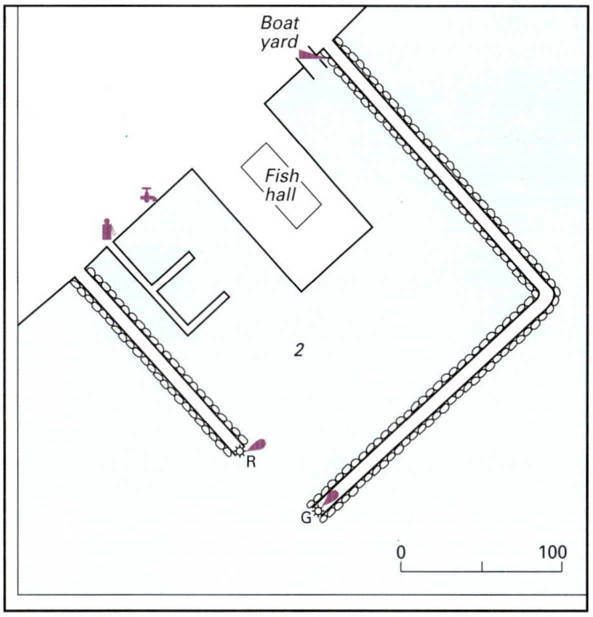

Approach
The fish market, breakwater and lights, together with the apartments on the sandy cliff 200m behind the port are conspicuous. It is only suitable for a daytime approach as the depths are uncertain and characteristics of the lights unknown.

Berthing
Alongside a fishing boat or vacant space on the quay, but expect to be moved.

Formalities
Garde national just outside the port.

Facilities
Water Available from a tap on the quay.
Fuel Diesel from a pump on the quay or petrol from 2 garages in the town.
Provisions 2 small shops in the port for basics only. A selection of shops and cafés in the town.
Post office, telephone and banks PTT, taxiphone and 2 banks in the town.

Weather forecasts
Available from the office (believed to be *APIP*) at vehicular entrance of the port.

Gabès

33°53'·5N 10°07'·1E

Distances
Sfax 75M – Houmt Souk 43M

Tides
MHWS MHWN MLWN MLWS
2·1m 1·3m 1·0m 0·3m

North Africa

Charts

	Approach	Port
Admiralty	3403	9
French	4240	4241
US	52164	52165

Lights
Approach
1. **Main light** 33°53'·6N 10°06'·8E
   Fl(2)6s13m20M 124°-vis-304° White 8-sided tower, black top R lights on pylon 0·9M SW

Harbour
2. **Jetée Nord head** Fl(2)G.9s10m6M
3. **Jetée Sud head** Fl.R.6·5s10m6M

General
The busy fishing port of Gabès is situated near the large oasis of Chenini. The port is big but there is not much room for visiting yachts. The Gulf of Gabès has rich fishing grounds and in mid-March when the prawn and tunny season begins, fishermen from all over Tunisia come for the tunny fishing for which large trawl nets are used. The pleasant town is a short walk from the port and has good shops to provision and restaurants and hotels of all categories. Gabès is also a good base for excursions into the desert.

The large commercial port of Ghannouche, 3M N of the fishing port, is far from the city and not suitable for yachts.

In winter time local depressions develop over the Gulf of Gabès and strong winds are frequent, mainly from SW to W or from NE to E and occasionally gales are recorded.

Approach
The coast around Gabès is fairly flat and low but the port is not hard to approach. There are no off-lying dangers and the industrial complex around the commercial port is conspicuous from a great distance. The breakwaters of the fishing port are large and fitted with good-sized light structures. The entrance channel between the breakwaters is fairly narrow and the heads should be given a wide berth in order to have an unobstructed view on entering. The entrance is dredged regularly and may, at worst, have depths of 2–2·5m at low water. In 1997, port officials reported that there was 4m in the entrance and main part of the harbour, but soundings along the quay NE of the fish hall revealed 2·3m at LW.

Berthing
The most likely space for visiting yachts is on the quay NE of the fish hall, alongside the *garde national* patrol boat. If entering at night (best avoided) there may be berths along the quays but keep in mind that they will probably be needed in the early morning for fishing boats.

Formalities
☎ 05 270367 VHF Ch 16 24hrs.
Port of entry. Friendly and helpful officials.

Facilities
Water From the fish market.
Electricity Power point which supplies patrol boats might be available to yachts.
Fuel Diesel pump in the port, petrol from service station in town.
Provisions Many small shops and a good local market for fresh produce, meat and fish. *Magasin général* and wine shop in the town. The port has 2 shops, including a fruit and vegetable shop and a café.
Post office, telephone and banks On Avenue Bour-guiba.
Repairs A boatyard with 200-ton travel-lift. Timber and mechanical repairs possible.
Laundry On a slightly hidden corner of Avenue Farhat Hached.

Weather forecast
Posted in Arabic at NE end of the fish market.

GABES

The fishing port of Gabès viewed from the red entrance light

Eating out
A wide selection of restaurants ranging from European style to the most simple Tunisian eating houses.

Transport
Major car rental agencies have offices in town as well as a *Land Rover* hire agency.

Tourism
Gabès was originally a Phoenician settlement, later becoming the most southern port of the Roman Empire in Africa. The relics of its Spanish, Ottoman and Arabic conquerors were destroyed between the French bombardment in 1904 and the Second World War, after which most of today's town was built. The most important religious monument is the new Mosque of Sidi Boulbaba, named after the *marabout* who brought peace and prosperity in the 7th century; nearby, an old mosque with beautifully decorated inner courtyard is worth visiting.

The main attraction of Gabès is the large oasis where one can still find a classic haven of peace and shade under the tall date palms. Bicycles can be hired at the youth hostel or alternatively one can rent a horse-drawn *calesh*.

Another interesting excursion is to visit the desert regions in the south. The most popular trip is to the underground Berber dwellings in Matmata. Staying in one of the pit hotels is a unique experience. Haddej, close to old Matmata, is less visited and gives a good idea what these underground villages were like. Take a torch to see olive presses and family dwellings and the pit house used for marriage ceremonies. From Matmata a picturesque but rough trail leads to Toujane, one of the most isolated Berber villages, built on two sides of a steep gorge in arid and wild mountains. The area was a battleground in the Second World War. Other interesting places in the same area are the extraordinary Berber village of Chenini (visit early in the morning before the tour buses arrive), Douirat and a hotel in converted storage rooms in Ksar Haddada.

The shortest way from Gabès to the true beginning of the Sahara is via the oasis of Douz. The *piste* route S of Douz to Sabria El Faouar loops through the desert and to isolated oases; in normal circumstances four-wheel drive is not necessary.

Other worthwhile excursions are across the Chott el Djerid to the large oases of Tozeur and Nefta, though these are popular destinations for tourist buses. The drive through the desolate salt pans of the Chott is a very special experience and it opens the way to another interesting desert trail to the Seldja Gorge via Tamerza.

In three days several of these places can be visited by car but a week or more will not be wasted. The landscape is spectacular and a glimpse of the unique lifestyle of the Berbers is a highlight of a visit to Tunisia. The *Rough Guide* covers these excursions extensively.

Zarat
33°42'·0N 10°21'·8E

Distances
Gabès 17M – Ajim 19M

Tides
MHWS	MHWN	MLWN	MLWS
2·1m	1·3m	1·0m	0·3m

Charts
	Approach	Port
Admiralty	3403, 9	–
French	7524, 4242	–
US	52160	–

Lights
Harbour
1. **NE breakwater head** Fl(3)G.10s6m5M
2. **SW breakwater head** LFl.R.10s6m5M

General
A recently finished, small fishing port in an isolated part of the coast between Gabès and Ajim. The port, at the end of a long dike, is situated near the site of an old tunny factory, called Sidi Marmora. The new village of Zarat is some 5km from the port close to the main road along the coast. In 1997 dredging was in progress and it was reported that both the approach and the harbour would be dredged to 2·5m LW but when visited, the harbour was still no more than 1·5m LW. Yachts rarely visit.

Approach
Approach is straightforward. A hill behind the port rises to 45m and the white tower of an old tunny factory on it is conspicuous. The port buildings are the only structures on the shore for miles.

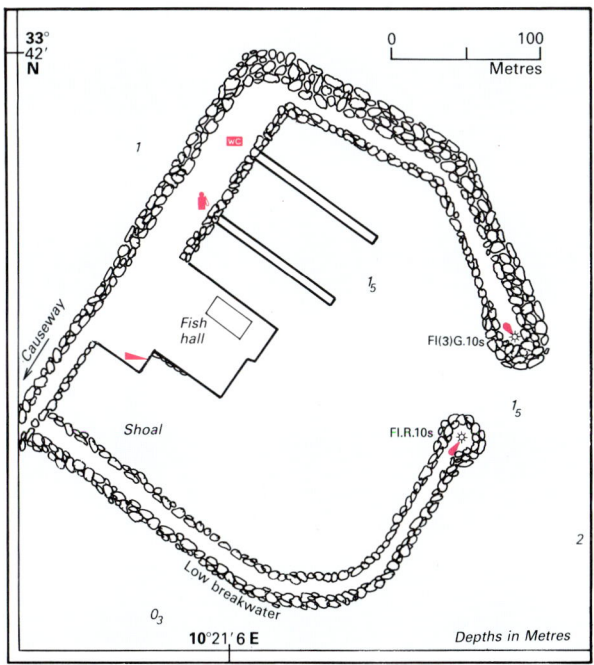

ZARAT

North Africa

The small port of Zarat at the end of a long dike viewed from the SE

Berthing
Tie up anywhere convenient on the two N piers. The part SW of the fish hall is very shallow. Not for yachts over 12m long.

Formalities
No authorities except for CGP representative.

Facilities
Water and diesel Available in the port.
Provisions The village has basic shops, cafés, hardware stores, PTT and bank.
Repairs A boatyard and 15-ton slip. There is a small crane on the quay. Timber and some mechanical repairs are possible.

Houmt Souk
33°53'·3N 10°51'·3E

Distances
Sfax 50M, Gabès 43M – Zarzis 42M

Tides
MHWS	MHWN	MLWN	MLWS
1·7m	1·2m	1·0m	0·7m

Charts
	Approach	Port
Admiralty	3403	–
French	7524, 4244	–
US	52160	–

Lights
Approach
1. **Bordj Djellidj** 33°53'·1N 10°44'·6E
   Fl.R.5s16m9M White 8-sided tower, black top, on building
2. **Ras Tourg-en-Nes** 33°49'·3N 11°02'·7E
   Fl.5s64m24M White tower, red bands
3. **Houmt Souk** 33°53'·1N 10°51'·2E
   Oc(2)7s9m14M 080°-vis-320° (existence doubtful)
   F.R on radio mast 0·5m SE
4. **No.0** R/W buoy in entrance channel Iso.6s

Harbour
5. **W breakwater head** F.G
6. **E breakwater head** F.R

Note Lights correct for colour but periods may differ.

General
Houmt Souk is the capital of Jerba and the only port on the island easily accessible to yachts. Over the years the fishing fleet, many of them not from the island, has outgrown the small port but yachts can usually find a berth alongside a fishing boat or the *garde national* patrol boat. The village is one of the nicest along the Tunisian coast and if only for this reason worth a visit. The interior of the low-lying, semi-desert island is interesting as well and, because it is flat, well suited for exploration by bicycle. Protection in the port is good but occasionally the quays flood in the winter when the sea level is raised by northerlies. In 1997 there were plans to build 4 pontoons for yachts extending from the west breakwater, and dredging the area to 4m. Construction scheduled to start in 1999/2000.

Approach
The N coast of Jerba is fringed with banks of sand and seaweed which extend up to 4M from the shore. Entrance to the port is through a buoyed dredged channel, 4M long on a course of 190° with depths at low water from 3–5m; stay well in the centre as depths around the beacons are less. Beware of strong tidal streams which transverse the channel. The N extremity is marked with a single buoy, well visible, but note that it is not in line with the centre of the channel, which is marked by several pairs of buoys. Do not confuse the palm fronds on the drying banks around the channel for buoys. The basin is protected by low breakwaters which are almost flooded at HW.

Landmarks on the N coast are from W to E.
- There is now a telecommunications tower approx 50m high just inland of the harbour and this, if approached on a bearing of 185/90°, will bring you to the entrance of the buoyed channel. This tower can be seen almost 10M off.
- A small fortress with light tower at Bordj Djellidj.
- The control tower of the airport (best landmark).
- A group of eucalyptus trees and the Bordj El Kebir fortress in the port.
- Some white hotels E of the port.

Visibility is often reduced to 5–6M during the summertime. The flood stream sets W and the ebb stream sets E.

Night entry is not recommended as the lights do not function reliably; anchor either close to the entrance of the channel or on the W side of the island SSW of the Bordj Djellidj light in depths which shoal gradually towards the shore. With the predominant summer easterlies, protection on the W side of the island is better.

Berthing
In the outer basin visitors can tie up to one of the larger fishing boats or the patrol boat from the *garde*

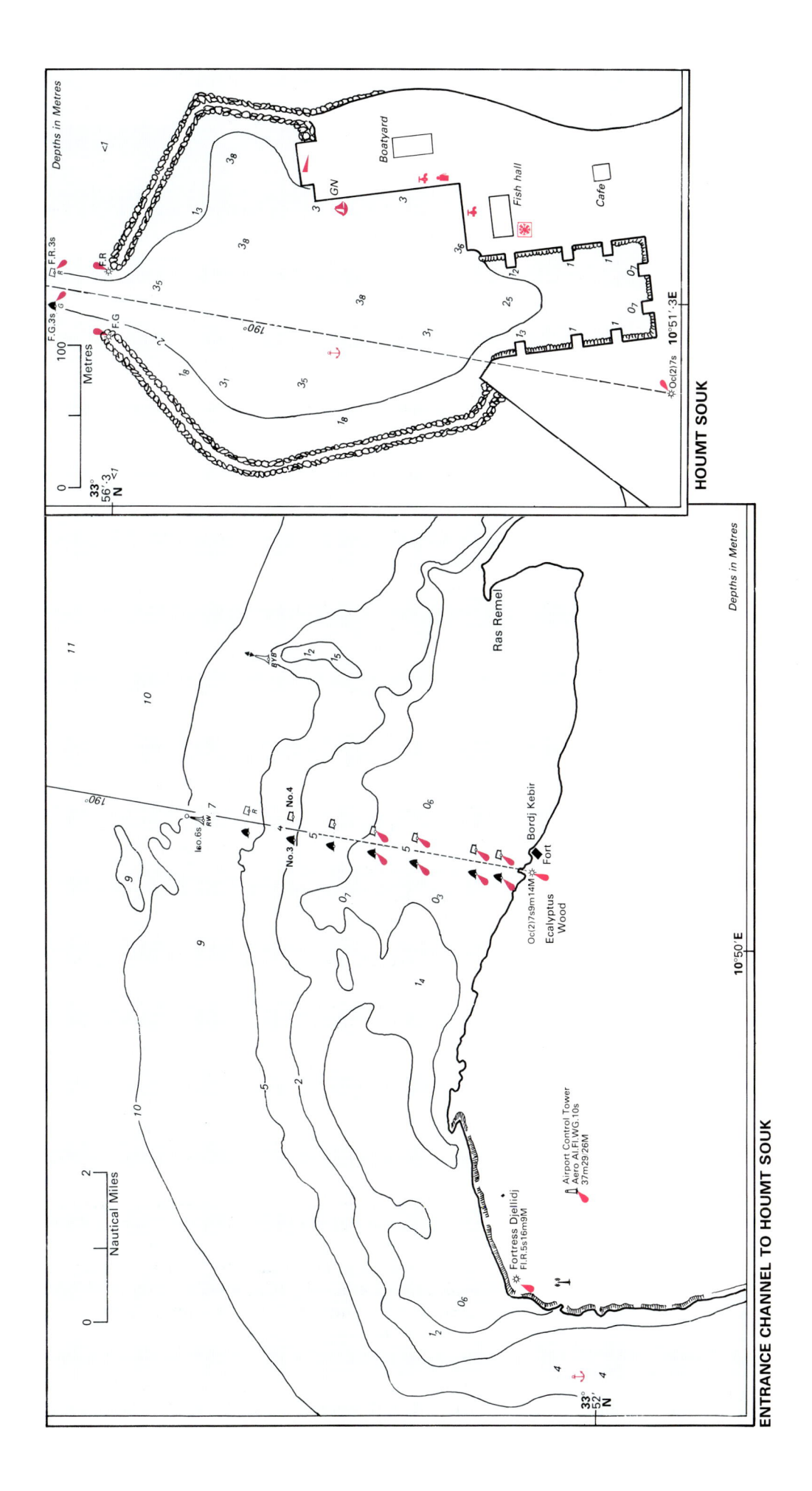

Tunisia

HOUMT SOUK

ENTRANCE CHANNEL TO HOUMT SOUK

195

North Africa

Fishing boats anchored off Bordj El Kebir, Houmt Souk

national. There is a temporary anchorage on the W side of the outer basin. The unquayed inner basin, aside from being shallow, is usually crammed with small fishing boats.

Formalities
☎ 05 650135 (0730–1330) VHF Ch 16.
Port of entry. Harbour dues at CGP rates. Police in the town, customs at the airport. *APIP* and *marine marchande* just outside the vehicular port entrance are helpful.

Facilities
Water Two water taps in the SE corner of the outer basin.
Electricity None readily available.
Fuel Diesel on the quay as indicated on harbour plan.
Repairs A boatyard with slip.
Provisions The village, 2km from the port, has a good local market and a *magasin général*. There is a small grocery shop, Magasin du Port, and a fruit stand about halfway between the port and village. English language newspapers are available in a book shop next to the main post office. There is a café in the port.
Post office, telephone and banks In the village.

Weather forecast
From Djeban Airport ☎ 05 650109 (24hr)

Eating out
A benefit of the tourist development in Jerba is that Houmt Souk has a wide choice of restaurants. Restaurant Haroun, just outside the port, with a French trained chef, has excellent fish specialities.

Transport
The major car hire agencies have offices in Houmt Souk.

Tourism
With its natural beauty, warm climate and wide sandy beaches, Jerba was a logical place for tourist development and it has become Tunisia's most successful endeavour in this field. In spite of the considerable number of visitors every year, the island has remained relatively unspoilt and the number of tourists is never objectionable except perhaps in mid-summer. All hotels are concentrated on the NE coast and because none of them are massive, they blend in with the surrounding landscape. Perhaps the special atmosphere of Houmt Souk is explained by the different population of Kharijites and Jews, who lived on the island for centuries. However, as is often the case with enterprising islanders, Jerbans have moved away from their island and settled on the mainland of Tunisia. Many of them operate grocery corner shops which are therefore called 'Djerbans'. There are still a few synagogues on the island but over the years most Jews have moved to Israel. In spite of these changes and the influx of tourists, Houmt Souk remains a charming place with its covered *souks*, narrow streets and shaded squares.

Ajim
33°42'·8N 10°44'·5E

Distances
Gabès 35M, Houmt Souk 33M

Tides
MHWS	MHWN	MLWN	MLWS
1·2m	0·7m	0·5m	0·1m

Charts
	Approach	Port
Admiralty	3403	–
French	7524, 4242	–
US	52160	–

Lights
Approach
1. **Passe Ouest** 33°42'·1N 10°36'·3E. Fl(2)9s5m8M
   Tank on masonry base
2. **No.1** buoy in port channel Fl(3)G.15s
   Green and white horizontal stripes on metal tripod
3. **No.2** buoy black and white horizontal stripes on metal tripod
4. **No.3** buoy – as No.1 light, unknown
5. **No.4** buoy – as No 2. light, unknown

Harbour
In 1997 there were no harbour lights

General
The small jetty at Ajim, which is used by the ferry to Tarf el Djorf on the mainland, has recently been upgraded into a proper fishing port. The port does not have breakwaters as it is between the drying banks of the Canal d'Ajim. This channel separates the island of Jerba from the mainland and leads to the Bahiret el Bou Grara, an enclosed gulf. The Gulf of Bou Grara is barred on the E side by a causeway which connects the SE point of Jerba with the mainland. Strong tidal streams flow through the Canal d'Ajim and the entrance is very difficult to negotiate. At least one yacht is known to have made the passage but not without running aground. The challenge is probably the only good reason to visit Ajim because the village, although not unattractive

Tunisia

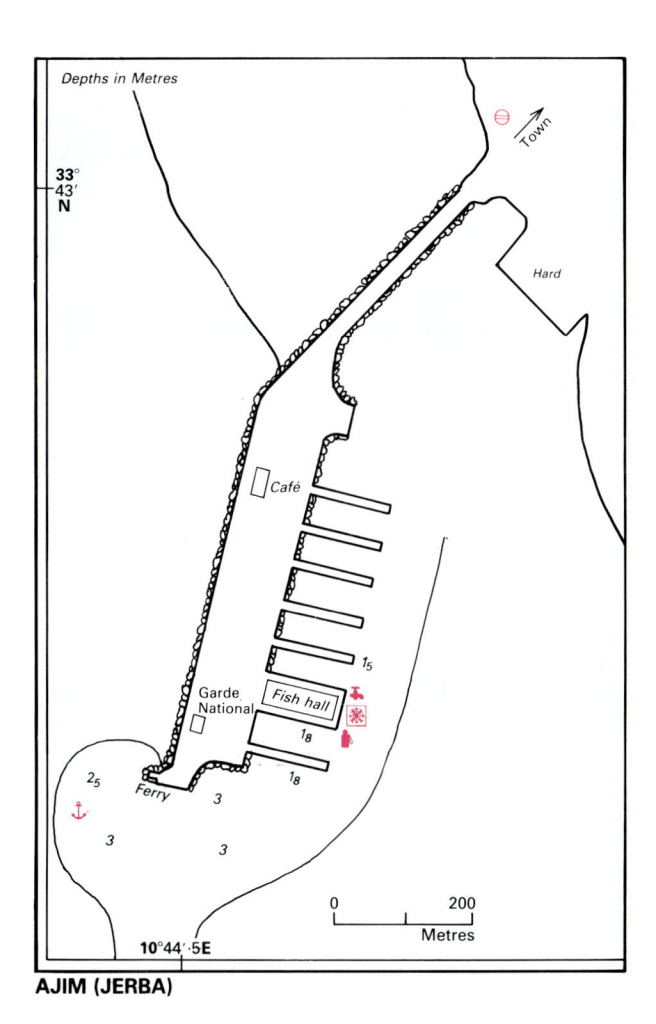

AJIM (JERBA)

with its white washed houses, is without any particular interest.

Approach
Two natural channels, Passe Nord and Passe Ouest, respectively 3 and 4M W of Tarf el Djorf, lead to Canal d'Ajim. Neither is clearly buoyed and certain buoys may be missing or displaced. Buoyage is particularly confusing where the two channels merge with the main channel. In the entrance channels the tidal stream can reach a spring rate of 3kts and in the main channel off Ajim 5kts. An unmarked rocky bank in the middle of the channel, 1½M W of Tarf el Djorf with depths of 1m has to be avoided. E of this bank the deep water is clear of dangers. From Canal d'Ajim a short dredged and buoyed channel leads to the port. There are two pairs of buoys marking the channel as indicated in the *Lights* section. This channel is used by the ferry and is dredged to 3m. Depths in the port are around 1·5m at MLWS. The fishermen of Ajim use these channels everyday as they go to their fishing grounds in the Gulf of Gabès but most of their boats do not draw more than 0·75m.

Berthing
The pier S of the fish hall probably has more than 1·5m as an old ferry was tied up there in 1989. Stay as close as practical to the quays since the E side of the port is shallow. Alternatively anchor SW of the ferry landing; good holding in sand and seaweed, but approach carefully as exact depths are uncertain. All suitable berths were taken by fishing boats in 1997.

Formalities
Garde national only.

Facilities
Water and diesel On the fish quay.
Provisions Only a café in the port. A selection of shops in the village plus PTT, bank and garage (diesel and petrol).
Repairs A small crane on the quay. Boatyard on the beach behind the port.

Bou Grara
33°32'·3N 10°41'·3E

Distances
Ajim 15M

Tides
MHWS	MHWN	MLWN	MLWS
0·8m	0·5m	0·5m	0·3m

Charts
	Approach	Port
Admiralty	3403	–
French	7524, 4245	–
US	52160	–

Lights
Harbour
Iso.2s7m8M

General
A very small fishing port, similar in layout to Zarat, set in an idyllic location in the remote SW corner of the Gulf of Bou Grara. Tall palm trees against a background of sandy cliffs and (rare nowadays) women and children searching for shellfish off the beach make Bou Grara look like a picture postcard. Visiting this port by sailing yacht presents the same sort of problems as visiting Ajim. From Ajim onward the Gulf has sufficient depths for any yacht,

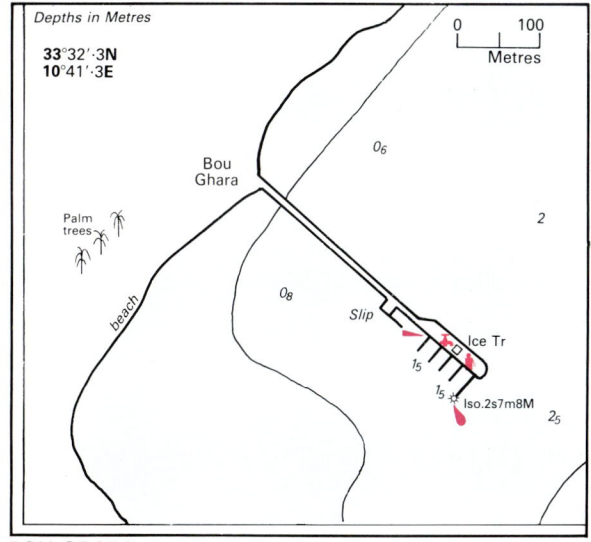

BOU GRARA

North Africa

The fishing-boat piers in Ajim

Women collecting shellfish in Bou Grara

but there are no buoys to mark the dangers. However with careful 'eye-ball' navigation and a suitable boat a visit to Bou Grara is possible and will be a unique experience.

Approach
Entrance to the Gulf of Bou Grara is as described under Ajim. French chart No. 4245 is required to cross the Gulf but buoyage in the channels marked 'Chenal Balise' is uncertain. The port buildings at the end of a long pier and a water tower and minaret in the village, 1km inland on low sandy cliffs, are conspicuous.

Berthing
Tie up where convenient. The port, dredged to 1·5m at MLWS, is not overcrowded.

Formalities
Garde national and *APIP*

Facilities
Water and diesel In the port but no petrol anywhere.
Provisions Only the most basic provisions are available in the hamlet of Bou Grara, 1km away. There is a small shop in the port.
Repairs A boatyard and small slip.

History
Though isolated today, Bou Grara has an interesting history. The Phoenicians were the first to establish a trading post in Bou Grara, then called Gightis, and the Romans took control after the campaign of Julius Caesar in 40BC. The Gulf of Bou Grara was a perfect natural harbour for their large fleet and the port was an important link in their trading route which went from Carthage via Puppet (Hammamet), El Djem and Tacape (Gabès) to Gightis and from there further S to Cydamus (Ghadames, in Libya). As a result of silting the port lost its importance and during the Arab invasions in the 7th century it was destroyed. Since that time the site was covered until excavated in 1906. The Roman ruins of Gightis are 2km from the port at the intersection of the road from the village with the main road between Djorf and Medenine and they are well worth a visit.

Zarzis
33°29'·9N 11°08'·5E

Distances
Sfax 77M, Houmt Souk 42M

Tides
MHWS	MHWN	MLWN	MLWS
1·0m	0·7m	0·5m	0·2m

Charts
	Approach	*Port*
Admiralty	3403	–
French	7524, 4245	–
US	52160	–

Lights
Approach
1. **LtHo** near customs house 33°29'·7N 11°07'·2E Oc(2+1)12s15m15M 180°-vis-090° Emergency light F.R.10M Obstn light on mast 3M WNW White 8-sided tower, black top

The fishing port of Zarzis viewed from SSE standing on the breakwater

North Africa

ZARZIS

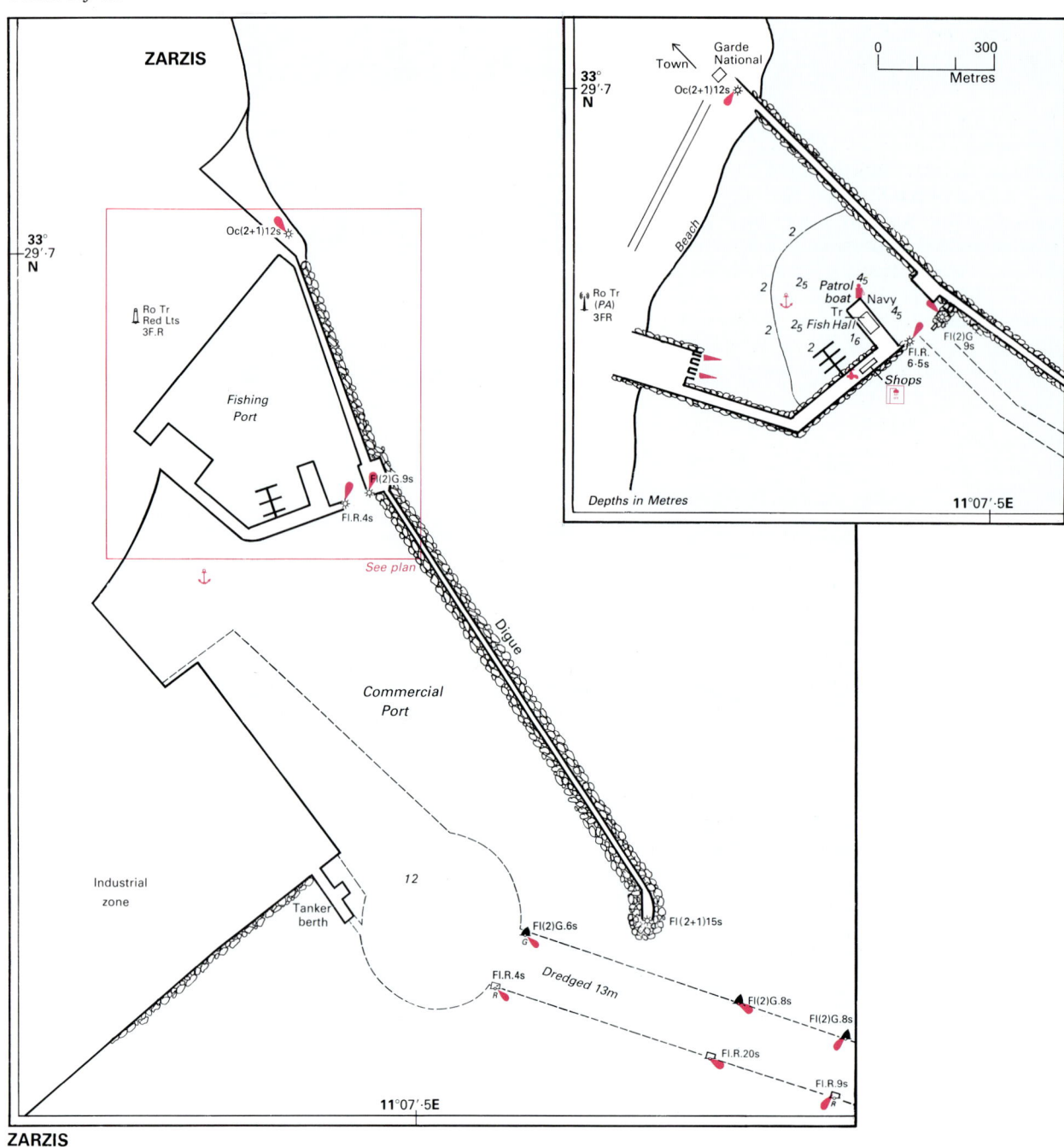

2. The dredged deep water entrance channel is marked with 4 buoys Fl(2)G.8s, Fl(2)G.8s and Fl.R.9s, Fl.R.20s

Harbour
3. **New breakwater head** Fl(2+1)15s11m12M Red and white tower
4. **Entrance fishing port** Fl(2)G.9s8m6M Green tower
5. **SW breakwater fishing port** Fl.R.6·5s10m6M red tower

General

Zarzis is the most southern port of Tunisia and probably more useful as a port of entry on passage from the eastern Mediterranean than as a place to visit when harbour-hopping along the coast but it is a good base to explore the Ksars in the south. The government has ambitious plans to develop Zarzis into a commercial port for oil and fertiliser products but a falling demand in world markets has delayed the construction of a potassium sulphate plant and consequently the new port, where a huge breakwater, quays and port buildings were finished in 1989, is only lightly used, in 1997 one Bulk Carrier and 3 large tugs occupied the port; the main activity is in the old fishing port. Protection is good and with the new breakwater entry can be made in any weather. The fishing port is busy. Yachts rarely visit.

Several new hotels line good beaches N of the town but they lack the surroundings and atmosphere of Jerba.

Approach
The coast N of Zarzis is backed by a chain of low hills, faced with cliffs, starting about 2M N of the town. The coast S of Zarzis, towards the Libyan border at Ras Ajdir, is low and backed by several lagoons. When approaching from the E avoid the shallows around Banc el Biban which extend up to 12M from the shore. The huge breakwater is probably the best landmark. At night, approach the entrance to the fishing port carefully as the starboard breakwater extends a considerable distance from the green light on it.

Note It is only 30M from the Libyan border and it is wise to stay well clear of Libyan territorial waters.

Berthing
Most likely visitors will find room around the fish hall. Alongside the patrol boat at the NW end of the fish quay is the most likely spot. Although the *APIP* recommended the small finger piers, these were crowded in 1997 and depths were no more than 2m on the outside. In strong northerly winds waves build up in the relatively large port. Alternatively anchor in the middle of the port. The basin shoals gradually towards the beach in the NW corner. Keep the tidal range in mind.

Formalities
☎ 05 680304 (0830–1300, 1500–1800) VHF Ch 10 24hrs. Control tower ☎ 05 680850.
Port of entry. Take paperwork ashore if anchored.

Facilities
Water Several water taps around the port.
Electricity None easily available.
Showers and WC As indicated in the plan.
Fuel Diesel pump in the port. Petrol from the town.
Provisions A good market, a *magasin général* and many small shops in the centre of the town, a good walk (3km) from the port. There is a café, shop and fruit and vegetable shop in the port.
Post office, telephone and bank In the town.
Repairs A boatyard and slip, workshops for mechanical repairs and Perkins agent.

Eating out
Throughout most of the Mediterranean the grouper (*mérou* in French) has disappeared but not so in Zarzis and this delicious fish can be found in the better restaurants.

Transport
Avis and Hertz have offices in the hotel area N of the town.

El Ketef
33°11'·1N 11°29'·3E

Distances
Zarzis 30M

In 1997 access to El Ketef was forbidden by the *garde national*, from the road, because of its proximity to Libya. Consequently it would be unwise to visit this port without getting permission first.

Tides
MHWS MHWN MLWN MLWS
1·0   0·6m 0·6m 0·3m

Lights
1. **Ras El Ketef** Iso.G.6s5M
2. **Ras El Ketef** Q(3)R.10s5M

General
El Ketef is a small fishing port in the middle of nowhere, near a minor cape called Ras el Ketef, 3M from the Libyan border. The port is built at the end of a long bridge-like pier in order to reach sufficiently deep water and is used by small fishing boats. It is planned to dredge the entrance and port to 2m. Once the port is finished, construction will start on a new village.

There is little reason to visit this port and it is only included for completeness.

North Africa

The Pelagie Islands

The Italian islands of Lampedusa, Linosa and Lampione are grouped together as the Pelagie Islands but geologically they are quite different. Lampedusa and Lampione are both low, flat, limestone islands situated on the edge of the Tunisian continental shelf while volcanic Linosa rises steeply from the sea bottom as the most southern volcano in the chain that starts north at Mount Etna.

The rocky islet of Lampione, only 700m long, has been uninhabited since the lighthouse-keeper left when the lighthouse was automated. A small landing, built during the Second World War, is used today by the occasional diving boat; it is not described further here.

Lampedusa and Linosa were both inhabited in ancient times but there are no historic remains. Unfortunately modern man has not been as careful about erasing the traces of his presence. In the past century, Lampedusa has turned into a barren island, bereft of practically all vegetation through careless soil management. It is hard to imagine that in 1800 the island had trees, fertile soil and wild boar. Lampedusa has over 4,000 inhabitants. A Loran station, operated by a small US navy crew, is located on the W end near Capo Ponente and when the American air force bombed Benghazi and Tripoli in 1986 the Libyans retaliated with an attack on these installations, which failed.

The fertile lava soil of Linosa proved less vulnerable to erosion and supports a variety of vegetation. In the 1880s the Italian government sent convicts to the islands, much to the dislike of the inhabitants. Today the Linosans, who number 450, live a peaceful existence. Fishing in this unpolluted part of the Mediterranean is the most important economic activity. Some income is made from tourism during the summer months and the terraced slopes between the dead craters are still farmed.

Lampedusa Island

35°29'·5N 12°36'E

Distances
Monastir 90M, Malta 107M

Tides
No data available.

Charts

	Approach	Port
Admiralty	2124	193
French	–	5023
US	53220	52170

Lights
Approach
1. **Capo Ponente** 35°31'·1N 12°31'·2E
   Fl(3)15s110m8M White metal pillar on pedestal 290°-vis-222° Iso.R on radio mast 740m E
   Note Several red lights in the top and green lights near the base of the radio tower for the Loran C station near Capo Ponente will be better visible from a distance.
2. **Capo Grecale** 35°31'·0N 12°37'·9E
   Fl.5s82m22M White 8-sided tower on dwelling 112°-vis-075°

Harbour
3. **Punta Maccaferri** Fl.G.3s17m8M
4. **Punta Guitgia** Fl.R.3s14m8M
5. **Punta Favalore breakwater head** Fl.R.5s7m7M
6. **Health Office Pier** F.R.7m3M

General
In recent years Lampedusa has become a popular holiday island for mainland Italians and a popular stopover between Monastir and Malta for yachtsmen. The rich grounds on the edge of the North African continental shelf are fished by large trawlers from Sicily and what is not processed on the island is shipped to Palermo. Many Italians are attracted by the good diving in the unpolluted waters around Lampedusa. In the summer season the port is busy with trawler traffic, a hydrofoil service, passenger and freight ferries and numerous small pleasure craft. It offers good protection but there is not much room on the quays and the anchorage is mediocre.

Approach
Straightforward but at night the lights on Capo Ponente can be confusing. The lights of the Loran station are likely to be seen before Capo Ponente light which is not very strong. With onshore winds the sea builds up and runs through the entrance.

Entrance
Depending on the wind direction, the daily ferry to Sicily sometimes runs a mooring line to the end of the Favalore breakwater, effectively blocking the entrance. The ferry usually docks between 0800–1000. Similarly Cala Guitgia is occasionally blocked for a day or two by the mooring line of the fuel tanker discharging near the fuel reservoirs.

Berthing
There is not much room for visiting yachts in the busy port. Try the inside of the west (Favalore) breakwater or the new extension of the short pier at Punta della Sanita. Depths from 3m at the end to 1·5m near the light No. 6. Anchoring is probably the best but holding is not very good: a thin layer of soft mud over limestone and in places the bottom is foul with old moorings. Leave enough room for the fishing boats moored in Cala Salina.

Formalities
None.

The Pelagie Islands

LAMPEDUSA

North Africa

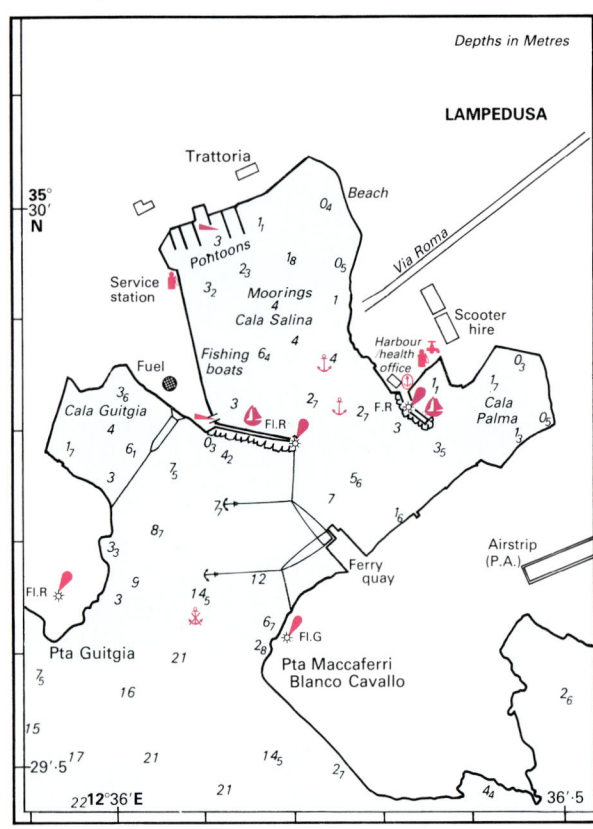

LAMPEDUSA

Anchorages around Lampedusa

Isola dei Conigli
35°30'·6N 12°33'·4E

There are pleasant anchorages on the W and E side of a small island on the S coast of Lampedusa with shelter from NW to NE. The island is not easily identified as such because it is almost attached to the shore. Beware of rocks on a bank 200m off the S side of the island. Good anchorage on either side in about 6m, sand.

Cala Calandra
35°30'·8E 12°37'·6E

A quiet, pretty anchorage tucked in the NW corner of Cala Creta on the E side of Lampedusa. Shelter from SW to NW. Anchor in sand, 6–10m.

Cala Pisana
35°30'·2N 12°37'·5E

Not a very picturesque anchorage but snug with good protection in case of strong westerlies. There is an emergency ferry landing on the S side. Do not proceed too far beyond this landing as the bay shallows gradually towards the head. Anchor in sand, 4–6m.

Linosa Island
35°52'N 12°52'·5E

Distances
Lampedusa 26M, Malta 85M

Charts

	Approach	Port
Admiralty	2124	193
French	–	5023
US	53220	52170

Lights
Approach
1. **Punta Arena Bianca** 35°51'·2N 12°51'·5E
   Fl.5s9m9M White square stone pillar and hut 276·5°-vis-150°
2. **Punta Beppe Tuccio** 35°52'·2N 12°52'·6E
   Fl(4)20s32m16M White round tower and dwelling 107°-vis-345° (arc varies with distance from light, at 6M 103°-vis-346°)

General
From seaward Linosa resembles Pantelleria but on a much smaller scale. The slopes between the dead craters are farmed and the island looks surprisingly green from the S. The N coast is more rugged and steep-to with large areas covered by black lava rocks. There is no port or anchorage with good all-round shelter but that need not prevent a visit in settled weather. Surprisingly, for such a remote island, the daily ferry drops off quite a few visitors during the summer but life in the small village is not much

Facilities
Water A water tap will be installed in the service station in Cala Salina but until then the attendant may run out on his scooter to fill containers which can also be filled at the service station in Cala Palma. Water quality is good as it is delivered from the mainland but there is also low purity local water on the island which is not for drinking.
Electricity None.
Fuel From the two service stations. The quay at the service station in Cala Salina has a depth of 2·3m.
Provisions Good provisions are available from a large Standa supermarket (opening hours 0830–1300 and 1700–2130) at the other end of the village and several smaller supermarkets along Via Roma. Photo and diving shops and several *gelaterias* in Via Roma.
Post office In the fifth block on Via Guglielmo Bontiglio, a right from Via Roma (towards the end).
Telephone Several card telephones.
Bank Three banks in Via Roma with ATMs.
Repairs Emergency engine repairs.

Eating out
Numerous *trattorias* around Cala Salina and in the village.

Transport
Daily ferry service to Porto Empedocle and thrice weekly to Trapani. Hydrofoil service to Porto Empedocle on Monday and Thursday between 1 June and 30 September. Flights to Palermo all year round and to Rome in July and August.

Cars and scooters may be hired near the service station in Cala Palma and in town. In the summer season reservations are necessary.

Anchorages around Lampedusa

The ferry and fishing quay with Cala Salina in the back, Lampedusa harbour viewed from the S

The small open ferry landing of Scalo Vecchio on Linosa

North Africa

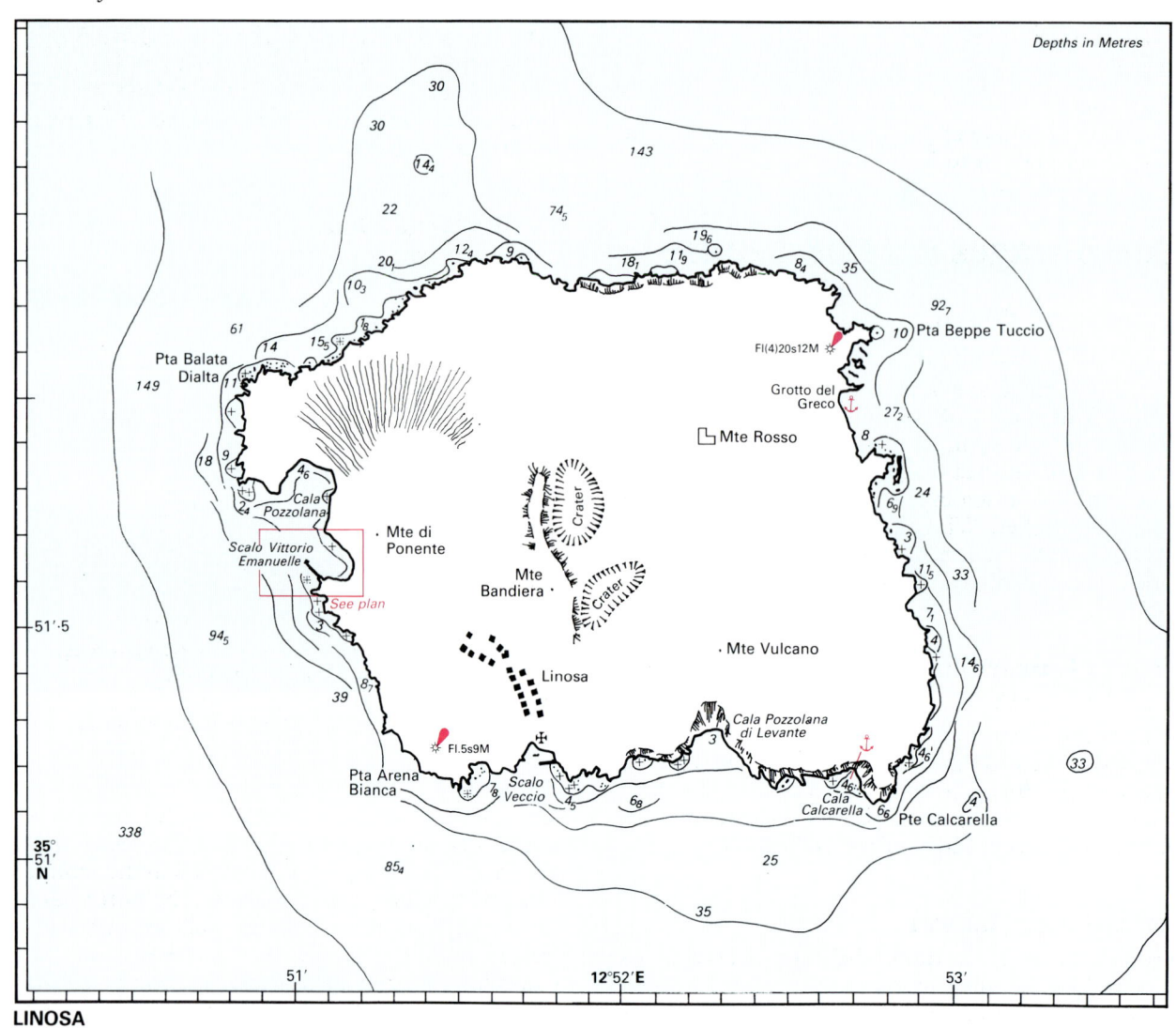

LINOSA

affected. Scalo Vecchio is a very small picturesque open port next to the village and the ferry landing provides the lifeline for the island.

Approach
No off-lying dangers.

Berthing
In settled weather one or two yachts could possibly lie stern-to a short quay in Scalo Vecchio. However there is not much room to drop the anchor and the bottom is rocky. A safer option is to anchor in Scalo Vittorio Emanuele. The large pier constructed for the ferry provides some additional protection but a swell from the NW would make the anchorage uncomfortable. Most of the quay on the inside of the pier is unusable because of submerged rocks but when there is no swell running, yachts can tie up at the end of the pier, leaving the ferry landing free for the hydrofoil. The anchorage is 3–5m deep, rocks, with reasonable holding. A further option is to anchor 400m N in Cala Pozzolana di Ponente in sand, with better protection from the NW swell. From the ferry landing a road leads to the village (about 20 minutes walk).

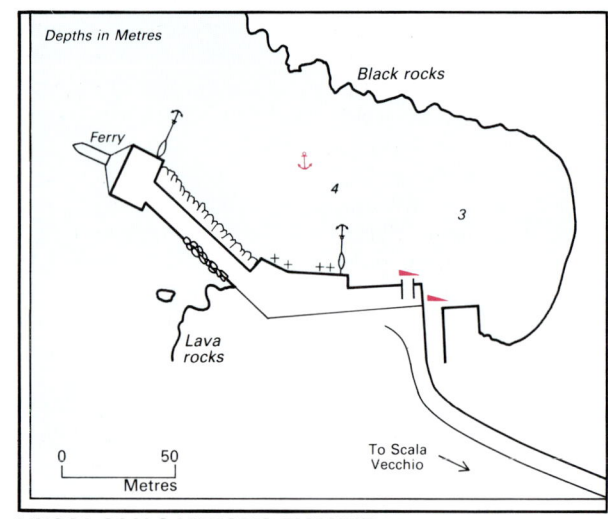

LINOSA SCALO VITTORIO EMANUELLE

206

Formalities
None

Facilities
There are a couple of grocery shops, a butcher and two restaurants (both facing the port) in the village.

Anchorages around Linosa

Grotto del Greco
35°52'·1N 12°52'·6E

A remote anchorage among rugged volcanic rocks 500m S of the lighthouse of Beppe Tuccio. The underwater caves in the N part of the bay are attractive to snorkel around. The bottom is large rocks with poor holding, 8–12m deep, only suitable in good weather. With no wind and leftover swell from the NW the anchorage is uncomfortable. A house on top of Mt Rosso can provide a useful bearing.

Punta Calcarella
35°51'·4N 12°52'·6E

A beautiful anchorage surrounded by steep rocks off the SE corner of the island. The sandy bottom shallows gradually towards the head of the bay, making anchoring easier and more secure than in Grotto del Greco. Shelter from NW to NE.

Pantelleria Island

Pantelleria is of a quite different character to Lampedusa because of its volcanic origins. The fertile soil on the terraced slopes is intensely farmed and even though tourism has grown considerably in the last 10 years, agriculture is still a major source of income. Capers and grapes are the main crops and Pantelleria has some good red and white wines. The island has two ports, the main harbour of Pantelleria in the NW corner and Porto Scauri on the W coast. Known human habitation goes back as far as the 18th century BC and the ruins of a Neolithic village from that time are found near Mursia, only a few kilometres from Pantelleria port. The island has been part of all the great Mediterranean empires but the Arabs were the first to start cultivation of the rich soil and they built the typical *dammuso* houses near their fields, still found all over the island. After the Arab period, Pantelleria was taken by the Normans and since that time it has been ruled from Sicily. During the Second World War the Allied Forces heavily bombed the island before they could advance from North Africa to Sicily and Pantelleria town was completely flattened.

There are good diving spots around the island and this is an important attraction for the mainly Italian visitors. Tourism has not reached an objectionable scale and outside of Pantelleria town the island is still rural and pretty. The Siremar ferry serves Pantelleria from Trapani, Monday through Saturday and daily in the months of July, August and September. The daily hydrofoil from Trapani to Kelibia (May–Oct.) stops in Pantelleria as well. There are daily flights from Palermo and Trapani all year round.

Pantelleria Port
36°50'N 11°56'·5E

Distances
Kelibia 40M, Malta 140M

Tides
No data available.

Charts

	Approach	Port
Admiralty	2122, 2123	193
French	4315	5023
US	53220	53223

Lights
Approach
1. **Punta San Leonardo** 36°50'·1N 11°56'·7E
   Fl.3s21m15M Yellow building Reserve light range 8M Fl.R.2·5s on radio mast 1·6M SSE

Harbour
2. **Porto di Pantellaria outer breakwater head**
   Fl.G.5s7m3M

General
An active and not particularly attractive port but an interesting contrast with Tunisia. The lively quays are lined with shops, restaurants and, in the summer time, with Italian holidaymakers. The port is used by a small fishing fleet as well as occasional freighters and the Siremar ferry. In recent years new quays have been built in Porto Vecchio and Porto Nuovo and in 1989 work was in progress on a large breakwater. Until finished, protection from the prevailing NW winds will remain poor. Swell from this direction easily enters Porto Vecchio. The floating pontoons for visiting yachts installed in Porto Nuovo offer better protection but they are further from the town centre and their nondescript surroundings will remain dusty as long as construction of the breakwater continues. Reasonable facilities are available in the town.

With NW winds over Force 7 Porto Nuovo is the only safe port on the island as in these conditions swell also enters Porto Scauri.

Approach
The island is quite high and Pantelleria is the only major town in the relatively flat NW corner. A night approach should definitely be avoided as the unlit, detached part of the new breakwater makes the entrance very confusing. There are no lights in the port and will probably be none until the new breakwater is finished

Entrances
Porto Vecchio Beware of the partially submerged remains of an old breakwater in the middle of the entrance.
Porto Nuovo Rocks barely awash extend off the N

The yacht quay in Porto Vecchio, Pantelleria viewed from NW

breakwater and the southern half of the entrance is shallow. Safe entry is made by rounding the N breakwater atj211
 a distance of between 10m and 25m. Do not enter in strong NW winds.

Berthing
In good weather the best berth is on your own anchor stern-to the quayed N breakwater in Porto Vecchio. Draught permitting, smaller yachts can tie up stern-to the E quays. In strong northwesterlies swell makes all berths in Porto Vecchio intolerable. Under these conditions the safest berth is on the new floating pontoons or on the quay (mooring lines planned) in Porto Nuovo.

Facilities
Water Two taps on the quays.
Electricity None.
Fuel From two service stations around Porto Vecchio.
Provisions Reasonable choice from several shops and a supermarket.
Post office and banks In the town with ATMs.

Repairs Limited possibilities but several repair shops for outboards and inflatables.

Eating out
Several restaurants around the port.

Local transport
Car hire in town.

Anchorages around Linosa

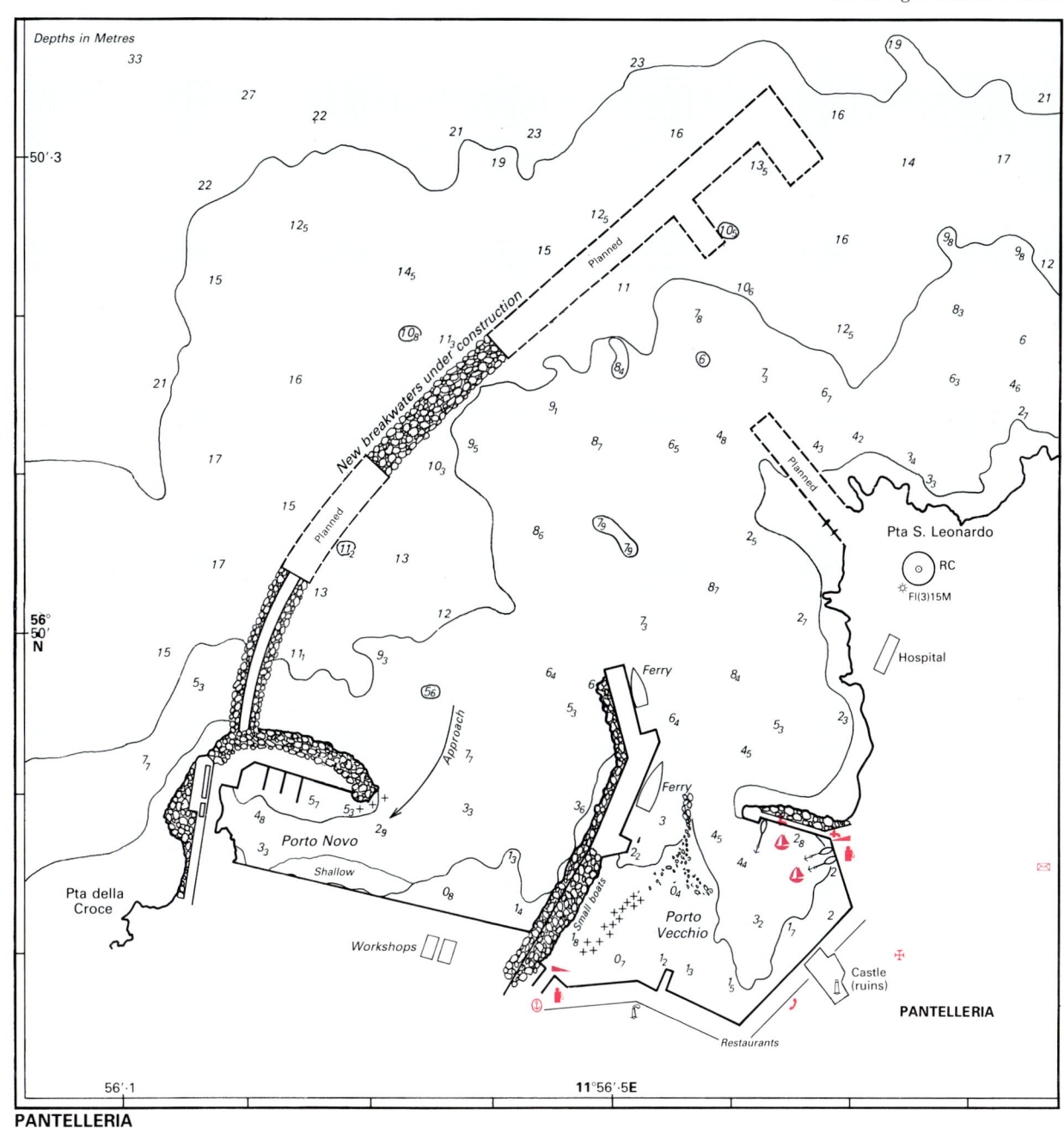

Porto Scauri
36°46'N 11°58'E

Distances
Pantelleria 6M

Lights
Approach
1. **Punta Tre Pietra** 36°46'·1N 11°57'·5E
   Fl.5s18m10M White metal column on pedestal
Harbour
2. **Marina W mole head** Fl.R.3s7m3M
3. **E mole head** Fl.G.3s7m3M

General
Although by no means a new port, its existence is not well known and it appears as though the Italians do not want to know about what seems to be a planning mistake. They refer to the port as 'Marina di Scauri' but there is nothing in the port and it is not maintained. It is mainly used by transient fishermen from Sicily and the occasional yacht that likes the tranquillity. Protection is good in normal weather. In summer time holidaymakers bathe in one corner. The small floating pontoons, with gutted electricity boxes and taps which do not work, are used to tie up inflatables and small craft. If tranquillity is a requirement and not supplies, it is a nice stop. In strong northwesterlies (Force 7 and

209

North Africa

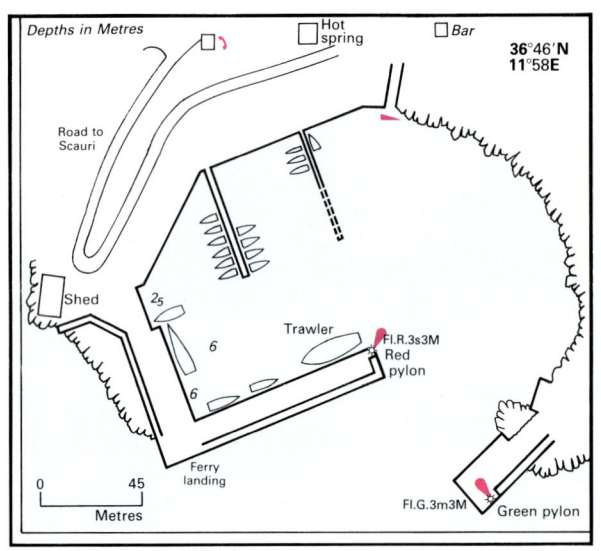

PORTO SCAURI

more) swell rolls around Punta Tre Pietra and into the port. Entry in strong southwesterlies is not recommended.

Approach
The small port is not easily visible from seaward as it is tucked in the corner of the bay and there are no buildings. A deserted white hotel with domed arches on top of Punta Tre Pietra is conspicuous from W to S. Even though the harbour lights will probably never be repaired, a night approach would not be too difficult as the port has good street lights to accommodate the fishing boats.

Berthing
Tie up alongside or with a stern anchor to the W or S quay. The floating pontoons are too small for yachts. The first pontoon and the inner part of the starboard breakwater have both been badly damaged by storms. The ferry landing is not in use.

If caught in a strong north or southwesterly lie along the S quay with a breast anchor or stern-to the W quay but neither will be very comfortable due to the swell. There is only room for a few yachts.

Formalities
No officials whatsoever but the port comes under the jurisdiction of Pantelleria.

Facilities
Water The warm spring water in the port can be used for a warm shower or laundry but it is not fit to drink.
Electricity No electricity.
Provisions There are no shops or other facilities in the port. However in the pleasant little village of Scauri on top of a steep hill (15 minutes walk from the port) there is a baker, an *alimentari*, a *pizzeria* and a *trattoria*. A visit is worth the effort if only for the pleasant walk. When there are enough fishing boats, bread is delivered to the port in a small truck.

Scauri village in mid-summer

Malta

This archipelago lies between latitudes 36°57'N to 35°48'N and 14°35'E to 14°11'E

Distances
Monastir 185M, Kelibia 180M, Lampedusa 107M, Crete 450M.

Tides

MHWS	MHWN	MLWN	MLWS
0·5m	0·5m	0·5m	0·4m

Charts

	Approach	Port
Admiralty	2124, 2537, 2538, 2623974	
French	–	–
US	53204, 53206	53205

Lights
Approaches
  Delimara Point (SE end) Fl(2)12s35m18M R lights on chimney 0·7M N
  Giordan (NW corner of Gozo) Fl.7·5s180m20M
Grand Harbour Approach
1. **St Elmo** 35°54'·2N 14°31'·2E Fl(3)15s49m19M Metal framework tower on Fort St Elmo
2. **St Elmo breakwater head** Q.G.16m7M White round tower, red band on E side
3. **Ricasoli breakwater** Q.R.11m6M 120°-obscd-157° when firing or searchlight practices are taking place Metal structure on white round stone tower, red bands on E side F.R radio mast 0·5M SE

Marsamxett Harbour Approach
4. **Dragut Point** has been extinguished for some years
5. **Msida Marina Jetty head** Q.G.5m2M

General

Malta, with an area of 316km2, has a population of 341,000 of whom 25,000 live on Gozo. Maltese and English are the official languages and Italian, French and German are widely spoken. (Maltese has Arabic roots but a Roman alphabet.) The time difference is UT+1 hour and UT+2 hours from the last Sunday in March until the last Sunday in September, but these dates may vary.

The Maltese Islands consist of the main island of Malta, where the majority of the population lives, Gozo, Comino and the uninhabited islets of St Paul's and Fifla. The latter is a nature reserve and landing is prohibited. With its central location in the Mediterranean, Malta is much used by yachts on their way to and from Tunisia and Sicily, and by yachts moving westwards from Crete. It is also a popular place to winter afloat.

The island used to be a major base for the Royal Navy and the American fleet, with full refit facilities, dry docks and a highly skilled workforce. However, when Dom Mintoff came to power in the 1970s he formed a preferential alliance with Libya, and subsequently ran down naval facilities. Malta has never really recovered from this, although the facilities were later offered to the Russian Navy and in recent times to commercial shipping. A reliance on trade with Libya is still an important part of the islands economy, with passenger ferries arriving daily from Tripoli; Malta provides one of the only possible destinations for Libyans with the current embargo on flights out of the country.

During the Mintoff era, it became very difficult to obtain permission to sail around the coast and anchoring was virtually forbidden. Since the Nationalist government took office in 1987, facilities for yachts have greatly improved and cruising restrictions around the islands have been removed.

Grand Harbour

Grand harbour is the main commercial harbour of the island with few facilities or concessions to yachtsmen.

The gap in the St Elmo Breakwater just under the Fort carries 5m in the western gap and 8m in the eastern one.

Formalities
The main customs point is on the NW side of the harbour at Hay Wharf, half a mile beyond the old unused customs house below the Barracca Gardens. From 1 July customs officials work longer hours and only late at night do yachts have to report to Grand Harbour. Customs and immigration officials are also located at Mgarr Harbour, Gozo, so that yachts can check out from there on the way to Sicily.

Facilities
Repairs There is a small yard in Kalkara Creek with laying up and repair facilities for yachts, and yards at the industrial and commercial end of the harbour at Marsa where work on large yachts could be undertaken. French and Dockyard Creeks contain dry docks and facilities for repairing the largest commercial vessels.

Marsamxett Harbours
35°54'·5N 14°31'E

Yachting facilities are concentrated in Lazaretto Creek and Msida Creek in Marsamxett harbour. Here are probably the best facilities in the Mediterranean for boat maintenance and repairs.

Protection in Marsamxett harbour is good in almost any weather except during a *gregale*, the feared NE wind. The natural harbour is completely open to this wind and strong *gregales* (Force 6 or more), which occur every winter, produce a heavy swell and considerable surge in the confines of the harbour, particularly in Lazaretto and Sliema Creeks. Msida Marina is more protected by its new breakwater which reduces the surge and there is more shelter from wind.

Beware of thieves, particularly in Lazaretto Creek where dinghies, outboards and bicycles are popular targets.

Manoel Island Yacht Yard and Msida Marina are guarded and more secure.

Approach
The Maltese Islands are low-lying with a maximum

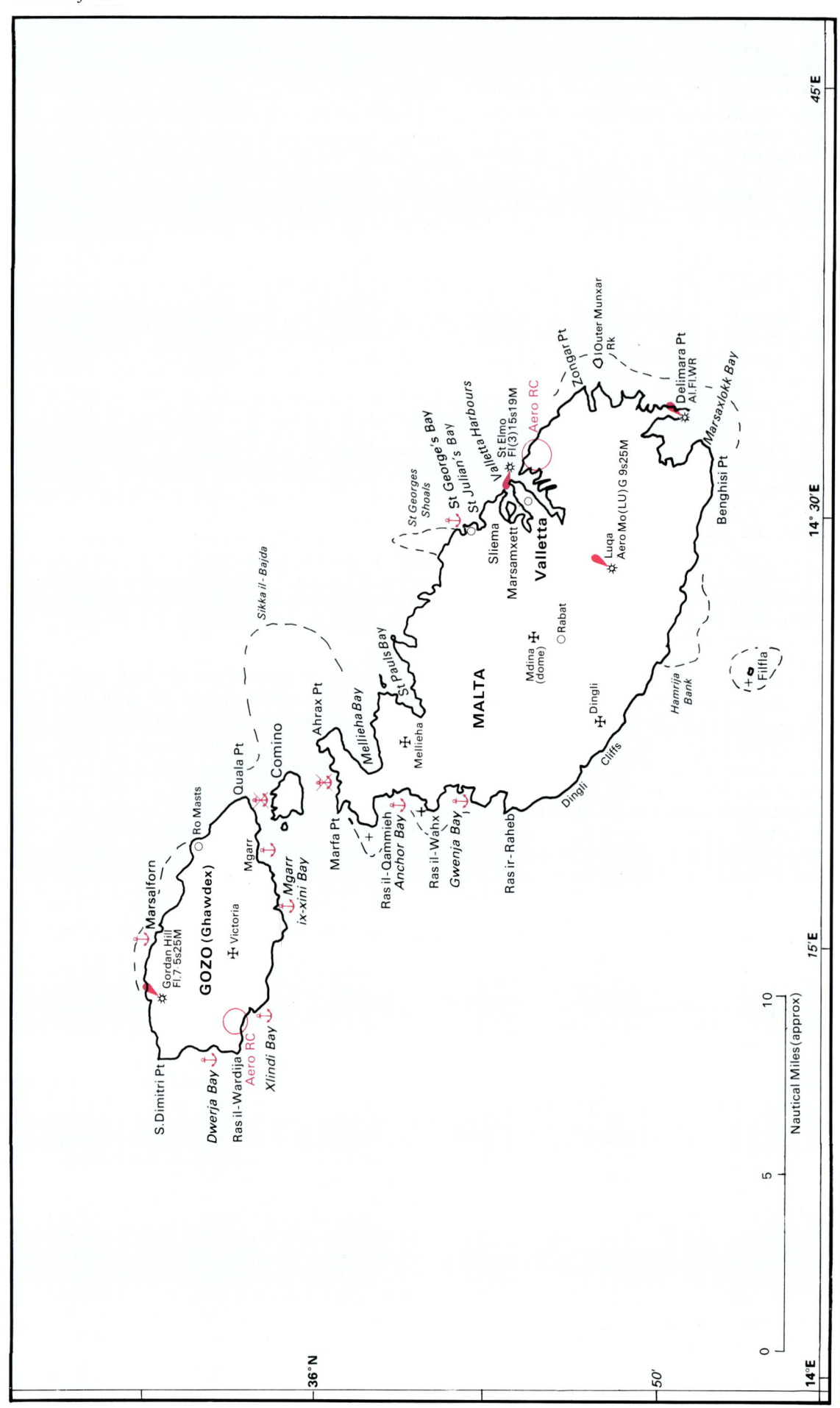

MALTA AND GOZO ISLANDS

elevation of 240m but the approach is not difficult as the coast is free from off-lying hazards, with the exception of Fifla Island S of Malta which is unlit. The passages between Gozo, Comino and Malta are free of dangers. The entrance to Marsamxett is not apparent until it opens up to the SW. Dragut Point, now unlit, should be given a wide berth. A night time approach from the Fairway buoy, (Fl.8s) having identified St Elmo and the main breakwater lights, should present no difficulties.

Formalities
Yachts should announce their arrival to Valletta Port Control on VHF Ch 12 to receive berthing instructions. Normally yachts are directed to Marsamxett Harbour but late at night or at the weekend yachts may be requested to proceed to the Grand Harbour to clear customs (see above).

Customs, immigration and the harbourmaster are all in Msida Marina. Pick up a berth immediately inside the marina breakwater by the green light tower. The offices are by the bows of a three-masted hulk masquerading as a restaurant. Ship's papers and all passports will be required but no visas. Stay is unlimited. Pets are not allowed and yachts with pets on board are usually given short notice to leave Maltese waters. They are occasionally allowed to anchor for a short time in mid-stream. Yachts in an unallocated berth should leave someone on board to warp clear if the owner of the berth returns. After clearing, a yacht is free to cruise the islands but note that harbour dues start from the time it ties up to a quay unless it leaves immediately after clearing. The intention to leave Malta should be announced 24 hours in advance in order to settle these bills and to receive customs clearance. Yachts moored in the port should at all times be under the charge of the master or someone duly authorised to assume full responsibility for the yacht.

Customs and immigration are also situated in Mgart Harbour, Gozo during the summer months.

Berthing
There are three areas available to berth: Msida Marina, Lazaretto Creek or Manoel Island Pier.

Msida Marina
Msida Marina has over 600 berths, mostly occupied, up to 15m in length, at pontoons with out-hauls provided.

This is the only reasonably safe berthing area afloat over the winter. Examples of berthing fees both here and in Lazaretto Creek in 1997 (including water and electricity) in Maltese pounds are
Season rates 1/5–30/9

	10–12m	12–14m
6 months	337	397
Monthly	81	95
Weekly	34	40
Daily	50	50

Live-aboards on season or annual (approx 75% of summer plus winter) are charged 30% extra).

Facilities
Water and electricity Available and metred.
Showers and toilets Free.
Fuel See section on *General Facilities*.

Lazaretto Creek
The old marina in Lazaretto Creek provides 130 berths along both Lazaretto Quay on Manoel Island and Ta'Xbiex Quay on the opposite side. Berthing can be confusing as there is no reception quay. Before selecting a berth call the harbourmaster on Ch 9. Yachts go bows or stern-to the quay. There is an amazing array of anchors, heavy ground tackle, anchor chains and lines. The heavy ground chain off both quays may or may not be marked by rusty oil drums secured to it by substantial but unreliable chain. If no obvious haul-off shows in the selected or allocated berth, use your own anchor; try to drop it well out and clear of the ground chain and always use a tripping line.

The bottom is mud and holding is good provided you don't select an area still littered with discarded ironwork.

An alternative is to anchor in the middle of the creek. This is a sensible choice if entering for the first time at night. In summer it is also cooler than alongside or in the marina; and more secure against thieving fingers.

Wintering
Unless the boat can be secured with very heavy tackle, enough room to swing and with a reliable guardian, Lazaretto Creek is not a place to leave a yacht for any length of time in the winter. The berths on the quays are subject to a heavy surge and movement during a *gregale*, and are not recommended even if living on board; reserve a place on the hard. If living aboard, particularly on a smaller yacht, Msida Marina will be found to be much more comfortable.

Manoel Island Pier, Sliema Creek
There are a few rather rough alongside berths at Manoel Island Pier and some yard moorings off it for boats waiting to slip at the yard or after launching. Water and electricity at the pier.
Apply to Manoel Island Yacht Yard for a berth.
☎ 334453/4, 334320 *Fax* 343900/80021.

Facilities
Water and electricity On the serviced quays metered water and electricity (120 or 240v/50Hz) can be hooked up on work days when staying longer than a few days. The water quality is quite reasonable.
Fuel A fuel barge selling duty-free diesel is moored 300m to the ENE of Misdi Marina entrance. Petrol and lubricants are also stocked. This is the best and most convenient way of fuelling. The alternative is to order delivery of duty-paid fuel by tanker through the Marina or your Agent or direct from the Falzon Service Station, Birkirkara ☎ 442763. Duty-free diesel from the same source can be ordered given

VALETTA HARBOUR

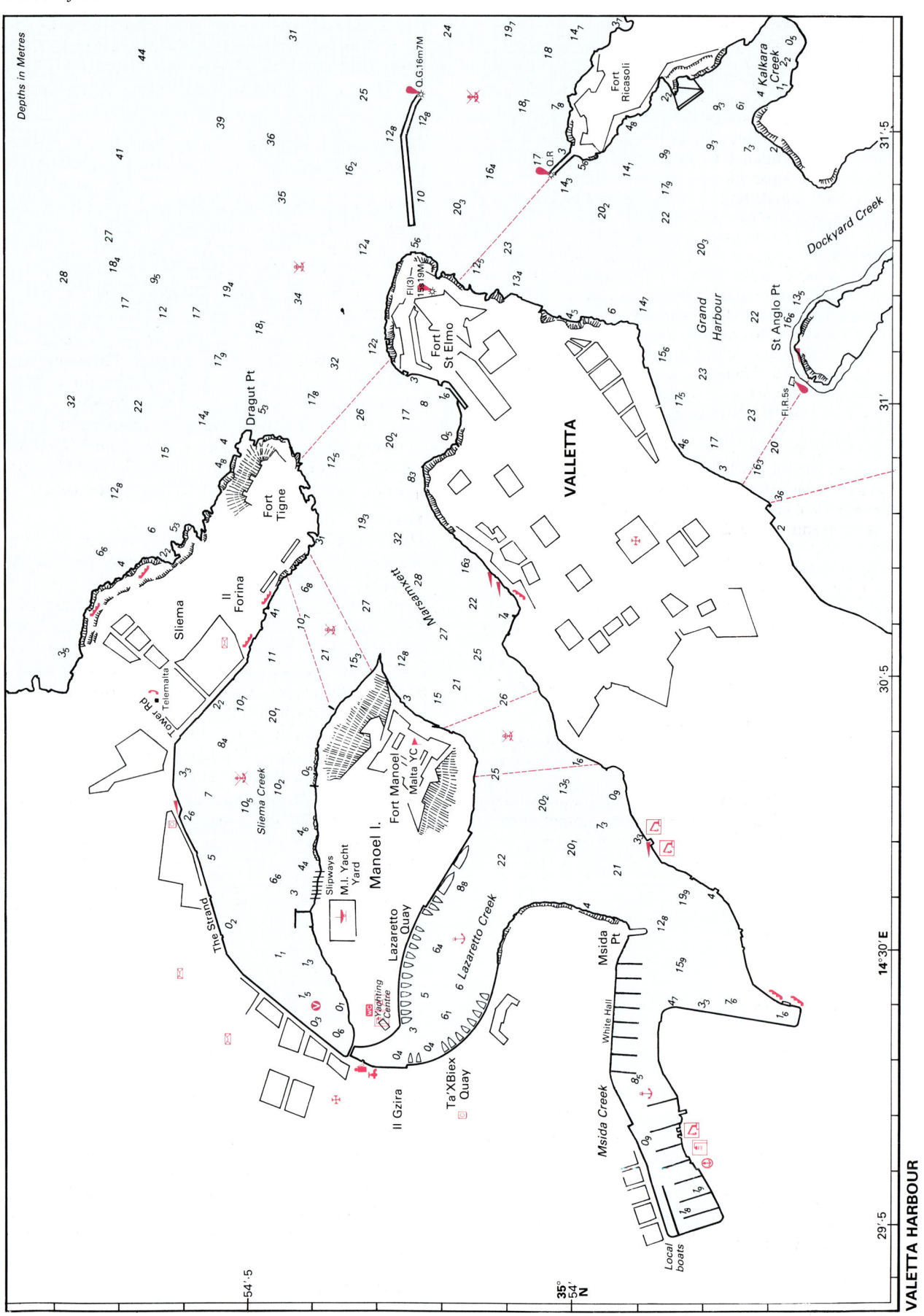

three days' notice prior to departure but will be subject to a minimum quantity.

Fuel may also be obtained in cans from the service station at the end of Manoel Island Bridge; this is closed on Sundays and public holidays.

Provisions Good provisions are available, although fruit and vegetables (only available from trucks) are seasonal and limited. Carefully check the prices, weights and quantities dispensed by the truck owners who have nimble fingers and a bazaar attitude. Also check for fruit about to turn rotten which he may slip in, especially if the vendor knows you are leaving! Excellent bread and very good, cheap frozen meat from Ireland, Australia and New Zealand. Not much fish which mostly goes to the restaurants. The best supermarket and well worth the walk, (20 minutes) is the Tower Self Service Store on Tower Road in Sliema. They will deliver to the boat if a sizeable order is placed. There is a good butcher, Charles nearby. There are some small shops on the Strand close to Manoel Island Bridge with a limited range but cheerful service.

Shopping Mon–Sat 0830–1245 1430–1730. Some small shops close for lunch between 1300 and 1600 and remain open later in the evening.

Duty free Alcoholic beverages can be ordered through the yacht agents. Allow 2–3 days for delivery.

Showers At Msidi Marina.

Post office Next to the Health Centre in Gzira and signposted from the Strand.

Telephone Overseas calls can be made from public telephones taking coins or telecards on The Strand or from Telemalta at the top of Tower Hill, Sliema. Private telephone connections are available at some of the serviced quays and in the marina is staying any length of time.

Mail Can be directed to and kept by your Agent.

Bank Banking hours are Mon–Thur 0830–1230, Fri 1700–1900, Sat 0830–1200. Several banks near the bridge to Manoel Island.

Medical The Health Centre in Gzira is 10 minutes walk from Manoel Island and is good for uncomplicated medical problems. If X-rays or special tests are required it is better to go to St Luke's hospital in Msida. In normal circumstances services are free of charge.

Laundry Around the corner from RLR chandlery with another launderette on the Strand shortly before Tower Road.

Weather forecast

Local weather forecast for Malta +50M is given on VHF Ch 12 and 04 in summer at 0803, 1203, 1803 and 2303 (local times) and in winter at 0703, 1103, 1703 and 2203. Unfortunately, channel 12 is not always audible on the far side of the islands. A forecast is available from the Meteorological office, ☎ 249170/2. German World Service has a relay station in Malta which broadcasts an extensive sea weather forecast for the entire Mediterranean on 1557kHz at about 1745 UT Monday to Saturday and between 1710 and 1715 UT on Sundays. On NAVTEX Malta is letter O for Oscar.

Eating out

Malta does not have a tradition of haute cuisine but the tourist trade has encouraged some good restaurants. In Paceville (about 20 minutes by bus from Gzira) there is a wide choice and there are fast food shops closer. The hospitable Valletta Yacht Club in Fort Manoel has good bar and dining facilities in one of the nicest locations on the island.

Transport

The old, colourfully decorated buses go everywhere in Malta and are cheap. Taxis in comparison are quite expensive as are *carrozzis*, the horse-drawn carriages which have reappeared to please the tourists. Sadly, the hundreds of colourful *dghaisas* (pronounced die-soes) which provided the main cross and inter-harbour transport have all but vanished following the withdrawal of the Royal Navy from Malta.

Air There are several flights daily to London and other destinations in the United Kingdom and Europe. Tunisavia (☎ 682234) flies three times a week to Tunis and once a week to Sfax.

Sea There is a weekly ferry to Naples, a thrice weekly service to Reggio Calabria and Syracuse and a catamaran service to Pozzallo and Catania.

Car hire Many agencies and not very expensive.

Tourism

Malta's history is long, rich and varied from Prehistoric times. It was well fortified by the Knights Templars, who used it as their base in the 14th century and the ancient fortifications and facilities were used during the Second World War. Apart from the books recommended in the introduction, it is worth seeing *The Malta Experience*, a multi-visual, multi-language show on the history of the islands, at the Mediterranean Conference Centre, Merchant's Street, Valletta. It is shown weekdays every hour between 1000 and 1600. There are many sites well worth a visit, including one of the oldest known temples in the world, dating from pre-historic times and some spectacular caves. The tourist office in the town centre has maps and information on all the sites. Rabat is an ancient and very beautiful town with spectacular architecture and a fine restaurant. Its narrow streets are usually deserted around sunset. The old fort of St Angelo, guarding the entrance of Grand Harbour is also worth a visit.

An excellent and cheap bus service operates throughout the island, giving access to all the sites, which are never very busy. Since the late 1970's Malta has primarily been sold as a package holiday resort, with its beaches the main attraction. Few tourists seem interested in venturing out of their hotels to explore its rich history to 1600.

Yacht facilities

Malta offers very good facilities for yachts. This claim is substantiated with the following listing which does not pretend to be complete but does give a good idea of the kind of services available. Only a selection of the services and products of the listed companies is given.

Yacht agencies

RLR/Yachtcare Services, Gzira. ☎ 331563/331192/ 331996 *Fax* 230708. The first to offer yacht services

North Africa

Marsamxett harbours viewed from SW. Sliema Creek, Lazaretto Creek and the new marina in Msida Creek

in Malta. Yacht Care is a subsidiary specialising in the care and maintenance of yachts. Brokers and boat builders. Also large chandlery.

S&D Yachts Ltd. Guiseppe Cali St, Ta'Xbiex Gzira. ☎ 320577/331515/339908 *Fax* 332259. Yacht Brokers and Agents, Charter Management, Engineering, Consultants, Registrations, *Guardiennage*. Agents for Tohatsu, Rotostay, Gib-Sea, Westerly Marine.

Nautica, Sliema ☎ 342286/7 *Fax* 342228. Small company started in 1988. Brokerage and Chartering. Chandlery in Gzira listed below.

Chandlers/Electronics/Services

D'Agata Marine/Nautilus Services Ltd, Gzira. Chandlery and importer of Force and Cruise n' Carry outboards, Plastimo, Extensor International paints, Wilks fendering, Imray pilots etc.

Gauci Borda Ltd, The Strand, Gzira/Msida. Good assortment of ropes, flags, rigging, shackles, hardware, stainless steel nuts and bolts, paints, varnishes, abrasives etc. Convenient to Manoel Island.

International Marine Centre Ltd, Gzira. Well assorted chandlery and importer of a wide range of products. Among them Avon Inflatables, ITT/Jabsco, Lavac, Blake, Whale, Henderson, Simpson Lawrence, Aqua Signal, Frigoboat, Morse Controls, Vire, VDO, Aqua Marine, Sestrel.

Camilleri Marine, Gzira. Chandlery and importer of Mercury, Morse, Shurflo, Guidi brass hardware, Inox-Mare stainless steel hardware etc. Specialist in welding/bending of stainless steel pipes, etc.

Data Marine Ltd, Gzira. Representative of Navico, SeaFresh, Neco Micrologic e.o. of prop shafts etc.

Fabian Enterprises, Gzira. Electronic repairs and supplier of communication equipment and electronic components.

Medcomms Ltd, Gzira. Electronics specialists. Sales and service of Cetrec, Furuno, Magnavox, Navionics, Sailor, Seafarer, Thrane & Thrane, Thomas Walker, SAIT/Skanti, Swiftech and V-tronic.

Medway, Gzira. Engine specialist and 'Jack of all trades' including stainless steel. Saab engines Representative.

Nautica Ltd, Gzira. Chandlery and importer of Vetus, Bombard, Davis, etc, Yamaha outboards and generators.

Ripard, Larvan & Ripard Ltd, (RLR) Gzira. The first chandlery in Malta, started by yachtsmen who still run the company. Wide range of chandlery items and importers of many nautical products: SPSystems, Lewmar, stainless hardware and yacht fittings, Mase, Sikkens, International paints, Musto, VDO, Autohelm, Zodiac, Jabsco, Hood, Norseman Gibb,

Johnson outboards, Volvo Penta, Simpson-Lawrence and Imray pilots.

Ronnie's Marine Services, Gzira. Engine/transmission specialist, engine spares, paints and very helpful in other matters. Tomos Outboards Representative.

Zarb Stores Ltd, Luqa. Chandlery with yachting hardware and accessories. Suzuki importer.

Thos. C. Smith & Co Ltd, Valletta. Stockist of Admiralty charts and publications.

Gaetano Bondin, Mellieha ☎ 472302. Refrigeration expert. Handles Taylor professional ice-making machines.

Action Sails, Cannon Road, Qormi. ☎ 623511. Sail makers.

Marine Services Ltd, Sliema. Young company specialising in boat care and maintenance.

Dolphin Forge, Msidia, opposite entrance to Marina. Galvanising, welding, shot-blasting on site, reconditioning of prop shafts.

Shipyards

Manoel Island Yacht Yard, Gzira ☎ 334453/4, 334320 *Fax* 343900. General Manager Mr Seguna. The largest facility for yacht repairs, maintenance, refitting, conversions, osmosis treatment for GRP hulls etc. Owned by the Maltese government together with Malta Drydocks who deal with commercial vessels or very large yachts. Conveniently located on Manoel Island, it has a 23-ton travel-lift and room for about 240 yachts on the hard and seven slips for yachts or commercial vessels up to 60m and 500-tonnes displacement. Anything larger can be accommodated in Malta Dry Docks in the Grand Harbour. Reservations are necessary.

Rates in 1997 for a 13m yacht were: Lift and launch: 104£M, Storage 13£M/week, service charge 25£M, electricity and water extra, high pressure wash-off inclusive. When less than 13 weeks are spent on the hard, work must be carried out by the yard but over this time permission can be granted for the Owner and one crew to do the work. No outside workers are allowed without permission. Except for one week before launching or after lifting, a charge will be made for living on board. Showers and toilets are free.

Kalkara Boatyard Co Ltd, Kalkara ☎ 781306. Yacht yard with winter storage on the hard and mobile crane for boats up to 50 tons. Lifting and storage rates are roughly the same as for Manoel Island Yacht Yard but fewer restrictions. Specialists in laying teak decks and joinery work.

The disadvantage of Kalkara is its distance from Marsa, Valetta and all the services in Gzira and Msida. In the absence of any *dghaisa* or boat link with Valetta and Sliema a hire car would be essential if doing own work and/or living on board.

Guzi Azzopardi, Marsa ☎ 234200. Boat Builders and Consultants.

Bezzina Ship Repair Yard Ltd, Marsa ☎ 824138/826283. Mostly for merchant vessels but they have worked on large private yachts up to 65m.

Cassar Enterprises Ltd, Marsa ☎ 225764 *Fax* 229761 One of the few yards, aside from Malta Drydocks, that does dry grit blasting. More suitable for smaller yachts than Malta Drydocks or Bezzina.

Manoel Island with the yacht yard on the left-hand side and the old marina in Lazaretto Creek to the right

North Africa

Anchorages around Malta
(Anti-clockwise from Valletta)

General
The NE coast of Malta slopes gradually to the shore and is indented with numerous bays. Because of easy access this part of Malta has the most tourist development. The increasing number of large local powerboats means that many of the anchorages are crowded, especially at weekends and on public holidays. In the summer months many local boats use these bays and consequently few, if any, are secluded. They all offer good protection from the W to SE and the anchorages are mostly sand or soft mud with seaweed in patches.

St Julian's Bay
35°55'·2N 14°29'·8E

A wide pleasant bay built up all round. Good protection and holding with room to swing. St Julian's and its neighbouring Balluta Bay are surrounded by restaurants and pubs. No stern-to moorings.

St George's Bay
35°55'·7N 14°29'·5E

A very good anchorage but surrounded by terraces and restaurants. A very busy tourist spot in summer and popular for watersports. If you like noise and bustle, this is the place.

Qala ta' san marku
35°56'·9N 14°27'·0E

A quiet and peaceful bay to the SE of Salina Bay. Good holding. No services. If proceeding from here to Salina Bay give the Ghallis Rocks a wide berth.

Salina Bay
35°57'·0N 14°29'·5E

Derives its name from the salt pans situated at the head of the bj165
ay which is shallow but with good holding. The NW side is covered with hotels and restaurants and there is a water sports centre.

St Paul's Bay
35°57'·3N 14°23'·7E

A large bay around which Malta's major tourist area has grown up which is noisy until the early hours. There is good holding and several small bays offer safe anchorages. Small boat moorings occupy some of Mistra Bay on the N side.

    St Paul's Island, marked by a conspicuous statue to the Saint is the site of his shipwreck while en route to Rome from Anatolia in AD60. This provided the opportunity to convert the islands to Christianity. The passage between St Paul's Island and the mainland should only be attempted by dinghy.

Good shelter in quiet surroundings in the NE corner of Mellieha Bay

Mgiebah or Selmun Bay
35°58'·0N 14°22'·0E

A shallow bay open to the N and holding in soft sand. No road access.

Mellieha Bay
35°58'·5N 14°21'·5E

The largest bay on the NE coast. It has one of the largest sandy beaches in Malta with many water sport facilities but some quiet anchorages along the N shore. Beware of a shoal patch and submerged rock in the middle.

Armier Bay
35°59'·5N 14°21'·5E

A large sandy beach with three restaurants, also known as the White Lido. If a quieter ambience is desired, Little Armier Bay just to the W is more tranquil. Both bays are open to the NW and the prevailing breeze.

Ramla Bay
35°59'·4N 14°20'·6E

Ramla Bay is dominated by a large hotel complex on the W side. The bottom is hard and sandy in the middle of the bay but weed and rocks at the sides. A water sports area.

Paradise Bay
35°59'·2N 14°19'·9E

Paradise Bay faces WNW and is open to the prevailing winds. A pretty bay with a small hotel and private beach. Soft sandy bottom.

Anchor Bay
35°57'·7N 14°20'·4E

A small, attractive bay on the NW coast surrounded

218

Anchor Bay on the W side of Malta with Mellieha Bay in the background

by steep hills, exposed to westerly winds. Approach carefully as the narrow entrance has submerged rocks on both sides. An unused ferry boat landing is located on the S side. The bottom is rocky with weed and sand patches. The village at the head of the bay was built by a film company for the Popeye cartoons. It is regularly visited by tour groups, either by boat or bus.

Ghajn Tuffieha
35°55'·9N 14°20'·4E

The largest sandy beach in Malta and popular. Sandy, regular bottom.

Gnenja Bay
35°55'·6N 14°20'·5E

A wide, beautiful bay in unspoilt surroundings, open to the NW. Small fishermens' cottages line the steep S shore and the beach at the head is frequented by swimmers at weekends but is quieter than Ghajn Tuffieha. The sandy bottom shoals gradually towards the head of the bay.

Fomm Ir-Rih Bay
35°54'·5N 14°20'·3E

A quiet if not desolate bay, open to the NW, just S of Gnenja Bay. Good holding but not comfortable with swell from the NW when the waves are reflected off the steep cliffs on the S side.

The SW coast of Malta consists of steep and dramatic cliffs which are well worth a sightseeing passage to visit. Unfortunately if offers no shelter. The only place that can be visited is:

Blue Grotto
35°49'·3N 14°27'·4E

It is not recommended to go into Wied iz-Zurrieq to visit the Blue Grotto and the water is too deep to anchor outside. It is better to stay under way and visit by tender. A number of small boats based in Wied iz-Zurrieq will be doing the same.

Fifla
35°47'·3N 14°24'·5E

This island lying 2½M S of Malta is a bird sanctuary and prohibited area. It was used as a target for many years by the Royal Navy and Fleet Air Arm and no doubt a quantity of unexploded ordnance still remains.

Marsaxlokk Bay
35°50'N 14°33'·3E

There are three bays within Marsaxlokk which is the second commercial port of Malta. There are still some quiet anchorages along the NE shore although the new power station casts a blight over the scenery. The bay offers good protection from prevailing wind directions. Beware of shallow patches both on this side and SE from the fort in the middle of the bay (marked with a beacon).

Marsaxlokk, the biggest fishing port of Malta, is located in the N corner of the bay. A picturesque village with some good restaurants, shops and services. Using the large scale chart (No.36) it is possible to get to one of the jetties at Marsaxlokk drawing up to 2·2m.

Qajjenza A south facing bay to the W of the fort with good holding.

Birzebugia A popular summer resort. There is a small jetty on the W side to which a few yachts can secure stern-to. Shops and restaurants ashore.

To the SE of Birzebugia lies the commercial and freeport of Kalafrana behind an extensive breakwater which will be of little interest to yachtsmen.

Natural surroundings in Gnenja Bay

North Africa

Il-Hofriet (or Armchair Bays)
35°50'·3N 14°34'E

Two pleasant quiet bays divided by a narrow spit, protected from SW through N to NE but open to the SE. Anchor in sand patches. Depths shoal gradually towards the head of the bay. Both anchorages are deserted and have no road access.

The transmitters of Deutsche Welle (German World Service) overlook the bay and have been known to play havoc with yacht electrics. DW usually starts transmitting at 1400.

The two Il Hofriet Bays also called Armchair Bay on the E side of Malta

The deep Marsascala Bay with numerous small-boat moorings at the head

Marsascala Bay
35°52'·0N 14°34'·5E

A small bay surrounded by the village with good protection from N to S through W. Shoals abruptly towards the head. Good holding. Numerous small boat moorings. Beware of the Munxar reef to the SE.

There are good fish restaurants, bars and pubs ashore. Grocers, butchers and greengrocers within walking distance.

Anchorages around Gozo
(Anticlockwise from Mgarr)

Mgarr
36°01'·5N 14°18'·1E

A pretty fishing and ferry harbour. Mgarr is Gozo's main port for car and passenger ferry services between the islands. There are frequent services from Cirkewwa across the Comino channel, a fast catamaran service and a ferry service from Marsamxett. Yachts must keep clear of them in the harbour and approaches. There is also a helicopter service to the island from Luqa airport.

There are now pontoons in the NE corner and along the N shore. If there is no space here, anchor in this corner clear of the fairway and moorings. Bottom mud/sand with good holding. A trip line is advisable due to the remains of old moorings. As this area is some distance from the village, use of the dinghy to get ashore will save a walk.

Shops and restaurants, ice and fuel are to be found in the village. Bus to the capital Rabat (Victoria). A customs and immigration office is situated in Mgarr and it may be more convenient to clear out here rather than in Marsamxett.

Tac-Cawl Rocks
36°01'·6N 14°19'·0E

A small bay surrounded by high rocks but good holding. 2 yachts would be a crowd.

Gebel tal-Halfa

Facing SE this is a beautiful little bay behind a big rock but very small and quickly crowded.

Mgarr harbour viewed from the W

Marsalforn Bay and fishing village viewed from the N

North Africa

Marsalforn
36°01'·8N 14°15'·7E

Good anchoring in a bay open to the N. The fishing village of Marsalforn is built around the bay and has been swallowed up to some extent by tourism. Usual services ashore. A small and shallow fishing port is located on the E shore.

Qala Dwejra
36°02'·9N 14°11'·2E

An interesting and beautiful anchorage in an almost circular bay surrounded by steep hills on the W side of Gozo. The entrance is partially closed off by Fungus Rock and entrance to the bay is by a narrow passage N and a wider one S of the rock. Anchorage is on rock and sand 5–12m. Good shelter from N to S through E.

An enchanting place whose only sounds at night are the wash of any swell against the cliffs, goat bells and owls.

Dwejra Inlet
36°03'·3N 14°11'·4E

A half mile to the N of Dwejra Point lies a tunnel through the cliffs to an inland bay. This is only accessible by road or through the channel. Anchoring outside is just possible in 25m; otherwise go by dinghy from Qala Dwejra or lie off. Dinghies can get through the tunnel or it is possible to swim through. Be very careful if there is any swell which can fill the tunnel with unfortunate results to any dinghy and occupants in it.

Between Qala Dwejra and Xlendi are the highest and most impressive cliffs in Malta, rising vertically for up to 500ft from the sea. There are no off-lying dangers and a close passage along them is impressive.

Xlendli Bay
36°01'·7N 14°12'·8E

Formerly a fishing village in a small narrow bay on the SW side of Gozo. It is open to the SW with a shallow area at the entrance (see chart 195). Beware of a rock, which is 1m awash, off the N point of the bay almost in the middle of the entrance. The S shore of the bay is clear of any dangers to yachts. Very little swinging room. Only suitable for small craft.

It is now a popular resort and the inner end of the bay is much cluttered with small boat moorings. There is still room to anchor outside the moorings. It is noisy in summer. Shops and restaurants ashore.

Mgarrix-Xini Bay
36°01'N 14°16'·5E

A peculiar, deep and narrow inlet cut out of the limestone cliffs on the S coast of Gozo. The entrance is marked by a tower on the E side and a *wied* (Maltese for river) flows into the natural bay.

Excellent protection in Xlendli Bay but beware of the submerged rock and fishing nets in the entrance

Good holding and almost all-round protection except from the S. Space is very restricted and it may be necessary to take a line ashore. There is a small beach at the head but beware of a rock with 1·5m and shoal patch on the western side near the head.

Anchorages around Comino

Santa Marija Bay
36°01'·3N 14°16'·5E

Good holding but much frequented by watersporters from the *club nautico*.

San Niklaw Bay
36°01'·3N 14°19'·9E

Good holding but fronted by a large hotel with a private beach.

Blue Lagoon
36°01'·1N 14°19'·3E

One of Malta's loveliest bays and heavily crowded by tour boats and people at weekends, public holidays and during the summer. Reasonable holding if you can find a space. Most of the tour boats go bows-to on the Comino side to disgorge the hordes. Nevertheless a sheltered and peaceful anchorage at night and out of season. The entrance from the S should not be used by deep draught yachts without a recce. The depths are marginal and changeable.

Appendix

Admiralty charts

Chart	Title	Scale
9	La Skhirra, Gabès and Ghannouch with approaches	
	Gabès and Ghannouch	30,000
	La Skhirra	50,000
	Gulf of Gabès	100,000
36	Marsaxlokk	10,000
45	Gibraltar harbour	3,600
92	Cabo de Sao Vicente to the Strait of Gibraltar	400,000
142	Strait of Gibraltar	100,000
	Tarifa	25,000
144	Gibraltar	10,000
165	Menorca to Sicilia including Malta	1,100,000
176	Cap Bon to Ra's At Tïn	1,175,000
178	Ports in Algeria	
	Port de Beni Saf	10,000
	Port de Ghazaouet: Port de Mostaganem: Port de Ténès	12,500
	Approaches to Beni Saf	125,000
193	Islands in the Sicilian Channel	
	Isola di Linosa	25,000
	Isola di Lampedusa	35,000
	Isola di Pantelleria	50,000
	Porto di Lampedusa; Porto di Pantelleria	75,000
194	Approaches to Malta and Ghawdex (Gozo)	100,000
195	Plans in Malta and Gozo	
	Xlendi bay	2,500
	Dwejra bay: Marsalforn	4,000
	St Paul's bay	12,000
252	Cap Corbelin to Cap Takouch	300,000
580	Al Hoceïma, Melilla and Port Nador with approaches	
	Al Hoceïma Melilla and Port Nador	10,000
	Approaches to Al Hoceïma	50,000
	Approaches to Melilla and Port Nador	60,000
773	Strait of Gibraltar to Isla de Alborán	300,000
812	Oran and Mers-el-Kebir	10,000
822	Approaches to Oran, Arzew and Mostaganem	120,000
838	Port of Arzew	15,000
855	Approaches to Alger and Skikda	
	Skikda	10,000
	Golfe de Stora	25,000
	Baie D'Alger	30,000
856	Oued Sébou to Casablanca	150,000
860	Approaches to Casablanca and Mohammedia	50,000
861	Mohammedia and Casablanca	
	Rade de Casablanca	12,500
	Mohammedia	15,000
862	Al Jadida, Jorf Lasfar, Safi and approaches	
	Safi	12,500
	Al Jadida	17,500

Chart	Title	Scale
	Jorf Lasfar	20,000
	Approaches to Al Jadida and Jorf Lasfar: Approaches to Safi	150,000
863	Essaouira, Anza and Agadir, Sidi Ifni and Laâyoune	
	Anza and Agadir: Essaouira	12,500
	Sidi Ifni: Laâyoune	30,000
	Approaches to Anza and Agadir	50,000
	Approaches to Essaouira	150,000
	Cap Rhir to Agadir: Approaches to Laâyoune	175,000
974	Valletta harbour	5,000
1162	Sfax and Sousse with approaches	25,000
	Port de Sfax: Port de Sousse	25,000
	Approaches to Sfax: Approaches to Sousse	125,000
1184	Baie de Tunis	65,000
	La Goulette and Tunis	25,000
1440	Adriatic Sea	1,100,000
1448	Gibraltar bay	25,000
	Puerto de Algeciras	12,500
1567	Approaches to Annaba	25,000
	Annaba	10,000
1569	Bizerte and approaches	50,000
	Port de Bizerte and Goulet du Lac: Port de Menzel Bourguiba	15,000
1710	Cherhell, Dellys and Bejaïa	
	Port de Cherchell	10,000
	Port de Dellys	12,500
	Port de Bejaïa	15,000
1712	Plans on the coasts of Algeria and Tunisia	
	Port of Jijel: Port de la Calle	12,000
	Collo anchorage	25,000
	Mersa Toukouch	25,000
	Port de la Calle	12,000
	Tabarka	25,000
	Île de la Galite	75,000
1909	Île Plane to Cherchell	300,000
1910	Cherchell to Bejaïa	300,000
1912	Tanger with approaches, Larache and Oued Sébou	
	Tanger: Larache	10,000
	Oued Sébou	20,000
	Approaches to Tanger	25,000
2121	Ras el Hadid to Îles Cani	300,000
2122	Bizerte to Capo San Marco	300,000
2123	Capo Granitola to Capo Passero	300,000
2124	Isola di Lampedusa to Capo Passero including Malta	300,000
2437	Cabo Quilates to Oran	300,000
2537	Ghawdex (Gozo), Kemmuna (Comino) and northern part of Malta	50,000
2538	Malta	50,000
2555	Alger	10,000
2623	Channels between Malta and Ghawdex (Gozo)	25,000
2717	Strait of Gibraltar to Barcelona and	1,100,000

North Africa

Map labels

- Atlantic Ocean
- Mediterranean Sea
- Strait of Gibraltar
- Ceuta
- Cap Spartel
- Tanger
- Pointe Nador
- Larache
- Mehdia
- Kénitra
- Cap de Fedala
- Rabat
- Pointe d'El Hank
- Mohammedia
- Sidi Bou Afi
- Casablanca
- El Jadida
- Cap Beddouza
- Cap Sim
- Cap Ghir
- Agadir
- Ilhas Selvagen
- Alegranza
- Lanzarote
- Sidi Ifni
- ISLAS CANARIAS
- Fuerteventura
- Cap Nachtigal
- Tenerife
- Gomera
- Gran Canaria
- Cap Tarfaya
- MOROCCO
- Port Laâyoune
- Cap Bojador
- Arciprés Grande
- Dakhla
- Cap Barbas
- Cap Blanc
- Cap Timiris

Chart numbers: 773, 142, 92, 3578, 856, 1831, 3132, 863, 3134, 3133

British Admiralty Chatrs

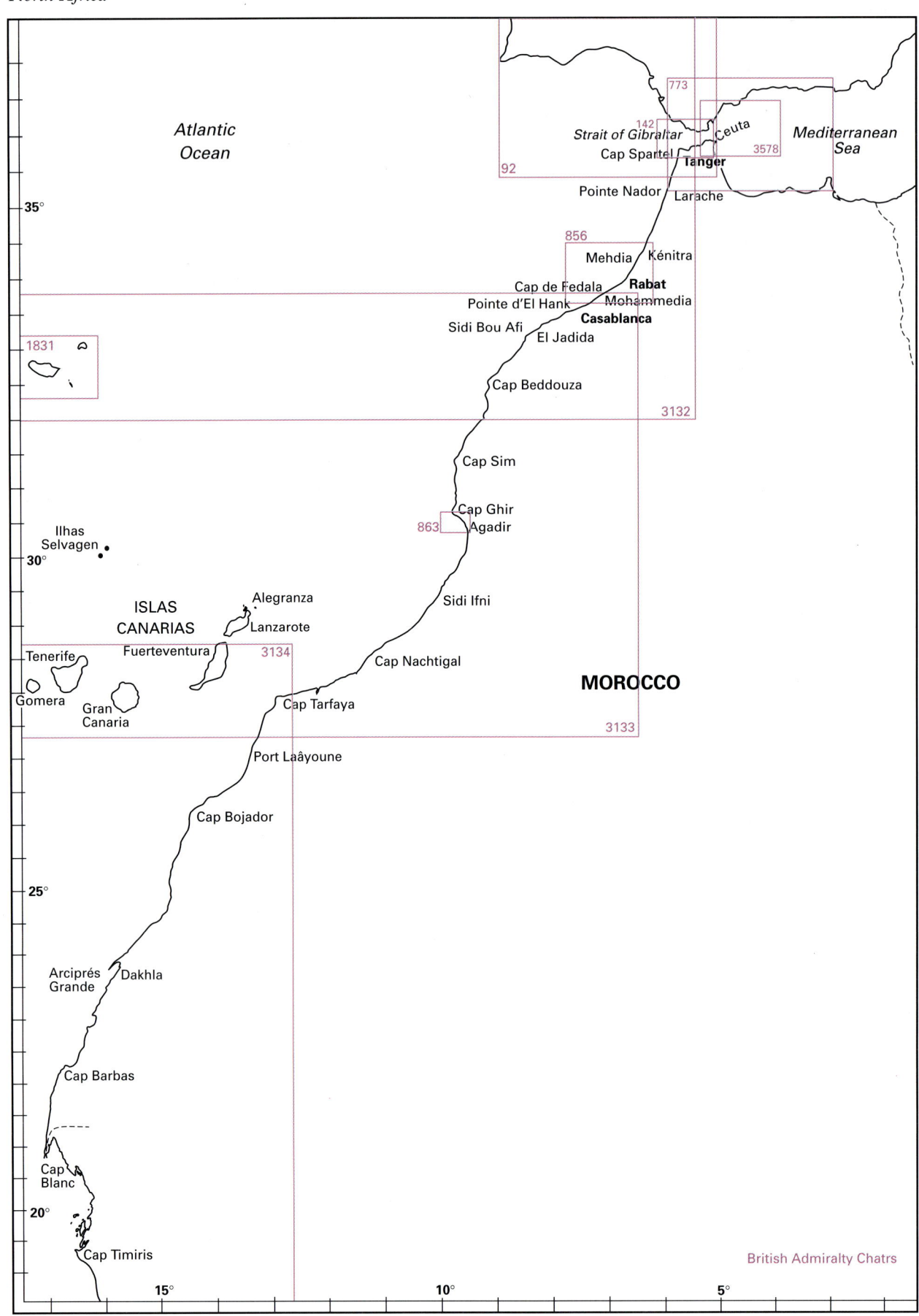

BRITISH ADMIRALTY CHARTS – MOROCCO ATLANTIC COAST

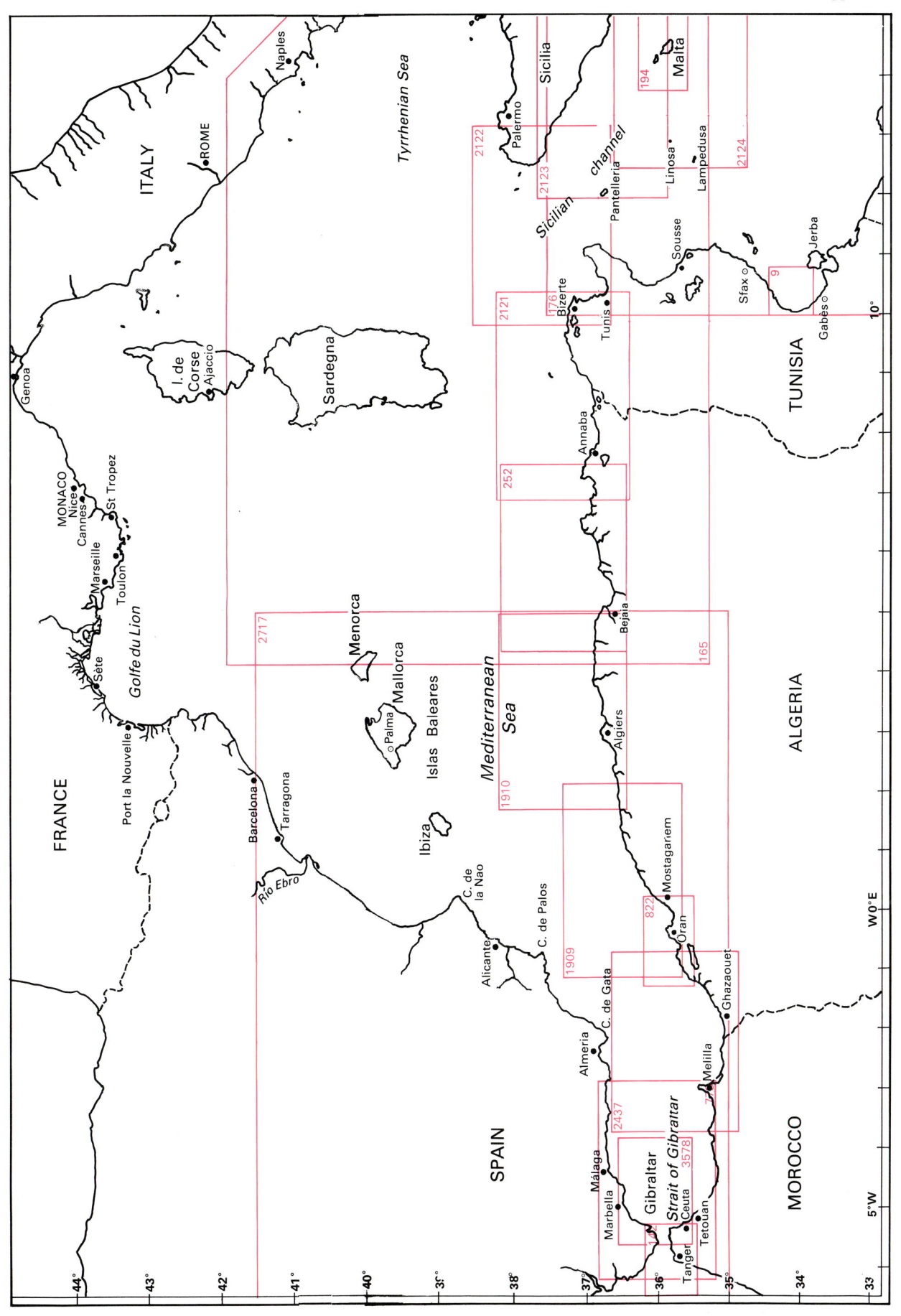

Appendix

North Africa

Chart	Title	Scale
	Alger including Islas Baleares	
2742	Puerto de Ceuta	10,000
3132	Strait of Gibraltar to Arquipélago da Madeira	1,250,000
3133	Casablanca to Islas Canarias	1,250,000
	Ilhas Selvagens	100,000
3403	Cap Afrique to Miṣratah	500,000
	Zuwarah	25,000
	Abu Kammash	30,000
	Az Zawiyah	40,000
3578	Eastern approaches to the Strait of Gibaltar	150,000
4301	Mediterranean Sea – western part	2,250,000

French charts

Service Hydrographique et Océanographique de la Marine

Chart	Title	Scale
1619	Mouillages de Tarifa	10,000
1700	Baie de Tétouan	25,000
1701	Tanger et ses atterrages	20,000
	Cartouche: Port de Tanger	10,000
1711	Côte Nord du Maroc	307,000
3023	De Djidjelli à Collo	100,000
3024	Du cap Toukouch au cap Rose	100,000
3029	Du cap Sigli à Djidjelli	100,000
3030	D'Alger à Cherchell	101,000
	Cartouches: Bou Aroun	5,000
	Chiffalo	5,000
3036	De Dellys au cap Sigli	102,000
	Cartouche: Port Gueydon	5,000
3043	D'Alger à Dellys	100,000
	Cartouche: Courbet-Marine	5,000
3061	Du cap Bougaroni au cap Axin	100,000
3202	De Cherchell à Ténès	101,000
3234	De la Point Kef el Assfer au cap Ténès	99,500
3405	D'Alger à la frontière de Tunisie	584,000
3424	Du cap Rose au cap Nègre	125,000
3678	Côte de l'Algérie (1ère feuille), d'Alger à la frontière du Maroc	596,000
4086	Al Mahdïyah	15,000
4087	Tabarca	15,300
4102	Sousse	25,000
	Cartouche: Port de Sousse	10,000
4129	Du cap Serrat au cap Blanc	61,600
4183	Tunisie côte Est, ports et mouillages	
	Cartouche: Rade de Kelibia	25,000
	Port de Kelibia	7,500
	Rade d'Hammamet	25,000
4191	De Ras-al-Fortas à Kelibia	61,700
4198	Du ras Enghela au cap Farina, baie et lac de Bizerte	61,100
4208	De Ksar Menara à Sousse	63,500
4219	Du cap Roux au cap Serrat (Tabarka et cap Négro)	61,700
4221	De Kilibia à ras Mamour	62,100
4222	Du cap Kamart au Ras-al-Fortas (Golfe de Tunis)	61,900
4225	De Kurba à la Sebkha Djiriba (Golfe d'Hammamet)	63,000
4226	Du ras Marsa au ras Dimas (Golfe de Sousse et de Monastir)	62,800
4227	Du ras Dimas au ras Kapudia	63,300
4228	De Sfax à Maharès	63,600
4235	Du ras Kapudia au ras Ungha (Iles et bancs Kerkennah)	152,000
4236	Du ras Kapudia à Sidi Makluf (Partie Nord du canal de Kerkennah)	63,500
4237	De Sidi Makluf à Sfax (Iles Kerkennah)	63,500
4238	Sfax	25,000
	Cartouche: Port de Sfax	10,000
4239	De Maharès à la Skhirra (Golfe de Gabès)	63,900
4240	De la Skhira à Gabès (Golfe de Gabès)	64,100
4241	Gabès (ancienne Tacape)	25,000
4242	De Gabès ou Bordj Djilidj (Golfe de Gabès)	64,300
4244	Du Bordj Djilidj à Sidi Garus (Partie Nord de l'île de Djerba)	64,200
4245	De Sidi Garus à Zarzis, Bahiret el Bou Grara	64,400
4247	De Zarzis au ras Ashdir (Bahiret el Biban)	64,700
4250	Du cap Farina au cap Carthage (Delta de Medjerda)	61,800
4314	De Bône à Tunis	328,000
4315	De Tunis à Sfax	335,000
4717	De Gibraltar à la pointe del Sabinal	250,000
	Cartouche: Port de Motril	10,000
	Mouillages de la Herradura, Los Berengueles, Almuźnécar, Belilla et Salobrena	80,000
4970	Lac de Bizerte	25,000
5023	Iles au Sud de la Sicile	
	Cartouches: Ile de Pantelleria	30,000
	Port de Pantelleria	7,500
	Port de Lampedusa	10,000
	Ile de Linosa	30,000
	Ile de Lampedusa	30,000
5281	Port de Bizerte et goulet du Lac	10,000
5617	Port d'Alger	10,000
	Cartouche: Mouillage de la Pointe Pescade	10,000
5638	Baie d'Alger	30,000
	Cartouche: Mouillage de La Pérouse	10,000
5640	Port de Dellys	10,000
5641	Port de Bejaia (Bougie)	15,000
5669	Port d'Annaba (Bône)	10,000
5670	Abords de Bône	25,000
5696	Port de Mostaganem	10,000
5697	Rade de Casablanca	10,000
5698	Ile de La Galite	27,500
5699	Port de Tipaza et baie de Chenoua	10,000
	Cartouche: Port de Cherchell	10,000
5708	Port de Ténès	10,000
	Cartouches: Baie des Beni-Haouas – Mouillage de Sidi Djilani	
	Baie et mouillage de Térarénia	10,000
	Baie des Souhalias – mouillage de Kef Doumia (Kef el Haouaci)	10,000
5787	Abords de Philippeville (Skikda)	25,000
	Cartouche: Port de Philippeville (Skikda)	10,000
5791	De Bizerte aux îles Cani	25,000
5864	Ports et mouillages sur la côte Nord du Maroc. Cartouche:	
	A – Baie de Al Hoceïma	120,000
	B – Port de Al Hoceïma	15,000
	C – Afraou	5,000
	D – Baie Tramontane	15,000
	E – Ile Alboran	20,000
	F – Ports de Melilla et de Nador	11,200
	G – Iles Zafarines et port de Ras Kebdana	15,000

Chart	Title	Scale
5873	Port de Nemours	10,000
5876	Ile Rachgoun, embouchure de la Tafna	10,000
	Cartouche: Béni-Saf	10,000
5886	Iles Habibas	10,000
	Cartouche: Mersa Ali Bou Nouar	10,000
5940	De la Tafna au cap Sigale	101,000
5942	Iles et récifs de Cani	10,000
5948	D'Arzew au cap Figalo	101,000
5951	Du Cap Ferrat à la pointe Kef el Asfer	100,000
5955	Rade et port d'Agadir	10,000
6011	Des îles Zafarines à la Tafna	102,000
6062	Ports de la Goulette et de Tunis	20,000
6070	Port de Sidi-Abdallah	10,000
6103	Rade de Safi	10,000
6111	Abords de Casablanca	49,900
6119	Rade de Mazagan	10,000
6120	Abords de Mazagan	50,000
6142	Abords de Mohammédia	15,000
	Cartouche: Port de Mohammédia	5,000
6145	De Moulay Bou Selham à Mohammédia	153,000
6169	Abords de Safi	50,600
6170	Du cap Magazan au cap Cantin	156,000
6178	Du cap Ghir à Agadir	51,600
6204	Rade d'Essaouira (Mogador)	10,000
6206	Du cap Hadid au cap Sim	51,100
6226	Du cap Cantin au cap Sim	158,000
6227	Du cap Sim à l'Oued Massa	160,000
6325	Baie de la Skhira ou des Sur-Kenis	35,000
6570	Mer d'Alboran, feuille Sud	203,000
6606	Canal de Sicile	674,000
6611	Entrée de la Méditerranée	674,000
7015	De Gibraltar aux îles Baléares (f.s. E 3)	1,000,000
7026	Baie de Algeciras (f.s. ES 445A)	25,000
7042	Détroit de Gibraltar (f.s. E 105)	100,000
7300	De cabo de São Vicente au Détroit de Gibraltar (f.s. ES 44)	350,000
7503	Baie et port de Ceuta	10,000
7524	Du cap Afrique à Miṣratah	494,00
	Cartouche:	
	A - Abu Kammash	30,000
	B - Az Zawiyah	40,000
	C - Zuwarah	25,000
7550	Du Détroit de Gibraltar à Kenitra	324,000
	Cartouche:	
	A - Embouchure de l'Oued Sebou	30,000
	B - Cours de l'Oued Sebou	30,000
7551	De Kenitra au cap Beddouza (cap Cantin)	331,000
	Cartouches: Port de Rabat	20,000
	Port de Jorf Lasfar	25,000

Spanish Charts

Chart	Title	Scale
44	De cabo de San Vicente al Estrecho de Gibraltar	350,000
44C	Costa Sur de España y Norte de Marruecos. De Broa de Sanlúcar a Estepona y de Larache a cabo Mazarí	175,000
45	Estrecho de Gibraltar y Mar de Alborán	350,000
45A	De punta Carnero a cabo Sacratif y de punta Cires a cabo Negro	175,000
46	De cabo de Gata a cabo de las Huertas y de cabo Milonia a cabo Ivi	350,000
	Plano inserto: Puerto de Ghazaouet	10,000
50	Rada y puerto de Casablanca	10,000
105	Estrecho de Gibraltar. De cabo Roche a punta de la Chullera y de cabo Espartel a cabo Negro	100,000
181	Rada y puerto de Agadir	10,000
215	De cabo Trafalgar a punta Europy de Ceuta a Kenitra (Port Lyautey)	350,000
216	De Kenitra a cabo Beddouza (Cantín)	350,000
	Planos insertos: Puerto de Rabat	20,000
	Puerto de Jorf-Lasfar	25,000
217	De cabo Safi a Sidi Ifni	350,000
254	Rada y puerto de Safi	10,000
	Puerto de Es-Suira (Mogador)	10,000
431	Bahía de Alhucemas	25,875
	Plano inserto: Puerto de Villa Sanjurjo	5,356
432	De cabo Abduna a puerto de Melilla	50,000
433	De Ras Tleta Madari (Cabo Tres Forcas) a Ras Cantara Run	50,000
	Plano inserto: Freu de los Farallones	10,000
434	De Ras Quiviana a la desembocadura del río Muluya	50,000
445	Estrecho de Gibraltar. De punta Camarinal a punta Europa y de cabo Espartel a punta Almina	60,000
445A	Bahía de Algeciras	25,000
445B	Bajo de los Caberos e Isla de Tarifa	2,500
446	De la bahía de Tánger a Asilah (Arcila)	52,500
447	De Asilah (Arcila) a El Aaraich (Larache)	52,500
451	De punta Leona a cabo Mazarí	50,000
453	De Punta Europa a la torre de las Bóvedas	50,000
	Planos insertos: Fondeadero de Estepona	12,500
	Fondeadero de la Sabinilla	12,500
527	De cabo Mohammedia (Fedala) a cabo El Jadida (Mazagán)	160,000
529	De cabo Cantín (Beddouza) a cabo Sim	160,000
530	De Es-Suira (Mogador) a Agadir	160,000
	Planos insertos: Fondeadero de cabo Sim	51,060
	Fondeadero de Tafelneh	51,241
	Bahía de Imsouane	51,446
532	Del río Asif Solguemat al río Asaca	75,000
4331	Puerto de Melilla	5,000
4341	Islas Chafarinas y Ras El Ma (Cabo del Agua)	10,000
4451	Bahía de Algeciras - zona oeste	10,000
4452	Bahía de Algeciras - zona este	10,000
4461	Bahía y puerto de Tánger	15,000
	Puerto de Asilah (Arcila)	10,000
	Barra y puerto de El Aairaich (Larache)	10,000
4511	Bahía y puerto de Ceuta	10,000
5271	Aproches de Mohammedia (Fédala)	15,000
	Plano inserto: Puerto de Mohammedia (Fédala)	5,000
5320	Puerto de Sidi Ifni	6,000

North Africa

US Charts

Chart	Title	Scale
51180	Cap Spartel to Moulay Bou Selham (Morocco)	150,000
51181	Plans on the west coast of Morocco	
	A. Baie de Tafelney	24,970
	B. Baie Imsouane	24,990
	C. Rabat and Sale	9,970
	D. Larache	9,930
	E. Asilah	9,990
51200	Moulay Bou Selham to Rabat and Sale	150,000
51201	Oued Sebou	
	Plans: A. Entrance to Oued Sebou	12,000
	B. Oued Sebou, continuation to Kenitra	12,000
51220	Rabat & Sale to El Jorf Lasfar	150,000
	Plan: El Jadida	20,000
51222	Rade de Casablanca	9,960
51223	Approaches to Casablanca and Mohammedia	75,000
51224	Rade de Safi and approaches	50,000
	Plan: Rade de Safi	10,000
51225	Agadir and approaches	50,000
	Plan: Port of Agadir	10,000
51240	El Jorf Lesfar to Rade de Safi	150,000
51280	Rade de Safi to Cap Rhir	150,000
52039	Strait of Gibraltar (Decca)	100,000
52040	Strait of Gibraltar to Cabo Gata and Cap Milonia (Loran-C)	300,000
52042	Baie de Tanger	15,500
	Plan: Harbour of Tanger	5,200
52047	Al Hoceïma, Melilla and Approaches	75,000
	Plans: Approaches to Al Hociema	10,000
	Port of Al Hoceïma	10,000
	Approaches to Melilla	75,000
	Port of Melilla	15,000
52048	Bahia de Ceuta (Morocco)	10,250
52060	Cabo de Gata to Cabo de Palos and Cap Milonia to Cap Ivi (Loran-C)	300,999
52069	Ghazaoulet, Beni Saf and Approaches	80,000
	Plans: Ghazaouet	12,500
	Beni Saf	10,000
52160	Sfax to Tarabulus (Loran-C)	300,000
	Plan: Houmt Souk-(Ile de Djerba)	100,000
52161	Sfax and Approaches	100,000
	Plan: Marsa Sfax	25,000
52164	Approaches to Skhira and Gabès	100,000
52165	Skhira (A) and Gabès (B)	25,000
52170	Rass el Melah to Sfax (Loran-C)	300,000
	Plans: Isola di Linosa	50,000
	Isola di Lampedusa	50,000
52172	Sousse and Approaches	100,000
	Plan: Sousse	15,000
52180	Strait of Sicily – Northern Reaches (Loran-C)	300,000
52183	Banzart and Manzil Bu Ruqaybah	15,000
52184	Approaches to Bizert	75,000
	Plan: Lac de Bizerte	35,000
52186	Approaches to Tunis	75,000
	Plan: Tunis	17,500
52200	Cap de Fer to Ras Engela including The Canal de Jalitah (Loran-C)	233,120
52202	Approaches to Annaba Harbour	25,000
	Plan: Annaba Harbour	10,000
52220	Cap Carbon to Cap de Fer	233,640
52221	Port of Bejaia (Algeria)	15,000
52223	Approaches to Skikda	100,000
	Plan: Port of Skikda	15,000
52240	Cherchel to Cap Carbon (Loran-C)	233,890

Chart	Title	Scale
52243	Alger (Algeria) and Approaches	50,000
	Plan: Alger	10,000
52260	Cap Ferrat to Cherchel (Loran-C)	235,150
52262	Port d'Arzew	15,000
52263	Golfe d'Arzew	50,000
52281	Approaches to Oran (Algeria)	37,500
52282	Ports of Oran and Mers El Kebir	10,000
53020	Tyrrhenian Sea (Loran-C)	754,300
53204	Northwest Malta	30,000
	Plans: St Paul's Bay	10,000
	Qala Tad-Dwejra	4,000
53205	Approaches to Valletta Harbours and Marsaxlokk	30,000
53206	Valletta and Marsaxlokk	
	Plans: Valletta	7,500
	Marsaxlokk	10,000
53220	Strait of Sicily – southern reaches	300,000
53223	Isola di Pantelleria (Italy)	25,000
	Plans: Pantelleria Harbour	7,500
	Ancoraggio di Scauri	7,500

Index

Agadir, 70-72
Ajim, 196-7, 198
Al Hoceima (Villa Sanjurjo), 85-7
Algeria, 93-126
  charts, 9
  coastal radio stations, 12
  entry formalities, 97-8
  general information, 1-17, 95-8
  history, 93-5
  radiobeacons, 11
  travel, 98
  weather forecasts, 10-11
Algiers, 95, 112
Anchor Bay, 218-19
anchoring, 7
Annaba (Bône), 95, 124-5
Anse Budmah (Cap Negro), 137-8
Anza, Port d' (Agadir), 71
Armchair Bays, 219
Armier Bay, 218
Arzew, 95, 105
Asilah, 42-5
El Ataya, 188-90
Atlantic coast, 36-73
Azzefoun (Port Gueydon), 115
bakhshish, 15, 34
bartering, 16
baths, public, 15
Bejaïa (Bougie), 115-17
Bekalta, 175
Beni Khiar, 159-60
Beni-Saf, 99-101
Berkane, 91
Birzebugia, 219
Bizerte, 141-3, 144
Blue Grotto, 219
Blue Lagoon, 222
Bône (Annaba), 95, 124-5
books and maps, 17
Bou Aroun, 109, 111
Bou Grara, 197-9
Bou-Zadjar, 101
Bougie (Bejaïa), 115-17
Budmah, Anse, 137-8
Bulla Regia, 137
buoyage, 10
business hours
  Algeria, 96
  Morocco, 33
  Tunisia, 131
Cala Calandra, 204
Cala Congrejo, 83
Cala Iris (Torres de Al Cala), 84
Cala Pisana, 204
Cala Tramontana, 87
Calcarella, Punta, 207
La Calle (El Kala), 125-6
Cani, Iles, 146
Cap Bon, 155-6
Cap Farina, 146, 147, 148
Cap Negro (Anse Budmah), 137-8

Cap Serrat, 139-40
Cap Zebib, 143-5
Carthage, 152
Casabianca, 119
Casablanca, 57-60
Ceuta (Sebta), 75-9
  crossing from Gibraltar, 27-9
Chafarinas, Islas, 91-2
chartering, 16
charts, 9, 223-8
La Chebba, 133, 179-81
Chefchaouen, 87
Cherchell, 107-9
Chergui, Ile, 184-90
Chetaibi (Mersa Takouch), 123-4
Chiffalo, 111
Ciris, 27
clearing, 10
climate, 2-4
coastal radio stations, 12
Collo, 119
Comino, 211, 222-3
Congrejo, Cala, 83
Conigli, Isola dei, 204
Conigliera, Ile, 171-2
Courbet Marine (Zemmouri Bahar), 112-13
currents, 4
  Atlantic coast, 38
  Straits of Gibraltar, 26-7
customs see entry formalities
Dakhla, 73-4
Dellys, 113-14
Dimas, Ras, 175
diving, 6, 7
Djen Djen, 118
Drek, Ras ed, 156
drugs, 34, 130-31
Dwejra Inlet, 222
eating out, 15-16
El Ataya, 188-90
El Fortras, Ras, 154
El Jadida, 60
El Jebha, 81, 83-4
El Kala (La Calle), 125-6
El Kantaoui, 163-5
El Ketef, 201
electricity
  Algeria, 96
  Malta, 213
  Morocco, 32
  Tunisia, 129-30
embassies
  Algeria, 97
  Morocco, 34-5
  Tunisia, 132
Ennajet, 187-8
entry formalities, 10
  Algeria, 97-8
  Malta, 211, 213
  Morocco, 33-4
  Tunisia, 131-3
equipment, 2, 7
Esrah, Pointe, 120
Essaouira, 67-70

Fes, 86-7
Fifla Island, 211, 219
fishing methods, 5-6
flora and fauna, 4-5
Fomm Ir-Rih Bay, 219
food and drink, 8, 15-16
formalities see entry formalities
El Fortras, Ras, 154
fuel, 7-8
  Algeria, 96
  Malta, 213-15
  Morocco, 32
  Tunisia, 130
Gabès, 133, 192-3
Galite, Ile de, 140-41
Gebel tal-Halfa, 220
Ghajn Tuffieha, 219
Ghar El Melh, 146-9
Ghazaouet, 98-9
Gibraltar, 18-29
  coastal radio station (ZDK), 12
  weather forecasts, 11
Gibraltar, Straits of, 26-9
glossary, 12-14
Gnenja Bay, 219
La Goulette, 152-3
Gozo, 211, 220-22
Grotto del Greco, 207
Habibas, Iles, 101-3
Hammamet, 160-61
hammams, 15
harbour charges
  Algeria, 96
  Malta, 213
  Morocco, 32
  Tunisia, 130
harpoon fishing, 6
health precautions
  Algeria, 96
  Morocco, 33
  Tunisia, 130
Hergla, 161-2
Houmt Souk, 133, 194-6
Il-Hofriet, 219
Ile Chergui, 184-90
Ile Conigliera, 171-2
Ile de Galite, 140-41
Ile Kuriat, 171-2
Ile Rharbi, 184
Iles Cani, 146
Iles Habibas, 101-3
inoculations, see health precautions
Iris, Cala (Torres de Al Cala), 84
Islam, 14-15
Islas Chafarinas, 91-2
Isles Purpuraires, 69
Isola dei Conigli, 204
Italy, *radiobeacons*, 11, 12
El Jadida, 60
El Jebha, 81, 83-4
Jerba, 194-6
Jijel, 117-18

Jorf Lasfar, 62-3
Kabila, Marina, 32, 79-80
El Kala (La Calle), 125-6
El Kantaoui, 163-5
Kelibia, 156-8
Kenitra, 48-51
Kerkennah Islands, 133, 184-90
Kerkouane, 158
El Ketef, 201
Kraten, 187-8
Ksar-es-Seghir, 74-5
Ksibet El Mdeiouni, 172-3
Kuriat, Ile, 171-2
La Calle (El Kala), 125-6
La Chebba, 133, 179-81
La Goulette, 152-3
La Louza (Port de Loueta), 181-2
La Pérouse, 112
La Skhira, 191
Laayoune, 73
Lampedusa Island, 202-204, 205
Lampione Island, 202
languages, 12-14
Larache, 46-8
Lazaretto Creek, 213
L'eau Chaud, 154
lights, 10
Linosa Island, 202, 204-10
Loueta, Port de (La Louza), 181-2
Ma, Ras el (Ras Kebdana), 90-91
Maharès, 190
Mahdia, 133, 175-8
Malabata, Punta, 27
Malta, 211-22
  entry formalities, 211, 213
  general information, 213-15
  radiobeacons, 12
  yacht facilities, 215-17
Manoel Island Pier, 213
maps and books, 17
Marina Bay (Gibraltar), 21
Marina Kabila, 32, 79-80
Marina Smir, 32, 77-9
marine life, 5
Maritime Mobile Net, 11
Marsalforn, 221, 222
Marsamxett Harbours, 211-13
Marsascala Bay, 220
Marsaxlokk Bay, 219
M'Diq, 80-82
Mehdia, 48-50
Melilla, 88-9
Melliha Bay, 218
Menzel Bourguiba, 141
Mers-el-Kébir, 103
Mersa Ali Bou Nouar, 101
Mersa Takouch (Chetaibi), 123-4
Mersa Zeitoun, 119
meteorology, 2-4
Mgarr, 220, 221

North Africa

Mgarrix-Xini Bay, 222
Mgiebah Bay, 218
Mohammedia, 55-7
Monaco Radio, 10, 11
Monastir, 133, 167-71
money
  Algeria, 96, 97-8
  Morocco, 31-2
  Tunisia, 129
Morocco, 30-92
  charts, 9
  coastal radio stations, 12
  crossing from Gibraltar, 26-9
  entry formalities, 33-4
  general information, 1-17, 31-6
  history, 30-31
  radiobeacons, 11
  tour guides, 35-6
  travel, 35-6
  weather forecasts, 10-11
Mostaganem, 105-6
Msida Marina, 213
Muslim culture, 14-17
Nador, 89, 90
navigation, 9
notices to mariners, 9
Oran, 95, 102, 103-5
Oualidia Lagoon, 63-7
Oujda, 91
Pantelleria Island, 207-10
Pantelleria Port, 207-8
paperwork, see entry formalities
Paradise Bay, 218
Pelagie Islands, 202-10
Peñón de Véléz de la Gomera, 84-5
Philippeville (Skikda), 122-3
photography
  Algeria, 97
  Morocco, 33
  Tunisia, 131
pilots, books and maps, 17
Pisana, Cala, 204
Pointe Esrah, 120
Port d'Anza (Agadir), 71
Port de Loueta (La Louza), 181-2
Port Gueydon (Azzefoun), 115
Porto Scauri, 208-10
precipitation, 3
provisioning, 7-9
  Algeria, 96
  Malta, 215
  Morocco, 32
  Tunisia, 129
public baths, 15
public holidays
  Algeria, 96
  Morocco, 33
  Tunisia, 131
Puerto Sotogrande, 32
Punta Calcarella, 207
Punta Malabata, 27
Purpuraires, Isles, 69
Qajjenza, 219
Qala Dwejra, 222
Qala ta' san marku, 218
Queensway Quay Marina (Gibraltar), 21-2
Rabat, 51-5
radio
  coastal stations, 12
  Maritime Mobile Net, 11
  weather forecasts, 10-11

radiobeacons, 11-12
rainfall, 3
Ramla Bay (Malta), 218
Ramla (Kerkennah Is), 187
Ras Dimas, 175
Ras ed Drek, 156
Ras El Fortras, 154
Ras el Ma (Ras Kebdana), 90-91
religion, 14-15
repairs, 8-9
  Algeria, 96
  Malta, 211, 215
  Morocco, 32
  Tunisia, 130
restaurants, 15-16
Restinga (Marina) Smir, 32, 77-9
Rharbi, Ile, 184
Sable D'Or, 54, 55
Safi Port, 63-7
Saidia, 92
St George's Bay, 218
St Julian's Bay, 218
St Paul's Bay, 218
St Paul's Island, 211
Salakta, 178-9
Sale, 53-5
Salina Bay, 218
San Niklaw Bay, 222
Santa Marija Bay, 222
Sardegna, *radiobeacons*, 11
Scauri, Porto, 208-10
scuba diving, 6, 7
sea conditions, 4
Sebta, *see* Ceuta
security
  Algeria, 97
  Malta, 211
  Morocco, 33
  Tunisia, 131
Selmun Bay, 218
Sfax, 133, 182-4
Sheppard's Marina (Gibraltar), 19-21
shopping, 16
Sicily, *radiobeacons*, 12
Sidi Bou Saïd, 149-52
Sidi Daoud, 154-5
Sidi Ferruch (Sidi Fredj), 95, 110, 111-12
Sidi Frej Anchorage (Ile Chergui), 186-7
Sidi Ifni, 72
Sidi Mechreg, 138-9
Sidi Youssef, 185-6
Skikda (Philippeville), 122-3
Sliema Creek, 213
Smir, Marina, 32, 77-9
snorkelling, 6
Sotogrande, Puerto, 32
Sousse, 165-7
Spain, *radiobeacons*, 11
steam baths, 15
Stora, 120-22
Straits of Gibraltar, 26-9
supplies, 7-9
swell, 4, 38
Tabarka, 135-7
Tac-Cawl Rocks, 220
Tan Tan, 72-3
Tanger (Tanger/Tangiers), 38-42
Tarfaya, 73
Tarifa, 26, 27
Teboulba, 173-5

telephones
  Algeria, 96
  Malta, 215
  Morocco, 32-3
  Tunisia, 130
temperatures, 4
Ténès, 106-7
Tetouan, 82
Thapsus, 175
tides, 4
  Atlantic coast, 38
  Straits of Gibraltar, 29
time zones
  Algeria, 96-7
  Morocco, 33
  Tunisia, 131
Tipasa, 109
tipping
  Algeria, 96
  Morocco, 33, 34
  Tunisia, 131
Tlemcen, 101
Torres de Al Cala (Cala Iris), 84
tourist information
  Algeria, 96
  Malta, 215
  Morocco, 33
  Tunisia, 131
Tramontana, Cala, 87
Tunis, 151, 152, 153
Tunisia, 127-201
  charts, 9
  coastal radio stations, 12
  entry formalities, 131-3
  general information, 1-17, 129-34
  history, 127-8
  radiobeacons, 11-12
  travel, 134
  weather forecasts, 10-11
  wintering, 128-9, 134
tunny nets, 5-6
Valletta, 211-17
Villa Sanjurjo (Al Hoceima), 85-7
visas, 10
  Algeria, 98
  Morocco, 34
  Tunisia, 132
visibility, 3-4
water supplies, 7
  Algeria, 96
  Malta, 213
  Morocco, 32
  Tunisia, 129
waterspouts, 3
weather, 2-4
  Atlantic coast, 38
weather forecasts, 10-11
  Gibraltar, 224
  Malta, 215
weatherfax, 38
winds, 2-3, 26-7
wintering, 16
  Tunisia, 128-9, 134
Xlendli Bay, 222
yacht and equipment, 2, 7-9
Zarat, 193-4
Zarzis, 133, 199-201
Zarzouna, 143
Zembra Island, 155
Zemmouri Bahar (Courbet Marine), 112-13